JOHN GOWER

Confessio Amantis

MIDDLE ENGLISH TEXTS SERIES

The Middle English Texts Series is designed for classroom use. Its goal is to make available to teachers and students texts that occupy an important place in the literary and cultural canon but have not been readily available in student editions. The series does not include authors, such as Chaucer, Langland, or Malory, whose English works are normally in print in good student editions. The focus is, instead, upon Middle English literature adjacent to those authors that teachers need in compiling the syllabuses they wish to teach. The editions maintain the linguistic integrity of the original work but within the parameters of modern reading conventions. The texts are printed in the modern alphabet and follow the practices of modern capitalization, word formation, and punctuation. Manuscript abbreviations are silently expanded, and *u/v* and *j/i* spellings are regularized according to modern orthography. Yogh (3) is transcribed as *g, gh, y,* or *s,* according to the sound in Modern English spelling to which it corresponds; thorn (þ) and eth (ð) are transcribed as *th.* Distinction between the second person pronoun and the definite article is made by spelling the one *thee* and the other *the,* and final *-e* that receives full syllabic value is accented (e.g., *charité*). Hard words, difficult phrases, and unusual idioms are glossed on the page, either in the right margin or at the bottom. Explanatory and textual notes appear at the end of the text, often along with a glossary. The editions include short introductions on the history of the work, its merits and points of topical interest, and brief working bibliographies.

JOHN GOWER

Confessio Amantis

Volume 1

Edited by
Russell A. Peck,
with Latin translations by
Andrew Galloway

SECOND EDITION

Published for TEAMS
(The Consortium for the Teaching of the Middle Ages)
in Association with the University of Rochester

by

MEDIEVAL INSTITUTE PUBLICATIONS
Kalamazoo, Michigan
2006

Library of Congress Cataloging-in-Publication Data

Gower, John, 1325?-1408.
  Confessio amantis / John Gower ; edited by Russell A. Peck, with Latin
translations by Andrew Galloway. -- 2nd ed.
     p. cm. -- (Middle English texts)
  Includes bibliographical references and index.
   ISBN 1-58044-102-5 (paperbound : v. 1 : alk. paper)
   1. Christian poetry, English (Middle) 2. Love poetry, English (Middle)
3. Christian ethics--Poetry. 4. Courtly love--Poetry.   I. Peck, Russell
A. II. Galloway, Andrew. III. Consortium for the Teaching of the
Middle Ages. IV. Title. V. Series: Middle English texts (Kalamazoo,
Mich.)
   PR1984.C6 2005
   821'.1--dc22

                                                          2005030793

ISBN 1-58044-102-5

 CONTENTS

❧ ACKNOWLEDGMENTS

ACKNOWLEDGMENTS FOR THE FIRST EDITION

I am greatly indebted to Professor Andrew Galloway for all the work that he has put into this volume. Not only has he translated Gower's Latin, which is no easy task in itself, but he has written explanatory notes for the Latin passages, read the whole manuscript twice, and made innumerable suggestions, both in glossing and with regard to critical issues. He has been a splendid colleague to work with. Quite simply, the edition could never have been completed without his expertise and support. I am also grateful to Derek Pearsall for years of encouragement in my Gower studies, from the time I first met him at York in 1967 until recent days when he still has had good advice to offer. The shape of this volume is his idea — a complete edition of the poem's narrative frame, that is, the Prologue, Book 1, and Book 8 — that includes a good number of Gower's most famous tales. Robert Yeager has likewise been a great friend over the past two decades. Over the years we have had many a conversation about Gower and shared a multitude of insights.

Eve Salisbury has provided a helpful critique of the Introduction. She has been particularly kind in pointing me to bibliography that I had not come across in my own readings. So too R. Allen Shoaf, who has helped me identify materials on Usk and Gower. Dana Symons, Ann Robinson, and Angela Gibson have also read the manuscript and offered useful criticism along the way. They have all checked my text against the Fairfax 3 manuscript, helping me to catch errors of transcription that might otherwise have slipped by. Dana has been responsible for formatting the volume and preparing the camera-ready copy. Her intelligence and patience in addressing editorial problems, carelessness, and inconsistencies in my several drafts of the volume have been all-surpassing; she has the eyes of Argos and the wisdom of Othea. Melissa Bernstein has made comments on the Introduction and, with Ann Robinson, has made an electronic check of the glosses cited in the *MED*. Mara Amster proofread the final copy.

I wish to thank Alan Lupack, the Associate Editor of the Middle English Texts Series, for his encouragement of the project from beginning to end and for his careful reading of the manuscript and the glosses, a task at which he is extraordinarily adept. Alan and the Robbins Library, of which he is curator, have proven to be resources of the first magnitude. Alan's care in helping me to find materials has been valuable beyond measure. At Kalamazoo the camera-ready copy has been reviewed by Tom Seiler who has shown steadfast devotion to the series over the years. Finally, I wish to thank my wife Ruth, who has seen me through two editions of Gower, and been supportive and reassuring even when my understanding of the poem wearies or seems too daunted to continue. Her counsel in finding the right tone and content for the Introduction has been much appreciated.

Thanks go to the National Endowment for the Humanities for its generous support of the Middle English Texts Series and this volume in particular. I am grateful to the Bodleian Library, University of Oxford, for permission to use the Fairfax 3 manuscript as my base text and also for the use of Bodley 902 and Bodley 294 for those portions of the earlier recension which I have included. I am likewise grateful for permission to reproduce the pictures from those manuscripts.

Since beginning work on Gower in 1967 I have developed an increasing admiration for the pioneering work of G. C. Macaulay. Even after a hundred years, his notes and carefully edited text stand as exemplars of fine scholarship that may be emulated but not surpassed. At Indiana University, as I was finishing up my dissertation on Chaucer in the early 1960s, John Hurt Fisher joined the faculty and first introduced me to Gower. For nearly four decades, he has been a kind friend. It is to him and the memory of G. C. Macaulay that I dedicate this edition.

ACKNOWLEDGMENTS FOR THE SECOND EDITION

First I would thank those who have used the METS edition of *Confessio Amantis* in their classes. Several have made helpful suggestions for the revision. Thanks go especially to Derek Pearsall who suggested a different format which would assist the reader in finding his or her way around in the volume. The Table of Contents has been greatly enlarged and new page headers make it easier to move about without going back to the contents page. Thanks next go to Michael Livingston, Assistant Editor of the Series, for his help at all phases of the revision. He converted the book to its new format, checked the Latin marginalia against Fairfax 3, catching several errors that had slipped past us in the earlier printing, and has been a good listener with forthright advice on various problems. Jacqueline Stuhmiller read the whole volume once again against Fairfax 3 and frequently consulted the Stafford manuscript (Huntington Library MS Ellesmere 26), St. John's College, Cambridge MS B.12 (34), and Bodleian Library MS Bodley 294 (*SC* 2449) as well. She caught many errors that had initially gone unheeded and was helpful in creating a number of new textual notes. Emily Rebekah Huber gave a careful reading of the explanatory notes, checking the accuracy of citations, and created the Index to References for the volume. John Chandler helped with the index and entered the final corrections. It has been a pleasure working with such accomplished people.

PREFACE

The *Confessio Amantis* has been an important part of my thinking for more than three decades. This volume, the first in a set of three, includes the frame of the poem; that is, the Prologue, Book 1, and Book 8. The three-volume edition provides readers with a complete text of Gower's poem, along with extensive glosses, bibliography, and explanatory notes. Volume 2 of the edition includes Books 2–4, and volume 3, Books 5–7. Books 2–4 follow one kind of development, following in its structure the outline of Vice and its children found in Gower's early French poem, the *Mirour de l'Omme*; then in volume 3 (Books 5–7) Gower offers another kind of development as he shifts his internal structure from romance banter and a formulaic confession to philosophical inquiry.

Despite the surface simplicity of the *Confessio*, the smoothness of its verse, and the apparent normality of its vocabulary, the poem is not easy to read. Gower's syntax is sometimes convoluted, using word order that is unfamiliar to modern readers, particularly in its placement of coordinating conjunctions in medial positions instead of at the head of the clause, but also occasionally imitating French idioms. Often we encounter inverted word order, and occasionally headless clauses and unusual use of hidden prepositions. Gower is a writer keenly aware of how to make language work for him, however, and he shapes the syntax pointedly toward his purpose. His vocabulary is not as broad as Chaucer's, but he uses words with distinctions of connotation that shift subtly from one context to another as shades of meaning change. One often encounters *rime riche*, which focuses attention on wordplay and the interiority of sense. Gower is alert to the innuendoes of language pertaining to law and legal matters. He also is well versed in French and Latin romance literature, which he uses with a grace and confidence that may slip past the casual reader. Thus this edition has sought to provide abundant glosses and notes to make his Middle English more fully clear to modern readers.

The *Confessio Amantis* is bilingual. This edition includes all Latin components of the poem along with translations. The Latin poetry is often graceful, although it sometimes seems to strive for difficulty and enigma; this opacity occasionally results in brilliantly significant ambiguities, at other times in collisions of partial metaphors. Both effects are challenging to translate. The Latin prose of the marginalia often has a legalistic ungainliness of style. But this quality provides congruities of idea that are important to the larger sense of Gower's poem. His Latin skills affect his English as he refashions the vocabulary with neologisms, such as "reprise"; likewise, his Latin is occasionally a calque of fourteenth-century English. For example, Gower will use the infinitive of "to desire" (*velle*) to mean the noun "desire" (normally this would be *desiderium* or *cupiditas* in Latin — words that do not scan well in iambic hexameter or its hemistiches used in elegiac couplets). But this is a case where in using *velle* he is thinking of the English word "wille," as in "to have your will," where in his Latin he says *habere velle*, the two words *wille* and *velle* sounding alike. When he writes English he is sometimes thinking in Latin, and when he writes Latin he is sometimes thinking in English.

Gower's poem is written in essentially the same dialect as Chaucer's poetry, that is, the literary dialect of cultivated Londoners of the late fourteenth century. The orthography of Fairfax 3 looks different from Chaucer's Ellesmere MS, however, largely because of the greater influence of French and Kentish spelling conventions in Fairfax. Commonly Gower (or his amanuensis) used *ie* as a digraph for /e/, a convention common in Anglo-Norman and in the Kentish dialect. So one finds *chiere, hiere, hiede, siek*, and the like in the *Confessio* where in Chaucer one would expect *chere* or *cheere, here* or *heere, hede* or *heede, sek* or *seek*. Gower's scribe will not hesitate to use both Chaucer's and the Kentish forms in rhymes like *dede/wommanhiede*, and so on. Where Chaucer uses *e* or *o*, Gower regularly uses the Anglo-Norman digraph *oe*, as in *poeple, proeved, moerdre*, and *coevere*. Gower probably pronounced the vowel as /e/ or /o/ as did Chaucer. In the *Confessio* one also finds spellings that reflect Romance etymology instead of actual pronunciation, such as *doubte* which rhymes with *aboute, deceipte* which rhymes with *conceite,* and *pleigne* which rhymes with *peine*.

One encounters a few Kentish phonemes in Chaucer, but in Gower they are frequent, especially Kentish *e* from Old English *y* where we would expect in Middle English *i* or *y*. So we find in Gower *ferst, senne, helle,* and *pet*, where we would normally find *first, sinne, hill*, and *pit* in Chaucer. Gower's scribes occasionally use *i* in all these instances, but we also find the Southern *u* for *i*, as in *hulles* or *puttes* for *hills* or *pits*. Finally, we find the Kentish participial ending *-ende* in the *Confessio*, where Chaucer normally uses *-inge*, though the latter form is also common in Gower.

In this edition of the *Confessio* I have followed the guidelines of the Middle English Texts Series and regularized *u/v* and *i/j* according to modern spelling conventions. I have also followed modern practices of punctuation and capitalization. As an aid to pronunciation I have placed an accent over *-é* if the vowel is long and given full syllabic value. So, instead of *charite, cite*, or *pite* the text will read *charité, cité*, and *pité*. According to this practice *honeste* and *honesté* will be distinguishable words, the adjective in two syllables, the noun in three. Sometimes unstressed *-e* is pronounced as *-ə* or not at all. In the fourteenth century, pronouns and prepositions are undergoing rapid change and thus often prove to be confusing. Gower commonly uses *hir* for "her," *her* for "their," *hem* for "them" or "themselves," and *him* for "him" or "himself." Distinction between the second person pronoun and the definite article is made by spelling the one *thee* and the other *the*. I have capitalized pronouns referring to the Christian deity along with proper names for the deity, though these capitalizations do not necessarily occur in the Middle English or among many modern stylists. But the practice saves on glossing and often makes hard passages clear where, in Middle English, no ambiguity seems to have been intended.

Illustration 1: MS Bodl. 902, fol. 8r. Bodleian Library, Oxford University. Confessio Amantis [The Confession of the Lover]. The representation of Amans as an old man is unique to this manuscript. (Contrast illustrations 3 and 5.) The artist seems knowledgeable of the conclusion to the poem where the lover sees his face defaced "[w]ith elde" [8.2828]. Some have argued that the portrait is of Gower himself as he points the way. See notes to Book 8.

ENTER GOWER

To sing a song that old was sung,
From ashes ancient Gower is come,
Assuming man's infirmities
To glad your ear, and please your eyes.
It hath been sung at festivals,
On ember-eves and holy-ales;
And lords and ladies in their lives
Have read it for restoratives:
The purchase is to make men glorious,
Et bonum quo antiquius, eo melius.[1]
If you, born in these latter times,
When wit's more ripe, accept my rimes,
And that to hear an old man sing
May to your wishes pleasure bring,
I life would wish, and that I might
Waste it for you like taper-light.

. . .

I tell you what mine authors say.
— William Shakespeare, *Pericles*, I.Prol.1–16, 20[2]

---

[1] "The older a good thing is, the better." The phrase is proverbial, though Hoeniger (Arden Shakespeare edition, p. 6) notes that *communius* is more common in the proverb than *antiquius*. Shakespeare's choice of *antiquius* is well attuned to the poet Gower's concerns. Ancient texts provide the purchase necessary for cultural amelioration and for their "restorative" value to the psyches of men and women "in their lives." The proverb with *communius* is found in T. Lodge, *Wits Miserie* (1576), where it is quoted as an axiom of Aristotle, and in Marston, *The Dutch Courtezan* (1605).

[2] Shakespeare, *Pericles*, ed. Hoeniger, pp. 5–6. For a brief discussion of Shakespeare's understanding and use of Gower in *Pericles*, see the Explanatory Note to Book 8, line 271 (below).

 **INTRODUCTION**

Scripture veteris capiunt exempla futuri,
Nam dabit experta res magis esse fidem.
[Writings of antiquity contain examples for the future,
For a thing experienced will afford greater faith.]
— Gower, *Vox Clamantis*, Prol. to Book I, lines 1–2[1]

Thanne telle I hem ensamples many oon
Of olde stories longe tyme agoon.
For lewed peple loven tales olde;
Swiche thynges kan they wel reporte and holde.
— Chaucer's Pardoner, *CT* VI(C)435–38[2]

GOWER, MAKER OF TALES

For Gower, old tales and their power to shape a "lewed peple" (to quote the Pardoner) are not something to be scorned.[3] Tales enable the mind to rethink itself. Coming as they do from outside one's immediate consciousness, they embody a culture's sense of order and help to place the reader within the ethical terms of the culture. They clarify the meanings of right and wrong and thus can serve as the restorative of which Shakespeare's Gower speaks. Tales forge identities. The *Confessio Amantis*, like the "writings of antiquity" that Gower mentions in the *Vox Clamantis*, is written to provide a bridge between the past and an anticipated future, a bridge that gives its audience a better sense of the present.[4] As

---

[1] The Latin text of *Vox Clamantis* is from Gower, *Complete Works*, ed. Macaulay, 4:20. The translation is based on that found in Gower, *Major Latin Works*, trans. Stockton.

[2] For discussion of these specific lines from the Pardoner's Prologue with regard to tale-telling, see Kolve, *Chaucer and the Imagery of Narrative*, pp. 18–19, who offers thoughtful considerations on "holding" tales in the memory for purposes of mental dialogue.

[3] Some portions of this introduction are adapted from the introduction to *Confessio Amantis*, ed. Peck (1968).

[4] As medieval writers frequently recognized, the present is an illusion. It can only be sensed. St. Augustine puts the matter succinctly: "it is in you, my mind, that I measure periods of time" (*Confessions* XI.xxvii.36). Having contemplated the "present" as a lifetime, a year, a day, or an hour — all of which measures are instantly more a matter of past than present, he observes, "if you can think of some bit of time which cannot be divided into even the smallest instantaneous moments, that alone is what we can call 'present'. And this time flies so quickly from future into past that it is an interval with no duration. If it has duration, it is divisible into past and future. But the present occupies no space" (*Confessions* XI.xv.20). Compare *The Cloud of Unknowing*'s theory of atoms of time which, if surpassed, place one momentarily in the presence of God, the only true present (see chs. 4 and 6).

1

Gower explains, the reading of old tales affords its participants "a thing experienced" (*experta*), a means of testing knowledge personally the way one might momentarily test any kind of sensual information, whether from nature or parchment, by trying it out in the mind to find out how it might be true.[5] In the *Confessio*, the experiencing of a tale equates with testing it. Each tale demarcates a trial through which one has the potential to learn and grow. In this sense, the plots of Gower's stories are deliberately *experiential*. They are *about* experience, but likewise they provide examples *to be tested in the mind*. Their plots develop through choices made by characters who, like the readers assessing them, anticipate some hoped-for denouement.[6]

Gower thinks within concepts of knowing that are ancient, though mainly articulated in the fourteenth century by writers steeped in the ideas of St. Augustine, who explored relentlessly the illusions people spin about themselves as they explore the interstices between time, memory, experience, consciousness of the present, and one's relationship with language.[7] All such ideas are crucial to Gower the storyteller.[8] In his attempt to understand temporal relationships and the psyche, Augustine takes his example from literary experience, as if reading affords the best means of perceiving how time and mind work:

---

[5] Fourteenth-century writers repeatedly insist that truth is relative to the perceiver. Consider Chaucer's *Book of the Duchess*, where the narrator rereads his Ovid to test it in his mind, wondering "yf hit were so" (line 233). See note 12. Petrarch's observations on the value of old sayings and ancient writings are useful in understanding what Gower means by *experta* and how a medieval reader might "experience" old books and ideas. In a letter to Giovanni Colonna di San Vito (25 September 1342) Petrarch writes: "Nothing moves me so much as the quoted maxims of great men. I like to rise above myself, to test my mind to see if it contains anything solid or lofty, or stout and firm against ill-fortune, or to find if my mind had been lying to me about itself. And there is no better way of doing this — except by direct experience, the surest mistress — than by comparing one's mind with those it would most like to resemble. Thus, as I am grateful to my authors who give me the chance of testing my mind against maxims frequently quoted, so I hope my readers will thank me" (*Letters from Petrarch*, p. 68).

[6] Hope, anticipation, and need of a good ending, despite the lack of certainty of where we are now or where we are going, is one of the most characteristic considerations of Middle English literature. It is found repeatedly in questions such as Chaucer's "not wot I . . . Ne where I am, ne in what contree" and his search for "any stiryng man / That may me telle where I am" (*House of Fame*, lines 474–79), or Will's perpetual search in *Piers Plowman*, or such poignant lyrics as "Kindely is now my coming" with its "Scharp and strong is my deying, / I ne woth whider schal I" (Luria and Hoffman, *Middle English Lyrics*, #237, lines 5–6).

[7] St. Augustine is the doctrinal authority most cited by philosophers such as Duns Scotus, William of Ockham, and Roger Bacon, theologians such as Wyclif, and writers such as Gower, Chaucer, Langland, and the author of *The Cloud of Unknowing*.

[8] For Augustine, time is movement, a "shuttling of the future into the past, moving through an immeasurable point" (Wills, "Augustine's Magical Decade," p. 30). That immeasurable point is the present, which we try to understand or make exist sensibly through the abridgments of mental acts. Augustine argues that "without creation, no time can exist" (*Confessions* XI.xxx.40). Being a phenomenon of creation, time can be understood only by measure, by relationships of moments (see *Confessions*, XI.xxvi.33 and XI.xxvi.34–36). Time is thus a kind of fiction — a tale, if you will — a distension of once-upon-a-time moments, stretching feeling according to measures made "real" as the mind expands itself through anticipation of the future and recollection of the past (*Confessions* XI.xxxi.41). Time enables one to frame the present even though we cannot know what it is. We make tales of time through which we imagine that we can grasp its being.

Say I am about to recite a psalm. Before I start, my anticipation includes the psalm in its entirety, but as I recite it, whatever I have gone over, detaching it from anticipation, is retained by memory. So my ongoing act is tugged [*distenditur*] between the memory of what I just said and the anticipation of what I am just about to say, though I am immediately engaged in the present transit from what was coming to what is past. As this activity works itself out, anticipation dwindles as memory expands, until anticipation is canceled and the whole transaction is lodged in memory. And what happens with the whole psalm is equally what happens with each verse of it, each syllable — and with the whole long liturgy of which the psalm may be a part, or with the whole of any man's life, whose parts are his own acts, or with the whole world, whose parts are the acts of men.[9]

Augustine privileges reading as a synecdoche for the mind's capacity to create a present in relation to the confines of the past and the anticipation of the future. Such a practice provides a useful substructure for Gower's ideas about tale-telling in relation to the moral goals of his *Confessio*. The present he wishes to understand is perpetually transitive. His tales are parts of a whole that offer diverse access to the present. In the *Confessio* tales testify through fiction what the case may be.[10]

Gower's conceptualization of literary "experience" as useful testimony compares well with Chaucer's. In the Prologue to *The Legend of Good Women*, Chaucer, like Gower, honors books as a key of "remembrance," observing, "Wel ought us thanne honouren and beleve / These bokes, there [where] we han noon other preve" (*LGW* Prologue, F.26–28). Initially, the juxtaposition seems to be between the experience of reading and that of daily practical experience, as if to say, we believe books until some better empirical proof may be found.[11] But upon reflection "the other preve" is, like a thing experienced (*experta*), better understood as the testing of any deeper understanding or perceptual revision, whether practical or theoretical. That is, books are understood mainly in the head; but so too is nature. Both nature and books are texts that perplex the viewer. Belief and thought are not, however, binary oppositions; rather, thought, with its perpetual reinvention of both past and present, challenges and sustains belief, whether in the writings of Gower or Chaucer.[12]

---

[9] *Confessions* XI.xxviii.38, as translated by Garry Wills, *St. Augustine*, p. 90; Wills' brackets.

[10] Garry Wills notes that Augustine's term *confessio* is synonymous with *testimonium, confiteri* meaning "to testify." For Augustine "even inanimate things confess — testify to — their Creator: 'Their beauty is their testimony' (*Pulchritudo eorum confessio eorum, Sermones* 241.2)" (*St. Augustine*, pp. xiv–xvi). Wills' explanation of Augustine's concept is useful in grasping the intentions of Gower's confessional tactic where telling serves a key part in a restorative procedure. The many parts of his poem challenge the reader even as Genius and Amans provoke and test each other.

[11] Compare Gower's *Nam dabit experta res magis esse fidem* (for a thing experienced will afford greater faith). See the opening epigram of this Introduction.

[12] For example, in Chaucer's *Book of the Duchess* the narrator reads a text from Ovid, then goes over it repeatedly ("[I] overloked hyt everydel") to discover "yf hit were so" (lines 232–33); that is, he rereads to get at what *might* be taken as the "truth" of the matter. That "truth" is, of course, contingent upon the capabilities of the perceiver, capabilities qualified by the reader's prejudice and intellectual capacities. Boethius puts the matter shrewdly: "alle thing that is iwist nis nat knowen by his nature propre, but by the nature of hem that comprehenden it" (Chaucer's translation, *Boece*, 5.pr.6.2–4). Gower works from a similar concept, fully cognizant of the relativity of experience to language. Although "experience" may be no authority, as Chaucer's Wife of Bath amusingly explains (*CT* III[D]1 ff.), it is the primary means available to people for testing the possibilities and proba-

Like *Vox Clamantis* and much of Chaucer's poetry, *Confessio Amantis* is deliberately a bookish poem, rooted in old texts — *scripture veteris*. But it is likewise empirical, albeit within the fictive framework of an imagined "lover of the world" quizzed by a responsive intellect, a "genius" that puts to the test memory in response to history (the texts of the past). Rooted in old texts, this testimonial confession is a poem *of* and *for* the present, a poem for King Richard *now* in 1390 or for England in 1392.[13] This precise historical positioning introduces a philosophical proposition akin to the problematics of understanding experience. Janet Coleman sees this locating of texts within specific historical contexts as a new and distinguishing feature of later fourteenth-century English literature.[14] The point is, of course, not simply to locate fiction within historical contexts; rather, it is part of an attempt to explore the relativity of time itself to fictive formulations within the mind. The mind is a perpetual plot-maker as it invents narratives it imagines to be the present (the way things are at the moment) within a metaphysic of temporality. In this regard, the *Confessio*, like so many other late-fourteenth-century poems,[15] creates a fiction of soul-searching. But it is soul-searching of a special kind. Gower's argument takes as its goal the accessing of the present by reconfiguring the past. Although the poem is ostensibly textual — that is, an interweaving of old maxims, proverbs, tales, social propositions, political alignments — it is also a subtly psychological work, a poem that through its rhetoric explores *how* the human psyche can understand itself within history — *now*.

Gower is the first English writer to use "history" as an English word.[16] He regularly rhymes the term with "memory," for to his way of thinking history and memory are correlative. That is, without history, there can be no memory; and without memory, there can be no history. But the point of historical knowledge is not to enable people to live in the past, or even to understand the past in the way we would expect a modern historian to proceed; rather, it is to enable people to live more vitally in the present — "The present time which now is" (*CA* 8.258), as Gower puts it. The present is, for Gower, a state of mind every bit as much as the past or future must be. And it is for this reason that the tales must be told and "experienced." Just as the past must be perpetually reinvented (and Gower is a master at such

----

bilities out of which they discover the relativity of knowledge. For discussion of the philosophical issues here see Peck, "Phenomenology of Make Believe," pp. 250–58.

[13] Gower first circulated the poem in 1390 with a dedication and concluding prayers addressed to King Richard. In 1392, he changed the dedication and conclusion to honor Henry of Derby (later King Henry IV) and to conclude with prayers for the state of England. See "Politics and Society," below, pp. 19 ff.

[14] Compare Chaucer's setting the Man of Law's Tale on April 18, or the dream in *HF* on the tenth day of the tenth month, or his frequent use of May 3 as an auspicious day. The effect is to relate fiction to historical moments in "real" time.

[15] For example, Chaucer's *Canterbury Tales*, *Troilus and Criseyde*, and *Book of the Duchess*; Langland's *Piers Plowman*; the anonymous *Pearl*; and Guillaume de Deguileville's *Pélerinage de la vie humaine*.

[16] Gower probably borrows the term from OF *estoire*, which is in turn derived from late Latin in the twelfth century to indicate "a (vernacular) narrative of past events, presented as true, and whose authenticity is attested by an authority" (Damian-Grint, "*Estoire* as a Word and Genre," p. 198). The term was perhaps borrowed to differentiate *romanz* from more "historical" kinds of writing. Chaucer never uses the word "history," though he does use the aphetic form, "storie" (which he rhymes with "memorie"), in *Troilus and Criseyde*, where Criseyde, considering her life, observes: "Men myght a book make of it, lik a storie" (5.585).

invention), so too must the present be perpetually reinvented if one is to have any notion of oneself in a locatable way. One claims the present by locating it within the terms of memory. In his tale-telling, Gower enters into a refined phenomenology where time, history, memory, and a fictionalizing of the past make discourse of the "now"-world presentable.

In *Confessio Amantis*, Gower is preeminently a storyteller. Through the voice of the poet and Genius, his surrogate contact with practical matters and the wisdom of antiquity, Gower revitalizes a treasury of old tales, thereby provisioning his new vessel with reclaimed ideas — a "tally" of tales for taking mental stock of the natural order of things.[17] Like Chaucer's Pardoner, who shrewdly uses tales to influence people — "For lewed peple loven tales olde" (VI[C]437) — Gower conjures old tales as a means of wooing an audience toward a confessional self-reassessment. Like the Pardoner, he is well aware that people use stories to "reporte and holde" (*CT* VI[C]438). He is also aware that tales can deceive. Genius' stories are full of manipulators who, like the Pardoner, tell tales as a means of satisfying their greed; in fact, Gower creates some of Middle English literature's most notorious deceivers, characters like Mundus in the Tale of Mundus and Paulina in Book 1 or Nectanabus in Book 6. But unlike Genius' villains or Chaucer's Pardoner, Gower's motive is not venal. That is, his tales are bound to the good intention of the teller and what he imagines the desirous intentions of his audience to be. Certainly Gower would entertain, but he is shrewdly aware that he has little control over his willful readers. He can only woo them and attempt to manipulate their responses through his rhetoric. The tales, he says, are to be "Somwhat of lust [pleasure], somewhat of lore [wisdom]" (Prol.19).[18] But, inevitably, his intention is intuitive — a feeling that people commonly yearn for the good and that the soul's welfare is generative within the outlines of a Christian doctrine that conforms with the goals of his society at large.

This earnest side of Gower's intention received adverse criticism in the early part of the twentieth century, which tended to view him as a moralist rather than as a poet of the first rank. But more recently the challenge of writing moral verse artfully has been better appreciated. John Fisher praises Gower's "absolute integrity, his coherent grasp of the ideals of his day, and his fearless expression of the moral judgments growing out of those ideals."[19] In his *Vox Clamantis*, a poem written c. 1378–82, Gower spoke as a moralist, delineating the ideals of social behavior through the genre of complaint. In the *Confessio* (c. 1386–90) he

---

[17] I make the "tally" pun to heighten the connotations of *tale* in Gower's usage. Both *tale* and *tally* have the same root, the Old Teutonic **tala*, as in the verb *taljan*, meaning to mention things in their natural or due order, to relate, enumerate, reckon (see *OED*). Both words, along with *tell*, imply a process of ordering, of taking account. When the wife in Chaucer's Shipman's Tale tells her husband to score the debt on her "taile" (*CT* VII[B²]416), she makes a triple pun on tail/tale/tally, with related puns on accounting. Gower regularly utilizes two components of the pun, those of tale and tally, in the economics of his narrative, though he does not make puns on *tail* as readily as Chaucer.

[18] The "lust" and "lore" phrasing is akin to Chaucer's telling of tales for "best sentence [wisdom] and moost solaas [entertainment]" (*CT* I[A]798). Coleman (*Medieval Readers and Writers*, p. 16) argues that most works in the period were written not merely to entertain but rather to inspire readers to criticize and eventually reform social practice. While this may be true, it is also true that the writers of the 1380s and 1390s were acutely aware of the limitations of literary assertion, as well as the dangers of political criticism and attempts by writers at reform. See Ferster, *Fictions of Advice*, on the use of Latin traditions as a means of disguising discontent in advice literature. See also Middleton, "Idea of Public Poetry," pp. 101–02, and Peter, *Complaint and Satire*, p. 70.

[19] *John Gower*, p. v.

now offers a new, more subtle formulation where moral assessment takes place through the nuances of fiction. As Kurt Olsson puts it, "This poem is as effectively moral in its 'game' as it is in its earnestness, and in both things together Gower will challenge and ultimately reward the careful reader."[20] Gower's tales stand as "ensamples" for stocktaking and are central to the poem's overall strategy of using entertainment for the winning of mental health and God's pardon. Though his own intention is good, Gower knows that the success of that triangulation between writer, text, and reader, and therefore the success of his whole enterprise, lies in the relativity of language and the intention of his reader.

For Gower, the value of a tale resides in its capacity to take its audience some place. Plots, like time, move, and they move people, stretching their feelings, as Augustine puts it;[21] they lay out an ethical geography and provide direction through an imaginary terrain. But the direction is never single-dimensional. The poem speaks with many voices simultaneously — the voices of Genius the confessor and Amans the lover, and with the voices of all the characters within the examples. These fictive voices are framed by another more subtle fiction, the voice of John Gower the poet, with his concerns about the welfare of England. Just as the voicing of the poem is multidimensional, so too are its settings. Sometimes the settings may be specifically identified places or times, or they may lie in the spaces between Genius' attempts to guide Amans in his confusion and erratic love and his efforts to account for that love. Although the voicing of "Gower the poet" functions in a narrative parameter within the poem larger than that of Genius, the poet's frame "story" is, nonetheless, akin to Genius' confessional scheme in that the "poet," like Genius, wishes to take his audience simultaneously in two directions: 1) toward a better understanding of the commonweal of the state, and 2) toward a better understanding of the welfare of the soul.

READING AS THERAPY

Hundreds of old stories will be envisioned in *Confessio Amantis* before the therapy of the distracted lover can be concluded. For Gower, reading is powerful medicine. As a concept, "reading" has provocative implications in Middle English. It connotes engagement of the reader through sight and (especially in a culture where books were commonly read aloud) hearing, as we might expect, but it likewise signifies engagement of the mind in a broad range of interior activities, such as learning, teaching, interpretation of riddles, dreams, and parables; it also denotes perception, discernment, deduction, and the ability to estimate, enumerate, count, or think. But it is further used with the sense of giving counsel and advice. It can mean to confer, advise, decide in council, or to agree or decide in the mind. The term has political implications as a word connoting acts of decreeing, guiding, governing, controlling, preparing, making ready, or exercising authority. And reading has a crucial psychological implication of carrying out one's intention. In the course of Gower's poem Amans learns to read by listening to tales and contemplating their implications. He is not an adept reader any more than he is an adept listener. The tales provide him with information, but, given his preoccupation, their significance often passes him by. Like all readers, he is obliged to be inventive — to find a personal means of framing the ideas of the tales within his unique consciousness.

---

[20] *Structures of Conversion*, p. 2.

[21] *Confessions* XI.xxxi.41.

Confession nurses by healing the cracks in the psyche which have come about through the degenerative anxieties of time and careless beholding. The one confessing must provide a narrative for his chaotic behavior, a "tale" that can be read and weighed by the interrogator. To approach the psychological demands of the poem, Gower introduces a debate between competing mental components — Amans, Venus, Genius, a mistress of the imagination who never appears but is ever yearned for, a forgotten sense of common profit, and so on — who are personified to give testimony to the ramifications of ill health. Augustine discusses the mental faculties at length, providing a terminological basis for analysis of aberrant human behavior, particularly of the brain enfeebled by the Fall.[22] Augustine argues that the mind of humankind was created to reflect the Trinity and thus consists of three principal agents: Memory, Intellect, and Will.[23] Early in his writing Augustine sees the Intellect (cognate with the Second Person) as the superior faculty upon whose right use healthy human behavior depends; later, as his theology becomes increasingly subtle, he shifts the primary focus of problems in human behavior to the Will (cognate with the Third Person).[24] It is to the later writings of Augustine that the fourteenth century, with its latent distrust of reason (though not of Christ), found itself most attracted. With the new fourteenth-century emphasis on empirical thought and an individual's responsibility for personal governance, attention in ethics is increasingly concentrated on free choice and the struggle to assess the intermingling of desire and moral behavior.

Augustine's focus on willful behavior was developed by Boethius into questions of intent,[25] which relocate Will (love) as a function of heart as well as brain. Intention is bound to desire — what one wants and wills — and often develops from an imagined deficiency that one wishes to remedy. By the eleventh century "brain science" had developed spatial models of the brain which are akin to Augustine's, but with some modifications deriving from Galen.[26] Medieval diagrams of the brain introduce a new faculty to Augustine's scheme, *ima-*

---

[22] It is perhaps noteworthy that medieval medical diagrams of the brain often label the figure as "Disease Man." The diagrams identify the areas of the brain where specific diseases might be located. See Clarke and Dewhurst, *Illustrated History of Brain Function*, figs. 5, 7, 9, 12, 13, 16, and 17.

[23] Augustine's most detailed discussion of mental faculties appears in *De Trinitate*, Books 9–11.

[24] A comparable shift of focus occurs in northern Europe between the twelfth and fourteenth centuries as the ideology of a monastic culture, focusing upon the Intellect, sees pride as the primary sin. But gradually, as the commercial revolution takes place and the educational centers shift from monasteries to universities, inns of court, and a culture of guildsmen, the focus shifts to the Will as the faculty most often abused, with sins of avarice and greed as the greatest threats to human welfare. See Little, "Pride Goes before Avarice"; Lopez, *Commercial Revolution*; Yunck, *Lineage of Lady Meed*; Bloomfield, *Seven Deadly Sins*; and Baldwin, "Medieval Merchant."

[25] On the prominence of intention in Boethius see *Consolation* 3.pr.11 and 12, 4.m.1 and pr.2, and 5.m.4 and pr.6. By the fourteenth century intention has become a central concern of civil law as well. See Chaucer's Parson's Tale on the complexity of self-adjudication as every aspect of motive becomes essential to the assessment of behavior. For general discussion of the concept see Bowers, *Crisis of Will in Piers Plowman*, and Dihle, *Theory of Will in Classical Antiquity*.

[26] See Clarke and Dewhurst, *Illustrated History of Brain Function*, pp. 10–48. The concept of three primary functions of the brain, namely, Imagination, Reason, and Memory, goes back to Galen, as far as medieval writers are concerned. Nemesius, bishop of Emesia (c. AD 390), and Augustine first propose a cell doctrine of brain function (Clarke and Dewhurst, p. 10), which dominates diagrams until well past the medieval period.

ginativa, which functions as a cognitive server for intellect and memory. A representative account of brain functions may be found in Bartholomaeus Anglicus' encyclopedia *De proprietatibus rerum*, written before 1250, but translated into English by John Trevisa in the later fourteenth century:

> The innere witte is departid aþre [into three] by þre regiouns of þe brayn, for in þe brayn beþ þre smale celles. Þe formest [the frontal cell] hatte [is called] *ymaginatiua*, þerin þinges þat þe vttir [outer] witte [i.e., the senses] apprehendiþ withoute beþ i-ordeyned and iput togedres withinne. . . . Þe middil chambre hatte *logica* þerin þe vertu estimatiue is maister. Þe þridde and þe laste is *memoratiua*, þe vertu of mynde. Þat vertu holdiþ and kepiþ in þe tresour of mynde þingis þat beþ apprehendid and iknowe by þe ymaginatif and *racio*.[27]

Ymaginative works with intuitions from the senses to create the mental experience of images in the brain, separate from the external forms. Under the influence of will, *ymaginative* can combine forms into new forms not found in nature. In some brain diagrams the first cell is subdivided between *sensus communis* and *ymaginative*.[28] This image-making component of the brain is particularly attuned to sight and hearing.[29] Gower draws upon the concept when he discusses the primacy of sight and hearing as the senses most influential in cognition. As he puts it in the Latin verses early in Book 1, before line 289: *Visus et auditus fragilis sunt ostia mentis*, "Vision and hearing are fragile gateways of the mind." Genius then goes on to excoriate abuse of these two senses which are deemed crucial to understanding.

As a personification in the *Confessio*, Genius is closely related to the frontal lobe of the brain, *ymaginative*, as he presents and manipulates images while putting tales together. In Chaucer's Second Nun's Tale, St. Cecile explains to Tiburce the "sapiences three" of the brain — "Memorie, engyn, and intellect also" (VIII[G]338–39). "Engyn," derived from *ingenium*, is that tale's term for *imaginative*, a term in whose jurisdiction Genius is an evident component. In Gower, Genius is the principal agent of therapy as he presents tales to the willful Amans in hope of engaging his intellect. Gower develops Genius from two well-known medieval counterparts, one in Alanus de Insulis' *De Planctu Naturae*, and the other in Jean de Meun's *Roman de la Rose*. In these two antecedents Genius represents a combination of natural reason, ingenuity (what we would call invention or "creativity"), and procreativity. He is subservient to Nature, and Nature, being God's creation, is essentially good. That she is subject to time and mortality is not her fault, but rather humankind's, who, in sinning, act "unnaturally." There is an essential ambiguity here: desire is natural and may lead to natural fulfillment; or, if ungoverned (i.e., willful), it may lead to "unnatural" disaster. The rightness

---

[27] Capitulum x [f. 21va], Bartholomaeus Anglicus, I.98.

[28] E.g., the three-cell diagram of the brain in Triumphus Augustinus de Anchona, in *Opusculum perutile de cognitione animae*, revised by Achillini (1503), printed by Kolve (*Chaucer and the Imagery of Narrative*, p. 25; discussed, p. 23). See also Clarke and Dewhurst, *Illustrated History of Brain Function*, p. 27.

[29] See the diagrams in Clarke and Dewhurst, *Illustrated History of Brain Function*. In some instances, the cells in the frontal lobe, identified with sensation and imagination, are linked directly to the eye. E.g., the drawing c. 1310 in Cambridge University Library Gg.l.l, fol. 490v (figure 39 in Clarke and Dewhurst; see also figures 24, c. 1410, and 32, c. 1501, which also link the eyes directly to the brain). One conclusion that might be drawn is that a diseased brain is simply an unbalanced one, often unbalanced by a failure to guard the eye or ear.

of desire depends upon the functions of both will and intention. Genius looks after Nature's mortal creatures; he is pleased when each finds satisfaction proper to its created purpose. So too in Gower, where Genius' primary means for judging behavior is to decide whether an act is natural or "unkynde." Genius is a most felicitous choice for analyzing the witless love crimes of Amans against Nature. It is to Genius that Amans must turn for penance, since, in his idleness, "genius" and his right use of inward visualization are what have become twisted.[30] The confessor, with his "lust and lore," attempts to help Amans re-create a more balanced view of himself.

Within the strictures of Gower's psychomachia, Genius serves as Venus' priest, but this does not make him necessarily subservient to her or even entirely sympathetic with her motives. In Alanus, Venus and her son Cupid help Genius to fulfill his office of replenishing Nature (that is to say, the sexual urge for singular pleasure which Venus and Cupid instill in creatures does help Nature to reproduce her kind). But although Gower's Genius enjoys the assistance of Venus and the god of love, he nevertheless objects scornfully to their selfish demands when they turn natural love into unnatural fantasies or mutually exclusive and unfruitful games. In fact, from the beginning of the poem it is clear that his interests are more imaginative than Venus'. He will speak of more things than love, at least love as cupidinous Amans has come to define the term. Usually he tells tales pertaining to specific sins, then, at Amans' request, tells additional tales pertaining to the lover's particular relationship with the sin. In order to help Amans see beyond his infatuation, Genius will, as the poem progresses, ultimately instruct him in all the humanities. The climax of his argument is Book 7, in which he explains the education of a king, lessons in governance which Amans must learn if he is to reclaim and rule the lost kingdom of his soul. Genius knows that love founded on mutuality, on what both Gower and Chaucer (among others) call "common profit," is the only love that is consistently satisfactory. Although Genius' understanding of higher love is limited, he can appreciate it as history has revealed it, just as Jean de Meun's Genius appreciates without fully understanding the "beau parc" of the good shepherd with its "fontaine de vie" toward the end of *Roman de la Rose*. Most certainly he can see from his natural vantage point that in the events of human behavior the love of Cupid is inconstant and that that of Venus usually ends in mockery. History demonstrates that this is so. That Venus would send Amans to Genius is understandable, however, in that she owes her very existence to the phenomena of time and nature over which Genius has perceptual jurisdiction.

Genius provides the impetus for Amans' therapy. His tales serve as a visual guide for the inner eye.[31] But the therapy itself can take place only through Amans' choices, under the guidance of his memory and intellect. Just as the first cell of the brain is subdivided into *sensus communis* and *ymaginativa*, likewise the second cell, that of the intellect, is divided into two parts too, namely *phantasia* and *aestimativa*. Intellect enables humankind to reason, estimate, and calculate. Some diagrams of the brain refer to this cell as the residence of *logica*,

---

[30] See Kolve's perceptive discussion of the role of the inner eye and seeing ear particularly as adjuncts to memory in the process of cognition (*Chaucer and the Imagery of Narrative*, pp. 27–58).

[31] See Kolve (*Chaucer and the Imagery of Narrative*) on the prominence of visual images and the inner eye in the therapeutic process of reading. Even the nose has an "inner eye" capable of projecting images in the brain. See illustration 63 in Clark and Dewhurst (*Illustrated History of Brain Function*, p. 43) for a fourteenth-century drawing of the eye in relation to the brain that also crudely depicts the eye of the nose.

others of *ratio*. This cell too is subject to will and intention. *Phantasia* is an especially volatile area and, like reason, can be perverse. That is, through misintent reason can become ratiocination, and fantasy, instead of providing a godlike, generative function, can become a foolish wishfulfiller of the sort that the lover commits himself so strongly to in the middle books of the *Confessio*, where he projects scenario after scenario on how he will win his lady or humiliate his opponents.

The third cell, *memoria*, which Augustine had compared to God the Father, the First Person of the Trinity from which all else comes, is more than simply a storehouse of past recollections. For Gower, memory is central to his psychopharmicon whereby, as in Boethius, the whole process of therapy might be seen as self-recovery after a severe case of forgetfulness.[32] Memory and motive are linked by Triumphus Augustinus de Anchona and others, *motiva* being the impulse toward the good that is deep-seated in memory. Augustine had linked the idea to what he called divine illumination, a Platonic recollection of eternity and divine purpose with which every person is born and for which every person unwittingly yearns. In the *Confessions,* Augustine uses container metaphors to describe memory — a treasury or storehouse, a vast hall (X.viii.14), caves and caverns (X.xvi.20), or "the stomach of the mind" (X.xiv.21–22).[33] Although, as we have seen, it may be difficult to realize the present within time, it certainly may be realized in memory, where a whole lifetime may be present, except for what is lost by forgetfulness (see Augustine, *Confessions* X.xvi.24). Memory is "an awe-inspiring mystery . . . a power of profound and infinite multiplicity," Augustine observes (X.xvii.26). For everyone, the desire for happiness is located in the memory. Memory enables the mind to put fragments together and in this regard is a primary source of happiness in the processes of therapy (see *Confessions* X.xx.29–xxv.31–32). Of all faculties, memory, more than any other, makes possible the grasp of numbers that helps satisfy the soul's need for right order.

Boethius and Augustine emphasize that confession is remembering. So too in Gower, where memory provides the key to Amans' restoration. It is his means of reclaiming his forgotten, natural self in order that he may be released from its fantastic, willfully unnatural substitutions. The *Confessio* begins by asserting that lore of the past needs to be drawn into "remembrance" (Prol.69, 93); by remembering we begin not only to perceive the agencies by which men have corrupted themselves but also to rediscover the meaning of "common profit." Repeatedly, Genius emphasizes that the tales are to be held in remembrance, and Amans again and again asks to be questioned so that he might recall what he has forgotten. The process of forgetting, confessing, and remembering is neatly epitomized in the account of Nebuchadnezzar's dream, based on Daniel 4. Gower places the story near the end of Book 1, as a model of therapy. In a vision Nebuchadnezzar saw what his fate would be if he continued in his vainglorious pride. He called Daniel to him, who explained what the dream meant. But the king forgot; he let the counsel "passe out of his mynde" (1.2951). The consequence of his forgetfulness is loss of human status. He is turned into a dumb ox and for seven years eats grass, drinks from the slough, and sleeps among the bushes, until finally

---

[32] See especially *Consolation* 1.pr.6, where the disconsolate narrator has been diagnosed as having forgotten who he is.

[33] Geoffrey of Vinsauf, in *Poetria Nova*, a work known to both Gower and Chaucer, devotes his concluding chapter to the metaphor of memory as stomach of the mind and to the right ways to feed it (ch. 5, trans. Nims, pp. 87–91).

he remembers what he has lost and prays for forgiveness. He makes a covenant with God and vows to follow humility, at which point, in the twinkling of an eye, just as he reformed his mind so too his body is reformed. Needless to say, when he returned to his throne he remembered to reform his behavior as a king also. Only his vainglory he forgot: "Evere afterward out of memoire / He let it passe"(1.3038–39).

Gower presents memory as the Lover's means of drawing the loose ends of his distracted self together. Memory enables him to see himself wholly. The antithesis of memory and unified vision is forgetfulness and "divisioun."[34] In the Prologue Gower uses the metaphor of division extensively to depict the decrepitude of fourteenth-century England. For Gower, sin is intimately tied to his concepts of memory and time. Sin equates with forgetting. Forgetting is the mind's willful divergence from the ordained order of things. As Gower puts it, sin is "moder of divisioun" (Prol.1030), and division is "moder of confusioun" (Prol.852). Time as we know it began with the Fall. As "moder of divisioun" sin substitutes illusion in place of divine presence. Genius' therapeutic tales are designed to provoke memory and serve as an antidote that makes possible the objectifying of illusion so that the deluded sinner might regain control of a just sense of being. By providing a position outside one's "confusioun," therapeutic tale-telling helps to make possible a reconsideration of the self-deceit of sin.[35]

To forget one's ordained purpose is to disintegrate into disjunctive fragments. Gower's favorite emblem of disintegration, an emblem he used in *Vox Clamantis* as well as the *Confessio*, he took from Daniel 2: the account of Nebuchadnezzar's dream of the monster of time, with its head of gold, chest of silver, belly of brass, and legs and feet of iron and clay (Prol.585 ff.).[36] Gower places the narrative immediately after his critique of the three estates. Although most of the scribes of Gower manuscripts place an image of the dreaming Nebuchadnezzar at the beginning of the story (c. lines 578–96), the illustrator of the Fairfax 3 manuscript begins the poem with the image, as if to establish the Prologue's central theme (see figure 2), namely, the degeneration of time in the divisive decades in England at the end of the fourteenth century. Like others, the Fairfax illustrator depicts the king asleep, dreaming of a monster who towers over him. Significantly, the monster is in the shape of man for, as Gower explains, the corruption of time is the consequence of man's severance from God: "al this wo is cause of man," who is himself "the lasse world" (Prol.905 ff.). Like the Bodley 294 illustrator, the Fairfax illustrator follows the marginal gloss to lines Prol.1031–41 and

---

[34] On the evils of division and dividedness see the Prologue, lines 127, 333, 576, 654, 782, 799, 830, 851, 889, 893, 966, 967, 971, 992, 996, 1010, 1022, and 1030.

[35] It is noteworthy that many of the manuscripts of *CA* include a miniature of Amans kneeling before Genius in hope of receiving a blessing. The image provides a visual meditation on the therapeutic ideal of reading the cultural ideology of Genius' orderly narratives as they, addressing Amans' confusion through his eye and ear, encourage moral reconsideration. See illustrations 1, 3, and 5.

[36] See Griffiths, "*Confessio Amantis*: The Poem and Its Pictures," pp. 163–78, and Emmerson, "Reading Gower in a Manuscript Culture," pp. 167–70, for discussion of the recurrent illuminations in Gower manuscripts. The illustration depicting Nebuchadnezzar's dream is the most often repeated of any representation. Griffiths refers to it as "the dream of precious metals," an inadequate title given Gower's pointed use of the image and the narrative on which it is based. Aside from the fact that iron and clay can scarcely be called precious metals, the point of the account in Daniel and Gower is to demarcate the divisive degeneration of time as human society becomes progressively fragmented by the monstrosities of sin. A preferable designation might be "the dream of the monster of time and the monstrosity of sin." See illustrations 2 and 4 for examples of this image.

picks up the detail from Daniel 2:34 that tells of a great stone cut from the mountain not by human hand that will crush to powder the clay feet of the monster (see illustrations 2 and 4). In both illustrations, the boulder hurtles toward the statue at that apocalyptic moment when time and the monstrosity of sin will instantly be destroyed and time and sin shall be no more.[37] In the text of the poem, as Genius introduces the story of Nebuchadnezzar, he reminds the reader of a perspective beyond time, where sits

> The hyhe almyhti pourveance   *foreknowledge*
> In whos eterne remembrance
> Fro ferst was every thing present. (Prol.585–87)

As people become increasingly forgetful, they lose that sense of the present to become progressively divided from God and eternal memory. Gower extends Daniel's exposition on the vanity of princes beyond that of the Bible so that it reaches even into the fourteenth century. The clay feet epitomize wars with France and civil strife in England as bitter divisions within Christendom crumble into such factions as the Great Schism and Lollardy.

By analogy, these times of division apply to "the lasse world" of the lover, as well. Through metaphors of division Gower links the romance plot of Books 1–8 with the estates critique of the Prologue. Like England, Amans too is a state at war with itself, unable to arrive at a treaty suitable to the demands of its many factions. He is, indeed, his own worst enemy. Toward the end of his confession, Genius will compare him to a burning stick that reduces itself to ashes.

Intimately related to Gower's views on memory and division are his views on poetry. He concludes his discussion of Nebuchadnezzar's monster of time with the story of Arion, the bard whose song was so sweet that it restored peace wherever it was heard:

> . . . of so good mesure   *meter/harmonic ratio*
> He song, that he the bestes wilde   *wild animals*
> Made of his note tame and milde,
> The hinde in pes with the leoun,   *deer*
> The wolf in pes with the moltoun,   *sheep*
> The hare in pees stod with the hound;
> And every man upon this ground
> Which Arion that time herde,
> Als wel the lord as the schepherde,
> He broghte hem alle in good acord;   *them*
> So that the comun with the lord,   *citizenry (common people)*
> And lord with the comun also,
> He sette in love bothe tuo
> And putte awey malencolie. (Prol.1056–69)

This second exemplum that concludes the Prologue functions with a thrust opposite to the fractiousness of Nebuchadnezzar's dream, introducing a poetic of amelioration within which

---

[37] See Apocalypse 21. In *VC* 7 Gower explores ideas of the apocalypse in detail; there he depicts his narrator as one who bears the name of John of the Apocalypse as he begins his diatribe against the ills of the fourteenth century. See Salisbury, "Remembering Origins," pp. 175–77, on Gower's riddling on his name.

the poem operates for the betterment of humankind. The poet is society's rememberer who sees with a unified vision to charm people out of their melancholy and "divisioun." He teaches people to laugh, not hate (Prol.1071). Gower must surely have seen his own purpose in the example. His poem, like the music of Arion, or like the songs of Apollonius and his daughter Thaise in Book 8, would provide therapy in troubled times. We shall see, in fact, that before the poem is over even Amans will smile and become England's poet.

GOWER'S RHETORIC OF ABRIDGMENT: THE "MIDDEL WEIE"

Gower's rhetorical strategy claims to locate the argument of his English poem along a "middel weie" (Prol.17), a pathway *between* rigorous instruction and entertainment. One might make much of the "in-betweenness" of Gower's poem. The *Confessio* mediates between audience and idea. But it is also in-between in its fictional relativity. Gower is sometimes labeled old-fashioned and conservative in his ethics,[38] but there are ways in which quite the opposite is the case. Gower's method is part of a radically new fourteenth-century philosophy of reading (albeit based on ancient literary principles), a method that might be labeled phenomenological epistemology, where one knows mainly by exploring spaces *between* fictions. His radical epistemology is akin to Chaucer's where the poet presents his persona as a figure caught indeterminately between magnets of equal strength (*Parliament of Fowls*, lines 148–49); or Boccaccio, attempting to know truth through fiction;[39] or Langland learning truth through peregrinations amidst the false; or the author of *The Cloud of Unknowing* attempting to unknow what is "known" because of the limitations of realizable knowledge. A middle way can never be stable. It is always configured by what it is between. Yet this relativity of middling may be the only means through which stability can be imagined in a temporal world. Betweenness is inevitably a matter of metonymy, where the name of one thing is used to get at the features of another. It should come as no surprise that the subjunctive mood is more prominent in Gower's poem than the imperative. Through its fictive propositions, the *Confessio* is more a study in possibilities than in moral certainties.

To travel his "middel weie" Gower claims that the style of his English poem, like that which is proper to confession, will be "plein" (see 1.357); that is, "me liketh to comune / And pleinly for to telle it oute" (1.70–71) in order to make the message more accessible to an untutored as well as a clerkish audience. From its stylistic medial point, the Prologue addresses all three estates; that is, although initially dedicated to the king, this poem addresses all people — the lewed as well as the learned. Its primary themes are similar to those of Chaucer in his contemporaneous ballade, "Lak of Stedfastnesse," with its strongly Boethian hope for security of place rather than permutation, stability rather than fickleness, truth rather than deceit, pity and mercy toward fellow men rather than covetousness and oppression. Chaucer's appeal to King Richard in the envoy to that poem puts the matter succinctly: "Dred God, do law, love trouthe and worthinesse, / And wed thy folk agein to stedfastnesse" (lines 27–28) — all themes recurrent in Gower.

In the *Confessio*, Genius' tales often admonish, but the strength of Gower's proposition, like Chaucer's, is that tales do have the capacity to "wed" people in a tie that, despite tur-

---

[38] Coleman, *Medieval Readers and Writers*, pp. 127–28.

[39] See *Boccaccio on Poetry*, ed. and trans. Osgood, especially Book 14, chs. 8–14, on the possibilities of knowing through fiction.

bulent times, could reunite social practices with ideologies. The fickle divisions within the state and within the soul perpetually require mending. Gower would have his tales participate in that remedy. When read carefully they may help to provide the only therapy possible for heart and soul, a therapy that comes from one's own assessment of the fictionally mediated experience. That is, the moral effect of Gower's argument can only be found in the most uncertain realm of all — the inceptive intuitions of his audience. How the audience will respond, Gower can only guess, and, like Chaucer, pray for the reader's good intent.[40] As Gower puts it in Book 8, "kep the sentence of my lore . . . [and] go ther vertu moral duelleth" (8.2923–25),[41] a sentiment exactly in keeping with the ethical economy of both Gower and Chaucer. But "keeping" is, he knows, a tricky business.

Part of the moral strength of the *Confessio* lies in Gower's mastery of his craft, a mastery of design that tallies the smallest of details. Measure defines his verses, a concept pivotal to the poem's utopian vision. There is a singing quality to Gower's tales. Indeed, in this poem he writes some of the most mellifluous, precisely measured verse in Middle English.[42] This textual richness contributes well to the keeping of the sense. Likewise, Genius' tales always have a strong storyline — a sense of going some place. His plots are as rich in invention and as carefully crafted as the narratives of the ancients rediscovered by Genius for his (and Gower's) particular purposes. He has, moreover, a keen awareness of differences of voice not only between characters and levels of fiction, but between himself and all constructed versions of himself as poet.[43] C. S. Lewis points out, "Gower everywhere shows a concern for

---

[40] In Book 8 Gower prays with "hol entente" (line 2968) that he and others will find a means of understanding the confusion of their lives. In the concluding section he prays for the state of England, first that the clergy act justly and "[a]ftir the reule of charité" in *hope* that men schuldyn se / This lond amende" (lines 3003–05; emphasis mine) and that the king will "entende" toward "rightwisnesse" (line 3069). As Gower laid out so clearly in the Prologue, after God destroyed the Tower of Babel, His *entente* (line 1023) was to isolate humankind within diverse languages. For comparison, see Chaucer who, like Gower, repeatedly invites his readers, trapped in their diverse personal languages, to amend his verse, the implication being that, given the instability of language and his own limited understanding, the most important text lies in the reader's perception. See the Retraction (*CT* I[X]1082), The Parson's Tale (I[X]60), and *Troilus and Criseyde* (3.1332); with an amusing variant in *HF* (lines 92–93). On the limitations of humankind's dullness of wit as a psychological inevitability as well as a modesty trope, see Lawton, "Dullness and the Fifteenth Century."

[41] The lines are spoken by Venus as she admonishes "Gower" to leave her court to return to his books. Gower may have got the idea from the Prologue to Chaucer's *Legend of Good Women* (F text), where Alceste sends Chaucer back to his books to work apart from Cupid's court, albeit still exploring the modes of courtesy within society.

[42] See Lewis, *Allegory of Love*, pp. 201–13, on the merits of Gower's plain style. It "has a sweetness and freshness which we do not find in the 'polite' style of later periods. Often a couplet in Gower sounds like a snatch of song" (p. 201). See also Burrow's *Ricardian Poetry*, especially pp. 50–51. Gower's metrical proficiency might be compared with that of Ben Jonson, who much admired Gower and often referred to him in his discussion of grammar in his treatise, *The English Grammar*. So attracted is Jonson to Gower and his more famous contemporary Chaucer that, in *Timber, or Discoveries*, he warns teachers to "beware of letting them [students] taste of *Gower*, or *Chaucer* at first, lest falling too much in love with Antiquity . . . they grow rough and barren in language onely. When their judgements are firme, and out of danger, let them reade both, the old and the new" (*Ben Jonson*, ed. Herford, Simpson, and Simpson, 8:618).

[43] Excellent examples of Gower's careful manipulation of fictive voicing of his persona occur in *Vox Clamantis* where, in the headnote, line 16, he presents himself *quasi in propria persona* [as if in his

form and unity which is rare at any time and which, in the fourteenth century in England, entitles him to all but the highest praise. He is determined to get in all the diversity of interests which he found in his model, and even to add to them his own new interest of tale-telling; but he is also determined to knit all these together into some semblance of a whole."[44] We should not think of this "whole" as an aesthetic absolute, however, though his poem certainly is well constructed. Its aesthetic is shaped not so much by its completeness as by its tangential probing. The tangents may contradict one another, though they proceed from common questions. From beginning to end, the *Confessio* is a cluster of tales (texts and propositions) that require one to respond. It is a poem best understood as a sequence of queries rather than an anthology of answers.

THE GENRE OF THE *CONFESSIO AMANTIS*

In setting up his romance narrative Gower creates an expository frame that, in the manner of complaint, excoriates the ills of the world as they are manifest in the three estates, and then, in the end, he returns to the persona of "John Gower" to pray for the welfare of the kingdom.[45] All but two of the tales are found in the "framed" portion of the poem, where Gower moves more intricately into his multilayered fiction. The two exceptions are the story of Nebuchadnezzar's dream of the statue of degenerative time (Prol.585–880), followed by the story of Arion (Prol.1053–88). Both tales are exemplary of key issues in the Prologue, namely, 1) the destructive effects of divisiveness in modern times, and 2) the need for imaginative amelioration through restorative tales. As we have seen, they identify the critical and salvific concepts that support the basic thesis of the poem's progress.

The interior section of the poem (Books 1–8), composed in the genre of confession/consolation, presents hundreds of tales in diverse subgenres drawn from dozens of sources and organized in terms of the seven deadly sins. Recent critics have referred to Gower as a "compiler," an archivist who collects examples according to some system of organization.[46]

---

own person] while speaking of the uprising of 1381. Macaulay observes: "The author takes care to guard his readers against a too personal application of his descriptions" (*Complete Works*, 4:377). But Gower also wants to keep his reader aware even in this expository moment of issues of fictive voicing. Compare the Latin gloss in the margin adjacent to lines 59 ff. in *CA* 1, where Gower explains *Hic quasi in persona aliorum, quos amor alligat, fingens se auctor esse Amantem* [Here the author, fashioning himself to be the Lover as if in the role of those others whom love binds]. See Galloway ("Gower in His Most Learned Role") on Gower's differentiations of persona in *VC*.

[44] *Allegory of Love*, pp. 198–99.

[45] See Dimmick, "'Redinge of Romance' in Gower's *Confessio Amantis*," for considerations of *CA* under the umbrage of romance conventions.

[46] On Gower as compiler see Minnis, "Late-Medieval Discussions of *Compilatio*," pp. 386–87, and *Medieval Theory of Authorship*, pp. 194–200; Olsson, *Structures of Conversion*, pp. 1–15; and Edwards, "Selection and Subversion." Minnis, *Medieval Theory of Authorship*, speaks of Gower as "a compiler who tried to present himself as an author" (p. 210). But Olsson challenges the imputation of failure in Minnis' assertion (p. 5); he finds in the term *compilator* "a means of identifying issues and strategies that become central to Gower in the work; the procedure of compilation impinges significantly on how he understands history and organizes moral experience itself." Such activities "energize his authorship" (p. 5) rather than weaken it. See Schutz, "Absent and Present Images," on the poem as a mixed genre that functions through mirroring.

It is a useful term, since Gower several times refers to himself as *compilator* in his Latin marginalia. But "compiler" scarcely gets at the poetic vision Gower is attempting to construct. Kurt Olsson has demonstrated a shift in terminology from compiler to author as the poem progresses, suggesting that Gower is becoming aware of what his work is capable of accomplishing as he gets further into it.[47] It may well be that the shift in terminology is part of the poem's dramatic design. What seems initially to be compilation — a treasury of lore for a culture-hungry audience — becomes upon reflection something much more "original." Every act of memory is a step toward originality as details of the past are reviewed. Gower must have been acutely aware of this creative dramatic process from the outset. I can think of no instance in which a "story" is simply retold as it is found in its source. Sometimes the transformations are broad, like his rewriting of the Tale of Narcissus; sometimes they are subtle, as in his adapting of biblical accounts. But the old material is always reworked according to his plan and re-presented, one might say, according to the new contexts of the present world. Divisive times require prolific exempla as remedy, along with a good bit of wit. Through the several personae that Gower manipulates one is perpetually alerted to what Anthony Farnham refers to as the poet's "keen awareness of the didactic value of misdirected seriousness" and an "almost perverse comic sense."[48]

The later fourteenth-century literary scene in England, newly attuned to incipient strategies of history, delights in diversity of signification. In rhetoric and the arts it is a time of multiple signifiers,[49] where, instead of *this* being equitable with *that*, the sign is equivocal, linked provocatively with *this*, *that*, and several *others*.[50] Gower himself is a master at multiple voicing. A tale may be read one way in terms of its immediate context, another way in

---

[47] *Structures of Conversion*, pp. 5–15.

[48] "Art of High Prosaic Seriousness," pp. 164–65.

[49] Part of the delight may be attributed to a new awareness of the relativity of knowledge and a loss of confidence in abstract equations. If direct knowledge of truth is impossible for temporal creatures, then one can only know through likenesses, which is a kind of knowing and not knowing simultaneously. See Myles, *Chaucerian Realism*, particularly the second chapter, and Peck (*Kingship and Common Profit* and "Phenomenology of Make Believe").

[50] A good example of delight in multiple possibilities of meaning may be found in Pierre Bersuire's "De formis figurisque deorum," the opening chapter to his *Ovidius Moralizatus*, in which he discusses numerous ways in which classical mythology may be interpreted. See Peck's discussion of Bersuire and the complexities of irony and multiple voicing in Gower ("Problematics of Irony, pp. 219–21). Behind such hermeneutics lie the playful practices of the Victorine school in the twelfth century, particularly works like Hugh of St. Victor's *De arca noe*, with its piling on of meanings for the ark in diverse contexts, or Anselm's propositions on the volatile relationships between fiction and perceived truth in the *Monologion*, or Boethius' representation of wordplay and the house of Dedalus, in the popular *Consolation of Philosophy* (3.pr.12). In the fourteenth century, contemporaneous with Gower, consider the heteroglossic ideation of *Margarete* in Usk's *Testament of Love*, or the daisy in the Prologue to Chaucer's *Legend of Good Women*, or the pearl in the poem of that name, or the perpetually shifting semantic valences of Piers in *Piers Plowman*. One is reminded of Duns Scotus in his use of suppositional logic in his development of an empirical science, where four quite different arguments are given to explain a proposition, an *if this, then that* strategy in which all propositions become correlative to the procedure of the argument. This "newe science," as Chaucer calls it (*Parliament of Fowls*, line 25), becomes a way of looking at things with results contingent upon the suppositional premises of initial propositions. What Usk called "delight in making" becomes a concept for reading as well as a formula for composing, a matter rather different from compiling.

relation to its source, another still in relation to its narrator (usually Genius), or in a further way in terms of Amans' prejudicial response to the tale; and finally it must be read in terms of the historical Gower and the several purposes of the whole poem.[51] Gower is perpetually conscious of the relativity of meaning to the different voices in his poem along with the alterable meanings of signs in relation to their sources and contexts. This hermeneutic of conditional perception anchored in diverse suppositions underlies the flexible choices of genre through which he makes particular statements.

There is, however, a distinctly definable plot to the fictive section of the poem — namely, the "tale" of Amans in debate with Genius. In a broad view, the *Confessio Amantis* is one of several Middle English poems that may be classified as poems of consolation. It is a genre with a powerful philosophical appeal to the later fourteenth century. The confessional aspect of the genre owes much to St. Augustine though, in the fourteenth century, the principal model behind the soul-searching is Boethius' *Consolation of Philosophy*. The likenesses of the group (which includes poems such as *Pearl*, Usk's *Testament of Love*, Chaucer's *Book of the Duchess*, *The Parliament of the Three Ages*, and, in a more complex way, Langland's *Piers Plowman*) lie in both subject matter and plot structure. Frequently consolation poems are dream visions, though the Boethian model is technically not a dream vision (nor is the *Confessio Amantis*, for that matter),[52] but rather a projected condition of displacement. In each the primary subject is the narrator's restless state of mind, which may, in turn, reflect upon some unstable social situation. The plot is the narrator/dreamer's search for repose, a search which, given the contingencies of time, can never be completed with full satisfaction. Given the uncertainty of circumstances, the means of argument within the plot is confrontational as well as confessional.[53]

The skeletal structure of a Boethian consolation plot normally follows four main steps.[54] 1) There will be an opening description of the narrator's physiological confusion and spiritual inertia, his displacement and alienation. His psychological turmoil will be presented as an illness he suffers within Fortune's domain. Usually, the illness will manifest itself in some form of death wish. The invalid may express a desire for help, but at the same time

---

[51] See Donaldson (*Speaking of Chaucer*, pp. 1–12) on the voicing in Chaucer, particularly in *CT*, which comes closest to the considerations required in the assessing of Gower's voicing. In the same vein see Olsson (*Structures of Conversion*), who, after observing that Gower, according to a Senecan model of voices in a chorus wherein multiple voices speak as one, observes that Gower, nonetheless, "works to separate, to create for the work an impression of *compilatio*, and does so by authoring divergent outlooks. Indeed, as he breaks his own voice out into many voices in his fiction of a compilation, he does by very different means what Chaucer does through his pilgrims in the *Canterbury Tales*" (p. 12).

[52] Though technically not a dream vision, Boethius' *Consolation* was consistently regarded as one, given the fact that the narrator is lying ill upon his bed and Philosophy comes to him as if in a vision. In setting up his exemplum Gower might have put his narrator to sleep, then had him meet Venus and Genius, but such a literalization of the shifting categories of mind was not necessary. All the poet needs to do is to project fictive situations which serve the same requirements as the discrete boundaries of a dream world. All thought is a kind of dream, and as Chaucer puts it in *HF*, "dreme he barefot, dreme he shod" (line 98), that is, whether he is sleeping or awake, he is still dreaming.

[53] The best discussion that I know of the debate components of the poem is Olsson's discussion of the *tumultuator* conventions through which Gower creates dispute and discord for the unbinding of ideas. See especially *Structures of Conversion*, pp. 13–15 and 70–72.

[54] This portion of my argument is adapted from my earlier edition of *CA* (1968), pp. ix–x.

acknowledge that he does not know where to find it. 2) The distracted, dis-eased narrator will then perform some act of choice that will precipitate a change of scene, whereupon new "characters" will appear which are projections of different fragments of his anxious self or his environment. The new setting is now in the realm of the mind, where the heart of the quest will take place. 3) The argument of the poem will be conducted through dialogue between the narrator and the new characters. This multiplication of voicing is the most elastic part of the genre. It enables the poet to explore conditional propositions through the suppositions of each, thus opening for the reader an intellectual playground in which problems may be dramatized. It is here and in the conclusion that the author will exercise the most originality as he chooses particular devices suitable to the intention of the argument. But regardless of the device, whether it be a hart hunt as in *The Book of the Duchess*, a walk beside a river coming from Paradise as in *Pearl*, a hunt by a poacher in a deep wood as in *The Parliament of the Three Ages*, a search for salvation amidst a field full of folk as in *Piers Plowman*, or a confessional debate with Genius as in the *Confessio Amantis*, the argument will most likely begin with questions of identity, such as "What or who am I?" "Where am I?" or "What is the trouble with my soul?" It will then progress through a series of partial revelations (tales, if you will) which present themselves dramatically and bear some similarity to Boethius' baring of his wound in order that Philosophy might apply the appropriate medicine. 4) The analysis and therapy will end with a tense moment in which the disturbed persona will waver, then achieve a revelation, usually partial, that will precipitate his return to the dilemma that initiated the search. The narrator may still be baffled by the meaning of the dreamlike experience, but he will, at least, have a better sense of what is at stake.

The *Confessio Amantis* is organized along the lines I have outlined, though Gower will, as we shall see, exercise a great deal of ingenuity in working within them. His most radical change is the introduction of a complex social analogue in the frame narrative that qualifies readings within the romance plot. Such a scheme is highly ambitious and even daring[55] as Gower attempts to conjoin social criticism presented in a nonfictional mode with fiction. At least the effect leaves no doubt in the reader's mind about Gower's convictions regarding the urgency of his argument; we find ourselves dealing with England as well as the Lover,[56] aware that the two are somehow interconnected. Since this political side of the poem's frame narrative is likely to give modern readers of the *Confessio* the greatest difficulty, I will preface my discussion of the poem's romance structure with an attempt to locate the concerns of the poem within the divisive political circumstances of the late 1380s to which the Prologue and the conclusion to the frame allude.

---

[55] The daring lies in criticizing people of higher social station in the fourteenth century but also in imagining that the moral force of the form might make a difference. See Ferster, *Fictions of Advice*, pp. 31–38 and 108–36, and Middleton, "Idea of Public Poetry," pp. 91–92 and 95–104, on the danger of such literary activities.

[56] His model for such a strategy might have been Chaucer or, perhaps, Jean de Meun in his continuation of *Le Roman de la Rose*. See Middleton, "Idea of Public Poetry," pp. 89–90, on the bridging of metaphysical and moral philosophy in fourteenth-century English literature.

POLITICS AND SOCIETY

The Prologue focuses emphatically on division within the state as cause of the woes of the times. As a social document the *Confessio* is securely anchored in the time of its origins — Gower has seen to that. The social concerns are not simply conservative or aristocratic,[57] though conservation of social structures is, for Gower, a primary concern. Few poets have been so deeply committed to the welfare of present times as Gower. That commitment was evident in his Anglo-Norman *Mirour de l'Omme*, where he first assesses English society within a gridwork of sins and remedies. Likewise, in his subsequent Latin work, the *Vox Clamantis*, one finds a comparable commitment toward understanding aberrations of the present time. Both of these earlier works are devoted to discursive analysis of the layout of social and political culture. The welfare of the kingdom remains a focal concern of the *Confessio Amantis*, especially in the Prologue and in the diatribe against war in Book 3 (Wrath), the discussions of labor in Book 4 (Sloth), of religion in Book 5 (Avarice), in the extended discourse on the pedagogy of the king of Book 7, and, finally, in the appeal for good rule in the conclusion to Book 8.[58] But the *Confessio Amantis* is more densely layered than Gower's earlier works. The frame narrative and the digressions of Books 4, 5, and 7, lay out what Gower perceives the sociological problems of the day to be, particularly factious aggressions within the three estates that disrupt the commonweal, peace, and unity.

In 1390, when Gower first completed and began circulating *Confessio Amantis*, England was at a relatively quiet moment between two turbulent decades. Peace after turbulence is indeed a concern of Gower's poem, from its beginning to its conclusion.[59] To a Londoner like Gower, living close to the seat of England's government, the decade of the 1380s had been an extended nightmare. The decade had begun with pervasive economic and political crises that led to the Uprising of 1381, a bloody protest that, as it descended upon London, reverberated through all levels of society but solved little. Gower might well have witnessed the burning of John of Gaunt's Savoy Palace and the siege of the Tower from his residence at St. Mary Overeys, across the river in Southwark. When young King Richard had shown

---

[57] As Gower's critique cuts across all three estates, his position is not too dissimilar from Langland's in *Piers Plowman* B.6, where Piers sets up rules of governance on his half acre. In Gower the commons is governed by the king and the church, though all three share responsibility for good rule. It is an evil time when the commons rebel, but an especially evil time if proud churchmen or aristocrats promote themselves at the cost of the kingdom. See Emmerson, "Reading Gower in a Manuscript Culture," pp. 171–75, on *CA* as a public poem.

[58] None of the expository sections — on the difficulty of justifying war, on the origins of labor and the professions, on the history of religion, and on the education of the king — appear in this volume, though they will occur in volumes 2 and 3 of this edition. For detailed summaries of the expository sections, see my one-volume edition of selections from *CA* (1968), pp. 192, 222–23, 242–48, and 368–414.

[59] Peace became for Gower almost a mania in his recurrent attempts to address the political chaos of England during his lifetime. It is not only central to his three major works, *Mirour de l'Omme*, *Vox Clamantis*, and *Confessio Amantis*; at the end of the 1390s, after the deposition of Richard, he wrote the *Tripartite Chronicle*, lamenting the greed of Richard's party and celebrating the justice of their overthrow. His final English poem is *In Praise of Peace*, c. 1400, a poem that hopes Henry's new administration can restore peace to the nation. The theme of peace is also found in such works of Chaucer as "Lak of Stedfastnesse" and The Tale of Melibee, both of which works bear close ties with *CA*.

his mettle in facing the rebels in Smithfield,[60] it must have seemed a demonstration of royal courage that Gower would have admired greatly, an action that might well have added a note of sincerity to the dedication to Richard in the Prologue and concluding dedication of the *Confessio* in 1390.

But the king had reason to admire Gower in return, which may have been a factor in his inviting the poet onto his royal barge (see Prol.*24–*92, the first recension account of the particular occasion out of which the *Confessio* grew). Earlier, in the late 1370s, Gower had attempted to address the factiousness of that "disastrous decade"[61] by means of the *Vox Clamantis* (c. 1377–81), a precautionary complaint against greed and private aggrandizement among the aristocracy as well as the unruly behavior manifested by the dissidents. In the 1370s the executive government of Edward III had been attacked on all sides by often vicious factions that assailed the clerical ministers of state, impeached the king's chamberlain and a number of lesser officials, murdered the chancellor and treasurer, and indiscriminately massacred officers of the law and minor civil servants. In the *Vox*, Gower's attack on such behavior is forthright and carefully reasoned, albeit in Latin. The social critique of *Vox Clamantis* was read primarily by ecclesiasts and men of law, though it must also have been known to some in the royal court and perhaps even the king himself. At least, he would most likely have known something of Gower's recounting of the terrors of the revolt in 1381.

As kings go, Richard was remarkably learned. In the prince's adolescence Simon Burley had served as his tutor, and it is possible that Richard's interest in books may have been instilled by Burley.[62] The extent to which he was affiliated with or encouraged writers in English in the younger days of his rule can only be surmised. He was evidently fond of Chaucer and may have been aware, at least, of the literary interests of others. Anne Middleton, in her discussion of Thomas Usk's *Testament of Love*, projects a literary coterie in London in the last two decades of the fourteenth century who took pride in the composing of vernacular literature and wrote for each other.[63] These wordcrafters — men like Chaucer, Langland,

---

[60] See Coleman, *Medieval Readers and Writers*, pp. 126–56, for an account of Gower as a witness to history in *VC*, and Staley, "Gower, Richard II, Henry of Derby, and the Business of Making Culture," for discussion of *CA* in its day. For a general survey of social events and responses to the "hurling time" of the uprising see Peck, "Social Conscience and the Poets." For a useful anthology of literature of protest from the period see Dean, ed., *Medieval English Political Writings*.

[61] The phrase is McKisack's, in *Fourteenth Century*; see p. 384, for a summary of the "disastrous" events.

[62] See Saul, *Richard II*, pp. 15–16, and Maude V. Clarke, *Fourteenth Century Studies*, pp. 120–23. Burley's library holdings included Egidio Colonna's *De regimine principum*, a book akin to *VC*. See Coleman, *Medieval Readers and Writers*, pp. 18–19, on Burley's book holdings. It is likely that Richard would have understood and appreciated the advice-to-princes genre, at which Gower was particularly adept. See also Michael J. Bennett, "Court of Richard II and the Promotion of Literature," and Kerby-Fulton and Justice, "Langlandian Reading Circles."

[63] The most thorough discussion of Gower's relationship with his fourteenth-century audience is Coleman, *Medieval Readers and Writers*, pp. 126 ff. The genius of Middleton's more succinct observations lies in its shifting of the audience of Gower from an aristocracy or coterie of ecclesiasts to a group of writers whose bond lies not in their social privilege but in their delight as men of letters in wordcrafting and the clerical arts of bookmaking, what Usk refers to as "perdurable letters" (3.923), those "sleigh inseer[s]" who "can souke hony of the harde stone, oyle of the drye rocke" and "lyghtly fele nobley of mater in my leude ymagination closed" (*Testament of Love* 3.104–06). See Middleton,

Gower, Usk, the *Pearl*-poet, Strode, Clanvowe, Hoccleve, and later Lydgate, along with the craftsmen of dozens of other anonymous literary gems, such as *The Alliterative Morte Arthure*, *The Stanzaic Morte Arthur*, *The Storie of Asneth*, and *The Pistel of Swete Susan* — wrote with the resourcefulness of a new Renaissance mentality that defined what Coleman calls "England's literary golden age."[64] Gower, along with Chaucer, was at the center of the group. We know something of the genius of these writers through their comments upon each other. Their reputation, particularly that of Chaucer, Gower, and Lydgate, lasted into the high Renaissance of the sixteenth and early seventeenth centuries, where they were praised for the marvelous inception in England of literary delight.

Although the degree to which the king was aware of such remarkable beginnings is unclear, he must have known something of what was happening. Gower's Latin *Vox Clamantis* may be the work to which Richard alludes in the 1390 Prologue to the *Confessio Amantis*, when he invited Gower aboard the royal barge on the Thames to encourage him to write "Som newe thing . . . That he himself it mighte looke / After the forme of my writyng" (lines *51–*53).[65] It is after this meeting that Gower presumably began working on the *Confessio Amantis*. Whether he actually began writing the poem with the Prologue we do not know. It is conceivable that the Prologue was written later, though certainly no later than 1389. Perhaps the meeting on the Thames that the Prologue refers to occurred c. 1385, before the machinations of the Appellants began, though the remainder of the Prologue probably alludes to the later events.

Like the *Vox*, the Prologue to the *Confessio* offers a critique of the times. The critique is similar to that of the *Vox*, perhaps not so much because Gower thinks in patterns as because the times of the 1380s are so similar in their factionalism to those of the 1370s. In the years immediately after the great revolt, England could scarcely be seen to be at peace, even though the unruly bloodshed had been quelled. The punitive and restrictive laws that were enacted offered little security or satisfaction to anyone. In 1386, baronial unrest in opposition to the young king spilled over into Parliament. Anticipation of the impending attack on the king and his counselors may explain Chaucer's resignation from his position in the Customs Office and his move out of London. Chaucer was certainly loyal to the king as he took up residence in Kent where the queen resided. He served in the Parliament of 1386 as a member from Kent, perhaps to act in support of the crown. But during the next year and the year following things did not go well for the king.[66] In November of 1387, three powerful barons — Gloucester, Arundel, and Warwick — attacked Richard through his counselors. With support from Derby (Henry of Lancaster) and Mowbray, they "appealed" five of Richard's administrators and principal supporters — Neville, De Vere, Suffolk, Tresilian, and

---

"Thomas Usk's 'Perdurable Letters,'" pp. 63, 68–70, 88n35, and 94–104, where she specifically considers Gower.

[64] *Medieval Readers and Writers*, p. 14.

[65] Another possibility of work by Gower known to the king might be early love poems (in French) which later were incorporated into the *Cinkante Balades*. See Macaulay, 1:lxxiii, on the history of the *Balades*.

[66] For succinct discussions of the events following 1386 and Usk's execution, see Saul, *Richard II*, pp. 193–94, and Scott, "Chaucer and the Parliament of 1386." For a more detailed analysis see McKisack, *Fourteenth Century*, pp. 424–61. See also Stow, "Richard II in John Gower's *Confessio Amantis*," pp. 13–24.

the Lord Mayor of London Nicholas Brembre, along with four knights of the royal household, including Thomas Usk, a man of letters friendly to Chaucer and Gower, and Simon Burley, young King Richard's friend and tutor. Suffolk and Neville fled. Tresilian and Brembre hid out in London. De Vere went to Chester to assemble an army. Burley wanted to go into hiding, but De Vere persuaded him to stand his ground firmly with the king. When De Vere and Richard's men were defeated at Radcot Bridge all were at the mercy of the Appellants. There was talk of deposing Richard, but that drastic action was opposed by Derby and Mowbray. Instead, the Appellants turned upon Richard's administration: On 3 February 1388, when the "Merciless Parliament" convened, they caught, tried, convicted, and executed Brembre and Tresilian. When Neville and Suffolk fled to the continent, the purge focused upon Burley, who was popular with Londoners and many of the baronry. As Scott puts it, Gloucester, his integrity on the line, forced a conviction "on the feeble charge of 'leading Richard in his youth to form a corrupt court,' the only charge out of eight on which he could force a confirmation. All the power which Derby exerted, and even the plea of Queen Anne on her knees at Gloucester's feet, failed to deter Gloucester's vengeance, and Burley went to the scaffold in the Tower."[67] On March 4, Thomas Usk, Chaucer's friend and associate in the arts, a man doubtless known to Gower, was likewise executed.[68] Condemned as a traitor "faux and malveise," Usk was sentenced to execution in a most brutal manner. After being drawn and hanged, he was "immediately taken down and, after about thirty strokes of the axe, beheaded."[69] Brutalities such as these demonstrated the trauma of the factious behavior that Gower had written about in *Vox* and which underlie the appeal for peace in the Prologue to the *Confessio Amantis*. But where in *Vox* the focus was on all three estates, particularly the commons, here the focus is more on the first estate — the baronry and the king.

After the ugly scenes of 1388, however, quieter days were in sight. In 1389 Richard declared himself free of tutelage and capable of rule as a monarch of full age. Chaucer returned to London to become Clerk of the King's Works. For the next few years there was some stability at court and its surrounding environs. After the atrocities earlier in the decade it seems that all parties were making an effort to cooperate. When Richard claimed his sovereignty the Appellants and their enforced administration withdrew quietly. Warwick retired to his estates, Arundel planned a crusade to the Holy Land, and Derby went to Prussia, where Gloucester followed. As May McKisack points out, Richard had been "carefully unprovocative," and with John of Gaunt's return from Portugal there seemed to be a "general restoration of unity."[70]

Some have thought that when Richard fell at odds with the city of London in 1392 Gower turned his loyalties away from the king to embrace Henry, count of Derby, who had been one of the Appellants at the time of the Merciless Parliament. But there is no sound evidence that Gower was hostile toward the king early in the decade. The dedication to

---

[67] Scott, "Chaucer and the Parliament of 1386," p. 85; see also Saul, *Richard II*, p. 194.

[68] See Strohm, "Politics and Poetics," pp. 83–112, on the politics surrounding Usk's execution; Kerby-Fulton and Justice, "Langlandian Reading Circles," pp. 59–83, for discussion of Usk's intellectual confreres; and Shoaf's introduction to his edition of Usk's *Testament of Love*, pp. 5–7, for a general survey of the issues. On possible links between Usk and Gower's *VC*, see Summers, "Gower's *Vox Clamantis* and Usk's *Testament of Love*," pp. 56–59.

[69] *The Westminster Chronicle*, ed. and trans. Hector and Harvey, p. 315.

[70] *Fourteenth Century*, pp. 464–65.

Henry is certainly sincere, but the poet is careful to keep that version separate from the earlier one. The Ricardian *Confessio* continued to be recopied until the end of the century when Richard was deposed. At that point Gower clearly was disappointed in the king and makes his disappointment evident in his attack on Richard and his courtiers in the *Tripartite Chronicle*, which he appended to the *Vox Clamantis*. But many tumultuous events transpired between 1390 and 1399. The world itself seemed to have changed.

THE ROMANCE PLOT OF THE *CONFESSIO AMANTIS*

After the Prologue, Gower mutes his critique on the turmoil of the times to focus, instead, on the mental tumult of a distracted lover. In the confessional section of the text Gower turns the crisis of political division into a psychological crisis that leads to a kind of schizophrenic behavior that the poet addresses through the therapy of tale-telling. The romance plot of the *Confessio* (in effect, the dream) begins as the poet, announcing in the Latin marginal gloss that he will assume the guise of a lover, tells how he, filled with "woful care" on a "wofull day" in May, puts his "wofull chance" (1.74–75) into the hands of Fortune as he sets out for the wood. Everything around him seems happy and gay but Amans is miserable. He is unhappy

> For I was further fro my love   *from*
> Than erthe is fro the hevene above. (1.105–06)

Once in the wood the lover throws himself to the ground and wishes he were dead. Then he awakens in his pain and, filled with self-pity, cries out to Cupid and Venus, who suddenly appear before him and transfix his heart on love's fiery dart.[71]

This opening description defines the lover's disorientation and thus establishes the main considerations of the romance plot. Trapped within the contradictions of Nature and his own desire, Amans, in his fantasy, has set himself apart from the mutual pleasures of Nature's domain in hope of enjoying singular pleasures. His main desire is to pamper his secretive emotions. The piercing of his heart by Cupid's dart clinches his loss of natural freedom. He is trapped by his amorous confusion, and many tales will pass before he returns home from dysfunctional spiritual exile.

When Venus first addresses Amans, she asks him questions of identity typical of the consolation genre: "What art thou, sone?" (1.154, 160). Amans replies, "A caitif that lith hiere: / What wolde ye, my ladi diere?" (1.161–62). The question is reminiscent of Boethius' *Consolation*, where Philosophy asked, "What are you?" of that narrator. The right answer is, of course, "A man."[72] But in his infatuation Amans has forgotten what a man should be.

---

[71] The romance devices here — the wandering in May, the music of the birds, the woeful frustration of the lovesick persona, the encounter with Venus and Cupid, and Cupid's fiery, captivating dart — are all found in the opening section of Guillaume de Lorris' *Roman de la Rose*, which sets the tone for many a *fin amor* love quest in France and England well into the fifteenth century and later. The love language signifies that the narrator has become "Amans" and that the subject of the poem will henceforth be the love fantasies of Fortune's child.

[72] Compare Philosophy's catechism for Boece as she attempts to identify the specifics of his illness (*Consolation* 1.pr.6): "'Whethir wenestow,' quod sche, 'that this world be governed by foolyssche happes and fortunows, or elles wenestow that ther be inne it ony governement of resoun?'" (lines 7–10, Chau-

Rather than a creature of free choice, he sees himself as a helpless, supine "caitif." He asks
to be cured of his affliction, but Venus says:

> "Tell thi maladie:
> What is thi sor of which thou pleignest?   *sorrow; complain*
> Ne hyd it noght, for if thou feignest,   *hide the truth*
> I can do thee no medicine."[73] (1.164–67)   *help you with*

Her question is reminiscent of Philosophy's request that Boethius bare his wound by reiter-
ating his illness truthfully (see *Consolation*, 1.pr.4). But Venus is no Dame Prudence or Lady
Philosophy. Her intention is quite the opposite, her demands a parody of Philosophy's. Her
motives are defensive and courtly, based on suspicion rather than mutual trust. She has
learned how to deal with "[f]aitours" (1.174). In her world nobody trusts anybody. Let
Amans explain his intentions!

Gower's use of confession as a device for developing his argument is a felicitous choice,
"a master-stroke which organizes the whole of Gower's material," C. S. Lewis observes.[74] The
device opens limitless possibilities for variety and dramatic effects. But Gower did not
choose the device for literary reasons alone. Confession, as Gower understood it, is an act
of self-discovery. It is for him what psychoanalysis is for us. Confession begins with a review
of experience in an effort to find out why it is that we are the way we are, in order that we
may ultimately reintegrate our minds and emotions. "You have forgotten what you are" (see
note 61), Philosophy tells Boethius: Amans' problem is precisely the same. Having displaced
his affection for the commonweal with a lover's doting alienation, he is not only far from his
heart's desire, but even uncertain of what that desire is. Venus sends him to a confessor
named Genius, who will become his attendant spirit. To Genius he appeals:

> "I prai thee let me noght mistime
> Mi schrifte, for I am destourbed   *confession*
> In al myn herte, and so contourbed,   *perturbed*
> That I ne may my wittes gete,
> So schal I moche thing forgete.
> Bot if thou wolt my schrifte oppose   *question me about my confession*
> Fro point to point, thanne, I suppose,
> Ther schal nothing be left behinde.   *left unexamined*

---

cer's translation). Boece is unable to answer the question reasonably, which brings Philosophy to her
next crucial move: "Remembrestow that thow art a man?" (lines 55–56). When the disconsolate Boece
stumbles on his definition of what a man is Philosophy knows where to begin her therapy: "'Now woot
I,' quod sche, 'other cause of thi maladye, and that ryght greet: thow hast left for to knowen thyselve
what thou art'" (lines 68–70).

[73] Venus raises an important consideration in the seeking of counsel, namely, that the suppliant
tell his tale truthfully: otherwise the adviser cannot address the problem accurately. Compare The
Tale of Melibee, where Dame Prudence insists that for the counsel to be of value the suppliant must
tell all truthfully. Contrast the summoner in The Friar's Tale, who boasts that he lies to his confessor
so that he can get away with whatever he wants.

[74] Lewis goes on to suggest that "the confession in the *Roman de la Rose* taught Gower nothing
except, possibly, the name and office of Genius." The confessional device "is, as far as I know, entirely
Gower's own and he has seldom received full credit for it" (*Allegory of Love*, p. 200n).

Bot now my wittes ben so blinde,
That I ne can miselven teche." (1.220–29)

Confessing, like tale-telling, is an exercise in timing. Given the confusion amidst temporalities of earth, mistiming is virtually inevitable. But at least his intention is good, and that is no small matter. Indeed, by the end of the poem nothing will be left behind: Genius, "with his wordes debonaire" (1.231), will search out the circumstances of Amans' soul, and through his questions redefine man in his rightful historical environment so that Amans may remember what he is and forget what he is not.

Amans' search for repose is, of course, analogous to England's search for peace and just administration. To regain his psychological homeland he must reclaim within himself each of the three estates. First he must reclaim his "commons," that is to say, his emotions which labor helps to regulate. The discussion on labor (Book 4.2363–2700) dwells mainly on alchemy and the writings of great men of letters. Amans does not take well to Genius' suggestion that he should study Ovid if he wants advice on dealing with his passion. He says he will heed no suggestions about giving up his lady. In the conclusion, after a long labor of penance, he changes his attitude, however, and, in Book 8, it is Ovid and the other men of letters who aid him in *his* final metamorphosis. Then a transformation as remarkable as any alchemy takes place, as we shall see, when Venus fixes up his kidneys (seat of the passions).

The discussion pertaining to the second estate (Book 5.729–1970) is more involved. Significantly Amans himself asks for instruction in the history of religions. His training begins with an outline of the pagan gods, then of Judaism, and then of Christianity. The sequence delineates the steps toward true revelation. That most of the exposition deals with the pagan deities is understandable if we keep in mind that the pagan world is simply the mutable world in which men spend most of their time. The tone of this portion of the poem is light, as Gower enjoys the incongruity of having Genius mock his godly accomplices, the classical deities. For Amans to discover objectively the ridiculousness of the pagan gods would be a crucial step toward recognizing the ridiculousness of his own pagan behavior as he attempts to do homage to Venus. But the lesson does not soak in yet. Only in the Epilogue, after he has recognized the old man in himself, does he get beyond pagan behavior to reinstate intelligently his second estate.

The hardest thing for the disconsolate rebel to accept is responsibility for his first estate, and, indeed, the instruction of Amans in the first estate (Book 7) provides the climax to the exposition, where Amans himself, out of curiosity, requests the discussion. The point seems to be that he has become sufficiently engaged in what Genius has to say to forget momentarily his infatuation. In Book 7 Genius' opening account of the universe defines the boundaries of the domain over which Amans should be king by natural right, and the discussion of man defines the rational creature Amans has forgotten. The ethical generalizations on Truth, Liberality, Justice, Pity, and Chastity define positive means for dealing with cupidity once Amans has realized what cupidity is. They provide the means through which a person cares for his soul. As Genius notes near the end of the poem:

For conseil passeth alle thing
To him which thenkth to ben a king;
And every man for his partie
A kingdom hath to justefie,
That is to sein his oghne dom.   *domain (judgment, head)*
If he misreule that kingdom,

He lest himself, and that is more	*loses*
Than if he loste schip and ore	*oar*
And al the worldes good withal:	
For what man that in special	
Hath noght himself, he hath noght elles,	
No mor the perles than the schelles. (8.2109–20)	*pearls; shells*

With the restoration of Amans' sense of right rule the romance comes to its conclusion.

THE TALES OF BOOK ONE

Several of the most memorable stories of the *Confessio* are found in Book 1. These tales, coming as they do immediately after Gower's disquisition on memory and the evils of forgetfulness, exemplify admirably Gower's idea of tales that "reporte and holde," to borrow the Pardoner's phrase, as a momentary stay against the "lewedness" of the post-lapsarian world. Book 1 is devoted to Pride and is arranged around that sin's five subdivisions — Hypocrisy, Murmur and Complaint, Presumption, Boasting, and Vain Glory.[75] Throughout the book Gower's remarkable powers of invention are evident in the variety of tales he tells — from short exempla like the Tale of Aspidis (lines 463–80) to tales of complex moral choice like the Tale of Mundus and Paulina, the Tale of Florent, the Trump of Death, the Tale of Albinus and Rosemund, or the Tale of Three Questions. One cannot help but be captivated by the stark composure of the Tale of Mundus and Paulina (lines 761–1059), a seduction narrative exposing Hypocrisy, where the deceitful Mundus (whose name *could* mean "pure," but ultimately proves to be a signifier of the corruption of the "world"),[76] under the sneaky posture of divine guide, attempts to destroy the innocent Paulina.[77] Even though she, with the assent of her husband, gives her body to the "god's" use (or thinks that she has done), she is the one who remains pure, despite the fact that she has been deceitfully dealt with by a corrupt man. The storyline is poignantly modulated with dramatic irony to demonstrate the power of family and community solidarity to underscore the point that innocence can be corrupted only by thought, not the hypocritical conniver.

The Tale of Florent (lines 1407–1861) is a loathly hag narrative, a likely source for Chaucer's Wife of Bath's Tale.[78] In this tale Genius claims to be focusing on the evils of Murmur and Complaint, though the crux of the plot hinges upon the virtue of being true

---

[75] These are the five subdivisions of Pride that Gower had outlined in the *Mirour de l'Omme*. The first four books of *CA* follow the arrangement of sin in the earlier poem; the last four vary the pattern extensively.

[76] For discussion of the pun on *mundus*:pure and *mundus*:world, see Peck, *Kingship and Common Profit*, pp. 41–45.

[77] For an unusual presentation of the tale see Hines, *Fabliau in English*, p. 215, who, in consideration of exempla and the fabliau, discusses fabliau components in the Tale of Mundus and Paulina. The tone of Gower's poem is, of course, altogether different from that of most fabliaux. That is, I do not think Gower means it as a joke, despite the peculiar sexual behavior.

[78] Gower wrote the tale sometime between 1386 and 1390. The Wife of Bath's Tale was most likely written after 1392 as part of that creative outburst that produced what Kittredge and others called "the marriage group."

to one's word.[79] Truth requires that one accept the responsibilities of one's decisions. Like the Tale of Mundus and Paulina, the Tale of Florent explores proper governance of the will. Neither Paulina nor Florent will, like Amans, fall captive to some absurd passion in an obscure wood through some misguided abuse of their wills, even though accidents beyond their ken befall them. In the story a young knight named Florent makes his way along a tortuous pathway defined by uncertainties. At the outset he seeks adventures in the western marches of England. Fortune leads him into a conflict in which he is "be strengthe take" (1.1423) and imprisoned in a castle. In the fighting he unfortunately slays Brachus, the son and heir of the "capitain" of the region (1.1419–30). The mother and grandmother of Branchus murmur and complain, demanding revenge, but fear that in exacting it they will incur the wrath of the emperor, to whom Florent is of "cousinage" (1.1437).[80] So they plan to entrap Florent through a cleverly contrived test of his character. Knowing that Florent is renowned as a knight who is true to his word, they plot to get him to commit himself to answering a question that he cannot understand. This compulsion to answer the unanswerable characterizes many of Gower's stories, thereby epitomizing the dilemma that Gower sees at the root of human need. If Florent is true to his word and returns without the answer, they can destroy him by law without fear of reprisal from the emperor. If he is false and does not return to his sentencing, then he will have destroyed himself by being untrue. For Gower, the issue here is not that Florent does not know the answer through his own cognizance — that had been true of Paulina, as well. Rather, the concern lies in *how* he deals with a problem that exceeds his grasp. A tale is by definition a test — a tally-taking — whether for the participants in the plot or the reader attempting to understand it. Every tale is paradigmatically a testing of the will. Florent's enemies have designs on his life. They imagine that he will fail to answer the impossible question and thus forfeit his life. The irony is that in Gower's moral scheme the old queen who puts the question to him is quite right: the only way he *can* be destroyed is by his own choice. The queen is wrong only insofar as she imagines that she can destroy him through subtle aggression. Florent is saved more by his integrity than by the queen's error or the old hag's answer. The hag knows this well and, in turn, counts upon his integrity for her own survival, just as he comes to count upon hers.

The grandame's test requires that Florent reveal what it is that women most desire. He searches for a year and is unable to discover an answer. On his return to his doom, filled with uncertainty, he meets a loathly hag whose hideousness is described. She tells him that she can supply the answer if he will agree to marry her. He at first refuses but then, thinking that she is old and cannot live long, agrees. She gives him the answer:

That thou schalt seie, upon this molde	*earth*
That alle wommen lievest wolde	*would most desire*
Be soverein of mannes love:	*To be*

---

[79] See Echard, "With Carmen's Help," pp. 32–34, on ambiguities of voicing in the tales of Florent and Albinus and Rosemond as revealed by various manuscript glosses. Echard demonstrates that the glosses, but often the text as well, deliberately displace the focus of the argument, particularly with regard to nature.

[80] Perhaps the point here supports the moral dimension of the tale, in that, in Christian ideology, all children of God hold "cousinage" to the "emperor" (i.e., to God, the ultimate authority and watchman). How God's kingship functions, however, is always an unknown. In this tale the key to familial solidarity lies in the keeping of one's word, which is the end toward which the moral speaks.

For what womman is so above,	*that woman [who] is thus of a higher rank*
Sche hath, as who seith, al hire wille;	*her desire*
And elles may sche noght fulfille	*For otherwise*
What thing hir were lievest have. (1.1607–13)	*she would most desire to have*

Armed with the answer he returns to the marches and is granted, perforce, his freedom. But being a man true to his word he is scarcely free, for, being now subcontracted,[81] he must return to the wood where he met the hag and fetch her to be his wife. They are married and he, that night, must perform his marriage duties. When he turns toward her in bed he sees a lovely woman of "eyhtetiene wynter age" (1.1803). Now, in the presence of beauty, he is eager to embrace, but she tells him that he must constrain his will and choose whether he would have her fair by night or by day. He leaves the choice to her and learns that in granting her sovereignty of choice he has rid her of a curse placed upon her by a hateful stepmother. She is, in truth, the daughter of the king of Sicily who is now, through Florent's obedience to his word, released from the curse. Thus, they live long and happily in joy together.

No summary can do justice to the wit of Gower's narrative — its efficiency of plot, its amusing descriptions, the playful tone in which the dilemmas of Florent are cast, and the skill with which Genius has recast a tale that "clerkes . . . this chance herde" (1.1856) and wrote down "in evidence" (1.1857). The narrative is very different from the Wife of Bath's more complexly narrated version of the story. But, given the demands of confessional interchange that Gower has established, the Tale of Florent is well-suited to its task. As in the case of Mundus and Paulina, personal and community welfare are inextricably interconnected. The true of heart bypass the hypocrite and murmurer. Despite the uncertainties of the fallen universe the community somehow remains coherent.

The Trump of Death, a tale exemplifying Presumption (Surquidry), differs in tone from the tales of Florent and of Mundus and Paulina, but shares similar concerns. Like the latter, its plot is austere. But it is deliberately more single-dimensional, with sharp focus on the chastening power of death. Like Mundus, the Trump of Death has a villain, but this time the villain is a member of the family — the king's brother, who does not, in fact, intend to be villainous. Instead of being motivated by lust, his motivation is a kind of presumptuous jealousy. The brother sees himself as superior to most of humankind, and when the king, upon meeting two ancient and decrepit pilgrims, gets down from his royal chair, embraces them hand and foot, and gives them gifts, the self-righteous brother feels humiliated that his kinsman would so abase himself. He complains that the king has dishonored the royal family by such behavior. The king, in return, teaches his proud brother a lesson in humility. He sends the Trump of Death to his kinsman's house.[82] The brother knows that once the

---

[81] This problem of being caught between contracts and subcontracts is a favorite issue in Middle English romances. See, for example, *Amis and Amiloun* and *Sir Amadace* for extreme situations, though double contracts, often in conflict with each other, show up in *The Wedding of Sir Gawain and Dame Ragnelle*, *Sir Gawain and the Green Knight*, *The Alliterative Morte Arthure*, *Athelstan*, *Sir Degaré*, and *Havelok the Dane*, to name a few. The will is perpetually subcontracted and required to make decisions without having the necessary information to differentiate between commitments. Ever since the serpent's subcontracting of Eve in the Garden of Eden, humankind is trapped by the need to choose amidst conditions that are not understood, and then be subjected to the necessities of consequence.

[82] The tale incorporates admirably a larger analogue wherein God, King of the Universe, having humbled himself by descending from his royal seat in carnal form, still permits Death to continue his

trumpet has sounded there is no reprise for him or his family. They all must die. The brother puts sackcloth on himself and his family and goes barefoot to the king to plead for his life. The king replies that when he (the king) saw the two pilgrims he was so reminded of his own death that he had honored them by bowing before them. Now it is the proud brother who brings "disgrace" to the household, as is evident by his going "despuiled [naked] thurgh the toun," dragging his wife and children with him "In sihte of alle men aboute" (1.2218–21). Were he wise, he would know that death awaits every person. Dignity resides only among the humble. I earlier referred to the tale as single-dimensional. That is its strength. As an exemplum against Surquidry the tale focuses unremittingly on presumption; there is little development of character except as it pertains to the crime. The pace is swift, the conclusion illustrious. The king leaves the brother to his own fate, albeit now chastened by the king's judgment upon him.

The Tale of Albinus and Rosemund (1.2459–2661), a tale of choice and its inevitable consequences, illustrates the sin of Boasting (Avantance). Albinus, king of Lombardy, defeats Gurmond, king of the Geptes. He smites off Gurmond's head and makes an ornate drinking cup of the skull. He then marries Gurmond's daughter, Rosemunde, "A fair, a freissh, a lusti on [one]" (1.2483). She proves to be a loving wife, until Venus "In al the hoteste of here [their] love" (1.2492) turns her wheel.[83] Albinus invites all his worthy knights to dinner and serves Rosemund from the cup: "Drink with thi fader," he orders (1.2551), and Rosemund drinks. When Albinus then boasts of what he has done, she feigns illness and withdraws, plotting the destruction of her boastful husband. Her maid Glodeside has taken Helmage, the king's butler, as her lover. Rosemund slips into her maid's bed, and when Helmage comes to "kepe his observance" (1.2605) Rosemund reveals herself and blackmails him into poisoning the king. The three then steal away to Ravenna, where the Duke, learning of Albinus' death, poisons all three of the fugitives. Like the Trump of Death, this tale moves forward swiftly and irrevocably. The king's boastful scorn destroys them all, as one presumption leads to another.

Book 1 ends with a summary narrative, the Tale of the Three Questions, a very complex story in contrast to the Trump of Death or the Punishment of Nebuchadnezzar discussed earlier; it is a story designed to tie all the subdivisions of Pride into a single, compelling narrative. As in the Tale of Mundus and Paulina, the Trump of Death, and the Tale of Albinus and Rosemund, the tale focuses on familial rapport — where one kind of gendered relationship (here a father and daughter) leads to another (husband and wife). The presentation of the daughter, upon whose wisdom the welfare of the whole family — and kingdom — depends, is truly remarkable. The wise Peronelle (for so she is named at the end, 1.3396) provides the pivotal wit that makes possible a felicitous conclusion. There is no villain in this tale. But there are many kinds of boundaries that are pressed to their limits, only to dissolve through verbal play. The antagonists are two men who take pride in their learning. Both are distinctly limited by their intellectual achievements. The one is the king, who rightly becomes learned (a good thing in a king, as Richard himself might attest), except that he becomes so enamored of his learning that he challenges all comers in the kingdom to contests of wit, which he, of course,

---

ways to serve as a reminder against pride. Humility, rather than pride, is the surest way of preparing for Death's trump.

[83] The turning of the wheel is normally the prerogative of Dame Fortune. Here Gower links Fortune's wheel to Venus, who "kepth the blinde whel" (line 2490) and turns it so that lovers fall (line 2493).

always wins. The other is a knight who, in solving one of the king's problems, makes the king envious and determined to destroy his rival for breach of decorum (i.e., kings are supposed to win). The king poses three difficult questions; the knight must answer all three within three weeks or be put to death. The questions seem unsolvable and, in grief, the knight returns to his home, certain that his lot is hopeless. When his fourteen-year-old daughter, whom he has trained in logic, asks if she may stand in for him, he, mainly because of pride in his fatherly office, refuses: no man would be foolish enough to put his life in the hands of his daughter. But she insists that there are some answers a woman can give that a man cannot (compare the Tale of Florent). She then thoughtfully solves all three of the riddles in the presence of the king, who is so impressed with her reasoning that he, being a bachelor himself, allows that he would wed her were she not a commoner. Nonetheless, he will give her one wish. Courteously, she asks nothing for herself, but wishes that her father, who has suffered so painfully for his presumption, be made a peer. The king immediately bestows a title upon him, whereupon the daughter then observes that the one obstacle between herself and the king has been removed — her father is a nobleman. The king, pleased with her wit, weds her.

This charming tale, perhaps the most popular of all tales in the *Confessio*,[84] celebrates wit, intellect, and familial love, which answer all the subdivisions of Pride to the mutual satisfaction of the whole community. It celebrates, moreover, the integrity of women, women with voices. All the disconcerting problems are solved through wordplay, wordplay that dissolves and re-establishes new boundaries that both contain and liberate people. Gower's heroes and heroines are perpetually challenged by life's riddles. In the relativity of their responses lies their only hope. The tale establishes a paradigm that defines for Gower the value of a well-disposed will in the semantics of salvation. As a summary tale, the Tale of the Three Questions is most akin to another summary tale, the Tale of Apollonius in Book 8, which serves as a romance epitome of the whole poem.

BOOK 8, THE TALE OF APOLLONIUS, AND THE CONCLUSION

The conclusion to the *Confessio* has afforded readers a great deal of difficulty. Book 8 poses four separate problems: 1) the discussion of incest; 2) the Tale of Apollonius; 3) the concluding sequence of the romance itself; and 4) the Epilogue. As Book 8 begins the reader is confronted with the question of why Gower does not deal with the seventh sin (Lechery) as he dealt with the other six. In Book 1 Genius had said he would exorcise Amans of all seven sins, but now, instead of discussing Lechery and its various servants (*Mirour de l'Omme* names five: *fornicioun, stupre, avolterie, incest,* and *fodelit*), he speaks briefly of the laws governing marriage, then discusses incest, and that is all. C. S. Lewis has suggested that Genius cannot speak of the sins of Venus since he is her priest. It is true that in Book 5 Genius tried to avoid talking about Venus when he described the Greek gods, but when he was specifically called upon to do so he showed little inhibition and minced no words. There may be other reasons for the apparent alteration of his plan as well.[85]

---

[84] In the fifteenth century, the Tale of the Three Questions is the most anthologized tale from *CA*, appearing apart from the rest of the poem in five manuscripts. See Edwards, "Selection and Subversion," pp. 259–66.

[85] See the explanatory notes to Book 8 of *CA* for detailed discussion on the issues of incest both in the poem and as an ethical and social problem.

First, a technical problem. In treating other sins, Genius had discussed each as a category of behavior and then (usually) had applied each to love. Thus many of the preceding tales deal with lechery. By Book 8 Genius has already told stories about fornication, adultery, and infatuation of various sorts. He has also told tales of incest. Why then would he single out incest as his final moral category for discussion? The answer may lie in the peculiar relationship of that vice to the illness of Amans.

Medieval writers commonly associated self-love and singular profit with incest. In *Roman de la Rose*, for example, the dreamer's self-indulgence, at first defined by Guillame de Lorris as Narcissism, is enlarged upon by Jean de Meun in the Pygmalion story where the narcissistic lover falls so greatly in love with his creation that consummation occurs, the progeny of which continues in incestuous love when Cinyrus and Myrrha beget Adonis. The term *incest* comes from Latin *in-* (not) *castus* (chaste); it commonly designated unnatural spiritual, as well as sexual, union. Its antidote, in the *Mirour*, at least, is Continence. Of all sins it preeminently typifies crime against family and thus against community. It is implied, then, in the selfishness of all sins. In fact, the word the Patristic Fathers generally used for sin — *cupiditas* — originates in the myth of Cupid, who incestuously loved his mother as if he were blind, the aftereffect being indeed loss of his wits. But the best illustration of this attitude towards incest may be found in Gower's own *Mirour de l'Omme*. That poem begins with an allegorical genealogy of Sin. She and all her unnatural brood are the products of incest. Born of Satan's selfish love, Sin is seduced by her father. She gives birth to Death, who in turn incestuously loves his mother, the get of this couple being the seven sins. Satan then takes his grandchildren and begets on them thirty-five subspecies of Sin. These are no true marriages: all are unnatural and motivated incestuously by lechery. Instead of creating harmony, they bring division of what should not be divided. We are reminded of the formula in the Prologue to the *Confessio*, where Sin is mother of division and division the mother of confusion.

Such an interpretation of incest is supported in the text of the *Confessio* itself. At the end of Book 7, after Genius finishes telling of the instruction of kings, Amans says his heart is still restless. He wonders if something pertaining to love has been "forgete or left behind" (7.5425). Genius acknowledges that one thing remains "Thi schrifte for to make plein" (7.5431) and that is to speak "Of love which is unavised" (7.5433). After a Latin epigram condemning the treachery of Venus' love, Genius summarizes the creation story, the fall of Lucifer, and the generations of humankind from Adam. His point is to explain how marriage laws developed and to show where men should place their love. Rather than isolating incest as a particular species of lechery Genius seems mainly concerned with exploring connotations. He speaks of "unavised" love, "mistimed" love, and "unkynde" love, and in the epigram to the story of Apollonius he speaks of excessive and immoderate love, though never does he specifically use the word incest. Although Genius is ostensibly talking about incest, and although Amans understands him only in its narrower sense, all of his generalizations seem designed to encourage the reader to look on this sin as an epitome of the selfish and unnatural qualities of cupidinous love in general. Two circumlocutions stand out particularly in this regard. Genius objects to men who passionately "taken wher thei take may" (8.152) and, again, to a man who knows no good "Bot takth what thing comth next to honde" (8.163). Here the focus is clearly on nearsighted love. After he has told the story of Apollonius, Genius observes that instead of taking whatever love is close at hand, men should "Tak love where it mai noght faile" (8.2086). His point seems to be that Amans should stop feeding morosely on his emotions and look to something more important.

The story of Apollonius dramatizes this idea superbly. Antiochus is the man who indulges himself myopically, taking where he may what is near at hand. But the effects are terrible. He becomes worse than a beast:

> The wylde fader thus devoureth
> His oghne fleissh, which non socoureth,   *whom no one helps*
> And that was cause of mochel care. (8.309–11)

Having abandoned his natural office of father, he corrupts his other office, that of king, and adjusts laws to satisfy his foolish desire. To avoid dealing with his inner anarchy he becomes a tyrant, slays his daughter's natural suitors, and puts their heads on the town gates. Sin breeds sin: "with al his pride" (8.2004), he slothfully ignores his natural responsibilities ("Him thoghte that it was no sinne," 8.346), lecherously gluts himself on his own flesh, enviously hides his daughter from other men, and then even becomes a murderer "full of rancour and of ire" (8.500). Ultimately he becomes too "unkynde," and God strikes him down with lightning.

Apollonius, on the other hand, shows what it means "to love in good manere" (8.2010). He fulfills admirably Genius' five points of policy (Truth, Liberality, Justice, Pity, Chastity) which should govern a king's behavior (see 7.1711–5397). He adheres to Truth, accepting responsibilities and fulfilling promises. He exemplifies Liberality in providing wheat for the starving people of Tharse and in properly rewarding the physician Cerymon for saving his wife. He understands the importance of Justice and brings wicked Dionise and Strangulio to trial according to the laws of their own land. He has Pity on the people of Tharse, first in giving them food and then in respecting their laws and judgment when their king has offended him. And he adheres to Chastity, not only in the winning of his wife and in the care of himself and her memory after her supposed death, but also in the care of his daughter. He is confronted with a situation like that which confronted Antiochus. When Thaise sings to him to woo him from his melancholy, he feels strong love for her. But he does not impose on her. Rather than taking what is near at hand and thus losing his daughter, as Antiochus did, he recovers his daughter by loving chastely. Diana rewards him for his chastity by enabling him to recover his wife. He in no way behaves *incaste*.

Apollonius' story is admirably suited to the conclusion of the *Confessio*. In addition to exemplifying good kingship and condemning incontinence, its plot provides a model for Amans at the end of his quest. Apollonius is a lover in exile who also is trying to regain his homeland. Fortune is a most bitter enemy, pursuing him with storms and assassins, stripping him of friends and possessions. She denies him his identity at every turn, making him a prince without a country, a husband without a wife, and a father without a child. Even so, he maintains his integrity. Although driven to the brink of despair, so far in fact that like Saul he strikes out, he recovers with the aid of his daughter. Thaise is his good seed. Like her father she too is victimized by Fortune, narrowly escaping murder only to end up in a brothel. But she, like her father, remembers her skill in music and science to save herself and also advance the community. Both she and Apollonius have learned to maintain their spiritual estates. The tale thus ends on a note of joy after woe: Apollonius finally achieves a happy homecoming. No more exile for him. He becomes king of all the lands he attended, and governs them "of on [one] assent" (8.1990).

Amans' homecoming differs from Apollonius' in that his exile is a spiritual exile. He has learned from Genius' examples, but at the same time he has not learned. He misses the point of Apollonius' story, though he does now ask directly for advice. He is at least that much closer to Truth. He speaks plainly: "teche [me] / What is my beste, as for an ende" (8.2058–59). Genius tells him to seek love which may not fail; let trifles be. He calls Amans' love sinful and says he should free himself before it is too late:

> "Yit is it time to withdrawe,
> And set thin herte under that lawe,
> The which of reson is governed
> And noght of will. And to be lerned,   *instructed*
> Ensamples thou hast many on   *many a one*
> Of now and ek of time gon,
> That every lust is bot a while;   *passing moment*
> And who that wole himself beguile,
> He may the rathere be deceived." (8.2133–41)   *sooner*

But Genius insists that Amans must make the decision himself; he can only show the way. He then poses his last question, the ultimate question of Christian humanism: "Now ches if thou wolt live or deie" (8.2148).

But Amans is simply not ready to make that choice. Although the preliminary questions have been asked and illustrated, their meaning has not yet come home. Again he dodges to protect his emotions. His defense is that characteristic "but you don't understand" of lovers:

> Mi wo to you is bot a game,
> That fielen noght of that I fiele. (8.2152–53)   *feel*

He wants sympathy. Yet at the same time he begins to realize rationally that Genius' advice makes sense. As he starts using reason the point of view of the poem shifts. Instead of dialogue and debate between Genius and Amans, we now have first-person narration.[86] The effect is to make the debate seem to be going on within Amans, while at the same time he seems to be looking down at himself:

> Tho was betwen mi prest and me
> Debat and gret perplexeté: *Conflict*
> Mi resoun understod him wel,
> And knew it was soth everydel   *altogether true*
> That he hath seid, bot noght forthi   *What; not even so*
> Mi will hath nothing set therby.   *will (desire)*
> For techinge of so wis a port   *wise a bearing*
> Is unto love of no desport;   *delight*
> Yit myhte nevere man beholde
> Reson, wher love was withholde;
> Thei be noght of o governance. (8.2189–99)   *the same (one)*

---

[86] It is perhaps noteworthy that Chaucer likewise uses the shift to first person in the conclusion to his *Canterbury Tales*, where, from the Prologue to The Canon Yeoman's Tale on, he uses first-person narrative in the Prologues and Retraction. As in Gower, Chaucer seems to be manipulating voice so that he moves back into the voice not simply of Geoffrey but of the poet himself and asks for prayers on his behalf in the Retraction as he puts fiction aside to consider more personal issues.

In this divided state of mind, Amans begs Genius to present his supplication to Venus. Genius agrees. Then Amans, quite objectively, tells how he sat upon a green and wrote with tears instead of ink his appeal. The appeal itself is clearly by a man "noght of o [one] governance" (line 2199): one voice pleads to Nature for release from love's cruelty, and the other pleads to Venus for satisfaction. Yet the effect of his writing is to formalize his dissatisfaction so that he can cope with it. The complaint stands sharply in contrast to his emotional outburst in Book 1 when Venus first appeared. Although Reason does not yet hold sway, she is at least present. His analysis of his malady is accurate, and although his desires are still at odds with his analysis, he is beginning, in these twelve stanzas of rhyme royal, to impose order on them.

The effect of Amans' prayer is immediate. Venus appears less than a mile away.[87] Again she asks, this time in mockery, who he is. "John Gower" (line 2321), he responds. The point here is not to let the world know who wrote the poem. Rather, it marks a new beginning. Amans has come a long way from "A caitif that lith hiere" (1.161). His homeland has been identified; what remains is the repossession. Venus acknowledges the schizophrenic intention of Amans' "bille" (8.2324 ff.) but offers no help. She leaves the dispute to Amans and Nature. Amans must reconcile himself with Nature or be refused any consolation. Gower cleverly has Amans recount her words in retrospect as he ponders her whimsical rejection of his appeal. It is he who acknowledges, now with keen awareness, that "olde grisel is no fole" (8.2407). Her only counsel is "Remembre wel hou thou art old" (8.2439). That acknowledgment causes Amans to faint, which brings him to the final step in his re-education.

In his swoon Amans envisions a parliament of lovers. These lovers are those whose stories Genius has just told. They pass in review before him — first those caught up in the heat of their desire, then those betrayed by love who are in sorrow. In contrast he sees the four constant women whose example of goodness the whole world remembers. This vision designates Amans' recognition of the moral implications of what he has learned. In this act of remembrance he incorporates the meaning of the past into himself. The scene shifts from the recollection of the examples from history to the historians themselves. Old Age approaches Venus, accompanied by his train of lovers — David, Aristotle, Virgil, Plato, "Sortes," and Ovid. These authors of the past pray for Amans' release. It is their prayer which is answered: Cupid removes the fiery dart. The wisdom of antiquity answers the needs of the present, once the present understands through its own experience. It is a matter of community regained.

The rest seems simple. As Amans comes out of his trance Venus places an ointment on his heart, his temples, and his kidneys, implying the restitution of his three estates (the kingdom of his soul, the sanctuary of his intelligence, and the residence of his passions). She also gives him a mirror that he might recognize the old man he has become. This time he does not swoon. He looks directly at himself, reason returns, and he is made "sobre and hol ynowh" (8.2869). Venus laughs at him and asks him what love was. Amans cannot answer: "be my trouthe I knew him noght" (8.2875). His fantasy has gone so far from him that it is as if Cupid had never been.

---

[87] The point here is another instance of Gower's insight into the relationship of time and space. When the right time is discovered space collapses. Compare Chaucer's *Book of the Duchess* where, after the long ordeal in the woods exploring the black knight's unconsolability, the wood, in an instant, disappears, and the "long castel" appears "from us but a lyte" (lines 1318, 1317), now that the knight has faced his grief and seen it through "be my trouthe" (line 1309). The dreamer has found the moment that he can now move "homwarde" (line 1315).

Genius gives Amans absolution — a "peire of bedes" (line 2904), with the motto *Por reposer* — and Venus tells him to return to his books, where moral virtue dwells.[88] Then she returns to the stars. Amans is on his own. For a brief but telling moment he stands in amazement:[89] has all his labor, all his lust come to this — an old man and some beads? Then, like Troilus at the end of his romance, he smiles at it all. The smile is the final clue to his release. In that moment,

> Homward a softe pas y wente,
> Wher that with al myn hol entente
> Uppon the poynt that y am schryve   *confessed (absolved)*
> I thenke bidde whil y live. (8.2967–70)   *pray*

This phase of the reiteration is complete: Amans has become "John Gower," poet. In that role he does what he can do — pray for the welfare of his other self, the kingdom of England.

The concluding sequences in the two main versions of the poem are quite different,[90] yet at the same time similar. In the 1390 Ricardian version, after an amusing admonition by Venus to Chaucer "upon his latere age" that he should leave off serving Venus in verse since the "lond fulfild is overal" with such "testament[s] of love" (8.*2941–*55),[91] the poet prays that the king "Richard by name the secounde" (8.*2987) be blessed by God the creator; like Chaucer in "Lak of Stedfastnesse," he exhorts the king to have pity on the people and rule in justice, peace, and accord. He then presents his poem to Richard, and, "feble and old" (8.*3070), makes his peace with the world — "Whan game is best, is best to leve" (8.*3087). In the Lancastrian ending the admonition to Chaucer is deleted and replaced by an eloquent prayer for the State of England. The prayer serves as a kind of Epilogue to the poem and grows quite naturally out of the romance plot, as Gower quite brilliantly fuses his larger social theme with Amans' story. This prayer for England's welfare stands in striking contrast to the infatuated pleas of Amans before he was shriven. Having regained his sense of kingdom Gower prays, now as poet, for common profit, right use of memory, and good governance.

> For if men takyn remembrance   *take notice*
> What is to live in unité,
> Ther ys no staat in his degree
> That noughte to desire pes . . . . (8.2988–91)

---

[88] The instruction to return to his books is reminiscent of Cupid's command to Geoffrey at the end of the Prologue to *LGW* F.556, 578.

[89] The dreamer's awakening in amazement is a prominent feature of dream visions and visionary poems like *CA* where the poet, returning to his first voice, is left to pick up the pieces as he returns home to everyday duties. Compare the conclusions to *Pearl*, *The Book of the Duchess*, and *The Parliament of the Three Ages*.

[90] Perhaps the best comparison of the two endings is that of Echard, "Pre-Texts."

[91] The phrase "testament of love" seems to echo the title given to Usk's Boethian apology that he wrote in prison while awaiting execution. Middleton ("Thomas Usk's 'Perdurable Letters,'" p. 88n35) argues persuasively that the phrase indirectly praises Usk and that Gower certainly knew Usk's treatise. See also Usk, *Testament of Love*, ed. Shoaf, p. 12.

It is a heartfelt desire for peace after the deep social wounds of the 1380s, a desire that was already by 1392 becoming threatened once again and would ultimately be utterly frustrated as the century came to its conclusion with the overthrow and execution of the king. In response to Richard's heavy-handed treatment of Henry by exiling him and confiscating his estates, Gower, like many others in England, turned against Richard. The king's irresponsible behavior seemed to annihilate the peace and accord Gower so desired. It was as if the events of time were once again demonstrating the wisdom of Gower's prophetic vision.

MANUSCRIPTS OF *CONFESSIO AMANTIS*

John Fisher lists and classifies forty-nine manuscripts of the *Confessio Amantis*, with an additional eight manuscripts which include excerpts from the poem.[92] The manuscripts are usually divided into three versions (recensions). The first recension was probably composed between 1386 and 1390. Thirty-two of the manuscripts fall into this category. After 1390 Gower continued working on the poem, adding lines and tales. Seven manuscripts fall into this category, which is sometimes referred to as the second recension. In 1392 Gower revised a first recension manuscript, changing the dedication of the poem from Richard II to Henry, count of Derby (later Henry IV). This version changes the account of his meeting Richard on the Thames, substituting instead verses in praise of England. It also deletes an encomium on Chaucer. Ten manuscripts survive that are based on the 1392 revision, referred to as the third recension.[93] A Spanish translation (dated 1400) which purports to be based upon a Portuguese translation of the poem survives in a single manuscript. I have consulted the following manuscripts in composing this volume:

- Fairfax 3. Bodleian Library 3883. Late-fourteenth century. [The premiere third recension manuscript. The manuscript has been carefully revised and corrected by the first hand, perhaps "under the direction of the author."[94] In addition to *CA*, the manuscript includes Gower's *Traitié* and *Carmen multiplici viciorum pestilencia*. There is some punctuation in the manuscript, which seems to be carefully carried out. The Latin verses usually occur in the columns of Middle English verse, with the Latin commentary in the margins. The manuscript also consistently marks in the margins changes of speaking voice in places where dialogue occurs. Genius is identified as *Confessor* and the lover as *Amans*. I have used Fairfax 3 as my base text and included all the Latin apparatus.]

- Bodley 902. Bodleian Library. Early-fifteenth century. [A revised first recension manuscript of high quality, used here and by Macaulay for the first recension conclusion to Book 8, which remarks on Chaucer and the "testament of love." The first leaf of this manuscript is missing, thus the need to rely on Bodley 294 for the Ricardian Prologue.]

- Bodley 294. Bodleian Library. Early-fifteenth century. [A second recension manuscript, used by Macaulay for the passages replaced in the Prologue of the third recension.]

---

[92] *John Gower*, pp. 303–09.

[93] For a detailed description of the individual manuscripts, see Gower's *Complete Works*, ed. Macaulay, 2:cxxxviii–clxvii.

[94] See Gower, *Complete Works*, ed. Macaulay, 2:cxxx.

• St. John's College, Cambridge, 34.B.12. First quarter of the fifteenth century. [A first recension manuscript similar to that used as the basis for the third recension. Includes *CA* only. The text and spelling are closer to Fairfax 3 than any other first recension manuscript. The punctuation usually agrees with Fairfax 3. This manuscript omits much of the Latin marginalia found variously in the other manuscripts.]

• Huntington El. 26 A.17 (the "Stafford Manuscript"). Late-fourteenth century. [A second recension manuscript of very high quality text. Includes *CA* only. Unfortunately, the manuscript is missing seventeen leaves.]

• Sidney Sussex College, Cambridge, 63. Mid-fifteenth century. [A second recension manuscript that is closely related to the Stafford manuscript. Includes *CA* and Cato's *Disticha*.]

MANUSCRIPTS OF GOWER'S OTHER MAJOR WORKS

Cinkante Balades (c. 1350–1400)
• Trentham Hall (Duke of Sutherland, Dunrobin Castle, c. 1400).

Mirour de l'Omme (c. 1376–78), also known as *Speculum Hominis* and *Speculum Meditantis*
• Cambridge University Library MS Additional 3035 (before 1400).

Vox Clamantis (c. 1377–81)
Twelve manuscripts survive:[95]
    Group A: Before the Great Uprising
    Group B: After the Great Uprising
    Group C: After 1400, including the *Tripartite Chronicle* at the end
    Modern printed editions are based on All Souls College, Oxford, MS 98 (c. 1400). Other important manuscripts include Bodleian MS Digby 138 (early-fifteenth century) and British Library Cotton Tiberius A.iv (c. 1408).

Tripartite Chronicle (c. 1400)
Five manuscripts, four of which are appended to *Vox Clamantis*. The manuscript favored by modern editors is All Souls College, Oxford, MS 98.

Laureate Poems (c. 1400)
Found in the five manuscripts of *Tripartite Chronicle*. Include "Rex celi deus," "H. aquile pullus," "O recolende," "Carmen super multiplici viciorum pestilencia," "Tractatus de lucis scrutinio," "Ecce patet tensus," "Est amor in glosa pax bellica," "Eneidos bucolis," "O Deus immense," and "Quicquid homo scribat."

In Praise of Peace (c. 1400)
• Trentham Hall manuscript (c. 1400).

---

[95] See Fisher, *John Gower*, pp. 306–08.

c. 1330   John Gower is born, probably in Kent or Yorkshire, into a family of considerable prominence and means, which held land in Kent, Yorkshire, Norfolk, and Suffolk; kin to Sir Robert Gower.

c. 1345   Geoffrey Chaucer born.

1365   Gower purchases Aldingdon Septvauns, an estate in Kent. The purchase was later contested by the crown, but in 1368 Gower's claim is adjudged just. During this decade Gower appears to have prospered, perhaps in some legal or civil office.

1368   Gower acquires a manor of Kentwell in Suffolk which formerly had belonged to Sir Robert Gower.

1373   Gower disposes of the manors of Aldingdon and Kentwell.

c. 1376–79   Gower writes *Mirour de l'Omme*, an allegory of about 32,000 octosyllabic lines composed in twelve-line stanzas. He appears not to have had the poem recopied, since only one fragmentary manuscript of the poem is known to exist. It may be that Gower wrote the work for his own pleasure in what turned out to be a trial run for his two greater poems, both of which draw on it. Although the poem is in French, Gower later changed its title to *Speculum Hominis*, then to *Speculum Meditantis*, so that it might correspond to the Latin titles of his other works.

    The *Mirour* is a commentary on the dilemma of fallen man. Its structure is panoramic, like a triptych which tells allegorically the genealogy of sin and the corruption of the time world, then offers a catalogue of vices and virtues that neatly classifies the errors of man and the remedies open to him, and finally presents an exaltation of the Virgin Mary, who offers frenzied man a realizable hope for extrication from the bewildering world. Like *Vox Clamantis*, it includes an extended section on the three estates.

1377   King Edward III dies; the regency for Richard II, age 10, is established.

c. 1377   Gower takes up residence at St. Mary Overeys Priory, where he spends most of the rest of his life. Tradition claims that in this year Gower financed repair and restoration of the priory, which had burned a century and a half earlier. The priory had its own scriptorium, where Gower may have supervised the copying of his poems.

1377–81   In about 1377 Gower begins work on *Vox Clamantis,* a moral essay of seven books written in Latin elegiac verse. The title is prophetic and derives from the gospel account of John the Baptist who comes as the voice crying in the wilderness. The tone throughout is apocalyptic. Gower seems to have begun composition with what is now Book 2 and to have completed the poem shortly after the Uprising, adding at that time the allegorical dream vision which constitutes Book 1. Eighteen years later, after the ascension of Henry IV to the throne, he added the *Tripartite Chronicle* to the poem.

   Book 2 announces the poem's title and defines man's loss of eminence in the universe: Fortune is not to blame; the fault of man's alienation lies in himself. Books 3 and 4 offer a bold diatribe against the corrupt clergy and religious orders. Book 5 is an attack on knighthood, which has also failed. Book 6 attacks those who have corrupted the laws themselves — lawyers, judges, and the king. Book 7 summarizes man's desperate condition by recounting Nebuchadnezzar's vision of the degeneration of the time world through incursions of Sin and Death. Book 1, written last, provides a brilliant dramatization of the consequences of irresponsible behavior of the upper echelons of society. By means of dream fable, Gower depicts the nightmarish world of a society gone berserk, where even the common men, in whom Gower elsewhere has great faith, turn themselves into animals ravaging each other. Book 1 ends with an emblem of chaos in which common profit has been totally obliterated. In a dramatically memorable scene, the narrator, unwillingly caught up in his narrative, finds himself isolated in a wilderness, afraid of all men about him, who seem surely bent on his destruction. This book should not be understood simply as an attack on the commons in revolt against hierarchy, but rather as a dramatic statement of the consequences of a whole society in disintegration, the causes of which Gower analyzes in the remaining books. To Gower the Peasants' Revolt must have seemed veritable proof of the validity of his prophetic attack on corrupt religious and civil authorities.

1378   Chaucer gives power of attorney to John Gower and Richard Forester while he travels abroad on the continent.

1381   The Rising of Essex and Kentishmen and their march on London in June. The burning of John of Gaunt's Savoy Palace and execution of Archbishop Simon Sudbury and others. The king's confrontation of the mob at Mile End and the killing of Wat Tyler.

1382   Gower is granted manors of Feltwell in Norfolk and Moulton in Suffolk, which he rents to Thomas Blakelake, parson, for £160 per annum.

c. 1385   Chaucer dedicates *Troilus and Criseyde* to "moral Gower" and "philosophical Strode." (The term "moral" should be understood to include that which pertains to the mores of society, as well as ethics.)

c. 1386   Gower begins work on *Confessio Amantis;* Chaucer begins work on the *Legend of Good Women.*

1388   The Merciless Parliament and the Lords Appellant defeat King Richard and his faction and execute Nicholas Brembre and Thomas Usk, both of whom were friends of Chaucer and known to Gower.

1389   Richard II declares himself monarch of full age, free of tutelage.

1390   Gower completes the first recension of the *Confessio Amantis* which he dedicates to the young King Richard, who had encouraged him to write the poem, and to his friend Geoffrey Chaucer. Thirty-one of the forty-nine known manuscripts of the poem follow this recension. It was popular because of the account of the king's commissioning of the poem and because of the dedication to Chaucer.

1390–92   Gower continues work on *Confessio Amantis.* During this period and, perhaps, beyond he does some revision of Books 5, 6, and 7 of the poem, adding new material and occasionally rearranging the old. In 1392 he issues a copy akin to Fairfax 3 which revises the conclusion of the poem to exclude praises of King Richard; to the Prologue of this edition he adds a dedication to Henry of Lancaster. That 1392 version, sometimes referred to as the third recension, was occasionally recopied, though not to the extent that the 1390 edition was. This Lancastrian recension of the poem does not include the passages which had been added to the middle books. The Fairfax 3 manuscript is the principal manuscript of this group, and although it is a relatively small group, it represents perhaps the most carefully prepared revision of the poem. It is conceivable that Gower himself supervised the corrections of Fairfax 3.

1393   In return for the issue of *Confessio Amantis* now dedicated to Henry of Lancaster, count of Derby, Henry presents Gower with an ornamental collar.

1394–97   Gower composes various lesser Latin poems, including "Carmen super multiplici viciorum pestilencia," "O Deus immense," and "De Lucis scrutino."

1397   Gower writes a sequence of eighteen French balades entitled *Traitié.* Each balade is of three stanzas in rhyme royal, without envoy; the eighteenth balade has a fourth stanza which functions as envoy to the whole sequence.

1398   Gower marries Agnes Groundolf. This may have been his second marriage. If so, the first marriage must have been in his younger days, some years prior to his residence at St. Mary Overeys. The marriage to Agnes Groundolf may have been a matter of convenience in order that someone might care for the aging poet who was, according to tradition, on the verge of blindness.

1399   Richard II is deposed by act of Parliament; Henry of Lancaster becomes King Henry IV. Five weeks after his coronation Henry grants Gower two pipes per annum of Gascony wine, perhaps in response to Gower's writing of the *Tripartite*

Chronicle, an allegorical attack on Richard's court and the rescue of England by Henry.

1399–1400 Gower dedicates and presents *Cinkante Balades* to King Henry. He also writes at this time his so-called laureate poems ("Rex celi deus," "H. aquile pullus," "O recolende"), praising the king in whom he placed such high hope, and also his last English poem, *In Praise of Peace*. This latter poem may have been written after the poet had become blind.

1400 Geoffrey Chaucer dies.

1408 John Gower dies and is buried in St. Mary Overeys Priory Church. He now lies in Southwark Cathedral.

Illustration 2: MS Fairfax 3, fol. 2r. Bodleian Library, Oxford University. Nebuchadnezzar's dream of the Monster of Time.

[handwritten top margin:] Pedigogy = the methods of teaching

CONFESSIO AMANTIS: PROLOGUE

i.   *Torpor, ebes sensus, scola parua labor minimusque*
            Causant quo minimus ipse minora canam:
        Qua tamen Engisti lingua canit Insula Bruti
            Anglica Carmente metra iuuante loquar
        Ossibus ergo carens que conterit ossa loquelis
            Absit, et interpres stet procul oro malus.[1]

                                                                    (see note)

INCIPIT PROLOGUS

            Of hem that writen ous tofore   *Of those who wrote before us*
            The bokes duelle, and we therfore   *remain*
            Ben tawht of that was write tho: *Are instructed from what; then*
            Forthi good is that we also   *Therefore*
5   In oure tyme among ous hiere   *us here*
            Do wryte of newe som matiere,   *Cause to be written anew*
            Essampled of these olde wyse,   *Exemplified by; wise [men/books]*
            So that it myhte in such a wyse,   *manner*
            Whan we ben dede and elleswhere,   *are dead*
10   Beleve to the worldes eere   *Be left behind for; ear*
            In tyme comende after this.   *coming*
            Bot for men sein, and soth it is,   *But since men say; true*
            That who that al of wisdom writ   *whoever writes only sententiously*
            It dulleth ofte a mannes wit   *Of the one who reads it all day*
15   To him that schal it aldai rede,
            For thilke cause, if that ye rede,   *that same; if you agree*
            I wolde go the middel weie
            And wryte a bok betwen the tweie,   *two*
            Somwhat of lust, somwhat of lore,   *pleasure; learning (wisdom)*
20   That of the lasse or of the more   *less*
            Som man mai lyke of that I wryte.   *be pleased with what*
☞   And for that fewe men endite   *since; compose (see note)*
            In oure Englissh, I thenke make   *plan to make*

[handwritten marginal notes:] we are going to leave this behind for those after us

BUT, doesn't want to sound too preachy

---

[1] *Listlessness, dull discernment, little schooling and least labor are the causes by which, I, least of all, sing things all the lesser. Nonetheless, in the tongue of Hengist in which the island of Brutus sang, with Carmentis' aid I will utter English verses. Let then the boneless one that breaks bones with speeches be absent, and let the interpreter wicked in word stand far away.*

	A bok for Engelondes sake,	*(see below, for first-recension verses)*
25	The yer sextenthe of Kyng Richard.	
	What schal befalle hierafterward	
	God wot, for now upon this tyde	*knows; time*
	Men se the world on every syde	*see*
	In sondry wyse so diversed,	*various ways; changed*
30	That it wel nyh stant al reversed,	*nearly stands*
	As for to speke of tyme ago.	*Compared to time past*
	The cause whi it changeth so	
	It needeth nought to specifie,	
	The thing so open is at ÿe	*eye*
35	That every man it mai beholde.	
	And natheles be daies olde,	*in the old days*
	Whan that the bokes weren levere,	*more dear*
	Wrytinge was beloved evere	
	Of hem that weren vertuous;	*those who*
40	For hier in erthe amonges ous,	
	If no man write hou that it stode,	*no one; how; stood*
	The pris of hem that weren goode	*reputation of those who*
	Scholde, as who seith, a gret partie	*as one may say*
	Be lost; so for to magnifie	
45	The worthi princes that tho were,	*then*

[The Ricardian recension of the poem reads as follows (lines *24–*92):]

	A book for King Richardes sake	
*25	To whom bilongeth my ligeance	*allegiance*
	With al myn hertes obeissance	
	In al that ever a liege man	
	Unto his king may doon or can;	
	So ferforth I me recomaunde	*myself admit*
*30	To him which al me may comaunde,	*all people may*
	Prayend unto the hihe regne	*Praying; high ruler (i.e., God)*
	Which causeth every king to regne,	
	That his corone longe stonde.	
	I thenke and have it understonde,	
*35	As it bifel upon a tyde,	*time*
	As thing which scholde tho bityde,	*then happen*
	Under the toun of newe Troye,	
	Which took of Brut his ferste joye,	
	In Temse whan it was flowende	*Thames; flowing*
*40	As I by bote cam rowende,	*came rowing by in a boat*
	So as Fortune hir tyme sette,	
	My liege lord par chaunce I mette;	
	And so bifel, as I cam neigh,	*near*
	Out of my bot, when he me seigh,	*saw*
*45	He bad me come into his barge.	

[handwritten: amiss]

46 The bokes schewen hiere and there,	
Wherof the world ensampled is;	
And tho that deden thanne amis	those who did
Thurgh tirannie and crualté	
50 Right as thei stoden in degré,	Just as
So was the wrytinge of here werk.	their
Thus I, which am a burel clerk,	ignorant clerk
Purpose for to wryte a bok	Intend to
After the world that whilom tok	About; once came about
55 Long tyme in olde daies passed.	Long ago
Bot for men sein it is now lassed,	since men see; lessened
In worse plit than it was tho,	plight; then
I thenke for to touche also	plan therefore to touch upon
The world which neweth every dai,	renews [itself]
60 So as I can, so as I mai.	Insofar as I am able and am allowed
Thogh I seknesse have upon honde	sickness
And longe have had, yit woll I fonde	attempt
To wryte and do my bisinesse,	
That in som part, so as I gesse,	estimate
65 The wyse man mai ben avised.	
For this prologe is so assised	composed
That it to wisdom al belongeth.	

[handwritten margin notes: "State of people just as bad as the writing"; "I intend to write a book about the world that once came about in the old days"; "worse than before"]

---

*46 And whan I was with him at large,	comfortably (without restraint)
Amonges othre thinges seyde	
He hath this charge upon me leyde,	
And bad me doo my busynesse	
*50 That to his hihe worthinesse	
Som newe thing I scholde booke,	compose
That he himself it mighte looke	
After the forme of my writyng.	
And thus upon his comaundyng	
*55 Myn hert is wel the more glad	
To write so as he me bad;	commanded
And eek my fere is wel the lasse	fear
That non envye schal compasse	
Without a resonable wite	
*60 To feyne and blame that I write.	misconstrue
A gentil herte his tunge stilleth,	
That it malice noon distilleth,	
But preyseth that is to be preised;	what
But he that hath his word unpeysed	unleashed
*65 And handeleth onwrong every thing,	meanly perverts
I pray unto the heven king	
Fro suche tunges He me schilde.	shield

68	What wys man that it underfongeth,	*understands*
	He schal drawe into remembrance	
70	The fortune of this worldes chance,	
	The which no man in his persone	
	Mai knowe, bot the god alone.	*except the good alone*
	Whan the prologe is so despended,	*finished*
	This bok schal afterward ben ended	*be finished up*
75	Of love, which doth many a wonder	*[As a book] about love*
	And many a wys man hath put under.	*has toppled many a wise person*
	And in this wyse I thenke trete	*way I plan to treat (make a discourse)*
	Towardes hem that now be grete,	*In respect to those who (In submission to those who)*
	Betwen the vertu and the vice	
80	Which longeth unto this office.	*pertain; social position*
	Bot for my wittes ben to smale	*But since; too small*
	To tellen every man his tale,	
	This bok, upon amendement	*for correction*
	To stonde at his commandement,	*To submit to*
85	With whom myn herte is of accord,	
	I sende unto myn oghne lord,	*own*
	Which of Lancastre is Henri named.	
	The hyhe God him hath proclamed	
	Ful of knyhthode and alle grace.	

Handwritten marginal note: Whatever wise man that understands the prologue he shall remember that no one will have insight into the world unless they are good

Handwritten marginal note: "All you need is love"

Handwritten marginal note: when the prologue is over

---

*68	And natheles this world is wilde	
	Of such jangling, and what bifalle,	*happens*
*70	My kinges heste schal nought falle,	*behest*
	That I, in hope to deserve	
	His thonk, ne schal his wil observe;	*obey*
	And elles were I nought excused,	
	For that thing may nought be refused	
*75	Which that a king himselve byt.	*ordered*
	Forthi the symplesce of my wit	
	I thenke if that it may avayle	
	In his service to travaile.	
	Though I seknesse have upon honde,	*illness*
*80	And long have had, yit wol I fonde,	*attempt*
	So as I made my byheste,	*promise*
	To make a book after his heste,	*command*
	And write in such a maner wise,	
	Which may be wisdom to the wise	
*85	And pley to hem that lust to pleye.	
	But in proverbe I have herd seye	
	That who that wel his werk begynneth	
	The rather a good ende he wynneth;	
	And thus the prologe of my book	

Thoseoya (handwritten, top margin)

90   So woll I now this werk embrace
       With hol trust and with hol believe.   _whole_
       God grante I mot it wel achieve.   _that I have the power to finish_

[THE STATE] — _Has become disordered. Follow more vices than virtue_ (handwritten)

ii.   _Tempus preteritum presens fortuna beatum_
        Linquit, et antiquas vertit in orbe vias.   _(see note)_
    Progenuit veterem concors dileccio pacem,
        Dum facies hominis nuncia mentis erat:
    Legibus vnicolor tunc temporis aura refulsit,
        Iusticie plane tuncque fuere vie.
    Nuncque latens odium vultum depingit amoris,
        Paceque sub ficta tempus ad arma tegit;
    Instar et ex variis mutabile Cameliontis   _(see note)_
        Lex gerit, et regnis sunt noua iura nouis:
    Climata que fuerant solidissima sicque per orbem
        Soluuntur, nec eo centra quietis habent.[1]

       If I schal drawe into my mynde   _In the past: world stood in wealth_ (handwritten)
☞   The tyme passed, thanne I fynde   _(see note)_
95   The world stod thanne in al his welthe.   _its wealth_
       Tho was the lif of man in helthe,   _Health, plenty,_ (handwritten)   _Then_
       Tho was plenté, tho was richesse,   _riches, fortune_ (handwritten)
Knighthood? (handwritten)   Tho was the fortune of prouesse,   _high time of virtue (strength)_
       Tho was knyhthode in pris be name,   _valued by report_
100   Wherof the wyde worldes fame —   _Worlds fame written in chronicles, maintained_ (handwritten)
       Write in cronique — is yit withholde.   _Written; chronicles; yet maintained_
       Justice of lawe tho was holde,   ➤ _Justice was then upheld by law_
       The privilege of regalie   _royalty_
       Was sauf, and al the baronie   _safe_
105   Worschiped was in his astat;   _No debate, conflict?_ (handwritten)   _Honored; its estate_
       The citees knewen no debat, —
       The poeple stod in obeissance   _people_
            obediance? (handwritten)

---

*90   After the world that whilom took,   _once came about_
       And eek somdel after the newe,
       I wol begynne for to newe.

---

[1] _Present-day Fortune has left behind the blessed times of the past, and overturned on her world-wheel the ancient ways. Harmonious love engendered the old-time peace, when the face was the messenger of a person's thought: then the unicolored air of the times was aglow with laws, and then the paths of justice were broad and even. But now hidden hatred presents a painted face of love, and clothes under false peace an age at arms. The law carries itself like the chameleon, changeable with every varied thing; and new laws are for new kingdoms. Regions that were most steady throughout the world's orb are unmoored, nor do they possess axis-points of quiet._

	Under the reule of governance,	
	And pes, which ryhtwisnesse keste,	*peace; justice kissed*
110	With charité tho stod in reste.	*then*
	Of mannes herte the corage	
	Was schewed thanne in the visage;	*shown; face (countenance)*
	The word was lich to the conceite	*like; concept*
	Withoute semblant of deceite.	
115	Tho was ther unenvied love,	*Then*
	Tho was the vertu sett above	
	And vice was put under fote.	
	Now stant the crop under the rote.	*top; root (i.e., upside down)*
	The world is changed overal,	
120	And therof most in special	*particular*
	That love is falle into discord.	*Whereby*
	And that I take to record	
	Of every lond, for his partie,	*From; part*
	The comune vois which mai noght lie;	*unanimous voice of the people*
125	Noght upon one bot upon alle	*one*
	It is that men now clepe and calle,	*what; make appeal*
	And sein the regnes ben divided:	*see kingdoms at odds*
	In stede of love is hate guided,	
	The werre wol no pes purchace,	*war; obtain*
130	And lawe hath take hire double face,	*lawyers; put on (donned) their*
	So that justice out of the weie	
	With ryhtwisnesse is gon aweie.	
	And thus to loke on every halve,	*all sides*
	Men sen the sor withoute salve,	*see the wound lacking healing ointment*
135	Which al the world hath overtake.	*has ruined*
	Ther is no regne of alle outtake,	*excepted*
	For every climat hath his diel	*has its share*
	After the tornynge of the whiel,	*According to*
	Which blinde Fortune overthroweth.	*turns over*
140	Wherof the certain no man knoweth.	*fact (certainty) no one*
	The hevene wot what is to done,	*knows*
	Bot we that duelle under the mone	*moon (i.e., amidst changeability)*
	Stonde in this world upon a weer,	*in doubt*
	And namely bot the pouer	*unless; power*
145	Of hem that ben the worldes guides —	*Of those who are*
	With good consail on alle sides —	
	Be kept upriht in such a wyse,	*way*
	That hate breke noght th'assise	*the court*
	Of love, whiche is al the chief	*principal means*
150	To kepe a regne out of meschief.	*kingdom*
	For alle resoun wolde this,	
	That unto him which the heved is	*who; head (see note)*
	The membres buxom scholden bowe,	*obedient*
	And he scholde ek her trowthe allowe,	*also their loyalty accept*

(handwritten annotations in margins)

155 With al his herte and make hem chiere,	*And welcome them with all his heart*
☞ For good consail is good to hiere.	*hear (see note)*
Althogh a man be wys himselve,	
Yit is the wisdom more of tuelve;	*Yet*
And if thei stoden bothe in on,	*one*
160 To hope it were thanne anon	
That God his grace wolde sende	
To make of thilke werre an ende,	*that war*
Which everyday now groweth newe.	
And that is gretly for to rewe	*repent*
165 In special for Cristes sake,	
Which wolde His oghne lif forsake	*Who; own life*
Among the men to geve pes.	*give peace*
But now men tellen natheles	*nonetheless*
That love is fro the world departed,	*from*
170 So stant the pes unevene parted	*peace unequally distributed*
With hem that liven now adaies.	
Bot for to loke, at alle assaies,	*at any rate*
To him that wolde resoun seche	*seek*
After the comun worldes speche	
175 It is to wondre of thilke werre,	*that strife*
In which non wot who hath the werre.	*no one knows; worse*
For every lond himself deceyveth	*itself*
And of desese his part receyveth,	*trouble its share*
And yet ne take men no kepe.	*men are indifferent (take no heed)*
180 Bot thilke Lord which al may kepe,	*But that very*
To whom no consail may ben hid,	
Upon the world which is betid,	*come to pass*
Amende that wherof men pleigne	*[May he] amend; complain*
With trewe hertes and with pleine,	*simple*
185 And reconcile love ageyn,	*[may he] reconcile*
As He which is king sovereign	
Of al the worldes governaunce,	
And of His hyhe porveaunce	*lofty overview*
Afferme pes betwen the londes	*Made*
190 And take her cause into Hise hondes,	*their*
So that the world may stonde appesed	*reconciled*
And His Godhede also be plesed.	

[THE CHURCH]

iii.   *Quas coluit Moises vetus aut nouus ipse Iohannes,*
       Hesternas leges vix colit ista dies.
   Sic prius ecclesia bina virtute polita
       Nunc magis inculta pallet vtraque via.   *(see note)*
   Pacificam Petri vaginam mucro resumens
       Horruit ad Cristi verba cruoris iter;

Nunc tamen assiduo gladium de sanguine tinctum
  Vibrat auaricia, lege tepente sacra.
Sic lupus est pastor, pater hostis mors miserator,
  Predoque largitor, pax et in orbe timor.[1]

	To thenke upon the daies olde,	*When thinking; days of old*
☞	The lif of clerkes to beholde,	*(see note)*
195	Men sein how that thei weren tho	*see; then*
	Ensample and reule of alle tho	*those*
	Whiche of wisdom the vertu soughten.	*Who; sought*
	Unto the God ferst thei besoughten	*prayed*
	As to the substaunce of her scole,	*For the material wealth of their community*
200	That thei ne scholden noght befole	*[So] that; besmirch*
	Her wit upon none erthly werkes,	*Their*
	Which were agein th'estat of clerkes,	*against*
	And that thei myhten fle the vice	*[so] that; might flee*
	Which Simon hath in his office,	
205	Wherof he takth the gold in honde.	
	For thilke tyme, I understonde,	
	The Lumbard made non eschange	*bankers had not [yet] financed*
	The bisschopriches for to change,	*purchase*
	Ne yet a lettre for to sende	*papal provision*
210	For dignité ne for provende,	*prebend*
	Or cured or withoute cure.	*Either with or without spiritual duties*
	The cherche keye in aventure	*power of the church*
	Of armes and of brygantaille	*brigands (irregular troops)*
	Stod nothing thanne upon bataille;	
215	To fyhte or for to make cheste	*strife*
	It thoghte hem thanne noght honeste.	*honorable*
	Bot of simplesce and pacience	
	Thei maden thanne no defence.	*prohibition*
	The court of worldly regalie	
220	To hem was thanne no baillie.	*jurisdiction*
	The vein honour was noght desired,	*empty (vain)*
	Which hath the proude herte fyred;	*heart inflamed*
	Humilité was tho withholde,	*practiced (held with)*
	And Pride was a vice holde.	*held to be a vice*
225	Of holy cherche the largesse	
	Gaf thanne and dede gret almesse	*Gave; distributed quantities of alms*
	To povere men that hadden nede;	*were needy*

---

[1] *The laws of yesterday that old Moses and new John — that one — cultivated, this day hardly keeps. Thus the church, formerly glittering with a double virtue and now instead disheveled, grows pale at either path. At the word of Christ the sword of Peter, regaining its peaceful sheath, abhorred the way of blood; now, however, with sacred law grown tepid, covetousness vigorously thrusts its blood-stained sword. Thus the wolf is the shepherd, the father the enemy, death the commiserator, the brigand the benefactor, and the peace on earth is fear.*

Thei were ek chaste in word and dede,   *also*

Wherof the poeple ensample tok;

230 Her lust was al upon the bok,   *Their desire*

Or for to preche or for to preie,   *Either; or; pray*

To wisse men the ryhte weie   *teach*

Of suche as stode of trowthe unliered.   *untaught in truth (untrained in loyalty)*

Lo, thus was Petres barge stiered   *St. Peter's ship guided*

235 Of hem that thilke tyme were,   *By those who at that time lived*

And thus cam ferst to mannes ere   *ear*

The feith of Crist and alle goode

Thurgh hem that thanne weren goode

And sobre and chaste and large and wyse.   *generous*

240 Bot now men sein is otherwise,   *But now [what] men say; contrarywise*

Simon the cause hath undertake,

The worldes swerd on honde is take;   *grasped*

And that is wonder natheles,

Whan Crist Himself hath bode pes   *proclaimed peace*

245 And set it in His Testament,

How now that holy cherche is went   *has departed*

Of that here lawe positif   *From what their [own] formal law*

Hath set, to make werre and strif   *Has established; war; contention*

For worldes good, which may noght laste.   *material wealth*

250 God wot the cause to the laste   *knows*

Of every right and wrong also;

But whil the lawe is reuled so

That clerkes to the werre entende,

I not how that thei scholde amende   *do not know how*

255 The woful world in othre thinges,

To make pes betwen the kynges

After the lawe of charité,   *According to*

Which is the propre dueté   *duty*

Belongende unto the presthode.

260 Bot as it thenkth to the manhode,   *seems to human beings*

The hevene is ferr, the world is nyh,   *far; near*

And veine gloire is ek so slyh,   *also so sly*

Which coveitise hath now withholde,   *retained [as servant]*

That thei non other thing beholde,

265 Bot only that thei myhten winne.   *Except what they*

And thus the werres thei beginne,   *wars*

Wherof the holi cherche is taxed,

That in the point as it is axed   *the moment it is requested*

The disme goth to the bataille,   *tithe (L. decima, "tenth")*

270 As thogh Crist myhte noght availe

To don hem riht be other weie.   *bring about justice by other means*

Into the swerd the cherche keie   *key*

Is torned, and the holy bede   *prayer*

Into cursinge, and every stede   *place*

275   Which scholde stonde upon the feith
        And to this cause an ere leyth,   ear
        Astoned is of the queréle.   quarrel
        That scholde be the worldes hele   What (i.e., the papacy); health
        Is now, men sein, the pestilence   say; plague
280   Which hath exiled pacience
        Fro the clergie in special.   priesthood
        And that is schewed overal,   revealed everywhere
        In eny thing whan thei ben grieved.   thwarted
        Bot if Gregoire be believed,
285   As it is in the bokes write,   written
        He doth ous somdel for to wite   causes us in part to know
        The cause of thilke prelacie,   such a priestly estate
        Wher God is noght of compaignie.
        For every werk as it is founded
290   Schal stonde or elles be confounded;
        Who that only for Cristes sake
        Desireth cure for to take,   benefice (curacy)
        And noght for pride of thilke astat,   such [priestly] estate
        To bere a name of a prelat,   title
295   He schal be resoun do profit   by reason give profit
        In holy cherche upon the plit   in the manner
        That he hath set his conscience.   established his conscience
☞   Bot in the worldes reverence   (see note)
        Ther ben of suche manie glade
300   Whan thei to thilke astat ben made,
        Noght for the merite of the charge,
        Bot for thei wolde hemself descharge   rid themselves
        Of poverté and become grete.
        And thus for pompe and for beyete   property
305   The Scribe and ek the Pharisee
        Of Moises upon the See   [Red] Sea
        In the chaiere on hyh ben set;
        Wherof the feith is ofte let,   released
        Which is betaken hem to kepe.   entrusted to them
310   In Cristes cause alday thei slepe,
        Bot of the world is noght forgete;   there is no forgetting
        For wel is him that now may gete
        Office in court to ben honoured.
        The stronge coffre hath al devoured
315   Under the keye of avarice
        The tresor of the benefice,
        Wherof the povere schulden clothe
        And ete and drinke and house bothe;
        The charité goth al unknowe,
320   For thei no grein of pité sowe;
        And slouthe kepeth the libraire

Which longeth to the saintuaire;   *belongs to the Church (sanctuary)*
To studie upon the worldes lore   *teaching*
Sufficeth now withoute more;

325 Delicacie his swete toth   *sweet tooth*
Hath fostred so that it fordoth   *destroys*
Of abstinence al that ther is.
And for to loken over this,
If Ethna brenne in the clergie   *burns among the clergy (see note)*
330 Al openly to mannes ȳe,   *people's eyes*
At Avynoun th'experience
Therof hath gove an evidence   *given; indication*
Of that men sen hem so divided.   *Since men see them*
And yit the cause is noght decided.

335 Bot it is seid and evere schal,
Betwen tuo stoles lyth the fal   *two stools lies the fall*
Whan that men wenen best to sitte.   *think*
In holy cherche of such a slitte   *division (schism)*
Is for to rewe unto ous alle;   *Is regrettable for us all*
340 God grante it mote wel befalle   *may well turn out*
Towardes him whiche hath the trowthe.   *In respect to whoever has*
Bot ofte is sen that mochel slowthe,   *sloth*
Whan men ben drunken of the cuppe,
Doth mochel harm, whan fyr is uppe,
345 Bot if somwho the flamme stanche;   *Unless someone should extinguish the flame*
And so to speke upon this branche,
Which proude Envie hath mad to springe,
Of Scisme, causeth for to bringe   *[it] causes*
This newe secte of Lollardie,
350 And also many an heresie
Among the clerkes in hemselve.   *themselves*
It were betre dike and delve   *to ditch; dig (i.e., work as a plowman)*
And stonde upon the ryhte feith,
Than knowe al that the Bible seith
355 And erre as somme clerkes do.
Upon the hond to were a schoo   *shoe*
And sette upon the fot a glove   *foot*
Acordeth noght to the behove   *Is not becoming; advantage*
Of resonable mannes us.   *usage*
360 If men behielden the vertus   *adhered to*
That Crist in erthe taghte here,
Thei scholden noght in such manere,
Among hem that ben holden wise,
The Papacie so desguise   *dress up*
365 Upon diverse eleccioun,
Which stant after th'affeccioun   *holds according to the inclination*
Of sondry londes al aboute.
Bot whan God wole, it schal were oute,   *wants, it [the schism] will wear away*

God determines the foolishness of the Scism (handwritten)

For trowthe mot stonde ate laste.   *must remain*
370 Bot yet thei argumenten faste   *They argue about the schism* (handwritten)   *debate vigorously*
Upon the Pope and his astat,
Wherof thei falle in gret debat;   *great conflict*
This clerk seith yee, that other nay,
And thus thei dryve forth the day,   *pass the time*
375 And ech of hem himself amendeth   *Want to know how they will benefit from the schism* (handwritten)   *improves*
Of worldes good, bot non entendeth   *In respect to*
To that which comun profit were.   *They don't care about the world's benefit* (handwritten)
Thei sein that God is myhti there,   *declare*
And schal ordeine what He wile,
380 Ther make thei non other skile   *argument*
Where is the peril of the feith,   *[About] where peril to faith exists*
Bot every clerk his herte leith   *They don't care about common interest, only* (handwritten)   *exerts his desire (lays his heart)*
To kepe his world in special,   *To support his own fortunes*
And of the cause general,
385 Which unto holy cherche longeth,   *belongs*
Is non of hem that underfongeth   *undertakes*
To schapen eny resistence.
And thus the riht hath no defence,   *The righteous are w/o friends* (handwritten)
Bot ther I love, ther I holde.   *Except where; there*
390 Lo, thus tobroke is Cristes folde,   *Christ's flock is →* (handwritten)   *broken to pieces*
Wherof the flock withoute guide
Devoured is on every side,
Careless shepherds (handwritten) In lacke of hem that ben unware   *want; those who; careless*
Schepherdes, whiche her wit beware   *who spend their wit*
395 Upon the world in other halve.   *On another part of the world*
The scharpe pricke in stede of salve   *They'll take all the wool from asleep & leave him w/ nothing simply for baudy, worldly bliss* (handwritten)   *goad*
Thei usen now, wherof the hele   *health*
Thei hurte of that thei scholden hele;   *heal*
And what schep that is full of wulle   *wool*
400 Upon his back, thei toose and pulle,   *shear*
Whil ther is eny thing to pile.   *plunder*
And thogh ther be non other skile   *reason*
Bot only for thei wolden wynne,   *make a profit*
Thei leve noght, whan thei begynne,   *cease*
405 Upon her acte to procede,   *their*
Which is no good schepherdes dede.   *Good shepherds don't act this way* (handwritten)   *behavior*
And upon this also men sein,
That fro the leese which is plein   *They drive their flock into the briars* (handwritten)   *pasture land; open*
Into the breres thei forcacche   *briars; drive out*
410 Her orf, for that thei wolden lacche   *Their sheep, because they would [like to] steal*
With such duresce, and so bereve   *By; cruelty; rob*
That schal upon the thornes leve   *What [the sheep] shall*
Of wulle, which the brere hath tore;   *briar*
Wherof the schep ben al totore   *fleeced*
415 Of that the hierdes make hem lese.   *what the shepherds; lose*

They'll sell cheese tho it is chalk

Lo, how thei feignen chalk for chese,   *something worthless for something good*
For though thei speke and teche wel, *(smooth tongue)*
Thei don hemself therof no del.   *exceptions to their words apply to themselves; part*
For if the wolf com in the weie,   *In danger, no help*
420   Her gostly staf is thanne aweie,   *Their spiritual*
Wherof thei scholde her flock defende;   *With which*
Quick to judge, slow to help Bot if the povere schep offende   *But if the sheep breaks a rule, they are in trouble*
In eny thing, thogh it be lyte,   *little*
They ben al redy for to smyte;
425   And thus, how evere that thei tale,   *reckon (tally)*
The strokes falle upon the smale,
And upon othre that ben grete
Hem lacketh herte for to bete.
So that under the clerkes lawe   *No fairness in the law*
430   Men sen the merel al mysdrawe   *lot (OF merel, "token," "coin")*
I wol noght seie in general,   *Sometimes There are good ones* *speak*
For ther ben somme in special   *a few here and there*
In whom that alle vertu duelleth,
☞   And tho ben, as th'apostel telleth,   *those are; [St. Paul] says (see note)*
435   That God of His eleccioun   *The ones*
Hath cleped to perfeccioun   *summoned (chosen)*
In the manere as Aaron was.
Thei ben nothing in thilke cas
Of Simon, which the foldes gate   *sheepfold's gate*
440   Hath lete, and goth in othergate,   *Have abandoned; behave contrarily*
Bot thei gon in the rihte weie.
Ther ben also somme, as men seie,
That folwen Simon ate hieles,   *Some follow Simon* *at Simon's heels*
Whos carte goth upon the whieles *(Greediness, worldly Pride)*
445   Of coveitise and worldes Pride,
And holy cherche goth beside,   *Neglect holy callings*
Which scheweth outward a visage   *Even tho they appear*
Of that is noght in the corage.   *"Holy", They have No virtue* *what; heart*
For if men loke in holy cherche,   *the clerical profession*
450   Betwen the word and that thei werche *B/w the word/ deeds*   *what*
Ther is a full gret difference. ◄
Thei prechen ous in audience   *to us; public assembly*
That no man schal his soule empeire,   *harm*
For al is bot a chirie feire   *cherry harvest fair*
455   This worldes good, so as thei telle;
Also thei sein ther is an helle,
Which unto mannes sinne is due,
And bidden ous therfore eschue
That wikkid is, and do the goode.   *What*
460   Who that here wordes understode,   *Whosoever; their*
It thenkth thei wolden do the same;   *One would think they would behave accordingly*
Bot yet betwen ernest and game

Ful ofte it torneth otherwise.

With holy tales thei devise — *pious stories*

465 How meritoire is thilke dede
Of charité, to clothe and fede
The povere folk and for to parte — *distribute*
The worldes good, bot thei departe — *detach [themselves]*
Ne thenken noght fro that thei have. — *And do not consider [distributing]*

470 Also thei sein, good is to save
With penance and with abstinence
Of chastité the continence;
Bot pleinly for to speke of that,
I not how thilke body fat, — *do not know how that fattened body*

475 Which thei with deynté metes kepe — *foods maintain*
And leyn it softe for to slepe,
Whan it hath elles al his wille, — *everything else to its desire*
With chastité schal stonde stille. — *can remain steady*
And natheles I can noght seie,

480 In aunter if that I misseye. — *On the chance that I am wrong*
Touchende of this, how evere it stonde,
I here and wol noght understonde, — *hear*
For therof have I noght to done. — *it is not my business*
Bot He that made ferst the mone, — *moon*

485 The hyhe God, of His goodnesse,
If ther be cause, He it redresce. — *may He redress it*
Bot what as eny man accuse,
This mai reson of trowthe excuse;
The vice of hem that ben ungoode, — *evil; unrighteous*

490 Is no reproef unto the goode.
For every man hise oghne werkes
Schal bere, and thus as of the clerkes — *bear; regarding churchmen*
The goode men ben to comende, — *righteous will be commended*
And alle these othre God amende. — *others may God improve*

495 For thei ben to the worldes ÿe — *eye*
The mirour of ensamplerie, — *example*
To reulen and to taken hiede — *guide; warn*
Betwen the men and the Godhiede.

[THE COMMONS]

iv.   *Vulgaris populus regali lege subactus*
       Dum iacet, vt mitis agna subibit onus.
    Si caput extollat et lex sua frena relaxet,
       Vt sibi velle iubet, Tigridis instar habet.

Ignis, aqua dominans duo sunt pietate carentes,
Ira tamen plebis est violenta magis.[1]   *(see note)*

	Now for to speke of the comune,	*commons (third estate)*
500	It is to drede of that fortune	
	Which hath befalle in sondri londes.	
	Bot often for defalte of bondes	
	Al sodeinliche, er it be wist,	
☞	A tonne, whanne his lye arist,	*tun (vessel); its lye boils over (see note)*
505	Tobrekth and renneth al aboute,	
	Which elles scholde noght gon oute;	
	And ek fulofte a litel skar	*crack (hole)*
	Upon a banke, er men be war,	*before; aware [of it]*
	Let in the strem, which with gret peine,	
510	If evere man it schal restreigne.	
	Wher lawe lacketh, errour groweth,	
	He is noght wys who that ne troweth,	*does not believe*
	For it hath proeved ofte er this.	
	And thus the comun clamour is	*noisy disapproval*
515	In every lond wher poeple dwelleth,	
	And eche in his compleignte telleth	
	How that the world is al miswent,	
	And therupon his jugement	
	Gifth every man in sondry wise.	*Every man gives; ways*
520	Bot what man wolde himself avise,	*consider*
	His conscience and noght misuse,	*And not misuse his conscience*
	He may wel ate ferste excuse.	
	His God, which evere stant in on,	*stands united*
	In Him ther is defalte non,	*no deficiency*
525	So moste it stonde upon ousselve	*ourselves*
	Nought only upon ten ne twelve,	
	Bot plenerliche upon ous alle,	*fully*
	For man is cause of that schal falle.	*what shall befall*
☞	And natheles yet som men wryte	*(see note)*
530	And sein that fortune is to wyte,	*blame*
	And som men holde oppinion	
	That it is constellacion,	*the stars*
	Which causeth al that a man doth.	
	God wot of bothe which is soth.	*knows; true*
535	The world as of his propre kynde	*its own nature*
	Was evere untrewe, and as the blynde	

(handwritten annotations in margin: "some men write that fortune is to blame. Some say fortune is in the stars & blame sun etc." and "'Doesn't' Matter")

---

[1] *So long as the commonfolk lies subjugated by royal law, it will bear its burden as meek as a ewe lamb; if its head should come up and the law relax its reins on it, as desire commands for itself, it becomes like a tiger [or, like the Tigris River]. Fire, domination by water are two things without mercy, but the wrath of the commoners is more violent.*

	Improprelich he demeth fame,	*judge*
	He blameth that is noght to blame	*what*
	And preiseth that is noght to preise.	
540	Thus whan he schal the thinges peise,	*weigh*
	Ther is deceipte in his balance,	
	And al is that the variance	
	Of ous, that schold ous betre avise.	*who should; consider*
	For after that we falle and rise,	*in accord with how*
545	The world arist and falth withal,	*likewise*
	So that the man is overal	
	His oghne cause of wel and wo.	
	That we fortune clepe so	*call*
	Out of the man himself it groweth	
550	And who that otherwise troweth,	*believes*
	Behold the poeple of Irael:	*Israel*
	For evere whil thei deden wel,	
	Fortune was hem debonaire,	*to them*
	And whan thei deden the contraire,	*adverse*
555	Fortune was contrariende,	*unfavorable*
	So that it proeveth wel at ende	
	Why that the world is wonderfull	*astonishing*
	And may no while stonde full,	
	Though that it seme wel besein.	*furnished*
560	For every worldes thing is vein,	
	And evere goth the whiel aboute,	
	And evere stant a man in doute:	
	Fortune stant no while stille,	*stands*
	So hath ther no man al his wille.	
565	Als fer as evere a man may knowe,	
	Ther lasteth nothing bot a throwe.	*moment*
☞	The world stant evere upon debat,	*in turmoil (see note)*
	So may be seker non astat:	*secure*
	Now hier now ther, now to now fro,	
570	Now up now doun, this world goth so,	
	And evere hath don and evere schal,	
	Wherof I finde in special	
	A tale writen in the Bible,	
	Which moste nedes be credible.	*true (believed)*
575	And that as in conclusioun	
	Seith that upon divisioun	
	Stant, why no worldes thing mai laste,	
	Til it be drive to the laste.	*end [of all things]*
	And fro the ferste regne of alle	
580	Into this day, hou so befalle,	
	Of that the regnes ben muable	*mutable*
	The man himself hath be coupable,	*has been to blame*

[Handwritten marginal note beside lines 549–550: "Fortune comes from the man himself."]

Which of his propre governance
Fortuneth al the worldes chance.

[NEBUCHADNEZZAR'S DREAM]

v.   *Prosper et aduersus obliquo tramite versus*   *(see note)*
       Immundus mundus decipit omne genus.
     Mundus in euentu versatur ut alea casu,
       Quam celer in ludis iactat auara manus.
     Sicut ymago viri variantur tempora mundi,
       Statque nichil firmum preter amare deum.[1]

585	The hyhe almyhti pourveance,	*foreknowledge*
	In whos eterne remembrance	
	Fro ferst was every thing present,	
	He hath his prophecie sent,	
	In such a wise as thou schalt hiere,	*manner; hear*
590	To Daniel of this matiere,	
☞	Hou that this world schal torne and wende	*change and decay (see note)*
	Til it befalle to his ende.	*its*
	Wherof the tale telle I schal,	
	In which it is betokned al.	
595	As Nabugodonosor slepte,	
	A swevene him tok, the which he kepte	*dream overwhelmed him; remembered*
	Til on the morwe he was arise,	
	For he therof was sore agrise.	*sorely terrified*
	To Daniel his drem he tolde,	
600	And preide him faire that he wolde	*asked him courteously what*
	Arede what it tokne may,	*Interpret; signify*
	And seide, "Abedde wher I lay,	
	Me thoghte I syh upon a stage	*saw*
	Wher stod a wonder strange ymage.	
605	His hed with al the necke also	*Its*
	Thei were of fin gold bothe tuo;	*both of them*
	His brest, his schuldres, and his armes	
	Were al of selver, bot the tharmes,	*silver; entrails*
	The wombe, and al doun to the kne,	*belly*
610	Of bras thei were upon to se;	*look*
	The legges were al mad of stiel,	*steel*
	So were his feet also somdiel,	*in part*
	And somdiel part to hem was take	*made*
	Of erthe which men pottes make.	

---

[1] *Fortunate and adverse, turning through its mazy trail, the unclean, disordered world deceives every sort. The world is overturned in its outcomes as a die in a toss, as quickly as the covetous hand throws at the games. Like an image of man do the ages of the world vary, and nothing besides the love of God stands firm.*

615	The fieble meynd was with the stronge,	*weak was mingled with*
	So myhte it wel noght stonde longe.	
☞	And tho me thoghte that I sih	*then it seemed to me (see note)*
	A gret ston from an hull on hyh	*hill on high*
	Fel doun of sodein aventure	
620	Upon the feet of this figure,	
	With which ston al tobroke was —	
	Gold, selver, erthe, stiel, and bras —	*clay, steel; brass*
	That al was into pouldre broght,	*So that; powder*
	And so forth torned into noght."	
625	This was the swevene which he hadde,	*dream*
☞	That Daniel anon aradde,	*explained (see note)*
	And seide him that figure strange	
	Betokneth how the world schal change	*Is an omen of (Portends); vary*
	And waxe lasse worth and lasse,	*grow less and less valuable*
630	Til it to noght al overpasse.	*becomes worthless*
	The necke and hed, that weren golde,	
	He seide how that betokne scholde	
	A worthi world, a noble, a riche,	
	To which non after schal be liche.	*like*
☞	Of selver that was overforth	*that [the gold] was directly above (see note)*
	Schal ben a world of lasse worth;	
☞	And after that the wombe of bras	*(see note)*
	Tokne of a werse world it was.	
☞	The stiel which he syh afterward,	*saw (see note)*
640	A world betokneth more hard.	
☞	Bot yet the werste of everydel	*of all (see note)*
	Is last, whan that of erthe and stiel	
	He syh the feet departed so,	*saw; divided*
	For that betokneth mochel wo.	
645	Whan that the world divided is,	
	It moste algate fare amis,	*must unceasingly go wrong*
	For erthe which is meynd with stiel	*alloyed (mingled)*
	Togedre may noght laste wiel,	*well*
	Bot if that on that other waste;	*Unless they both consume one another*
650	So mot it nedes faile in haste.	
☞	The ston, which fro the hully stage	*mountainous location (see note)*
	He syh doun falle on that ymage,	
	And hath it into pouldre broke,	*powder smashed*
	That swevene hath Daniel unloke,	*dream; interpreted (unlocked)*
655	And seide how that is Goddes myht,	*explained*
	Which whan men wene most upryht	*think*
	To stonde, schal hem overcaste.	
	And that is of this world the laste,	
	And thanne a newe schal beginne,	
660	Fro which a man schal nevere twinne.	*depart*

☞   Or al to peine or al to pes   *Either entirely for pain or peace (see note)*
            That world schal lasten endeles.   *forever*

[DANIEL'S PROPHECIES FULFILLED]

            Lo thus expondeth Daniel
            The kynges swevene faire and wel   *dream*
665   In Babiloyne the cité,
            Wher that the wiseste of Caldee
            Ne cowthen wite what it mente;   *Could not figure out; meant*
            Bot he tolde al the hol entente,   *whole meaning*
            As in partie it is befalle.   *As in part it has [already] come to pass*
☞   Of gold the ferste regne of alle   *(see note)*
671   Was in that kinges time tho,   *then*
            And laste manye daies so,
            Therwhiles that the monarchie
            Of al the world in that partie   *region*
675   To Babiloyne was soubgit;   *subjected*
            And hield him stille in such a plit,   *plight*
            Til that the world began diverse.   *began to change*
            And that was whan the king of Perse,   *Persia*
            Which Cirus hyhte, agein the pes   *Cyrus was named, against the peace*
680   Forth with his sone Cambises
            Of Babiloine al that empire,
            Ryht as thei wolde hemself desire,
            Put under in subjeccioun
            And tok it in possessioun,
685   And slayn was Baltazar the king,
            Which loste his regne and al his thing.   *kingdom; possessions*
            And thus whan thei it hadde wonne,
☞   The world of selver was begonne   *(see note)*
            And that of gold was passed oute.
690   And in this wise it goth aboute   *proceeds*
            Into the regne of Darius;
            And thanne it fell to Perse thus,
            That Alisaundre put hem under,   *overthrew them*
            Which wroghte of armes many a wonder,   *Who*
695   So that the monarchie lefte   *remained*
            With Grecs, and here astat uplefte,   *their estate elevated*
            And Persiens gon under fote,
            So soffre thei that nedes mote.   *suffer what needs must be*
☞   And tho the world began of bras,   *(see note)*
700   And that of selver ended was.
            Bot for the time thus it laste,
            Til it befell that ate laste
            This king, whan that his day was come,
            With strengthe of deth was overcome.

705	And natheles yet er he dyde,	*before; died*
	He schop his regnes to divide	*arranged for (shaped); to be divided*
	To knyhtes whiche him hadde served,	
	And after that thei have deserved	*according to what they*
	Gaf the conquestes that he wan;	*Distributed; booty; won*
710	Wherof gret werre tho began	*war*
	Among hem that the regnes hadde,	*those who*
	Thurgh proud Envie which hem ladde,	*motivated them*
	Til it befell agein hem thus.	
	The noble Cesar Julius,	
715	Which tho was king of Rome lond,	
	With gret bataille and with strong hond	*armed might*
	Al Grece, Perse, and ek Caldee	
	Wan and put under, so that he	
	Noght al only of th'orient	*Not only all of the East*
720	Bot al the marche of th'occident,	*territories of the West*
	Governeth under his empire,	
	As he that was hol lord and sire,	*absolute*
	And hield thurgh his chivalrie	*prowess in warfare*
	Of al this world the monarchie,	
725	And was the ferste of that honour	*of such honor*
	Which tok the name of Emperour.	
	Wher Rome thanne wolde assaille,	*attack*
	Ther myhte nothing contrevaille,	*resist with equal force*
	Bot every contré moste obeie.	
730	Tho goth the regne of bras aweie,	
☞	And comen is the world of stiel,	*(see note)*
	And stod above upon the whiel.	*[Fortune's] wheel*
	As stiel is hardest in his kynde,	
	Above alle othre that men finde	
735	Of metals, such was Rome tho	
	The myhtieste, and laste so	
	Long time amonges the Romeins	
	Til thei become so vileins,	*depraved (villainous)*
	That the fals Emperour Leo	
740	With Constantin his sone also	
	The patrimoine and the richesse,	
	Which to Silvestre in pure almesse	
	The ferste Constantinus lefte,	
	Fro holy cherche thei berefte.	*stole*
745	Bot Adrian, which Pope was,	
	And syh the meschief of this cas,	
	Goth into France for to pleigne,	*complain*
	And preith the grete Charlemeine,	
	For Cristes sake and soule hele	*health*
750	That he wol take the querele	*quarrel*
	Of holy cherche in his defence.	

And Charles for the reverence
Of God the cause hath undertake,
And with his host the weie take
755 Over the montz of Lombardie; *Alps*
Of Rome and al the tirandie *tyrants*
With blodi swerd he overcom
And the cité with strengthe nom *by force took*
In such a wise; and there he wroghte *manner*
760 That holy cherche agein he broghte
Into franchise, and doth restore *sovereignty; causes to be restored*
The Popes lost, and gaf him more. *loss of property*
And thus whan he his God hath served,
He tok, as he wel hath deserved,
765 The diademe and was coroned.
Of Rome and thus was abandoned *surrendered*
Th'empire, which cam nevere agein
Into the hond of no Romein;
Bot a long time it stod so stille
770 Under the Frensche kynges wille,
Til that Fortune hir whiel so ladde, *controlled*
That afterward Lombardy it hadde,
Noght be the swerd, bot be soffrance *by; permission*
Of him that tho was kyng of France,
775 Which Karle Calvus cleped was; *was called*
And he resigneth in this cas
Th'empire of Rome unto Lowis
His cousin, which a Lombard is. *relative*
☞ And so hit laste into the yeer *(see note)*
780 Of Albert and of Berenger;
Bot thanne upon dissencioun
Thei felle, and in divisioun
Among hemself that were grete, *themselves*
So that thei loste the beyete *possession*
785 Of worschipe and of worldes pes, *peace*
Bot in proverbe natheles
Men sein, ful selden is that welthe *seldom [it] is*
Can soffre his oghne astat in helthe, *tolerate its own; to be healthy*
And that was on the Lombardz sene; *seen in the case of the*
790 Such comun strif was hem betwene
Thurgh coveitise and thurgh Envie
That every man drowh his partie, *seduced his followers*
Which myhte leden eny route, *Whoever might; mob*
Withinne burgh and ek withoute. *city*
795 The comun ryht hath no felawe, *common law*
So that the governance of lawe
Was lost, and for necessité,
Of that thei stode in such degré *Since*

	Al only thurgh divisioun,	
800	Hem nedeth in conclusioun	*They had need finally*
	Of strange londes help beside.	*foreign*
	And thus for thei hemself divide	*since they*
	And stonden out of reule unevene,	
	Of Alemaine princes sevene	*From Germany*
805	Thei chose in this condicioun,	
	That upon here eleccioun	*their*
	Th'empire of Rome scholde stonde.	
	And thus thei lefte it out of honde	
	For lacke of grace, and it forsoke,	
810	That Alemans upon hem toke.	*[So] that*
	And to confermen here astat,	*strengthen their property*
	Of that thei founden in debat	*that [which]; in turmoil*
	Thei token the possessioun	*gained rulership over*
	After the composicioun	*According to the agreement*
815	Among hemself, and therupon	
	Thei made an emperour anon,	
	Whos name as the cronique telleth	
	Was Othes; and so forth it duelleth,	*Otto*
	Fro thilke day yit unto this,	*that*
820	Th'empire of Rome hath ben and is	
	To th'Alemans. And in this wise,	*Under jurisdiction of the Germans*
	As ye tofore have herd divise	*prior to this have heard explained*
	How Daniel the swevene expondeth	*dream*
	Of that ymage, on whom he foundeth	*established by interpretation*
825	The world which after scholde falle,	
	Come is the laste tokne of alle.	
	Upon the feet of erthe and stiel	
	So stant this world now everydiel	
	Departed, which began riht tho,	
830	Whan Rome was divided so.	
	And that is for to rewe sore,	
	For alway siththe more and more	*thereafter*
	The world empeireth every day.	*worsens*
	Wherof the sothe schewe may,	*truth*
835	At Rome ferst if we beginne.	
	The wall and al the cit withinne	*city*
	Stant in ruine and in decas;	*Stands; decay*
	The feld is wher the paleis was,	*field*
	The toun is wast, and overthat,	*ruined; moreover*
840	If we beholde thilke astat	*condition*
	Which whilom was of the Romeins,	
	Of knyhthode and of citezeins,	*freemen*
	To peise now with that beforn,	*compare (weigh)*
	The chaf is take for the corn.	*accepted*
845	As for to speke of Romes myht,	*Rome's power*

Unethes stant ther oght upryht   *Scarcely stands; anything*
Of worschipe or of worldes good,
As it before tyme stod.
And why the worschipe is aweie,
850   If that a man the sothe seie,   *sees the truth*
The cause hath ben divisioun,
Which moder of confusioun
Is wher sche cometh overal,
Noght only of the temporal
855   Bot of the spirital also.
The dede proeveth it is so,
And hath do many day er this,
Thurgh venym which that medled is   *mingled*
In holy cherche of erthly thing.
860   For Crist Himself makth knowleching   *declares*
That no man may togedre serve
God and the world, bot if he swerve   *unless he*
Froward that on and stonde unstable;   *Away from that one (God)*
And Cristes word may noght be fable.
865   The thing so open is at ẙe,   *so evident to the eye*
It nedeth noght to specefie
Or speke oght more in this matiere;
Bot in this wise a man mai lere   *learn*
Hou that the world is gon aboute,
870   The which wel nyh is wered oute,   *worn*
After the forme of that figure
Which Daniel in his scripture
Expondeth, as tofore is told.
Of bras, of selver, and of gold
875   The world is passed and agon,   *come to naught (gone to ruin)*
And now upon his olde ton   *toes*
It stant of brutel erthe and stiel,   *brittle (untrustworthy)*
The whiche acorden nevere a diel;   *not at all*
So mot it nedes swerve aside   *come apart*
880   As thing the which men sen divide.
☞   Th'apostel writ unto ous alle   *(see note)*
And seith that upon ous is falle
Th'ende of the world; so may we knowe,
This ymage is nyh overthrowe,   *nearly overthrown*
885   Be which this world was signified,   *By*
That whilom was so magnefied,
And now is old and fieble and vil,   *feeble; vile*
Full of meschief and of peril,
And stant divided ek also
890   Lich to the feet that were so,   *Like*
As I tolde of the statue above.
And this men sen, thurgh lacke of love

Where as the lond divided is,

It mot algate fare amis.   *must continually*

895   And now to loke on every side,

A man may se the world divide,

The werres ben so general   *conflicts (wars)*

Among the Cristene overal,

That every man now secheth wreche,   *seeks vengeance*

900   And yet these clerkes alday preche

And sein, good dede may non be

Which stant noght upon charité.

I not hou charité may stonde,   *I do not know how*

Wher dedly werre is take on honde.

905   Bot al this wo is cause of man,   *caused by*

The which that wit and reson can,   *Who has understanding and intelligence*

And that in tokne and in witnesse

That ilke ymage bar liknesse

Of man and of non other beste.   *creature*

910   For ferst unto the mannes heste   *command (dominion)*

Was every creature ordeined,   *created*

Bot afterward it was restreigned.

Whan that he fell, thei fellen eke,   *also*

Whan he wax sek, thei woxen seke;   *sick*

915   For as the man hath passioun,

Of seknesse, in comparisoun   *similarly*

So soffren othre creatures.

☞   Lo, ferst the hevenly figures,   *(see note)*

The sonne and mone eclipsen bothe.

920   And ben with mannes senne wrothe;   *mankind's sins made angry*

The purest eir for senne alofte   *air; on high*

Hath ben and is corrupt ful ofte,   *infected*

Right now the hyhe wyndes blowe,

And anon after thei ben lowe,

925   Now clowdy and now clier it is.   *clear*

So may it proeven wel be this,

A mannes senne is for to hate,   *sin; to be hated*

Which makth the welkne to debate.   *causes; heavens to be in turmoil*

And for to se the propreté

930   Of every thyng in his degree,

Benethe forth among ous hiere   *On earth*

Al stant aliche in this matiere.

The see now ebbeth, now it floweth,   *sea*

The lond now welketh, now it groweth,   *withers*

935   Now be the trees with leves grene,   *are*

Now thei be bare and nothing sene,

Now be the lusti somer floures

Now be the stormy wynter shoures,

Now be the daies, now the nyhtes,

940	So stant ther nothing al upryhtes.	
	Now it is lyht, now it is derk,	
	And thus stant al the worldes werk	
	After the disposicioun	
	Of man and his condicioun.	
945	Forthi Gregoire in his *Moral*	*(see note)*
	Seith that a man in special	
	The lasse world is properly,	*smaller (microcosmic)*
	And that he proeveth redely.	*proves skillfully*
	For man of soule resonable	
950	Is to an angel resemblable,	
	And lich to beste he hath fielinge,	*sensory perception*
	And lich to trees he hath growinge;	
	The stones ben and so is he.	
	Thus of his propre qualité	
955	The man, as telleth the clergie,	*as learning teaches us*
	Is as a world in his partie,	*for his part*
	And whan this litel world mistorneth,	
	The grete world al overtorneth.	
	The lond, the see, the firmament,	
960	Thei axen alle jugement	
	Agein the man and make him werre.	*make war against him*
	Therwhile himself stant out of herre,	*stands out of kilter (ME herre, "hinge")*
	The remenant wol noght acorde.	
	And in this wise, as I recorde,	
965	The man is cause of alle wo,	
	Why this world is divided so.	

[DIVISION AND EVIL]

☞	Division, the Gospell seith,	*(see note)*
	On hous upon another leith,	*One; lays*
	Til that the regne al overthrowe.	*realm*
970	And thus may every man wel knowe,	
	Division aboven alle	
	Is thing which makth the world to falle,	
	And evere hath do sith it began.	*since*
☞	It may ferst proeve upon a man;	*(see note)*
975	The which, for his complexioun	*since his*
	Is mad upon divisioun	
	Of cold, of hot, of moist, of drye,	
	He mot be verray kynde dye,	*must by [his] very nature die*
	For the contraire of his astat	*contrariness*
980	Stant evermor in such debat,	
	Til that o part be overcome,	
	Ther may no final pes be nome.	*peace be attained*
	Bot otherwise, if a man were	

	Mad al togedre of o matiere	*Made; one*
985	Withouten interrupcioun,	*separation of parts*
	Ther scholde no corrupcioun	*disintegration*
	Engendre upon that unité.	
	Bot for ther is diversité	*because*
	Withinne himself, he may noght laste,	*survive*
990	That he ne deieth ate laste.	*But that he ultimately dies*
☞	Bot in a man yit over this	*(see note)*
	Full gret divisioun ther is,	
	Thurgh which that he is evere in strif,	
	Whil that him lasteth eny lif.	
995	The bodi and the soule also	
	Among hem ben divided so,	*themselves*
	That what thing that the body hateth	
	The soule loveth and debateth;	*fights [against the body]*
	Bot natheles fulofte is sene	
1000	Of werre which is hem betwene	
	The fieble hath wonne the victoire.	
☞	And who so drawth into memoire	*(see note)*
	What hath befalle of old and newe,	
	He may that werre sore rewe,	*war sorely lament*
1005	Which ferst began in Paradis.	
	For ther was proeved what it is,	*demonstrated*
	And what desese there it wroghte;	
	For thilke werre tho forth broghte	
	The vice of alle dedly sinne,	
1010	Thurgh which division cam inne	
☞	Among the men in erthe hiere,	*(see note)*
	And was the cause and the matiere	
	Why God the grete flodes sende,	*sent*
	Of al the world and made an ende	
1015	Bot Noë with his felaschipe,	*Except Noah*
	Which only weren saulf be schipe.	*safe by*
	And over that thurgh senne it com	*besides that; came about*
☞	That Nembrot such emprise nom,	*enterprise undertook (see note)*
	Whan he the Tour Babel on heihte	
1020	Let make, as he that wolde feihte	*Had made; fight*
	Agein the hihe Goddes myht,	
	Wherof divided anon ryht	*immediately*
	Was the langage in such entente,	
	Ther wiste non what other mente,	*none knew*
1025	So that thei myhten noght procede.	
	And thus it stant of every dede	
	Wher senne takth the cause on honde	
	It may upriht noght longe stonde;	
	For senne of his condicioun	
1030	Is moder of divisioun	*mother*

☞   And tokne whan the world schal faile.   *signifies (see note)*
       For so seith Crist withoute faile,
       That nyh upon the worldes ende   *close to (nigh)*
       Pes and acord awey schol wende   *shall depart*
1035   And alle charité schal cesse   *cease*
       Among the men, and hate encresce;
       And whan these toknes ben befalle,
       Al sodeinly the ston schal falle,
       As Daniel it hath beknowe,   *foreseen*
1040   Which al this world schal overthrowe,
       And every man schal thanne arise   *be resurrected*
       To joie or elles to juise,   *justice*
       Wher that he schal for evere dwelle,
       Or straght to hevene or straght to helle.
1045   In hevene is pes and al acord,
       Bot helle is ful of such descord
       That ther may be no loveday.
       Forthi good is, whil a man may,
       Echon to sette pes with other
1050   And loven as his oghne brother;   *own*
       So may he winne worldes welthe
       And afterward his soule helthe.

[EXAMPLE OF ARION]   We need a new Arion, Gower wants it to be him

☞   Bot wolde God that now were on   *(see note)*
       An other such as Arion,
1055   Which hadde an harpe of such temprure,   *tunefulness*
       And therto of so good mesure   *meter/harmonic ratio?*
       He song, that he the bestes wilde   *wild animals*
       Made of his note tame and milde,
       The hinde in pes with the leoun,   *deer*
1060   The wolf in pes with the moltoun,   *sheep*
       The hare in pees stod with the hound;
       And every man upon this ground
       Which Arion that time herde,
       Als wel the lord as the schepherde,
1065   He broghte hem alle in good acord;   *them*
       So that the comun with the lord,   *citizenry (common people)*
       And lord with the comun also,
       He sette in love bothe tuo
       And putte awey malencolie.
1070   That was a lusti melodie,
       Whan every man with other low;   *laughed*
       And if ther were such on now,   *such a person*
       Which cowthe harpe as he tho dede,   *Who*
       He myhte availe in many a stede   *place*

1075	To make pes wher now is hate;	
	For whan men thenken to debate,	*engage in conflict*
	I not what other thing is good.	*do not know*
	Bot wher that wisdom waxeth wod,	*goes mad*
	And reson torneth into rage,	
1080	So that mesure upon oultrage	*So that moderation has put licentiousness*
	Hath set his world, it is to drede;	*In charge of his world*
	For that bringth in the comun drede,	
	Which stant at every mannes dore.	*door*
	Bot whan the scharpnesse of the spore	*spur*
1085	The horse side smit to sore,	*horse's; pierced too sorely*
	It grieveth ofte. And now nomore,	
	As for to speke of this matiere,	
	Which non bot only God may stiere.	*guide (govern)*

EXPLICIT PROLOGUS

Illustration 3: MS Fairfax 3, fol. 8r. Bodleian Library, Oxford University. The Confession of the Lover to Genius.

🌿 CONFESSIO AMANTIS: BOOK 1 (PRIDE)

INCIPIT LIBER PRIMUS

[ON LOVE]

i.   *Naturatus amor nature legibus orbem*   (see note)
       Subdit, et vnanimes concitat esse feras: (see note)
     Huius enim mundi Princeps amor esse videtur,
       Cuius eget diues, pauper et omnis ope.
     Sunt in agone pares amor et fortuna, que cecas
       Plebis ad insidias vertit vterque rotas.
     Est amor egra salus, vexata quies, pius error,
       Bellica pax, vulnus dulce, suaue malum.[1]

	I may noght strecche up to the hevene	
	Min hand, ne setten al in evene	
	This world, which evere is in balance:	*Aware of his limits*
	It stant noght in my sufficance	stands not; ability
5	So grete thinges to compasse,	undertake
	Bot I mot lete it overpasse	must; go by
	And treten upon othre thinges.	discourse on
	Forthi the stile of my writinges	Therefore; style
	Fro this day forth I thenke change	plan to (see note)
	And speke of thing is noght so strange,	something [that] is not; foreign
	Which every kinde hath upon honde,	nature has at hand
	And wherupon the world mot stonde,	must
	And hath don sithen it began,	since
	And schal whil ther is any man;	
15	And that is love, of which I mene	
	To trete, as after schal be sene.	
	In which ther can no man him reule,	no one can govern himself
	For loves lawe is out of reule,	unruly passion causes disorder

He'll talk of something on ☞ everyone's mind

Not Taught in school

---

[1] *Love fashioned for nature's ends subjects the world to the laws of nature, and incites harmonized ones to wildness [or: incites wild ones to harmony]. Love is seen to be the prince of this world, whose bounty rich man, poor man, and every man demand. Equal in the contest are Love and Fortune, both of which turn their blind wheels to entrap the people. Love is a sharp salvation, a troubled quiet, a pious error, a warring peace, a sweet wound, a soothing ill.*

	That of to moche or of to lite	*too much; too little*
20	Wel nyh is every man to wyte,	*blame*
	And natheles ther is no man	*For, in truth,*
	In al this world so wys, that can	
	Of love tempre the mesure,	
	Bot as it falth in aventure.	*falls by chance*
25	For wit ne strengthe may noght helpe,	*Neither intelligence nor*
	And he which elles wolde him yelpe	*who otherwise; boast*
	Is rathest throwen under fote,	*most quickly; foot*
	Ther can no wiht therof do bote.	*Where no one; be of help*
	For yet was nevere such covine,	*conspiracy*
30	That couthe ordeine a medicine	*Who knew how to concoct*
	To thing which God in lawe of kinde	*natural law*
	Hath set, for ther may no man finde	
	The rihte salve of such a sor.	*remedy; ailment*
	It hath and schal ben everemor	
35	That love is maister wher he wile,	
	Ther can no lif make other skile;	*no creature do otherwise*
	For wher as evere him lest to sette,	*wherever he chooses to set himself*
	Ther is no myht which him may lette.	*power that may stop him*
	Bot what schal fallen ate laste,	
40	The sothe can no wisdom caste,	*truth; wise man forecast*
	Bot as it falleth upon chance.	*Except; accidentally*
	For if ther evere was balance	
	Which of fortune stant governed,	
	I may wel lieve as I am lerned	*believe; taught*
45	That love hath that balance on honde,	
	Which wol no reson understonde.	
	For love is blind and may noght se,	
	Forthi may no certeineté	*reliance*
	Be set upon his jugement,	
50	Bot as the whiel aboute went	*wheel [of Fortune] turns*
	He gifth his graces undeserved,	*gives*
	And fro that man which hath him served	
	Ful ofte he takth aweye his fees,	*winnings*
	As he that pleieth ate dees;	*dice*
55	And therupon what schal befalle	
	He not, til that the chance falle,	*knows not; happens*
	Wher he schal lese or he schal winne.	*Whether; lose*
	And thus ful ofte men beginne,	
	That if thei wisten what it mente,	*knew*
☞	Thei wolde change al here entente.	*their (see note)*
	And for to proven it is so,	
	I am miselven on of tho,	*myself one of those*
	Which to this scole am underfonge.	*made a member of*
	For it is siththe go noght longe,	*since*
65	As for to speke of this matiere,	

[Handwritten annotations in margin:]
There is No man that is wise enough to temper love because it is by Chance.

Wit wont help, if you think that you will fail.

Can't remedy love

        I may you telle, if ye woll hiere,   *hear*
        A wonder hap which me befell,   *wondrous adventure*
        That was to me bothe hard and fell,   *cruel*
        Touchende of love and his fortune,   *its*
70   The which me liketh to comune   *explain (communicate)*
        And pleinly for to telle it oute.
        To hem that ben lovers aboute
        Fro point to point I wol declare
        And wryten of my woful care,
75   Mi wofull day, my wofull chance,
        That men mowe take remembrance   *may*
        Of that thei schall hierafter rede: *what; read next*
        For in good feith this wolde I rede,   *advise*
        That every man ensample take
80   Of wisdom which him is betake,   *to him is allotted*
        And that he wot of good aprise   *knows by sound learning*
        To teche it forth, for such emprise   *enterprise*
        Is for to preise; and therfore I   *praiseworthy*
        Woll wryte and schewe al openly
85   How love and I togedre mette
        Wherof the world ensample fette   *obtain (fetch)*
        Mai after this, whan I am go,   *gone*
        Of thilke unsely jolif wo,   *unfortunate happy woe*
        Whos reule stant out of the weie,
90   Nou glad and nou gladnesse aweie,   *Now*
        And yet it may noght be withstonde
        For oght that men may understonde.

[COMPLAINT TO CUPID AND VENUS]

ii.   *Non ego Sampsonis vires, non Herculis arma*   *(see note)*
        Vinco, sum sed vt hii victus amore pari.
     Vt discant alii, docet experiencia facti,
        Rebus in ambiguis que sit habenda via.
     Deuius ordo ducis temptata pericla sequentem
        Instruit a tergo, ne simul ille cadat.
     Me quibus ergo Venus, casus, laqueauit amantem,
        Orbis in exemplum scribere tendo palam.[1]

        Upon the point that is befalle
        Of love, in which that I am falle,

---

[1] *I do not indeed outdo Sampson's powers or Hercules' arms; but I am conquered as they were, by an equal love. Experience of the deed teaches so that others might learn what path should be held amidst uncertain circumstances. The twisting progress of one leading instructs another following at his back in the dangers already met, so that he too should not fall. Therefore, those disasters by which Venus ensnared me as a lover I strive to write, publicly, as example for the world.*

95	I thenke telle my matiere:	
	Now herkne, who that wol it hiere,	
	Of my fortune how that it ferde.	*happened (fared)*
☞	This enderday, as I forthferde	*other day; went forth (see note)*
	To walke, as I yow telle may,	
100	And that was in the monthe of Maii,	
	Whan every brid hath chose his make	*bird; mate*
	And thenkth his merthes for to make	
	Of love that he hath achieved;	*obtained*
	Bot so was I nothing relieved,	
105	For I was further fro my love	*from*
	Than erthe is fro the hevene above.	
	As for to speke of eny sped,	*any success*
	So wiste I me non other red,	*know; council*
	Bot as it were a man forfare	*worn out with travel*
110	Unto the wode I gan to fare,	*wood; go*
	Noght for to singe with the briddes,	*birds*
	For whanne I was the wode amiddes,	
	I fond a swote grene pleine,	*sweet*
	And ther I gan my wo compleigne	
115	Wisshinge and wepinge al myn one,	*alone by myself*
	For other merthes made I none.	
	So hard me was that ilke throwe,	*[for] me; very pain (circumstance)*
	That ofte sithes overthrowe	*many times*
	To grounde I was withoute breth;	
120	And evere I wisshide after deth,	
	Whanne I out of my peine awok,	
	And caste up many a pitous lok	
	Unto the hevene, and seide thus:	
[Amans]	"O thou Cupide, O thou Venus,	
125	Thow god of love and thou goddesse,	
	Wher is pité? wher is meknesse?	
	Now doth me pleinly live or dye,	
	For certes such a maladie	
	As I now have and longe have hadd,	
130	It myhte make a wis man madd,	
	If that it scholde longe endure.	
	O Venus, queene of loves cure,	
	Thou lif, thou lust, thou mannes hele,	*life; delight; well-being*
	Behold my cause and my querele,	*complaint*
135	And yif me som part of thi grace,	
	So that I may finde in this place	
	If thou be gracious or non."	*Whether*
	And with that word I sawh anon	
	The kyng of love and qweene bothe;	
140	Bot he that kyng with yhen wrothe	*angry eyes*
	His chiere aweiward fro me caste,	*countenance*

	And forth he passede ate laste.	
	Bot natheles er he forth wente	*before he left*
	A firy dart me thoghte he hente	*seized*
145	And threw it thurgh myn herte rote:	*deepest part of my heart*
	In him fond I non other bote,	*relief (reward)*
	For lenger list him noght to duelle.	*[it] pleased; dwell*
	Bot sche that is the source and welle	*well*
	Of wel or wo, that schal betide	*gladness (weal); happen*
150	To hem that loven, at that tide	*them; time*
	Abod, bot for to tellen hiere	*Awaited; speak of here*
	Sche cast on me no goodly chiere:	*regard*
	Thus natheles to me sche seide,	
[Venus]	"What art thou, sone?" and I abreide	*started*
155	Riht as a man doth out of slep,	
	And therof tok sche riht good kep	*notice*
	And bad me nothing ben adrad:	*afraid*
	Bot for al that I was noght glad,	
	For I ne sawh no cause why.	
160	And eft scheo asketh, what was I:	*then (after) she*
[Amans]	I seide, "A caitif that lith hiere:	*captive (wretch); lies*
	What wolde ye, my ladi diere?	
	Schal I ben hol or elles dye?"	*be made well (whole); die*
[Venus]	Sche seide, "Tell thi maladie:	
165	What is thi sor of which thou pleignest?	*sorrow; complain*
	Ne hyd it noght, for if thou feignest,	*hide the truth*
	I can do thee no medicine."	*help you with*
[Amans]	"Ma dame, I am a man of thyne,	
	That in thi court have longe served,	
170	And aske that I have deserved,	
	Som wele after my longe wo."	
	And sche began to loure tho,	*scowl then*
[Venus]	And seide, "Ther is manye of yow	
	Faitours, and so may be that thow	*Imposters (OF faiteor, "contriver")*
175	Art riht such on, and be feintise	*by deceit*
	Seist that thou hast me do servise."	*Say*
	And natheles sche wiste wel,	*knew*
	Mi world stod on an other whiel	*wheel [of Fortune]*
	Withouten eny faiterie:	*false pretense*
180	Bot algate of my maladie	*in any case*
	Sche bad me telle and seie hir trowthe.	
[Amans]	"Ma dame, if ye wolde have rowthe,"	*compassion*
	Quod I, "thanne wold I telle yow."	
[Venus]	"Sey forth," quod sche, "and tell me how;	
185	Schew me thi seknesse everydiel."	
[Amans]	"Ma dame, that can I do wel,	
	Be so my lif therto wol laste."	*Provided that; should last to that extent*
	With that hir lok on me sche caste,	

[Venus]	And seide: "In aunter if thou live,	*In doubt*
190	Mi will is ferst that thou be schrive;	*be confessed/absolved*
	And natheles how that it is	
	I wot miself, bot for al this	*know*
	Unto my prest, which comth anon,	*priest, who will arrive immediately*
	I woll thou telle it on and on,	*one thing at a time*
195	Bothe all thi thoght and al thi werk.	
	O Genius myn oghne clerk,	
	Com forth and hier this mannes schrifte,"	*hear; confession*
	Quod Venus tho; and I uplifte	*then; raised up*
	Min hefd with that and gan beholde	
200	The selve prest which as sche wolde	*self-same*
	Was redy there and sette him doun	*himself*
	To hiere my confessioun.	

[Confessio Amantis, the Lover's Confession]

iii.	*Confessus Genio si sit medicina salutis*	
	Experiar morbis, quos tulit ipsa Venus.	
	Lesa quidem ferro medicantur membra saluti,	
	Raro tamen medicum vulnus amoris habet.[1]	*(see note)*

	This worthi prest, this holy man	
	To me spekende thus began,	*speaking*
[Confessor]	And seide: "Benedicité,	*Bless you*
	Mi sone; of the felicité	
	Of love and ek of all the wo	*also*
	Thou schalt thee schrive of bothe tuo.	
☞	What thou er this for loves sake	*before (see note)*
210	Hast felt, let nothing be forsake,	
	Tell pleinliche as it is befalle."	
	And with that word I gan doun falle	
	On knees, and with devocioun	
	And with full gret contricioun	
[Amans]	I seide thanne: "Dominus,	*Lord*
	Min holi fader Genius;	
	So as thou hast experience	
	Of love, for whos reverence	
	Thou schalt me schriven at this time,	
220	I prai thee let me noght mistime	
	Mi schrifte, for I am destourbed	*confession*
	In al myn herte, and so contourbed,	*perturbed*
	That I ne may my wittes gete,	

---

[1] *Having confessed to Genius, I will try to discover whether that is the healing medicine for the diseases that Venus herself has transmitted. Even limbs wounded by the knife may be brought to health by treatment; yet rarely does the wound of love have a physician.*

So schal I moche thing forgete.

225 Bot if thou wolt my schrifte oppose   *question me about my confession*
Fro point to point, thanne, I suppose,
Ther schal nothing be left behinde.   *left unexamined*
Bot now my wittes ben so blinde,
That I ne can miselven teche."

230 Tho he began anon to preche,   *Then; soon*
And with his wordes debonaire
He seide to me softe and faire:

[**Confessor**] "Thi schrifte to oppose and hiere,
Mi sone, I am assigned hiere

235 Be Venus the godesse above,   *By*
☞   Whos prest I am touchende of love.   *pertaining to (see note)*
Bot natheles for certein skile   *But nonetheless; specific reasons*
I mot algate and nedes wile   *must continuously*
Noght only make my spekynges

240 Of love, bot of othre thinges,
That touchen to the cause of vice.
For that belongeth to th'office
Of prest, whos ordre that I bere,
So that I wol nothing forbere,   *leave out*

245 That I the vices on and on   *point by point*
Ne schal thee schewen everychon;
Wherof thou myht take evidence
To reule with thi conscience.
Bot of conclusion final

250 Conclude I wol in special
For love, whos servant I am,
And why the cause is that I cam.
So thenke I to don bothe tuo,
Ferst that myn ordre longeth to,

255 The vices for to telle arewe,   *in succession (a row)*
Bot next above alle othre schewe
Of love I wol the propretes,
How that thei stonde be degrees   *by*
After the disposicioun

260 Of Venus, whos condicioun
I moste folwe, as I am holde.   *bound*
For I with love am al withholde,   *in bondage*
So that the lasse I am to wyte,   *less; blame*
Thogh I ne conne bot a lyte   *know only a little*

265 Of othre thinges that ben wise: *prudent*
I am noght tawht in such a wise;   *way*
For it is noght my comun us   *custom (use)*
To speke of vices and vertus,
Bot al of love and of his lore,   *teaching*

270 For Venus bokes of no more

	Me techen nowther text ne glose.	commentary
	Bot for als moche as I suppose	
	It sit a prest to be wel thewed,	becomes; instructed
	And schame it is if he be lewed,	ignorant
275	Of my presthode after the forme	
	I wol thi schrifte so enforme,	
	That ate leste thou schalt hiere	
	The vices, and to thi matiere	
	Of love I schal hem so remene,	recount (bring back)
280	That thou schalt knowe what thei mene.	
	For what a man schal axe or sein	ask
	Touchende of schrifte, it mot be plein,	Regarding confession; must be complete
	It nedeth noght to make it queinte,	strange
	For trowthe hise wordes wol noght peinte:	cover over
285	That I wole axe of thee forthi,	That [which]; ask you therefore
	My sone, it schal be so pleinly,	
	That thou schalt knowe and understonde	
	The pointz of schrifte how that thei stonde."	

[SENSES OF SIGHT AND SOUND]

iv.   *Visus et auditus fragilis sunt ostia mentis,*
        Que viciosa manus claudere nulla potest.
    Est ibi larga via, graditur qua cordis ad antrum
        Hostis, et ingrediens fossa talenta rapit.   (see note)
    Hec michi confessor Genius primordia profert,
        Dum sit in extremis vita remorsa malis.
    Nunc tamen vt poterit semiviua loquela fateri,
        Verba per os timide conscia mentis agam.[1]

	Betwen the lif and deth I herde	
290	This prestes tale er I answerde,	before
	And thanne I preide him for to seie	speak
	His will, and I it wolde obeie	
	After the forme of his apprise.	teaching
☞	Tho spak he to me in such a wise,	Then; manner (see note)
295	And bad me that I scholde schryve	confess
	As touchende of my wittes fyve,	senses
	And schape that thei were amended	see to it that
	Of that I hadde hem mispended.	In whatever way I had abused (misspent) them
	For tho be propprely the gates,	those are

---

[1] *Vision and hearing are fragile gateways of the mind, which no vice-weakened hand can keep shut. A wide path is there by which an enemy strides to the inner cave of the heart and, entering, seizes the buried coin. These first principles Genius the Confessor offers me, while my vexed life is in deadly peril. But now in order that a half-living speech might be able to be uttered, I will fearfully press out through my mouth words privy to my thoughts.*

300	Thurgh whiche as to the herte algates	*assuredly*
	Comth alle thing unto the feire,	*our dealings (market-fair)*
	Which may the mannes soule empeire.	*harm*
	And now this matiere is broght inne:	

[Confessor] "Mi sone, I thenke ferst beginne

305	To wite how that thin yhe hath stonde,	*know; your eye has fared*
	The which is, as I understonde,	
	The moste principal of alle,	*of all [the senses]*
	Thurgh whom that peril mai befalle.	
	And for to speke in loves kinde,	*nature*
310	Ful manye such a man mai finde,	
	Whiche evere caste aboute here yhe,	*their eye*
	To loke if that thei myhte aspie	
	Ful ofte thing which hem ne toucheth,	*that does not pertain to them*
	Bot only that here herte soucheth	*their heart suspects*
315	In hindringe of an other wiht;	*creature*
	And thus ful many a worthi knyht	
	And many a lusti lady bothe	
	Have be ful ofte sythe wrothe.	*been many times angry*
	So that an yhe is as a thief	*eye*
320	To love, and doth ful gret meschief;	
	And also for his oghne part	*its own*
	Ful ofte thilke firy dart	*that same fiery*
	Of love, which that evere brenneth,	*burns*
	Thurgh him into the herte renneth:	*Through; runs (pierces)*
325	And thus a mannes yhe ferst	*eye first*
	Himselve grieveth alther werst,	*worst of all*
	And many a time that he knoweth	
	Unto his oghne harm it groweth.	
	Mi sone, herkne now forthi	*listen to; therefore*
330	A tale, to be war therby	*made aware*
	Thin yhe for to kepe and warde,	*guard*
	So that it passe noght his warde.	*its domain*

[TALE OF ACTEON]

	Ovide telleth in his bok	
☞	Ensample touchende of mislok,	*inappropriate looking (see note)*
335	And seith hou whilom ther was on,	*how once there was one*
	A worthi lord, which Acteon	
	Was hote, and he was cousin nyh	*Was named; near-relative*
	To him that Thebes ferst on hyh	*high*
	Up sette, which king Cadme hyhte.	*Cadmus was called*
340	This Acteon, as he wel myhte,	
	Above alle othre caste his chiere,	*set his heart*
	And used it fro yer to yere,	*customarily*
	With houndes and with grete hornes	

	Among the wodes and the thornes	
345	To make his hunting and his chace:	*chase*
	Where him best thoghte in every place	
	To finde gamen in his weie,	
	Ther rod he for to hunte and pleie.	*amuse himself*
	So him befell upon a tide	*time*
350	On his hunting as he cam ride,	*came to ride*
	In a forest alone he was:	
	He syh upon the grene gras	
	The faire freisshe floures springe,	
	He herde among the leves singe	
355	The throstle with the nyhtingale:	
	Thus er he wiste into a dale	*Thus, before he knew it*
	He cam, wher was a litel plein,	*clearing*
	All round aboute wel besein	*furnished*
	With buisshes grene and cedres hyhe;	*green bushes; tall cedars*
360	And ther withinne he caste his yhe.	*eye*
	Amidd the plein he syh a welle,	
	So fair ther myhte no man telle,	
	In which Diana naked stod	
	To bathe and pleie hire in the flod	*bathe herself; play; water*
365	With many a nimphe, which hire serveth.	*who served her*
	Bot he his yhe awey ne swerveth	*eye did not turn away*
	Fro hire which was naked al,	*From her who was stark naked*
	And sche was wonder wroth withal.	*intensely angry*
	And him, as sche which was godesse,	
370	Forschop anon, and the liknesse	
	Sche made him taken of an hert,	*take on [the likeness] of*
	Which was tofore hise houndes stert,	*in front of; was surprised*
	That ronne besiliche aboute	
	With many an horn and many a route,	*horn-blast; company of hunters*
375	That maden mochel noise and cry:	*Who made great hue and cry*
	And ate laste, unhappely,	
	This hert his oghne houndes slowhe	*his own hounds slew the hart*
	And him for vengance al todrowhe.	*utterly tore him apart*
Confessor	Lo now, my sone, what it is	
380	A man to caste his yhe amis,	*eye*
	Which Acteon hath dere aboght;	*dearly bought*
	Be war forthi and do it noght.	
	For ofte, who that hiede toke,	
	Betre is to winke than to loke.	
385	And for to proven it is so,	
	Ovide the poete also	
	A tale which to this matiere	
	Acordeth seith, as thou schalt hiere.	

[TALE OF MEDUSA]

	In Metamor it telleth thus,	
390	How that a lord which Phorceus	
☞	Was hote, hadde dowhtres thre.	*Was called (see note)*
	Bot upon here nativité	*their nativity*
	Such was the constellacioun,	
	That out of mannes nacioun	
395	Fro kynde thei be so miswent,	*From nature; askew*
	That to the liknesse of serpent	
	Thei were bore, and so that on	*born; one*
	Of hem was cleped Stellibon,	*them was called*
	That other soster Suriale,	
400	The thridde, as telleth in the tale,	
	Medusa hihte, and natheles	*was called*
	Of comun name Gorgones	
	In every contré ther aboute,	
	As monstres whiche that men doute,	*fear*
405	Men clepen hem; and bot on yhe	*only one eye*
	Among hem thre in pourpartie	*to share*
	Thei hadde, of which thei myhte se:	
	Now hath it this, now hath it sche;	
	After that cause and nede it ladde,	
410	Be throwes ech of hem it hadde.	*By turns*
	A wonder thing yet more amis	
	Ther was, wherof I telle al this.	
	What man on hem his chiere caste	*countenance cast*
	And hem behield, he was als faste	*beheld them*
415	Out of a man into a ston	
	Forschape, and thus ful manyon	*Transformed; full many a one*
	Deceived were, of that thei wolde	
	Misloke, wher that thei ne scholde.	
	Bot Perseus that worthi knyht,	
420	Whom Pallas of hir grete myht	*Pallas Athena*
	Halp, and tok him a schield therto,	*gave him*
	And ek the god Mercurie also	
	Lente him a swerd, he, as it fell,	*as it happened*
	Beyende Athlans the hihe hell	*Beyond Atlas; high hill*
425	These monstres soghte, and there he fond	
	Diverse men of thilke lond	
	Thurgh sihte of hem mistorned were,	*disfigured*
	Stondende as stones hiere and there.	
	Bot, he, which wisdom and prouesse	
430	Hadde of the god and the godesse,	
	The schield of Pallas gan enbrace,	*placed on his arm*
	With which he covereth sauf his face,	*safely*
	Mercuries swerd and out he drowh,	

	And so he bar him that he slowh	*he so carried himself*
435	These dredful monstres alle thre.	
Confessor	Lo now, my sone, avise thee,	*take heed*
	That thou thi sihte noght misuse:	
	Cast noght thin yhe upon Meduse,	
	That thou be torned into ston:	
440	For so wys man was nevere non,	
	Bot if he wel his yhe kepe	
	And take of fol delit no kepe,	*wanton delight*
	That he with lust nys ofte nome,	*is not often taken*
	Thurgh strengthe of love and overcome.	
445	Of mislokynge how it hath ferd,	
	As I have told, now hast thou herd,	
	Mi goode sone, and tak good hiede.	
	And over this yet I thee rede	*advise you*
	That thou be war of thin heringe,	*hearing*
450	Which to the herte the tidinge	
	Of many a vanité hath broght,	
	To tarie with a mannes thoght.	*With which to vex*
	And natheles good is to hiere	
	Such thing wherof a man may lere	*learn*
455	That to vertu is acordant,	*What; in agreement*
	And toward al the remenant	
	Good is to torne his ere fro;	*ear [away] from*
	For elles, bot a man do so,	*unless*
	Him may ful ofte mysbefalle.	
460	I rede ensample amonges alle,	
	Wherof to kepe wel an ere	
	It oghte pute a man in fere.	

[ASPIDIS THE SERPENT]

	A serpent, which that Aspidis	
	Is cleped, of his kynde hath this,	
465	That he the ston noblest of alle,	
☞	The which that men carbuncle calle,	*(see note)*
	Berth in his hed above on heihte.	*Bears; in the upper part of his body*
	For which whan that a man be sleyhte	*by cunning*
	The ston to winne and him to daunte,	*overwhelm*
470	With his carecte him wolde enchaunte,	*conjuration (charm)*
	Anon as he perceiveth that,	*As soon as*
	He leith doun his on ere al plat	*places; one ear; flat*
	Unto the ground, and halt it faste,	*holds*
	And ek that other ere als faste	*also; ear just as tightly*
475	He stoppeth with his tail so sore,	*assiduously*
	That he the wordes lasse or more	*[So] that*
	Of his enchantement ne hiereth;	*doesn't hear*

	And in this wise himself he skiereth,	*manner; defends*
	So that he hath the wordes weyved	*excluded (avoided)*
480	And thurgh his ere is noght deceived.	

[SIRENS]

	An othre thing, who that recordeth,	*if one calls it to mind*
	Lich unto this ensample acordeth,	
☞	Which in the tale of Troie I finde.	*(see note)*
	Sirenes of a wonder kynde	*marvellous nature*
485	Ben monstres, as the bokes tellen,	
	And in the grete se thei duellen:	*sea*
	Of body bothe and of visage	
	Lik unto wommen of yong age	
	Up fro the navele on hih thei be,	*above*
490	And doun benethe, as men mai se,	
	Thei bere of fisshes the figure.	
	And over this of such nature	
	Thei ben, that with so swete a stevene	*voice*
	Lik to the melodie of hevene	
495	In wommanysshe vois thei singe,	
	With notes of so gret likinge,	*delight*
	Of such mesure, of such musike,	
	Wherof the schipes thei beswike	*deceive*
	That passen be the costes there.	
500	For whan the schipmen leie an ere	*give ear*
	Unto the vois, in here avys	*their judgment*
	Thei wene it be a paradys,	*think*
	Which after is to hem an helle.	
	For reson may noght with hem duelle,	*stay with them*
505	Whan thei tho grete lustes hiere;	*those great delights hear*
	Thei conne noght here schipes stiere,	*do not know how to steer their ships*
	So besiliche upon the note	*busily; song*
	Thei herkne, and in such wise assote,	*listen; are befuddled*
	That thei here rihte cours and weie	
510	Forgete, and to here ere obeie,	*to their ear obey*
	And seilen til it so befalle	*sail*
	That thei into the peril falle,	
	Where as the schipes be todrawe,	*broken apart*
	And thei ben with the monstres slawe.	*slain*
515	Bot fro this peril natheles	
	With his wisdom king Uluxes	*Ulysses*
	Ascapeth and it overpasseth;	*gets past*
	For he tofor the hond compasseth	*beforehand devises*
	That no man of his compaignie	
520	Hath pouer unto that folie	
	His ere for no lust to caste;	

For he hem stoppede alle faste,
That non of hem mai hiere hem singe.   *[So] that none of them; them*
So whan thei comen forth seilinge,
525   Ther was such governance on honde,
That thei the monstres have withstonde
And slain of hem a gret partie.   *slew a great many of them*
Thus was he sauf with his navie,   *ships*
This wise king, thurgh governance.
Confessor   Wherof, my sone, in remembrance
Thou myht ensample taken hiere,
As I have told, and what thou hiere
Be wel war, and gif no credence,
Bot if thou se more evidence.
535   For if thou woldest take kepe
And wisly cowthest warde and kepe   *know how to protect and preserve*
Thin yhe and ere, as I have spoke,
Than haddest thou the gates stoke   *gates (eyes and ears) locked up*
Fro such sotie as comth to winne   *foolishness*
540   Thin hertes wit, which is withinne,
Wherof that now thi love excedeth
Mesure, and many a peine bredeth.   *breeds*
Bot if thou cowthest sette in reule   *Unless; understand how to govern*
Tho tuo, the thre were eth to reule: *Those two; [other] three; easy*
545   Forthi as of thi wittes five
I wole as now no more schryve,   *interrogate*
Bot only of these ilke tuo.
Tell me therfore if it be so,
Hast thou thin yhen oght misthrowe?"   *eyes ever misused*
Amans   "Mi fader, ye, I am beknowe,   *I admit guilt*
I have hem cast upon Meduse,
Therof I may me noght excuse:
Min herte is growen into ston,
So that my lady therupon
555   Hath such a priente of love grave,   *mark of love engraved*
That I can noght miselve save."
Opponit Confessor   "What seist thou, sone, as of thin ere?"
Respondet Amans   "Mi fader, I am gultyf there;   *guilty there [too]*
For whanne I may my lady hiere,   *hear*
560   Mi wit with that hath lost his stiere: *its rudder*
I do noght as Uluxes dede,
Bot falle anon upon the stede,   *collapse immediately on the spot*
Wher as I se my lady stonde;   *Where [I am] when I see*
And there, I do yow understonde,
565   I am topulled in my thoght,   *pulled to pieces*
So that of reson leveth noght,   *remains nothing*
Wherof that I me mai defende."   *defend myself*

Confessor   "Mi goode sone, God th'amende!   *God help you*
         For as me thenketh be thi speche
570   Thi wittes ben riht feer to seche.   *far to seek*
         As of thin ere and of thin yhe
         I woll no more specefie,
         Bot I woll axen over this   *ask beyond this*
         Of othre thing how that it is."

[HYPOCRISY]

v.   *Celsior est Aquila que Leone ferocior ille,*
               Quem tumor elati cordis ad alta mouet.
           Sunt species quinque, quibus esse Superbia ductrix
               Clamat, et in multis mundus adheret eis.
           Laruando faciem ficto pallore subornat
               Fraudibus Ypocrisis mellea verba suis.
           Sicque pios animos quamsepe ruit muliebres
               Ex humili verbo sub latitante dolo.[1]

[Confessor]   "Mi sone, as I thee schal enforme,
☞   Ther ben yet of an other forme   *(see note)*
             Of dedly vices sevene applied,   *assigned*
             Wherof the herte is ofte plied   *bent*
             To thing which after schal him grieve.
580   The ferste of hem thou schalt believe
             Is Pride, which is principal,
             And hath with him in special
             Ministres five ful diverse,
             Of whiche, as I thee schal reherse,
585   The ferste is seid Ypocrisie.   *called Hypocrisy*
             If thou art of his compaignie,
             Tell forth, my sone, and schrif thee clene."   *confess yourself completely*
[Amans]   "I wot noght, fader, what ye mene:
             Bot this I wolde you beseche,
590   That ye me be som weie teche
             What is to ben an ypocrite;
             And thanne if I be for to wyte,   *to blame*
             I wol beknowen, as it is."   *understand*
[Confessor]   "Mi sone, an ypocrite is this:
595   A man which feigneth conscience,   *who feigns*
             As thogh it were al innocence

---

[1]   *Higher than an eagle and more fierce than a lion is that one whom the swelling of a heart, borne upwards, moves to the heights. There are five species over which Pride clamors that she is the leader, and the world clings to those in many ways. By enchanting the face with a feigned paleness, Hypocrisy decks out honey-sweet words with his frauds. And thus time and again he overwhelms pious, womanly souls by means of humble speech with deceit hidden underneath.*

	Withoute, and is noght so withinne;	
	And doth so for he wolde winne	*in order that he might gain*
	Of his desir the vein astat.	*vain*
600	And whanne he comth anon therat,	*as soon as he arrives at [his goal]*
	He scheweth thanne what he was.	*reveals*
	The corn is torned into gras,	
	That was a rose is thanne a thorn,	
	And he that was a lomb beforn	
605	Is thanne a wolf, and thus malice	
	Under the colour of justice	*disguise*
	Is hid; and as the poeple telleth,	*hidden*

Ipocrisis Religiosa   These ordres witen where he duelleth,   *clerks know; he (the hypocrite)*

	As he that of here conseil is,	*their*
610	And thilke world which thei er this	*the same; that they before*
	Forsoken, he drawth in agein:	
	He clotheth richesse, as men sein,	*disguises wealth*
	Under the simplesce of poverte,	
	And doth to seme of gret decerte	*causes; value*
615	Thing which is litel worth withinne:	
	He seith in open, fy! to sinne,	*openly*
	And in secre ther is no vice	*secretly*
	Of which that he nis a norrice:	*is not nurse*
	And evere his chiere is sobre and softe,	*countenance*
620	And where he goth he blesseth ofte,	
	Wherof the blinde world he dreccheth.	*destroys*
	Bot yet al only he ne streccheth	
	His reule upon religioun,	*religious orders*
	Bot next to that condicioun	
625	In suche as clepe hem holy cherche	
	It scheweth ek how he can werche	*appears also*

Ipocrisis Ecclesiastica   Among tho wyde furred hodes,   *[of monks]*

	To geten hem the worldes goodes.	
	And thei hemself ben thilke same	
630	That setten most the world in blame,	*most accuse; of fault*
	Bot yet in contraire of her lore	*contradiction of their teaching*
	Ther is nothing thei loven more;	
	So that semende of liht thei werke	
	The dedes whiche are inward derke.	
635	And thus this double Ypocrisie	
	With his devolte apparantie	*devout appearance*
	A viser set upon his face,	*places (sets)*
	Wherof toward this worldes grace	
	He semeth to be riht wel thewed,	*mannered*
640	And yit his herte is al beschrewed.	*evilly disposed*
	Bot natheles he stant believed,	
	And hath his pourpos ofte achieved	*accomplished*
	Of worschipe and of worldes welthe,	

And takth it, as who seith, be stelthe
645 Thurgh coverture of his fallas.   *By concealment of his falsity*
And riht so in semblable cas   *similar manner*
This vice hath ek his officers

Ipocrisis Secularis Among these othre seculers   *men of the world also*
Of grete men, for of the smale
650 As for t'acompte he set no tale,   *He makes no reckoning (tally) in his account*
Bot thei that passen the comune   *surpass the ordinary*
With suche him liketh to comune,
And where he seith he wol socoure
The poeple, there he woll devoure;
655 For now aday is manyon   *many a person*
Which spekth of Peter and of John
And thenketh Judas in his herte.
Ther schal no worldes good asterte   *escape*
His hond, and yit he gifth almesse   *alms*
660 And fasteth ofte and hiereth Messe: *Mass*
With *mea culpa*, which he seith,
Upon his brest fullofte he leith   *places*
His hond, and cast upward his yhe,   *eyes*
As thogh he Cristes face syhe;   *saw*
665 So that it semeth ate syhte,
As he alone alle othre myhte
Rescoue with his holy bede.   *prayer*
Bot yet his herte in other stede   *place*
Among hise bedes most devoute   *prayers*
670 Goth in the worldes cause aboute,
How that he myhte his warisoun   *property*
Encresce.

[HYPOCRISY OF LOVERS]

And in comparisoun
Ther ben lovers of such a sort,   *in like manner*
☞ That feignen hem an humble port,   *bearing (see note)*
675 And al is bot Ypocrisie,
Which with deceipte and flaterie
Hath many a worthi wif beguiled.
For whanne he hath his tunge affiled,   *polished*
With softe speche and with lesinge,   *lies*
680 Forth with his fals pitous lokynge,
He wolde make a womman wene   *think*
To gon upon the faire grene,
Whan that sche falleth in the mir.   *mire*
For if he may have his desir,
685 How so falle of the remenant,   *Whatever happens as a consequence*
He halt no word of covenant;   *agreement*

	Bot er the time that he spede,	
	Ther is no sleihte at thilke nede,	
	Which eny loves faitour mai,	
690	That he ne put it in assai,	
	As him belongeth for to done.	
	The colour of the reyni mone	watery (pale)
	With medicine upon his face	
	He set, and thanne he axeth grace,	
695	As he which hath sieknesse feigned.	
	Whan his visage is so desteigned,	discolored
	With yhe upcast on hire he siketh,	eye; sighs
	And many a contenance he piketh,	expressive posture he assumes
	To bringen hire into believe	
700	Of thing which that he wolde achieve,	
	Wherof he berth the pale hewe;	the [lover's] pallid complexion
	And for he wolde seme trewe,	
	He makth him siek, whan he is heil.	makes himself [seem] sick; well
	Bot whanne he berth lowest the seil,	sail
705	Thanne is he swiftest to beguile	
	The womman, which that ilke while	at that same moment
	Set upon him feith or credence.	

Opponit Confessor Mi sone, if thou thi conscience

	Entamed hast in such a wise,	Wounded
710	In schrifte thou thee myht avise	
	And telle it me, if it be so."	

Respondet Amans   "Min holy fader, certes no.

	As for to feigne such sieknesse	As regards feigning
	It nedeth noght, for this witnesse	There is no need
715	I take of God, that my corage	
	Hath ben mor siek than my visage.	sick; countenance
	And ek this mai I wel avowe,	also
	So lowe cowthe I nevere bowe	I could never bow so low
	To feigne humilité withoute,	
720	That me ne leste betre loute	That I did not want to bow better
	With alle the thoghtes of myn herte;	
	For that thing schal me nevere asterte,	will never occur to me
	I speke as to my lady diere	[That] I [would]
	To make hire eny feigned chiere.	countenance
725	God wot wel there I lye noght,	
	Mi chiere hath be such as my thoght;	
	For in good feith, this lieveth wel,	believe
	Mi will was betre a thousendel	desire was a thousand-times better
	Than eny chiere that I cowthe.	expression (cheer) I knew
730	Bot, sire, if I have in my yowthe	
	Don otherwise in other place,	
	I put me therof in your grace:	
	For this excusen I ne schal,	I shall not declare

That I have elles overal
735   To love and to his compaignie
      Be plein withoute Ypocrisie.   *Been direct*
      Bot ther is on the which I serve,   *one*
      Althogh I may no thonk deserve,
      To whom yet nevere into this day
740   I seide onlyche or ye or nay,   *said only yes or no*
      Bot if it so were in my thoght.
      As touchende othre seie I noght   *other [kinds of hypocrisy]*
      That I nam somdel for to wyte   *am not somewhat to blame*
      Of that ye clepe an ypocrite."   *With regard to what you call*
Confessor "Mi sone, it sit wel every wiht   *behooves; person*
      To kepe his word in trowthe upryht
      Towardes love in alle wise.
      For who that wolde him wel avise
      What hath befalle in this matiere,
750   He scholde noght with feigned chiere
      Deceive love in no degré.
      To love is every herte fre,
      Bot in deceipte if that thou feignest
      And therupon thi lust atteignest,   *desire obtain*
755   That thow hast wonne with thi wyle,   *your deviousness*
      Thogh it thee like for a whyle,
      Thou schalt it afterward repente.
      And for to prove myn entente,
      I finde ensample in a croniqe   *chronicle*
760   Of hem that love so beswike.   *Of those who thus defraud love*

[TALE OF MUNDUS AND PAULINA]

      It fell be olde daies thus,
      Whil th'emperour Tiberius
☞   The monarchie of Rome ladde,   *(see note)*
      Ther was a worthi Romein hadde   *Roman citizen [who] had*
765   A wif, and sche Pauline hihte,   *was called*
      Which was to every mannes sihte
      Of al the cité the faireste,
      And as men seiden, ek the beste.   *also the most virtuous*
      It is and hath ben evere yit,
770   That so strong is no mannes wit,
      Which thurgh beauté ne mai be drawe
      To love, and stonde under the lawe
      Of thilke bore frele kinde,   *Of such nature, created frail*
      Which makth the hertes yhen blinde,   *heart's eyes*
775   Wher no reson mai be comuned: *shared*
      And in this wise stod fortuned
      This tale, of which I wolde mene;   *speak*

	This wif, which in hire lustes grene	*her youthful charm*
	Was fair and freissh and tendre of age,	
780	Sche may noght lette the corage	*hinder the sexual desire*
	Of him that wole on hire assote.	*on her become besotted*
	Ther was a duck, and he was hote	*duke; called*
	Mundus, which hadde in his baillie	*charge (duty)*
	To lede the chivalerie	*horsemen*
785	Of Rome, and was a worthi knyht;	
	Bot yet he was noght of such myht	
	The strengthe of love to withstonde,	
	That he ne was so broght to honde,	*But that he was so reined in [by love]*
	That malgré wher he wole or no,	*despite whether he would*
790	This yonge wif he loveth so,	
	That he hath put al his assay	*effort*
	To wynne thing which he ne may	*might not*
	Gete of hire graunt in no manere,	*Obtain with her consent*
	Be gifte of gold ne be preiere.	*By; nor by supplication*
795	And whanne he syh that be no mede	*bribery*
	Toward hir love he myhte spede,	*succeed*
	Be sleyhte feigned thanne he wroghte;	*By sneaky tricks; proceeded*
	And therupon he him bethoghte	*recalled*
	How that ther was in the cité	
800	A temple of such auctorité,	
	To which with gret devocioun	
	The noble wommen of the toun	
	Most comunliche a pelrinage	*on pilgrimage*
	Gon for to preie thilke ymage	*in order to pray to that*
805	Which the godesse of childinge is,	*childbirth*
	And cleped was be name Ysis:	*was called by*
	And in hire temple thanne were,	
	To reule and to ministre there	
	After the lawe which was tho,	*In conformity with; then*
810	Above alle othre prestes tuo.	*two*
	This duck, which thoghte his love gete,	*duke who thought to obtain*
	Upon a day hem tuo to mete	
	Hath bede, and thei come at his heste;	*requested; came; command*
	Wher that thei hadde a riche feste,	*feast*
815	And after mete in privé place	*secret*
	This lord, which wolde his thonk pourchace,	*gratitude purchase*
	To ech of hem gaf thanne a gifte,	*them gave*
	And spak so that be weie of schrifte	*confession*
	He drowh hem unto his covine,	*secret plan (conspiracy)*
820	To helpe and schape how he Pauline	
	After his lust deceive myhte.	
	And thei here trowthes bothe plyhte,	*their troth; pledged*
	That thei be nyhte hire scholden wynne	*succeed in bringing*
	Into the temple, and he therinne	

825	Schal have of hire al his entente;	
	And thus acorded forth thei wente.	*agreed*
	Now lest thurgh which ypocrisie	*Now hear*
	Ordeigned was the tricherie,	
	Wherof this ladi was deceived.	
830	These prestes hadden wel conceived	
	That sche was of gret holinesse;	
	And with a contrefet simplesse,	
	Which hid was in a fals corage,	
	Feignende an hevenely message	*Pretending*
835	Thei come and seide unto hir thus:	
	"Pauline, the god Anubus	
	Hath sent ous bothe prestes hiere,	
	And seith he woll to thee appiere	*will appear to you*
	Be nyhtes time himself alone,	
840	For love he hath to thi persone:	
	And therupon he hath ous bede,	*commanded us*
	That we in Ysis temple a stede	*place*
	Honestely for thee pourveie,	*ordain*
	Wher thou be nyhte, as we thee seie,	*say*
845	Of him schalt take avisioun.	*shall have a vision*
	For upon thi condicioun,	*personal character*
	The which is chaste and ful of feith,	
	Such pris, as he ous tolde, he leith,	*value; puts*
	That he wol stonde of thin acord;	*agree in sentiment with you*
850	And for to bere hierof record	
	He sende ous hider bothe tuo."	*sent*
	Glad was hire innocence tho	
	Of suche wordes as sche herde	
	With humble chiere, and thus answerde,	
855	And seide that the goddes wille	
	Sche was al redy to fulfille,	
	That be hire housebondes leve	*permission*
	Sche wolde in Ysis temple at eve	
	Upon hire goddes grace abide,	*await*
860	To serven him the nyhtes tide.	
	The prestes tho gon hom agein,	
	And sche goth to hire sovereign,	*lord (husband)*
	Of goddes wille and as it was	
	Sche tolde him al the pleine cas,	
865	Wherof he was deceived eke,	*also*
	And bad that sche hire scholde meke	*should submit herself*
	Al hol unto the goddes heste.	*Wholly; command*
	And thus sche, which was al honeste	*virtuous*
	To godward after hire entente,	*Toward the god with full integrity*
870	At nyht unto the temple wente,	
	Wher that the false prestes were;	

	And thei receiven hire there	
	With such a tokne of holinesse,	
	As thogh thei syhen a godesse,	*saw*
875	And al withinne in privé place	
	A softe bedd of large space	
	Thei hadde mad and encourtined,	*prepared; draped*
	Wher sche was afterward engined.	*seduced*
	Bot sche, which al honour supposeth,	
880	The false prestes thanne opposeth,	*questioned*
	And axeth be what observance	*asked by*
	Sche myhte most to the plesance	
	Of godd that nyhtes reule kepe.	
	And thei hire bidden for to slepe,	*bade her*
885	Liggende upon the bedd alofte,	*lying*
	For so, thei seide, al stille and softe	
	God Anubus hire wolde awake.	
	The conseil in this wise take,	*manner given*
	The prestes fro this lady gon;	
890	And sche, that wiste of guile non,	*who knew of no treachery*
	In the manere as it was seid	
	To slepe upon the bedd is leid,	
	In hope that sche scholde achieve	
	Thing which stod thanne upon bilieve,	*which then was thought to be possible*
895	Fulfild of alle holinesse.	
	Bot sche hath failed, as I gesse,	*suppose*
	For in a closet faste by	*private room near by*
	The duck was hid so prively	*duke; secretly*
	That sche him myhte noght perceive;	
900	And he, that thoghte to deceive,	
	Hath such arrai upon him nome,	*put such clothing upon himself*
	That whanne he wolde unto hir come,	
	It scholde semen at hire yhe	*eyes*
	As thogh sche verrailiche syhe	*truly saw*
905	God Anubus, and in such wise	
	This ypocrite of his queintise	*cunning*
	Awaiteth evere til sche slepte.	
	And thanne out of his place he crepte	
	So stille that sche nothing herde,	
910	And to the bedd stalkende he ferde,	*stalking he went*
	And sodeinly, er sche it wiste,	*before she knew it*
	Beclipt in armes he hire kiste:	*Embraced in arms, he kissed her*
	Wherof in wommanysshe drede	*terror*
	Sche wok and nyste what to rede;	*knew not what to think*
915	Bot he with softe wordes milde	
	Conforteth hire and seith, with childe	
	He wolde hire make in such a kynde	*impregnate her [with a child] of such a nature*
	That al the world schal have in mynde	

	The worschipe of that ilke sone;	*same son*
920	For he schal with the goddes wone,	*dwell*
	And ben himself a godd also.	
	With suche wordes and with mo,	*more*
	The whiche he feigneth in his speche,	
	This lady wit was al to seche,	*lady's wit was gone*
925	As sche which alle trowthe weneth:	*faith believes*
	Bot he, that alle untrowthe meneth,	*unfaithfulness intends*
	With blinde tales so hire ladde,	*deceitful tales; seduced*
	That all his wille of hire he hadde.	
	And whan him thoghte it was ynowh,	*enough*
930	Agein the day he him withdrowh	*At dawn; withdrew himself*
	So prively that sche ne wiste	*did not know*
	Wher he becom, bot as him liste	*Where he went; pleased him*
	Out of the temple he goth his weie.	
	And sche began to bidde and preie	*pray; pray*
935	Upon the bare ground knelende,	
	And after that made hire offrende,	*offering*
	And to the prestes giftes grete	
	Sche gaf, and homward be the strete.	*gave; [goes] homeward by*
	The duck hire mette and seide thus:	*duke*
940	"The myhti godd which Anubus	
	Is hote, he save thee, Pauline,	*called; may he save you*
	For thou art of his discipline	
	So holy, that no mannes myht	
	Mai do that he hath do to nyht	
945	Of thing which thou hast evere eschuied.	*That thing; avoided*
	Bot I his grace have so poursuied,	
	That I was mad his lieutenant:	*made*
	Forthi be weie of covenant	
	Fro this day forth I am al thin,	
950	And if thee like to be myn,	
	That stant upon thin oghne wille."	*depends; your own determination*
	Sche herde his tale and bar it stille,	*bore it quietly*
	And hom sche wente, as it befell,	
	Into hir chambre, and ther sche fell	
955	Upon hire bedd to wepe and crie,	
	And seide: "O derke ypocrisie,	
	Thurgh whos dissimilacion	
	Of fals ymaginacion	
	I am thus wickedly deceived!	
960	Bot that I have it aperceived	*perceived*
	I thonke unto the goddes alle;	
	For thogh it ones be befalle,	*once has happened*
	It schal nevere eft whil that I live,	*again (after)*
	And thilke avou to godd I give."	*this vow*
965	And thus wepende sche compleigneth,	*mourns*

Hire faire face and al desteigneth	*stains*
With wofull teres of hire ye,	*eyes*
So that upon this agonie	
Hire housebonde is inne come,	
970 And syh how sche was overcome	
With sorwe, and axeth what hire eileth.	*asks what ails her*
And sche with that hirself beweileth	*laments*
Welmore than sche dede afore,	*before*
And seide, "Helas, wifhode is lore	*lost*
975 In me, which whilom was honeste,	*who once was virtuous (chaste)*
I am non other than a beste,	*beast*
Now I defouled am of tuo."	*two*
And as sche myhte speke tho,	*then*
Aschamed with a pitous onde	*sigh*
980 Sche tolde unto hir housebonde	
The sothe of al the hole tale,	*truth; whole story*
And in hire speche ded and pale	*deathlike*
Sche swouneth wel nyh to the laste.	*faints nearly to death*
And he hire in hise armes faste	
985 Uphield, and ofte swor his oth	
That he with hire is nothing wroth,	
For wel he wot sche may ther noght:	*could do nothing*
Bot natheles withinne his thoght	
His herte stod in sori plit,	
990 And seide he wolde of that despit	
Be venged, how so evere it falle,	
And sende unto hise frendes alle.	
And whan thei weren come in fere,	*together sent (in company)*
He tolde hem upon this matiere,	
995 And axeth hem what was to done:	*asked them*
And thei avised were sone,	
And seide it thoghte hem for the beste	*it seemed best to them*
To sette ferst his wif in reste,	*reassure his wife*
And after pleigne to the king	*subsequently complain*
1000 Upon the matiere of this thing.	
Tho was this wofull wif conforted	*Then*
Be alle weies and desported,	*ways; cheered*
Til that sche was somdiel amended;	
And thus a day or tuo despended;	*passed*
1005 The thridde day sche goth to pleigne	*went to lament*
With many a worthi citezeine,	*worthy female citizen*
And he with many a citezein.	*male citizen*
Whan th'emperour it herde sein,	*heard the account*
And knew the falshed of the vice,	
1010 He seide he wolde do justice:	
And ferst he let the prestes take	*had the priests arrested*
And, for thei scholde it noght forsake,	*in order that they; deny*

He put hem into questioun; *them under interrogation*
Bot thei of the suggestioun *accusation*
1015 Ne couthen noght a word refuse, *deny*
Bot for thei wolde hemself excuse, *wanted to excuse themselves*
The blame upon the duck thei leide. *duke they laid*
Bot theragein the conseil seide
That thei be noght excused so,
1020 For he is on and thei ben tuo, *he (the duke) is one [person]*
And tuo han more wit then on,
So thilke excusement was non. *that excuse*
And over that was seid hem eke, *And beyond that*
That whan men wolden vertu seke,
1025 Men scholde it in the prestes finde; *Their; noble*
Here ordre is of so hyh a kinde,
That thei be duistres of the weie: *guides*
Forthi, if eny man forsueie *Therefore; goes astray*
Thurgh hem, thei be noght excusable. *Because of them*
1030 And thus be lawe resonable *by law*
Among the wise jugges there
The prestes bothe dampned were, *were condemned*
So that the privé tricherie
Hid under fals Ipocrisie
1035 Was thanne al openliche schewed, *shown*
That many a man hem hath beschrewed. *[So] that; cursed*
And whan the prestes weren dede, *executed*
The temple of thilke horrible dede
Thei thoghten purge, and thilke ymage, *thought to purge; that same*
1040 Whos cause was the pelrinage, *aim (end); [Paulina's] journey*
Thei drowen out and als so faste
Fer into Tibre thei it caste,
Wher the rivere it hath defied:
And thus the temple purified
1045 Thei have of thilke horrible sinne,
Which was that time do therinne.
Of this point such was the juise, *justice*
Bot of the duck was other wise: *duke was treated differently*
For he with love was bestad, *Since; beset*
1050 His dom was noght so harde lad; *judgment*
For love put reson aweie
And can noght se the rihte weie.
And be this cause he was respited,
So that the deth him was acquited, *relieved of the death penalty*
1055 Bot for al that he was exiled,
For he his love hath so beguiled,
That he schal nevere come agein:
For who that is to trowthe unplein, *dishonest*
He may noght failen of vengance.

1060	And ek to take remembrance	*pay attention*
	Of that Ypocrisie hath wroght	*To what*
	On other half, men scholde noght	
	To lihtly lieve al that thei hiere,	*believe*
	Bot thanne scholde a wis man stiere	
1065	The schip, whan suche wyndes blowe:	
	For ferst, thogh thei beginne lowe,	*at first; they (winds of hypocrisy)*
	At ende thei be noght menable,	*In the end; not fit to guide [the ship]*
	Bot al tobroken mast and cable,	
	So that the schip with sodein blast,	
1070	Whan men lest wene, is overcast,	*least expect*
	As now ful ofte a man mai se.	*see*
	And of old time how it hath be	*from time past how it has been*
	I finde a gret experience,	*demonstration*
	Wherof to take an evidence	*get a clue*
1075	Good is, and to be war also	*beware*
	Of the peril, er him be wo.	*before disaster befalls him*

[TROJAN HORSE]

	Of hem that ben so derk withinne,	*Concerning those who are so blind within*
	At Troie also if we beginne,	*therefore*
	Ipocrisie it hath betraied:	*it (Troy)*
1080	For whan the Greks hadde al assaied,	*tried everything*
☞	And founde that be no bataille	*by (see note)*
	Ne be no siege it myhte availe	
	The toun to winne thurgh prouesse,	*prowess*
	This vice feigned of simplesce	
1085	Thurgh sleyhte of Calcas and of Crise	*trickery*
	It wan be such a maner wise:	*conquered in this way*
	An hors of bras thei let do forge,	*had forged*
	Of such entaile, of such a forge,	*design; workmanship*
	That in this world was nevere man	
1090	That such an other werk began.	*undertook*
	The crafti werkman Epius	
	It made, and for to telle thus,	
	The Greks, that thoghten to beguile	
	The kyng of Troie, in thilke while	
1095	With Anthenor and with Enee,	*Antenor; Aeneas*
	That were bothe of the cité	
	And of the couseil the wiseste,	
	The richeste and the myhtieste,	
	In privé place so thei trete	*secret; negotiate*
1100	With fair beheste and giftes grete	*promises*
	Of gold, that thei hem have engined	*[so] that; deceived*
	Togedre; and whan thei be covined,	*agreed*
	Thei feignen for to make a pes,	*peace*

	And under that yit natheles	
1105	Thei schopen the destruccioun	*fashioned*
	Bothe of the kyng and of the toun.	
	And thus the false pees was take	*arranged*
	Of hem of Grece and undertake.	*By; agreed upon*
	And therupon thei founde a weie,	
1110	Wher strengthe myhte noght aweie,	*avail*
	That sleihte scholde helpe thanne;	
	And of an ynche a large spanne	*from an inch; span (fabrication)*
	Be colour of the pees thei made,	*By deceptive appearance*
	And tolden how thei weren glade	
1115	Of that thei stoden in acord;	
	And for it schal ben of record,	
	Unto the kyng the Gregois seiden,	
	Be weie of love and this thei preiden,	
	As thei that wolde his thonk deserve,	
1120	A sacrifice unto Minerve,	
	The pes to kepe in good entente,	
	Thei mosten offre er that thei wente.	
	The kyng, conseiled in this cas	
	Be Anthenor and Eneas,	*By*
1125	Therto hath goven his assent:	*given*
	So was the pleine trowthe blent	*concealed (darkened; blinded)*
	Thurgh contrefet Ipocrisie	*deceitful Hypocrisy*
	Of that thei scholden sacrifie.	
	The Greks under the holinesse	
1130	Anon with alle besinesse	
	Here hors of bras let faire dihte,	*Their; had beautifully constructed*
	Which was to sen a wonder sihte;	
	For it was trapped of himselve,	*furnished with its own trap-doors*
	And hadde of smale whieles twelve,	
1135	Upon the whiche men ynowe	
	With craft toward the toun it drowe,	*drew*
	And goth glistrende agein the sunne.	*glistening against*
	Tho was ther joye ynowh begunne,	
	For Troie in gret devocioun	
1140	Cam also with processioun	
	Agein this noble sacrifise	
	With gret honour, and in this wise	
	Unto the gates thei it broghte.	
	Bot of here entré whan thei soghte,	
1145	The gates weren al to smale;	*entirely too*
	And therupon was many a tale,	*much discussion*
	Bot for the worschipe of Minerve,	
	To whom thei comen for to serve,	
	Thei of the toun, whiche understode	
1150	That al this thing was do for goode,	

For pes, wherof that thei ben glade,
The gates that Neptunus made
A thousend wynter ther tofore,
Thei have anon tobroke and tore;   *broken to pieces; torn down*
1155   The stronge walles doun thei bete,   *fortified*
So that in to the large strete
This hors with gret solempnité
Was broght withinne the cité,
And offred with gret reverence,
1160   Which was to Troie an evidence
Of love and pes for everemo.
The Gregois token leve tho   *Greeks departed then*
With al the hole felaschipe,   *whole company*
And forth thei wenten into schipe
1165   And crossen seil and made hem yare,   *set the sails; made them (sails) ready*
Anon as thogh thei wolden fare: *go [home]*
Bot whan the blake wynter nyht
Withoute mone or sterre lyht
Bederked hath the water stronde,   *Enveloped in darkness; shore*
1170   Al prively thei gon to londe   *secretly*
Ful armed out of the navie.
Synon, which mad was here aspie   *was made their spy*
Withinne Troie, as was conspired,   *prearranged*
Whan time was a tokne hath fired;   *signal [light]; lit*
1175   And thei with that here weie holden,   *take their way*
And comen in riht as thei wolden,
Ther as the gate was tobroke.   *Where*
The pourpos was full take and spoke:
Er eny man may take kepe,   *care*
1180   Whil that the cité was aslepe,
Thei slowen al that was withinne,   *slew*
And token what thei myhten wynne
Of such good as was sufficant,
And brenden up the remenant.   *burnt*
1185   And thus cam out the tricherie,   *became known*
Which under fals Ypocrisie
Was hid, and thei that wende pees
Tho myhten finde no reles
Of thilke swerd which al devoureth.
1190   Ful ofte and thus the swete soureth,   *sweet becomes sour*
Whan it is knowe to the tast.
He spilleth many a word in wast
That schal with such a poeple trete;
For whan he weneth most begete,   *thinks to gain the most*
1195   Thanne is he schape most to lese.   *destined to lose most*
And riht so if a womman chese   *should choose*
Upon the wordes that sche hiereth   *hears*

Som man, whan he most trewe appiereth,
Thanne is he forthest fro the trowthe:

1200   Bot yit ful ofte, and that is rowthe,   *that is a pity*
Thei speden that ben most untrewe   *succeed who are*
And loven every day a newe,
Wherof the lief is after loth   *beloved is later the enemy*
And love hath cause to be wroth.

1205   Bot what man that his lust desireth
Of love, and therupon conspireth
With wordes feigned to deceive,
He schal noght faile to receive
His peine, as it is ofte sene.   *pain (punishment)*

Confessor   Forthi, my sone, as I thee mene,   *advise you*
It sit thee wel to taken hiede   *It behooves; heed*
That thou eschuie of thi manhiede   *[So] that; avoid*
Ipocrisie and his semblant,
That thou ne be noght deceivant,

1215   To make a womman to believe
Thing which is noght in thi believe: *conviction*
For in such feint Ipocrisie   *false*
Of love is al the tricherie,
Thurgh which love is deceived ofte;

1220   For feigned semblant is so softe,   *so quiet*
Unethes love may be war.   *Scarcely may love beware*
Forthi, my sone, as I wel dar,
I charge thee to fle that vice,
That many a womman hath mad nice;   *has made many a woman foolish*

1225   Bot lok thou dele noght withal."

Amans   "Iwiss, fader, no mor I schal."   *Indeed*

Confessor   "Now, sone, kep that thou hast swore:
For this that thou hast herd before
Is seid the ferste point of Pride.   *called*

1230   And next upon that other side,
To schryve and speken over this   *confess*
Touchende of Pride, yit ther is
The point seconde, I thee behote,   *assure*
Which Inobedience is hote."   *called*

[DISOBEDIENCE]

vi.   *Flectere quam frangi melius reputatur, et olle*
      Fictilis ad cacabum pugna valere nequit.   *(see note)*
   Quem neque lex hominum, neque lex diuina valebit
      Flectere, multociens corde reflectit amor.
   Quem non flectit amor, non est flectendus ab vllo,
      Set rigor illius plus Elephante riget.
   Dedignatur amor poterit quos scire rebelles,

Et rudibus sortem prestat habere rudem;
Set qui sponte sui subicit se cordis amore,
Frangit in aduersis omnia fata pius.[1]

1235	"This vice of Inobedience	
	Agein the reule of conscience	
	Al that is humble he desalloweth,	*censures*
	That he toward his God ne boweth	
	After the lawes of His heste.	*command*
1240	Noght as a man bot as a beste,	
☞	Which goth upon his lustes wilde,	*follows (see note)*
	So goth this proude vice unmylde,	
	That he desdeigneth alle lawe:	*disdains*
	He not what is to be felawe,	*does not know what it is*
1245	And serve may he noght for pride;	
	So is he badde on every side,	
	And is that selve of whom men speke,	*same thing*
	Which wol noght bowe er that he breke.	*bend before he is broken*
	I not if love him myhte plie,	*do not know; might bend*
1250	For elles for to justefie	
	His herte, I not what mihte availe.	
Confessor	Forthi, my sone, of such entaile	*disposition*
	If that thin herte be disposed,	
	Tell out and let it noght be glosed:	*concealed*
1255	For if that thou unbuxom be	*disobedient*
	To love, I not in what degree	*do not know*
	Thou schalt thi goode world achieve."	*acquire*
Amans	"Mi fader, ye schul wel believe,	
	The yonge whelp which is affaited	*trained*
1260	Hath noght his maister betre awaited,	
	To couche, whan he seith 'Go lowe!'	*cower timidly; Lie down!*
	That I, anon as I may knowe	*as soon as I may know*
	Mi ladi will, ne bowe more.	*My lady's wish, nor [does a trained dog]*
	Bot other while I grucche sore	*grumble wretchedly*
1265	Of some thinges that sche doth,	
	Wherof that I woll telle soth:	*the truth*
	For of tuo pointz I am bethoght,	*reminded*
	That, thogh I wolde, I myhte noght	
	Obeie unto my ladi heste;	*my lady's command*
1270	Bot I dar make this beheste,	*promise*

---

[1] *To bend is thought better than to break, and the attack of the earthen pot cannot prevail over the cauldron. Many a time the man whom neither human nor divine law is strong enough to bend is bent over in his heart by love. The man whom love cannot bend cannot be bent by anything, for his inflexibility stands more rigid than an elephant. Love disdains those he can recognize as rebels, and he sees to it that the uncivil have an uncivil fate. But he who, a pious man, freely subjects himself to Love in his heart, in adversities shatters all fates.*

	Save only of that ilke tuo	*That except for these same two*
	I am unbuxom of no mo."	*disobedient; more*
Opponit Confessor	"What ben tho tuo? tell on," quod he.	*those two*
Respondet Amans	"Mi fader, this is on, that sche	*one*
1275	Comandeth me my mowth to close,	
	And that I scholde hir noght oppose	*question*
	In love, of which I ofte preche,	
	Bot plenerliche of such a speche	*fully*
	Forbere, and soffren hire in pes.	
1280	Bot that ne myht I natheles	
	For al this world obeie ywiss;	*certainly*
	For whanne I am ther as sche is,	
	Though sche my tales noght alowe,	*should not allow*
	Agein hir will yit mot I bowe,	
1285	To seche if that I myhte have grace:	
	Bot that thing may I noght enbrace	
	For ought that I can speke or do;	
	And yit ful ofte I speke so,	
	That sche is wroth and seith, 'Be stille.'	*angry*
1290	If I that heste schal fulfille	*command*
	And therto ben obedient,	
	Thanne is my cause fully schent,	*lost*
	For specheles may no man spede.	*succeed*
	So wot I noght what is to rede;	*advise*
1295	Bot certes I may noght obeie,	
	That I ne mot algate seie	*But that I must certainly say*
	Somwhat of that I wolde mene;	
	For evere it is aliche grene,	*fresh*
	The grete love which I have,	
1300	Wherof I can noght bothe save	
	Mi speche and this obedience:	
	And thus ful ofte my silence	
	I breke, and is the ferste point	
	Wherof that I am out of point	*out of step*
1305	In this, and yit it is no pride.	
	Now thanne upon that other side	*second point*
	To telle my desobeissance,	
	Ful sore it stant to my grevance	
	And may noght sinke into my wit;	
1310	For ofte time sche me bit	*orders*
	To leven hire and chese a newe,	*new [lover]*
	And seith, if I the sothe knewe	
	How ferr I stonde from hir grace,	
	I scholde love in other place.	
1315	Bot therof woll I desobeie;	*with respect to that*
	For also wel sche myhte seie,	*she might as well say*
	'Go tak the mone ther it sit,'	*moon where*

	As bringe that into my wit:	
	For ther was nevere rooted tre,	
1320	That stod so faste in his degré,	
	That I ne stonde more faste	*But that I stood*
	Upon hire love, and mai noght caste	
	Min herte awey, althogh I wolde.	
	For God wot, thogh I nevere scholde	*God knows*
1325	Sen hir with yhe after this day,	*eye*
	Yit stant it so that I ne may	
	Hir love out of my brest remue.	*remove*
	This is a wonder retenue,	*engagement of service*
	That malgré wher sche wole or non	*despite whether she*
1330	Min herte is everemore in on,	*steadfast*
	So that I can non other chese,	*choose*
	Bot whether that I winne or lese,	*Regardless whether*
	I moste hire loven til I deie;	
	And thus I breke as be that weie	*by that manner*
1335	Hire hestes and hir comandinges,	
	Bot trewliche in non othre thinges.	
	Forthi, my fader, what is more	
	Touchende to this ilke lore	
	I you beseche, after the forme	*according to the proper procedure*
1340	That ye pleinly me wolde enforme,	
	So that I may myn herte reule	
	In loves cause after the reule."	

[MURMUR AND COMPLAINT]

vii.   *Murmur in aduersis ita concipit ille superbus,*
       Pena quod ex bina sorte perurget eum.
    Obuia fortune cum spes in amore resistit,
       Non sine mentali murmure plangit amans.[1]

	[Confessor] "Toward this vice of which we trete	*vice (i.e., Pride)*
☞	Ther ben yit tweie of thilke estrete,	*the same extraction (see note)*
1345	Here name is Murmur and Compleignte:	*Their*
	Ther can no man here chiere peinte	*their countenance depict*
	To sette a glad semblant therinne,	
	For thogh fortune make hem wynne,	*even if; succeed*
	Yit grucchen thei, and if thei lese,	*grumble; lose*
1350	Ther is no weie for to chese	*choose*
	Wherof thei myhten stonde appesed.	*Whereby; appeased*

---

[1] *The proud man generates grumbling in adversities in such a way that the penalty from a twofold fate presses down upon him. When ready hope in love struggles against fortune, not without a grumbling in the mind does the lover complain.*

	So ben thei comunly desesed;	*distressed*
	Ther may no welthe ne poverté	
	Attempren hem to the decerte	*merit*
1355	Of buxomnesse be no wise:	*obedience by any means*
	For ofte time thei despise	
	The goode fortune as the badde,	*as [well as]*
	As thei no mannes reson hadde,	*As if*
	Thurgh pride, wherof thei be blinde.	
1360	And ryht of such a maner kinde	
	Ther be lovers, that thogh thei have	
	Of love al that thei wolde crave,	
	Yit wol thei grucche be som weie,	*grumble about something*
	That thei wol noght to love obeie	*[So] that*
1365	Upon the trowthe, as thei do scholde;	
	And if hem lacketh that thei wolde,	*desire*
	Anon thei falle in such a peine,	*Instantly; discomfort*
	That evere unbuxomly thei pleigne	*complain*
	Upon fortune, and curse and crie,	
1370	That thei wol noght here hertes plie	*[So] that; their hearts submit*
	To soffre til it betre falle.	
	Forthi if thou amonges alle	
	Hast used this condicioun,	*manner of behavior*
	Mi sone, in thi confessioun	
1375	Now tell me pleinly what thou art."	
Amans	"Mi fader, I beknowe a part,	
	So as ye tolden hier above	
	Of Murmur and Compleignte of love,	
	That for I se no sped comende,	*success coming*
1380	Agein fortune compleignende	
	I am, as who seith, everemo:	
	And ek ful ofte tyme also,	
	Whan so is that I se and hiere	
	Or hevy word or hevy chiere	*Either; or*
1385	Of my lady, I grucche anon;	
	Bot wordes dar I speke non,	
	Wherof sche myhte be desplesed.	
	Bot in myn herte I am desesed	
	With many a Murmur, God it wot;	
1390	Thus drinke I in myn oghne swot,	*sweat*
	And thogh I make no semblant,	*I show no sign of it*
	Min herte is al desobeissant;	
	And in this wise I me confesse	
	Of that ye clepe unbuxomnesse.	*you call inobedience*
1395	Now telleth what youre conseil is."	
Confessor	"Mi sone, and I thee rede this,	*advise*
	What so befalle of other weie,	
	That thou to loves heste obeie	*command*

	Als ferr as thou it myht suffise:	
1400	For ofte sithe in such a wise	*often times*
	Obedience in love availeth,	*provides help*
	Wher al a mannes strengthe faileth;	
	Wherof, if that thee list to wite	*if you desire to know*
	In a cronique as it is write,	
1405	A gret ensample thou myht fynde,	
	Which now is come to my mynde.	

[TALE OF FLORENT]

	Ther was whilom be daies olde	*once in days of old*
☞	A worthi knyht, and as men tolde	*(see note)*
	He was nevoeu to th'emperour	*nephew*
1410	And of his court a courteour.	
	Wifles he was, Florent he hihte.	*Wifeless; was called*
	He was a man that mochel myhte;	*who had great power*
	Of armes he was desirous,	
	Chivalerous and amorous,	
1415	And for the fame of worldes speche,	
	Strange aventures for to seche,	*Foreign; seek*
	He rod the marches al aboute.	*borderlands*
	And fell a time, as he was oute,	
	Fortune, which may every thred	
1420	Tobreke and knette of mannes sped,	*Sever and tie; success*
	Schop, as this knyht rod in a pas,	*Contrived; narrow passageway*
	That he be strengthe take was,	*forceably captured*
	And to a castell thei him ladde,	
	Wher that he fewe frendes hadde.	
1425	For so it fell that ilke stounde	*befell at that time*
	That he hath with a dedly wounde	
	Feihtende, his oghne hondes slain	*Fighting, by his own military prowess slain*
	Branchus, which to the capitain	*military governor of the castle*
	Was sone and heir, wherof ben wrothe	*are angry*
1430	The fader and the moder bothe.	
	That knyht Branchus was of his hond	*in his military prowess*
	The worthieste of al his lond,	
	And fain thei wolden do vengance	*eagerly*
	Upon Florent, bot remembrance	
1435	That thei toke of his worthinesse	
	Of knyhthod and of gentilesse,	
	And how he stod of cousinage	
	To th'emperour, made hem assuage,	*made them grow calm*
	And dorsten noght slen him for fere.	*slay him because of fear*
1440	In gret desputeisoun thei were	*debate*
	Among hemeself, what was the beste.	*themselves*
	Ther was a lady, the slyheste	*most sly*

	Of alle that men knewe tho,	*then*
	So old sche myhte unethes go,	*scarcely get about*
1445	And was grantdame unto the dede:	*grandmother to the dead man (Branchus)*
	And sche with that began to rede,	*advise*
	And seide how sche wol bringe him inne,	*him (Florent)*
	That sche schal him to dethe winne	*lure him to his death*
	Al only of his oghne grant,	*Exclusively by his own consent*
1450	Thurgh strengthe of verray covenant	*true (binding)*
	Withoute blame of eny wiht.	*any man*
	Anon sche sende for this kniht,	*sent*
	And of hire sone sche alleide	*alleged*
	The deth, and thus to him sche seide:	
1455	"Florent, how so thou be to wyte	*even though you are to blame*
	Of Branchus deth, men schal respite	*For; delay*
	As now to take vengement,	*For the time being*
	Be so thou stonde in juggement	*Provided that you*
	Upon certein condicioun,	
1460	That thou unto a questioun	
	Which I schal axe schalt ansuere;	*ask [you] shall answer*
	And over this thou schalt ek swere,	*And in addition to this you; also*
	That if thou of the sothe faile,	*right answer (truth)*
	Ther schal non other thing availe,	
1465	That thou ne schalt thi deth receive.	*But that you shall*
	And for men schal thee noght deceive,	*so that men*
	That thou therof myht ben avised,	*[In order] that; advised*
	Thou schalt have day and tyme assised	*allotted*
	And leve saufly for to wende,	*permission safely to go*
1470	Be so that at thi daies ende	*Provided that*
	Thou come agein with thin avys."	*your opinion*
	This knyht, which worthi was and wys,	
	This lady preith that he may wite,	*know*
	And have it under seales write,	
1475	What questioun it scholde be	
	For which he schal in that degree	
	Stonde of his lif in jeupartie.	*jeopardy*
	With that sche feigneth compaignie,	
	And seith: "Florent, on love it hongeth	*depends*
1480	Al that to myn axinge longeth:	*question pertains*
	What alle wommen most desire	
	This wole I axe, and in th'empire	
	Wher as thou hast most knowlechinge	
	Tak conseil upon this axinge."	*question*
1485	Florent this thing hath undertake,	
	The day was set, the time take,	*determined*
	Under his seal he wrot his oth,	
	In such a wise and forth he goth	
	Hom to his emes court agein;	*uncle's*

1490	To whom his aventure plein	*fully*
	He tolde, of that him is befalle.	
	And upon that thei weren alle	
	The wiseste of the lond asent,	*sent for*
	Bot natheles of on assent	*one*
1495	Thei myhte noght acorde plat,	*agree entirely*
	On seide this, an othre that.	*One*
	After the disposicioun	
	Of naturel complexioun	
	To som womman it is plesance,	
1500	That to an othre is grevance;	
	Bot such a thing in special,	
	Which to hem alle in general	*them*
	Is most plesant, and most desired	
	Above alle othre and most conspired,	*craved for*
1505	Such o thing conne thei noght finde	
	Be constellacion ne kinde:	*By the stars nor by nature*
	And thus Florent withoute cure	*remedy*
	Mot stonde upon his aventure,	*Must take his fortune*
	And is al schape unto the lere,	*prepared for his death*
1510	As in defalte of his answere.	*default*
	This knyht hath levere for to dye	*would rather die*
	Than breke his trowthe and for to lye	*break his pledge and lie*
	In place ther as he was swore,	
	And schapth him gon agein therfore.	*prepared himself to return again*
1515	Whan time cam he tok his leve,	
	That lengere wolde he noght beleve,	*tarry*
	And preith his em he be noght wroth,	*uncle that he not be angry*
	For that is a point of his oth,	*oath*
	He seith, that no man schal him wreke,	*avenge*
1520	Thogh afterward men hiere speke	*Even though*
	That he par aventure deie.	*by chance should die*
	And thus he wente forth his weie	
	Alone as knyht aventurous,	
	And in his thoght was curious	*eager*
1525	To wite what was best to do:	*know*
	And as he rod alone so,	
	And cam nyh ther he wolde be,	
	In a forest under a tre	
	He syh wher sat a creature,	
1530	A lothly wommannysch figure,	
	That for to speke of fleisch and bon	
	So foul yit syh he nevere non.	*hitherto saw*
	This knyht behield hir redely,	*carefully*
	And as he wolde have passed by,	
1535	Sche cleped him and bad abide;	*called to him and told him to stop*
	And he his horse heved aside	*horse's head*

Tho torneth, and to hire he rod, *Then turned; rode*
And there he hoveth and abod, *paused and waited*
To wite what sche wolde mene. *To find out what she intended*
1540 And sche began him to bemene, *to take pity on him*
And seide: "Florent be thi name.
Thou hast on honde such a game,
That bot thou be the betre avised, *unless; better informed*
Thi deth is schapen and devised,
1545 That al the world ne mai thee save, *may not save you*
Bot if that thou my conseil have." *Unless*
  Florent, whan he this tale herde,
Unto this olde wyht answerde *creature*
And of hir conseil he hir preide.
1550 And sche agein to him thus seide:
"Florent, if I for thee so schape, *for you so devise*
That thou thurgh me thi deth ascape
And take worschipe of thi dede, *achieve honor for your behavior*
What schal I have to my mede?" *as my reward*
1555 "What thing," quod he, "that thou wolt axe."
"I bidde nevere a betre taxe," *ask for; payment*
Quod sche, "bot ferst, er thou be sped, *are helped*
Thou schalt me leve such a wedd, *grant me such a pledge*
That I wol have thi trowthe in honde *vow*
1560 That thou schalt be myn housebonde."
"Nay," seith Florent, "that may noght be."
"Ryd thanne forth thi wey," quod sche,
"And if thou go withoute red, *counsel*
Thou schalt be sekerliche ded." *certainly be killed*
1565 Florent behihte hire good ynowh *promised her plenty of goods*
Of lond, of rente, of park, of plowh, *land; income; game-reserve; plowland*
Bot al that compteth sche at noght. *counts she as nothing*
Tho fell this knyht in mochel thoght,
Now goth he forth, now comth agein,
1570 He wot noght what is best to sein, *say*
And thoghte, as he rod to and fro,
That chese he mot on of the tuo, *must one*
Or for to take hire to his wif *Either to*
Or elles for to lese his lif. *Or else to lose*
1575 And thanne he caste his avantage, *perceived*
That sche was of so gret an age,
That sche mai live bot a while,
And thoghte put hire in an ile, *island*
Wher that no man hire scholde knowe,
1580 Til sche with deth were overthrowe.
And thus this yonge lusti knyht
Unto this olde lothly wiht *loathly creature*
Tho seide: "If that non other chance *opportunity*

Mai make my deliverance,

1585   Bot only thilke same speche

Which, as thou seist, thou schalt me teche,

Have hier myn hond, I schal thee wedde."   *here*

And thus his trowthe he leith to wedde.   *gave as a pledge*

With that sche frounceth up the browe: *wrinkled up*

1590   "This covenant I wol allowe,"   *agreement; accept*

Sche seith; "if eny other thing   *if any other means*

Bot that thou hast of my techyng   *Except that [which]*

Fro deth thi body mai respite,   *save*

I woll thee of thi trowthe acquite,   ·   *release you of your vow*

1595   And elles be non other weie.   *But by no other means*

Now herkne me what I schal seie.

Whan thou art come into the place

Wher now thei maken gret manace

And upon thi comynge abyde,   *await*

1600   Thei wole anon the same tide   *will swiftly at that very moment*

Oppose thee of thin answere.   *Ask you for*

I wot thou wolt nothing forbere   *not at all hold back*

Of that thou wenest be thi beste,   *From what you think your best [effort]*

And if thou myht so finde reste,

1605   Wel is, for thanne is ther no more.   *That is fine; no more [to do]*

And elles this schal be my lore,   *But otherwise; teaching*

That thou schalt seie, upon this molde   *earth*

That alle wommen lievest wolde   *would most desire*

Be soverein of mannes love: *To be*

1610   For what womman is so above,   *that woman [who] is thus of a higher rank*

Sche hath, as who seith, al hire wille;   *her desire*

And elles may sche noght fulfille   *For otherwise*

What thing hir were lievest have.   *she would most desire to have*

With this answere thou schalt save

1615   Thiself, and other wise noght.

And whan thou hast thin ende wroght,   *achieved*

Com hier agein, thou schalt me finde,

And let nothing out of thi minde."   *i.e., do not forget*

    He goth him forth with hevy chiere,   *glum looks*

1620   As he that not in what manere   *does not know*

He mai this worldes joie atteigne: *attain*

For if he deie, he hath a peine,

And if he live, he mot him binde   *must bind himself*

To such on which of alle kinde   *such a one who*

1625   Of wommen is th'unsemylieste: *the most unbecoming*

Thus wot he noght what is the beste:

Bot be him lief or be him loth,   *glad; sad*

Unto the castell forth he goth

His full answere for to give,

1630   Or for to deie or for to live.   *Either; or*

Forth with his conseil cam the lord,
The thinges stoden of record,
He sende up for the lady sone,   *at once*
And forth sche cam, that olde mone.   *consort (OE gemana, "intercourse")*
1635   In presence of the remenant
The strengthe of al the covenant
Tho was reherced openly,
And to Florent sche bad forthi   *accordingly*
That he schal tellen his avis,   *opinion*
1640   As he that woot what is the pris.   *reward*
Florent seith al that evere he couthe,   *knew*
Bot such word cam ther non to mowthe,
That he for gifte or for beheste   *promise*
Mihte eny wise his deth areste.   *prevent*
1645   And thus he tarieth longe and late,
Til that this lady bad algate   *demanded continuously*
That he schal for the dom final   *final judgment (doom)*
Gif his ansuere in special   *Give; precisely*
Of that sche hadde him ferst opposed;   *first asked*
1650   And thanne he hath trewly supposed
That he him may of nothing yelpe,   *boast*
Bot if so be tho wordes helpe,
Whiche as the womman hath him tawht;
Wherof he hath an hope cawht
1655   That he schal ben excused so,
And tolde out plein his wille tho.   *then*
And whan that this matrone herde
The manere how this knyht ansuerde,
Sche seide, "Ha! Treson! Wo thee be,   *Woe be to you*
1660   That hast thus told the privité,   *Who have; secret*
Which alle wommen most desire!
I wolde that thou were afire."   *in flames*
Bot natheles in such a plit   *dilemma*
Florent of his answere is quit: *justified in his answer*
1665   And tho began his sorwe newe,   *then his grief began to renew*
For he mot gon, or ben untrewe,   *must*
To hire which his trowthe hadde.   *who had his promise*
Bot he, which alle schame dradde,   *shame feared*
Goth forth in stede of his penance,   *Goes forth on behalf of*
1670   And takth the fortune of his chance,   *endures*
As he that was with trowthe affaited.   *governed*
    This olde wyht him hath awaited   *creature*
In place wher as he hire lefte:
Florent his wofull heved uplefte   *woeful head raised up*
1675   And syh this vecke wher sche sat,   *saw; hag*
Which was the lothlieste what   *thing*
That evere man caste on his yhe: *cast his eye upon*

	Hire nase bass, hire browes hyhe,	nose low; brows high-arched
	Hire yhen smale and depe set,	i.e., beady eyes
1680	Hire chekes ben with teres wet,	
	And rivelen as an emty skyn	wrinkled
	Hangende doun unto the chin,	
	Hire lippes schrunken ben for age,	
	Ther was no grace in the visage.	
1685	Hir front was nargh, hir lockes hore,	forehead; narrow; gray
	Sche loketh forth as doth a More,	Moor
	Hire necke is schort, hir schuldres courbe —	stooped (curved)
	That myhte a mannes lust destourbe!	
	Hire body gret and nothing smal,	
1690	And schortly to descrive hire al,	
	Sche hath no lith withoute a lak;	limb; deficiency
	Bot lich unto the wollesak	woolsack
	Sche proferth hire unto this knyht,	offered herself
	And bad him, as he hath behyht,	promised
1695	So as sche hath ben his warant,	guarantor
	That he hire holde covenant,	
	And be the bridel sche him seseth.	[horse's] bridle; seizes him
	Bot Godd wot how that sche him pleseth	Only God knows; pleases him
	Of suche wordes as sche spekth:	
1700	Him thenkth wel nyh his herte brekth	It seems to him
	For sorwe that he may noght fle,	flee
	Bot if he wolde untrewe be.	
	Loke, how a sek man for his hele	sick; health
	Takth baldemoine with canele,	gentian root; cinnamon
1705	And with the mirre takth the sucre,	myrrh
	Ryht upon such a maner lucre	sort of gain
	Stant Florent, as in this diete:	
	He drinkth the bitre with the swete,	
	He medleth sorwe with likynge,	pleasure
1710	And liveth, as who seith, deyinge;	
	His youthe schal be cast aweie	
	Upon such on which as the weie	whey
	Is old and lothly overal.	
	Bot nede he mot that nede schal:	
1715	He wolde algate his trowthe holde,	
	As every knyht therto is holde,	bound
	What happ so evere him is befalle.	
	Thogh sche be the fouleste of alle,	
	Yit to th'onour of womanhiede	the honor
1720	Him thoghte he scholde taken hiede;	It seemed to him
	So that for pure gentilesse,	
	As he hire couthe best adresce,	Providing for her as best he could array
	In ragges, as sche was totore,	since she was all tattered
	He set hire on his hors tofore	before [him]

1725	And forth he takth his weie softe.	*quietly*
	No wonder thogh he siketh ofte	*often sighs*
	Bot as an oule fleth be nyhte	*owl flies by night*
	Out of alle othre briddes syhte,	*birds*
	Riht so this knyht on daies brode	*in broad daylight*
1730	In clos him hield, and schop his rode	*Kept himself hidden; did his riding*
	On nyhtes time, til the tyde	*At night; time*
	That he cam there he wolde abide;	
	And prively withoute noise	*secretly*
	He bringth this foule grete coise	*ugly woman (rump; OF cuisse, "thigh")*
1735	To his castell in such a wise	
	That no man myhte hire schappe avise,	*her figure observe*
	Til sche into the chambre cam:	
	Wher he his privé conseil nam	*took*
	Of suche men as he most troste,	*trusted*
1740	And tolde hem that he nedes moste	*them*
	This beste wedde to his wif,	*best (lovely lady)/beast*
	For elles hadde he lost his lif.	
	The privé wommen were asent,	*personal serving women; sent for*
	That scholden ben of his assent:	
1745	Hire ragges thei anon of drawe,	*soon took off*
	And, as it was that time lawe,	
	Sche hadde bath, sche hadde reste,	
	And was arraied to the beste.	*dressed*
	Bot with no craft of combes brode	
1750	Thei myhte hire hore lockes schode,	*hoary locks comb through (divide)*
	And sche ne wolde noght be schore	*did not want to be shorn*
	For no conseil, and thei therfore,	
	With such atyr as tho was used,	*attire as then was the custom*
	Ordeinen that it was excused,	*Decided; it (the custom)*
1755	And hid so crafteliche aboute,	*craftily covered*
	That no man myhte sen hem oute.	*them (her hoary locks)*
	Bot when sche was fulliche arraied	*dressed*
	And hire atyr was al assaied,	*inspected*
	Tho was sche foulere on to se.	*more foul to look on [than before]*
1760	Bot yit it may non other be:	
	Thei were wedded in the nyht.	
	So wo begon was nevere knyht	
	As he was thanne of mariage.	
	And sche began to pleie and rage,	
1765	As who seith, I am wel ynowh;	
	Bot he therof nothing ne lowh,	*laughed*
	For sche tok thanne chiere on honde	*began to be merry*
	And clepeth him hire housebonde,	*called*
	And seith, "My lord, go we to bedde,	*let us go*
1770	For I to that entente wedde,	
	That thou schalt be my worldes blisse,"	

And profreth him with that to kisse,   *offers to kiss him*
As sche a lusti lady were.
His body myhte wel be there,
1775   Bot as of thoght and of memoire
His herte was in purgatoire.
Bot yit for strengthe of matrimoine
He myhte make non essoine,   *excuse*
That he ne mot algates plie   *But that he need[s] must comply*
1780   To gon to bedde of compaignie.   *companionably*
And whan thei were abedde naked,   *amorously in bed*
Withoute slep he was awaked;   *lay awake*
He torneth on that other side,   *turned his back to her*
For that he wolde hise yhen hyde   *eyes hide*
1785   Fro lokynge on that fole wyht.   *ugly creature*
The chambre was al full of lyht,
The courtins were of cendal thinne,   *(OF cendal, a costly fabric)*
This newe bryd which lay withinne,   *bride*
Thogh it be noght with his acord,   *consent*
1790   In armes sche beclipte hire lord,   *embraced*
And preide, as he was torned fro,   *prayed; turned away*
He wolde him torne ageinward tho;   *[That] he would turn himself; then*
"For now," sche seith, "we ben bothe on."   *one*
And he lay stille as eny ston,
1795   Bot evere in on sche spak and preide,   *steadfastly (insistently)*
And bad him thenke on that he seide,   *what he had said*
Whan that he tok hire be the hond.   *married her*
   He herde and understod the bond,
How he was set to his penance,
1800   And, as it were a man in trance,
He torneth him al sodeinly
And syh a lady lay him by
Of eyhtetiene wynter age,
Which was the faireste of visage
1805   That evere in al this world he syh:
And as he wolde have take hire nyh,
Sche put hire hand and be his leve
Besoghte him that he wolde leve,   *wait*
And seith that for to wynne or lese   *lose*
1810   He mot on of tuo thinges chese,   *must one of two things choose*
Wher he wol have hire such on nyht,   *Whether; by night*
Or elles upon daies lyht,   *daylight*
For he schal noght have bothe tuo.
And he began to sorwe tho,   *then*
1815   In many a wise and caste his thoght,
Bot for al that yit cowthe he noght
Devise himself which was the beste.
And sche, that wolde his hertes reste,   *who wanted his peace of mind*

	Preith that he scholde chese algate,	*chose nevertheless*
1820	Til ate laste longe and late	
	He seide: "O ye, my lyves hele,	*life's salvation*
	Sey what you list in my querele,	*Say what you please; debate*
	I not what ansuere I schal give:	*do not know*
	Bot evere whil that I may live,	
1825	I wol that ye be my maistresse,	
	For I can noght miselve gesse	*discern*
	Which is the beste unto my chois.	
	Thus grante I yow myn hole vois,	*my whole voice*
	Ches for ous bothen, I you preie;	*Choose*
1830	And what as evere that ye seie,	
	Riht as ye wole so wol I."	*Just as you might wish*
	"Mi lord," sche seide, "grant merci,	
	For of this word that ye now sein,	
	That ye have mad me soverein,	*Since you have made*
1835	Mi destiné is overpassed,	*fulfilled*
	That nevere hierafter schal be lassed	*diminished*
	Mi beauté, which that I now have,	
	Til I be take into my grave;	
	Bot nyht and day as I am now	
1840	I schal alwey be such to yow.	
	The kinges dowhter of Cizile	*Sicily*
	I am, and fell bot siththe awhile,	*it befell but a while ago*
	As I was with my fader late,	
	That my stepmoder for an hate,	*out of hatred*
1845	Which toward me sche hath begonne,	
	Forschop me, til I hadde wonne	*transformed; until*
	The love and sovereineté	
	Of what knyht that in his degré	
	Alle othre passeth of good name.	
1850	And, as men sein, ye ben the same,	*you are that one*
	The dede proeveth it is so.	
	Thus am I youres evermo."	
	Tho was plesance and joye ynowh,	*Then; enough*
	Echon with other pleide and lowh;	*Each; played; laughed*
1855	Thei live longe and wel thei ferde,	*fared together*
	And clerkes that this chance herde	
	Thei writen it in evidence,	
	To teche how that obedience	
	Mai wel fortune a man to love	
1860	And sette him in his lust above,	*in a state of prosperity*
	As it befell unto this knyht.	
Confessor	Forthi, my sone, if thou do ryht,	
	Thou schalt unto thi love obeie,	
	And folwe hir will be alle weie."	*desire in all ways*

Amans	"Min holy fader, so I wile:	
	For ye have told me such a skile	*reasonable thing*
	Of this ensample now tofore,	
	That I schal evermo therfore	
	Hierafterward myn observance	*Henceforth*
1870	To love and to his obeissance	
	The betre kepe: and over this	
	Of pride if ther oght elles is,	
	Wherof that I me schryve schal,	
	What thing it is in special,	
1875	Mi fader, axeth, I you preie."	
Confessor	"Now lest, my sone, and I schal seie:	*listen*
	For yit ther is Surquiderie,	*Presumption*
	Which stant with Pride of compaignie;	
	Wherof that thou schalt hiere anon,	
1880	To knowe if thou have gult or non	
	Upon the forme as thou schalt hiere:	
	Now understond wel the matiere."	

[PRESUMPTION]

viii.	*Omnia scire putat, set se Presumpcio nescit,*
	Nec sibi consimilem quem putat esse parem
	Qui magis astutus reputat se vincere bellum,
	In laqueos Veneris forcius ipse cadit.
	Sepe Cupido virum sibi qui presumit amantem
	Fallit, et in vacuas spes redit ipsa vias.[1]

[Confessor]	"Surquiderie is thilke vice	*Presumption is that [particular]*
	Of Pride, which the thridde office	
1885	Hath in his court, and wol noght knowe	
	The trowthe til it overthrowe.	*until it falls into calamity*
☞	Upon his fortune and his grace	*(see note)*
	Comth 'Hadde I wist' ful ofte aplace;	*Had I known*
	For he doth al his thing be gesse,	*carries out all his business by supposition*
1890	And voideth alle sikernesse.	*drives away all certainty*
	Non other conseil good him siemeth	
	Bot such as he himselve diemeth;	*judges*
	For in such wise as he compasseth,	
	His wit alone alle othre passeth;	
1895	And is with pride so thurghsoght,	*[he] is; pervaded*

---

[1] *All things Presumption thinks he knows, but he does not know himself, nor does he think that anyone similar to him is his equal. He who thinks himself more astute in winning the battle falls all the more tightly into Venus's snares. Often Cupid betrays the man who presupposes a lover for himself, and Hope itself turns back down empty roads.*

That he alle othre set at noght,

And weneth of himselven so,   *thinks*

That such as he ther be no mo,   *more*

So fair, so semly, ne so wis;   *nor so wise [as he is]*

1900   And thus he wolde bere a pris   *take the prize*

Above alle othre, and noght forthi   *nevertheless*

He seith noght ones 'grant mercy'

To Godd, which alle grace sendeth,

So that his wittes he despendeth   *used up*

1905   Upon himself, as thogh ther were

No godd which myhte availe there.

Bot al upon his oghne witt

He stant, til he falle in the pitt

So ferr that he mai noght arise.

1910   And riht thus in the same wise

☞   This vice upon the cause of love   *(see note)*

So proudly set the herte above,

And doth him pleinly for to wene   *causes him; think*

That he to loven eny qwene

1915   Hath worthinesse and sufficance;

And so withoute pourveance   *prudence*

Ful ofte he heweth up so hihe,   *chops so high up*

That chippes fallen in his yhe;   *eye*

And ek ful ofte he weneth this: *also very often he thinks*

1920   Ther as he noght beloved is,   *Where [i.e., by whom]*

To be beloved alther best.   *best of all*

Now, sone, tell what so thee lest   *you wish*

Of this that I have told thee hier."   *you here*

Amans   "Ha, fader, be noght in a wer!   *doubt*

1925   I trowe ther be no man lesse,

Of eny maner worthinesse,

That halt him lasse worth thanne I

To be beloved; and noght forthi   *nevertheless*

I seie in excusinge of me,   *myself*

1930   To alle men that love is fre.

And certes that mai no man werne;   *prevent*

For love is of himself so derne,   *secret*

It luteth in a mannes herte.   *lurks*

Bot that ne schal me noght asterte,   *that [idea] will not occur to me*

1935   To wene for to be worthi   *think that I am*

To loven, bot in hir mercy.   *except at her authority*

Bot, sire, of that ye wolden mene,   *intend*

That I scholde otherwise wene   *I should think differently*

To be beloved thanne I was,

1940   I am beknowe as in that cas."   *I admit [my guilt] in that case*

Confessor   "Mi goode sone, tell me how."

Amans	"Now lest, and I wol telle yow,	*listen*
	Mi goode fader, how it is.	
	Ful ofte it hath befalle or this	*before now*
1945	Thurgh hope that was noght certein,	
	Mi wenynge hath be set in vein	*thinking has been determined in vain*
	To triste in thing that halp me noght,	*To trust*
	Bot onliche of myn oughne thoght.	
	For as it semeth that a belle	
1950	Lik to the wordes that men telle	
	Answerth, riht so ne mor ne lesse,	
	To yow, my fader, I confesse,	
	Such will my wit hath overset,	*desire my intellect has*
	That what so hope me behet,	*whatever hope might promise*
1955	Ful many a time I wene it soth,	*believe it true*
	Bot finali no spied it doth.	*success it brings about*
	Thus may I tellen, as I can,	
	Wenyng beguileth many a man.	*Thinking beguiles*
	So hath it me, riht wel I wot:	
1960	For if a man wole in a bot	
	Which is withoute botme rowe,	
	He moste nedes overthrowe.	*go down*
	Riht so wenyng hath ferd be me,	
	For whanne I wende next have be,	*what would happen next*
1965	As I be my wenynge caste,	*by my thinking imagined*
	Thanne was I furthest ate laste,	
	And as a foll my bowe unbende,	*fool*
	Whan al was failed that I wende.	
	Forthi, my fader, as of this,	
1970	That my wenynge hath gon amis	
	Touchende to Surquiderie,	
	Gif me my penance er I die.	
	Bot if ye wolde in eny forme	
	Of this matiere a tale enforme,	*recount*
1975	Which were agein this vice set,	
	I scholde fare wel the bet."	

[TALE OF CAPANEUS]

[Confessor]	"Mi sone, in alle maner wise	
☞	Surquiderie is to despise,	*(see note)*
	Wherof I finde write thus.	
1980	The proude knyht Capaneus	
	He was of such Surquideric,	*Presumption*
	That he thurgh his chivalerie	*military prowess*
	Upon himself so mochel triste,	*In himself so much trusted*
	That to the goddes him ne liste	*it pleased him not*
1985	In no querele to beseche,	*conflict to pray*

	Bot seide it was an ydel speche,	*it [prayer] was a useless utterance*
	Which caused was of pure drede,	*fear*
	For lack of herte and for no nede.	
	And upon such presumpcioun	
1990	He hield this proude opinioun,	
	Til ate laste upon a dai,	
	Aboute Thebes wher he lay,	
	Whan it of siege was belein,	*besieged*
	This knyht, as the Croniqes sein,	
1995	In alle mennes sihte there,	
	Whan he was proudest in his gere,	*armor*
	And thoghte how nothing myhte him dere,	*wound*
	Ful armed with his schield and spere	
	As he the cité wolde assaile,	
2000	Godd tok himselve the bataille	
	Agein his Pride, and fro the sky	
	A firy thonder sodeinly	*thunderbolt*
	He sende, and him to pouldre smot.	*powder pulverized*
	And thus the Pride which was hot,	
2005	Whan he most in his strengthe wende,	*most trusted in his strength*
	Was brent and lost withouten ende:	
	So that it proeveth wel therfore,	*proves clearly*
	The strengthe of man is sone lore,	*lost*
	Bot if that he it wel governe.	*Unless*
2010	And over this a man mai lerne	*moreover*
	That ek ful ofte time it grieveth,	*it is injurious*
	Whan that a man himself believeth,	
	As thogh it scholde him wel beseme	*be proper for him*
	That he alle othre men can deme,	*judge*
2015	And hath forgete his oghne vice.	*forgotten his own*
	A tale of hem that ben so nyce,	*those who are so stupid*
	And feigne hemself to be so wise,	
	I schal thee telle in such a wise,	
	Wherof thou schalt ensample take	
2020	That thou no such thing undertake.	

[TRUMP OF DEATH]

	I finde upon Surquiderie,	
	How that whilom of Hungarie	*once*
	Be olde daies was a king	
	Wys and honeste in alle thing:	*honorable*
2025	And so befell upon a dai,	
	And that was in the monthe of Maii,	*May*
	As thilke time it was usance,	*custom*
	This kyng with noble pourveance	*provision*
	Hath for himself his charr araied,	

2030 Wherinne he wolde ride amaied	*a-maying*
☞ Out of the cité for to pleie,	*(see note)*
With lordes and with gret nobleie	
Of lusti folk that were yonge:	
Wher some pleide and some songe,	*played [games]*
2035 And some gon and some ryde,	*were walking; were riding*
And some prike here hors aside	*were spurring their; alongside*
And bridlen hem now in now oute.	*now reining them in, now releasing the reins*
The kyng his yhe caste aboute,	*eye*
Til he was ate laste war	*became aware*
2040 And syh comende agein his char	*saw coming toward*
Two pilegrins of so gret age,	
That lich unto a dreie ymage	*withered effigy*
Thei weren pale and fade hewed,	
And as a bussh which is besnewed,	*covered with snow*
2045 Here berdes weren hore and whyte;	*Their beards; hoary*
Ther was of kinde bot a lite,	*so little natural vitality left*
That thei ne semen fulli dede.	*they seemed almost totally dead*
Thei comen to the kyng and bede	*made supplication for*
Som of his good par charité;	
2050 And he with gret humilité	
Out of his char to grounde lepte,	
And hem in bothe hise armes kepte	*took*
And keste hem bothe fot and hond	*kissed them*
Before the lordes of his lond,	
2055 And gaf hem of his good therto:	*gave them*
And whanne he hath this dede do,	
He goth into his char agein.	
Tho was Murmur, tho was Desdeign,	*Then; Disdain*
Tho was Compleignte on every side,	
2060 Thei seiden of here oghne Pride	*in their own Pride*
Eche until othre: "What is this?	
Oure king hath do this thing amis,	*wrongly*
So to abesse his realté	*degrade his kingship*
That every man it myhte se,	
2065 And humbled him in such a wise	*himself; manner*
To hem that were of non emprise."	*worth*
Thus was it spoken to and fro	
Of hem that were with him tho	*By those who*
Al prively behinde his bak;	*secretly*
2070 Bot to himselven no man spak.	
The kinges brother in presence	
Was thilke time, and gret offence	
He tok therof, and was the same	*He took in response to that, and*
Above alle othre which most blame	*who*
2075 Upon his liege lord hath leid,	*sovereign had laid*
And hath unto the lordes seid,	

	Anon as he mai time finde,	*As soon as*
	Ther schal nothing be left behinde,	
	That he wol speke unto the king.	
2080	Now lest what fell upon this thing.	*listen to what befell*
	The day was merie and fair ynowh,	
	Echon with othre pleide and lowh,	*laughed*
	And fellen into tales newe,	
	How that the freisshe floures grewe,	
2085	And how the grene leves spronge,	
	And how that love among the yonge	
	Began the hertes thanne awake,	
	And every bridd hath chose hire make:	*bird; her mate*
	And thus the Maies day to th'ende	
2090	Thei lede, and hom agein thei wende.	*went*
	The king was noght so sone come,	*had no sooner come [home]*
	That whanne he hadde his chambre nome	*Than that when; taken*
	His brother ne was redi there,	*His brother was already there*
	And broghte a tale unto his ere	*ear*
2095	Of that he dede such a schame	
	In hindringe of his oghne name,	*own*
	Whan he himself so wolde drecche,	*debase*
	That to so vil a povere wrecche	*vile*
	Him deigneth schewe such simplesce	*It seemed to him worthy to show such humility*
2100	Agein th'astat of his noblesce:	*nobility*
	And seith he schal it no mor use,	*behave that way no more*
	And that he mot himself excuse	*must excuse himself*
	Toward hise lordes everychon.	*To each one of his lords*
	The king stod stille as eny ston,	
2105	And to his tale an ere he leide,	*listened carefully to his tale*
	And thoghte more than he seide.	
	Bot natheles to that he herde	*to what he heard*
	Wel cortaisly the king answerde,	
	And tolde it scholde be amended.	*said it should*
2110	And thus whan that her tale is ended,	*their complaint*
	Al redy was the bord and cloth,	
	The king unto his souper goth	
	Among the lordes to the halle;	
	And whan thei hadden souped alle,	
2115	Thei token leve and forth thei go.	
	The king bethoghte himselve tho	*thought to himself then*
	How he his brother mai chastie,	*may reprove (chasten)*
	That he thurgh his Surquiderie	
	Tok upon honde to despreise	
2120	Humilité, which is to preise,	*praiseworthy*
	And therupon gaf such conseil	
	Toward his king that was noght heil;	*wholesome*
	Wherof to be the betre lered,	*taught*

	He thenkth to maken him afered.	*It occurred to him to frighten him*
2125	It fell so that in thilke dawe	*that time*
	Ther was ordeined be the lawe	
	A trompe with a sterne breth,	*trumpet; fierce sound*
	Which cleped was the trompe of deth:	*called; trumpet of death*
	And in the court wher the king was	
2130	A certein man this trompe of bras	
	Hath in kepinge, and therof serveth,	*in [his] keeping, and has the job of using it*
	That whan a lord his deth deserveth,	*[Such] that*
	He schal this dredful trompe blowe	
	Tofore his gate, and make it knowe	*Before*
2135	How that the jugement is gove	*given*
	Of deth, which schal noght be forgove.	*reprieved*
	The king, whan it was nyht, anon	
	This man asente and bad him gon	*sent for*
	To trompen at his brother gate;	
2140	And he, which mot so don algate,	*who must do so regardless*
	Goth forth and doth the kynges heste.	*command*
	This lord, which herde of this tempeste	
	That he tofore his gate blew,	
	Tho wiste he be the lawe and knew	*Then he understood by the law*
2145	That he was sikerliche ded:	*assuredly dead*
	And as of help he wot no red	*since for help he knew no plan*
	Bot sende for hise frendes alle	*Except [that he should] send*
	And tolde hem how it is befalle.	*And [that he should] tell them*
	And thei him axe cause why	*asked*
2150	Bot he the sothe noght forthi	*truth*
	Ne wiste, and ther was sorwe tho:	*Knew not*
	For it stod thilke tyme so,	
	This trompe was of such sentence,	
	That theragein no resistence	
2155	Thei couthe ordeine be no weie,	*by no means*
	That he ne mot algate deie,	*might not have to die nonetheless*
	Bot if so that he may pourchace	*Unless he succeed*
	To gete his liege lordes grace.	*In getting; forgiveness*
	Here wittes therupon thei caste,	*Their; inclined*
2160	And ben apointed ate laste.	*came to a decision*
	This lord a worthi ladi hadde	
	Unto his wif, which also dradde	
	Hire lordes deth, and children five	
	Betwen hem two thei hadde alyve,	
2165	That weren yonge and tendre of age,	
	And of stature and of visage	
	Riht faire and lusty on to se.	
	Tho casten thei that he and sche	*Then they planned*
	Forth with here children on the morwe,	*their*
2170	As thei that were full of sorwe,	

Al naked bot of smok and sherte,   *except for*
To tendre with the kynges herte,   *move to tenderness*
His grace scholden go to seche
And pardoun of the deth beseche.
2175   Thus passen thei that wofull nyht,
And erly, whan thei sihe it lyht,
Thei gon hem forth in such a wise
As thou tofore hast herd devise,
Al naked bot here schortes one.   *except for their shirts alone*
2180   Thei wepte and made mochel mone,   *great lament*
Here her hangende aboute here eres;   *Their hair hanging about their ears*
With sobbinge and with sory teres
This lord goth thanne an humble pas,
That whilom proud and noble was;   *once*
2185   Wherof the cité sore afflyhte,   *became sorely distressed (afflicted)*
Of hem that sihen thilke syhte: *On the part of those who*
And natheles al openly   *publicly*
With such wepinge and with such cri
Forth with hise children and his wif
2190   He goth to preie for his lif.   *pray*
Unto the court whan thei be come,
And men therinne have hiede nome,   *taken heed*
Ther was no wiht, if he hem syhe,   *person [who] if he saw them*
Fro water mihte kepe his yhe
2195   For sorwe which thei maden tho.
The king supposeth of this wo,   *anticipates*
And feigneth as he noght ne wiste;   *feigns as if he knew nothing*
Bot natheles at his upriste   *arising*
Men tolden him how that it ferde:
2200   And whan that he this wonder herde,
In haste he goth into the halle,
And alle at ones doun thei falle,
If eny pité may be founde.   *[To see] if*
The king, which seth hem go to grounde,   *who sees them drop to the ground*
2205   Hath axed hem what is the fere,   *fear*
Why thei be so despuiled there.   *despoiled (naked)*
His brother seide: "Ha! lord, mercy!   *Ah!*
I wot non other cause why,   *know*
Bot only that this nyht ful late
2210   The trompe of deth was at my gate
In tokne that I scholde deie;   *As a sign; had to die*
Thus be we come for to preie   *pray*
That ye mi worldes deth respite."   *my earthly death cancel*
     "Ha! fol, how thou art for to wyte,"   *fool; blame*
2215   The king unto his brother seith,
"That thou art of so litel feith,
That only for a trompes soun

Hast gon despuiled thurgh the toun,   *naked*
Thou and thi wif in such manere
2220   Forth with thi children that ben here,
In sihte of alle men aboute,
For that thou seist thou art in doute   *Because you see; in fear*
Of deth, which stant under the lawe
Of man, and man it mai withdrawe,
2225   So that it mai par chance faile.   *With the result that it (the law) may*
Now schalt thou noght forthi mervaile   *therefore marvel*
That I doun fro my charr alihte,   *chariot got down*
Whanne I behield tofore my sihte   *before*
In hem that were of so gret age
2230   Min oghne deth thurgh here ymage,   *own; their features*
Which God hath set be lawe of kynde,   *established by nature's law*
Wherof I mai no bote finde: *respite (remedy)*
For wel I wot, such as thei be,
Riht such am I in my degree,
2235   Of fleissh and blod, and so schal deie.
And thus, thogh I that lawe obeie   *that [human] law*
Of which the kinges ben put under,
It oghte ben wel lasse wonder
Than thou, which art withoute nede
2240   For lawe of londe in such a drede,   *Because of common law [to be]*
Which for t'acompte is bot a jape,   *by evaluation is*
As thing which thou miht overscape.   *That is to say, a thing you might escape from*
Forthi, mi brother, after this   *moreover*
I rede, sithen that so is   *advise since*
2245   That thou canst drede a man so sore,
Dred God with al thin herte more.
For al schal deie and al schal passe,
Als wel a leoun as an asse,
Als wel a beggere as a lord,
2250   Towardes deth in on acord   *in steadfast accord*
Thei schullen stonde." And in this wise
The king hath with hise wordes wise
His brother tawht and al forgive.
Confessor   Forthi, mi sone, if thou wolt live
2255   In vertu, thou most vice eschuie,   *eschew*
And with low herte humblesce suie,   *humble heart follow humility*
So that thou be noght surquidous."   *presumptuous*
Amans   "Mi fader, I am amorous,
Wherof I wolde you beseche
2260   That ye me som ensample teche,
Which mihte in loves cause stonde."
Confessor   "Mi sone, thou schalt understonde,
In love and othre thinges alle
If that Surquiderie falle,

2265   It may to him noght wel betide
       Which useth thilke vice of Pride,   *this same vice*
       Which torneth wisdom to wenynge   *wishful thinking*
       And sothfastnesse into lesynge   *truth into lying*
       Thurgh fol ymaginacion.   *foolish*
2270   And for thin enformacion,
       That thou this vice as I thee rede
       Eschuie schalt, a tale I rede,
       Which fell whilom be daies olde,   *in olden days*
       So as the clerk Ovide tolde.   *man of letters*

[TALE OF NARCISSUS]

2275   Ther was whilom a lordes sone,   *once*
       Which of his Pride a nyce wone   *foolish attitude*
       Hath cawht, that worthi to his liche,   *[namely] that worthy as his peer*
       To sechen al the worldes riche,   *world's territory*
☞   Ther was no womman for to love.   *(see note)*
2280   So hihe he sette himselve above   *high*
       Of stature and of beauté bothe,
       That him thoghte alle wommen lothe: *loathsome*
       So was ther no comparisoun   *equal*
       As toward his condicioun.   *moral disposition*
2285   This yonge lord Narcizus hihte: *was called*
       No strengthe of love bowe mihte   *might humble*
       His herte, which is unaffiled.   *untrained*
       Bot ate laste he was beguiled,
       For of the goddes pourveance   *provision*
2290   It fell him on a dai par chance,   *by chance*
       That he in all his proude fare   *bearing*
       Unto the forest gan to fare,
       Amonges othre that ther were
       To hunte and to desporte him there.   *entertain himself*
2295   And whanne he cam into the place
       Wher that he wolde make his chace,   *hunt*
       The houndes weren in a throwe   *instantly*
       Uncoupled and the hornes blowe.
       The grete hert anon was founde,   *hart soon*
2300   Which swifte feet sette upon grounde,
       And he with spore in horse side
       Him hasteth faste for to ride,   *[Narcissus] hastened himself*
       Til alle men be left behinde.
       And as he rod, under a linde   *tree*
2305   Beside a roche, as I thee telle,
       He syh wher sprong a lusty welle:
       The day was wonder hot withalle,
       And such a thurst was on him falle,

	That he moste owther deie or drinke;	*either*
2310	And doun he lihte and be the brinke	*alighted*
	He teide his hors unto a branche,	*tied*
	And leide him lowe for to stanche	
	His thurst: and as he caste his lok	
	Into the welle and hiede tok,	*took heed*
2315	He sih the like of his visage,	*saw; likeness (peer)*
	And wende ther were an ymage	
	Of such a nimphe as tho was faie,	*magical (enchanted/of fairy)*
	Wherof that love his herte assaie	*assault*
	Began, as it was after sene,	
2320	Of his sotie, and made him wene	*From his besottedness; think*
	It were a womman that he syh.	*saw*
	The more he cam the welle nyh,	*near*
	The nerr cam sche to him agein;	*nearer*
	So wiste he nevere what to sein;	*knew; to say*
2325	For whanne he wepte, he sih hire wepe,	
	And whanne he cride, he tok good kepe,	
	The same word sche cride also:	
	And thus began the newe wo,	*woe*
	That whilom was to him so strange.	
2330	Tho made him love an hard eschange:	*love made with him; exchange*
	To sette his herte and to beginne	
	Thing which he mihte nevere winne.	
	And evere among he gan to loute,	*bow down*
	And preith that sche to him come oute;	
2335	And otherwhile he goth a ferr,	*sometimes; away*
	And otherwhile he draweth nerr,	
	And evere he fond hire in o place.	
	He wepth, he crith, he axeth grace,	
	There as he mihte gete non;	
2340	So that agein a roche of ston,	*against*
	As he that knew non other red,	*As one who; counsel*
	He smot himself til he was ded.	*dashed*
	Wherof the Nimphes of the welles,	
	And othre that ther weren elles	
2345	Unto the wodes belongende,	
	The body, which was ded ligende,	
	For pure pité that thei have	
	Under the grene thei begrave.	*grass; buried*
	And thanne out of his sepulture	
2350	Ther sprong anon par aventure	
	Of floures such a wonder syhte,	
	That men ensample take myhte	
	Upon the dedes whiche he dede,	*deeds; did*
	As tho was sene in thilke stede;	*that place*
2355	For in the wynter freysshe and faire	

	The floures ben, which is contraire	*flowers are present*
	To kynde, and so was the folie	*To nature*
	Which fell of his Surquiderie.	
Confessor	Thus he, which love hadde in desdeign,	
2360	Worste of alle othre was besein,	*endowed*
	And as he sette his pris most hyhe,	*premium most high*
	He was lest worth in loves yhe	*least; eye*
	And most bejaped in his wit:	*tricked*
	Wherof the remembrance is yit,	
2365	So that thou myht ensample take,	
	And ek alle othre for his sake."	
Amans	"Mi fader, as touchende of me,	
	This vice I thenke for to fle,	*avoid*
	Which of his wenynge overtroweth;	*Of one who believes too much in his thinking*
2370	And nameliche of thing which groweth	*generates*
	In loves cause or wel or wo.	*either gladness or sadness*
	Yit pryded I me nevere so,	*prided myself never*
	Bot wolde God that grace sende,	*[if only] God would send that grace*
	That toward me my lady wende	*lady should turn wishful thinking*
2375	As I towardes hire wene!	*As I do toward her*
	Mi love scholde so be sene,	
	Ther scholde go no pride a place.	
	Bot I am ferr fro thilke grace,	
	As for to speke of tyme now;	
2380	So mot I soffre, and preie yow	
	That ye wole axe on other side	
	If ther be eny point of Pride,	
	Wherof it nedeth to be schrive."	
Confessor	"Mi sone, Godd it thee forgive,	
2385	If thou have eny thing misdo	
	Touchende of this, bot overmo	
	Ther is an other yit of Pride,	*other [aspect] yet*
	Which never cowthe hise wordes hide,	
	That he ne wole himself avaunte;	*[Such] that; boast*
2390	Ther mai nothing his tunge daunte,	
	That he ne clappeth as a belle:	*makes noise*
	Wherof if thou wolt that I telle,	
	It is behovely for to hiere,	*suitable*
	So that thou myht thi tunge stiere,	*guide*
2395	Toward the world and stonde in grace,	
	Which lacketh ofte in many place	
	To him that can noght sitte stille,	
	Which elles scholde have his wille."	

[BOASTING]

<table>
<tr><td>ix.</td><td>Magniloque propriam minuit iactancia lingue
   Famam, quam stabilem firmat honore cilens.
Ipse sui laudem meriti non percipit, vnde
   Se sua per verba iactat in orbe palam.
Estque viri culpa iactancia, que rubefactas
   In muliere reas causat habere genas.[1]</td></tr>
</table>

[Confessor]	"The vice cleped Avantance	*Boasting*
2400	With Pride hath take his aqueintance,	
	So that his oghne pris he lasseth,	*worth he diminishes*
	When he such mesure overpasseth	
	That he his oghne herald is.	
	That ferst was wel is thanne mis,	*What at first; amiss*
2405	That was thankworth is thanne blame,	*worthy of thanks; blameworthy*
☞	And thus the worschipe of his name	*fame (see note)*
	Thurgh pride of his avantarie	
	He torneth into vilenie.	
	I rede how that this proude vice	
2410	Hath thilke wynd in his office,	*official function*
	Which thurgh the blastes that he bloweth	
	The mannes fame he overthroweth	
	Of vertu, which scholde elles springe	
	Into the worldes knowlechinge;	
2415	Bot he fordoth it alto sore.	*destroys it all too sorely*
	And riht of such a maner lore	
	Ther ben lovers: forthi if thow	
	Art on of hem, tell and sei how.	*one of them*
	Whan thou hast taken eny thing	
2420	Of loves gifte, or nouche or ring,	*either brooch or*
	Or tok upon thee for the cold	*chilling anguish [of love]*
	Som goodly word that thee was told,	
	Or frendly chiere or tokne or lettre,	
	Wherof thin herte was the bettre,	
2425	Or that sche sende thee grietinge,	*sent you greeting*
	Hast thou for Pride of thi likinge	
	Mad thin avant wher as thee liste?"	*boast; it pleased you*
Amans	"I wolde, fader, that ye wiste,	
	Mi conscience lith noght hiere:	
2430	Yit hadde I nevere such matiere,	
	Wherof myn herte myhte amende,	*improve in spirit*

---

[1] *The boasting of a bombastic tongue diminishes the genuine fame that being silent would, with honor, confirm as stable. That one does not perceive praise of his merit, so he openly extolls himself in his own words to the world. There is moreover the sinful boasting of a man, which makes the guilty cheeks on a woman redden.*

Noght of so mochel that sche sende
Be mowthe and seide, "Griet him wel!"   *By mouth*
And thus for that ther is no diel   *nothing (no portion)*
2435   Wherof to make myn avant,
It is to reson acordant
That I mai nevere, bot I lye,   *unless I lie*
Of love make avanterie.
I wot noght what I scholde have do,
2440   If that I hadde encheson so,   *grounds for so [doing]*
As ye have seid hier manyon;   *many times*
Bot I fond cause nevere non:
Bot daunger, which wel nyh me slowh,   *[her] aloofness; has nearly killed me*
Therof I cowthe telle ynowh,   *could tell plenty*
2445   And of non other Avantance.
Thus nedeth me no repentance.
Now axeth furthere of my lif,
For hierof am I noght gultif."   *guilty*
Confessor   "Mi sone, I am wel paid withal;   *pleased*
2450   For wite it wel in special   *know*
That love of his verrai justice
Above alle othre agein this vice
At alle times most debateth,   *combats*
With al his herte and most it hateth.
2455   And ek in alle maner wise
Avantarie is to despise,
As be ensample thou myhte wite,   *know*
Which I finde in the bokes write.

[TALE OF ALBINUS AND ROSEMUND]

Of hem that we Lombars now calle   *those who*
2460   Albinus was the ferst of alle
Which bar corone of Lombardie,   *the crown*
☞   And was of gret chivalerie   *prowess (see note)*
In werre agein diverse kinges.   *war against*
So fell amonges othre thinges,
2465   That he that time a werre hadde
With Gurmond, which the Geptes ladde,   *who led the Geptes*
And was a myhti kyng also,
Bot natheles it fell him so,   *turned out for him thus [that]*
Albinus slowh him in the feld: *slew*
2470   Ther halp him nowther swerd ne scheld,
That he ne smot his hed of thanne,   *But that he smote his head off*
Wherof he tok awey the panne,   *cut off the brain-pan*
Of which he seide he wolde make
A cuppe for Gurmoundes sake,   *Gurmond's destruction*
2475   To kepe and drawe into memoire

Of his bataille the victoire.
And thus whan he the feld hath wonne,
The lond anon was overronne
And sesed in his oghne hond,   *"legally" transferred to his own use*
2480   Wher he Gurmondes dowhter fond,
Which maide Rosemounde hihte,   *was called*
And was in every mannes sihte
A fair, a freissh, a lusti on.
His herte fell to hire anon,
2485   And such a love on hire he caste,
That he hire weddeth ate laste.
And after that long time in reste   *at peace*
With hire he duelte, and to the beste   *to the highest degree*
Thei love ech other wonder wel.
2490   Bot sche which kepth the blinde whel,   *wheel*
Venus, whan thei be most above,   *on high*
In al the hoteste of here love,   *most passionate condition of their love*
Hire whiel sche torneth, and thei felle
In the manere as I schal telle.
2495   This king, which stod in al his welthe
Of pes, of worschipe, and of helthe,   *peace; fame*
And felte him on no side grieved,   *in no respect unhappy*
As he that hath his world achieved,
Tho thoghte he wolde a feste make;   *Then*
2500   And that was for his wyves sake,
That sche the lordes ate feste,   *[So] that*
That were obeissant to his heste,   *command*
Mai knowe: and so forth therupon   *Might know [the lords]*
He let ordeine, and sende anon   *gave orders*
2505   Be lettres and be messagiers,   *By*
And warnede alle hise officiers
That every thing be wel arraied:
The grete stiedes were assaied   *steeds were readied*
For joustinge and for tornement,
2510   And many a perled garnement
Embroudred was agein the dai.   *in preparation for the day*
The lordes in here beste arrai   *their*
Be comen ate time set:
On jousteth wel, an other bet,   *One; better*
2515   And otherwhile thei torneie,
And thus thei casten care aweie
And token lustes upon honde.   *grew interested in pleasures*
And after, thou schalt understonde,
To mete into the kinges halle   *feast*
2520   Thei come, as thei be beden alle: *all had been invited to do*
And whan thei were set and served,
Thanne after, as it was deserved,

	To hem that worthi knyhtes were,	those who
	So as thei seten hiere and there,	
2525	The pris was gove and spoken oute	prize was given; announced
	Among the heraldz al aboute.	
	And thus benethe and ek above	below and above [according to social status]
	Al was of armes and of love,	
	Wherof abouten ate bordes	Whereof in several places
2530	Men hadde manye sondri wordes,	
	That of the merthe which thei made	
	The king himself began to glade	rejoice
	Withinne his herte and tok a pride,	
	And sih the cuppe stonde aside,	saw; standing out of the way
2535	Which mad was of Gurmoundes hed,	
	As ye have herd, whan he was ded,	
	And was with gold and riche stones	
	Beset and bounde for the nones,	
	And stod upon a fot on heihte	
2540	Of burned gold, and with gret sleihte	skill
	Of werkmanschipe it was begrave	engraved
	Of such werk as it scholde have,	
	And was policed ek so clene	polished
	That no signe of the skulle is sene,	
2545	Bot as it were a gripes ey.	[the size of] a griffin's egg
	The king bad bere his cuppe awey,	ordered to be borne away
	Which stod tofore him on the bord,	
	And fette thilke. Upon his word	[ordered] that other one to be fetched
	This skulle is fet and wyn therinne,	brought
2550	Wherof he bad his wif beginne:	
	"Drink with thi fader, Dame," he seide.	
	And sche to his biddinge obeide,	obeyed
	And tok the skulle, and what hire liste	the amount that pleased her
	Sche drank, as sche which nothing wiste	knew
2555	What cuppe it was: and thanne al oute	
	The kyng in audience aboute	
	Hath told it was hire fader skulle,	
	So that the lordes knowe schulle	
	Of his bataille a soth witnesse,	true
2560	And made avant thurgh what prouesse	boast; prowess
	He hath his wyves love wonne,	
	Which of the skulle hath so begonne.	Which with
	Tho was ther mochel Pride alofte,	
	Thei speken alle, and sche was softe,	quiet
2565	Thenkende on thilke unkynde Pride,	Thinking; cruel (disrespectful)
	Of that hire lord so nyh hire side	
	Avanteth him that he hath slain	
	And piked out hire fader brain,	
	And of the skulle had mad a cuppe.	

2570	Sche soffreth al til thei were uppe,	*finished (got up)*
	And tho sche hath seknesse feigned,	*illness*
	And goth to chambre and hath compleigned	
	Unto a maide which sche triste,	*whom she trusted*
	So that non other wyht it wiste.	*person knew it*
2575	This mayde Glodeside is hote,	*called*
	To whom this lady hath behote	*promised*
	Of ladischipe al that sche can,	
	To vengen hire upon this man,	
	Which dede hire drinke in such a plit	*Who made her drink; circumstance*
2580	Among hem alle for despit	
	Of hire and of hire fader bothe;	
	Wherof hire thoghtes ben so wrothe,	*angry*
	Sche seith, that sche schal noght be glad,	
	Til that sche se him so bestad	*situated (beset)*
2585	That he no more make avant.	*[So] that he should boast no more*
	And thus thei felle in covenant,	*agreement*
	That thei acorden ate laste,	
	With suche wiles as thei caste	
	That thei wol gete of here acord	*their*
2590	Som orped knyht to sle this lord:	*valiant*
	And with this sleihte thei beginne,	*deceit*
	How thei Helmege myhten winne,	
	Which was the kinges boteler,	*chief servant in charge of drink*
	A proud, a lusti bacheler,	
2595	And Glodeside he loveth hote.	*passionately*
	And sche, to make him more assote,	*besotted*
	Hire love granteth, and be nyhte	
	Thei schape how thei togedre myhte	
	Abedde meete: and don it was	
2600	This same nyht; and in this cas	
	The qwene hirself the nyht secounde	
	Wente in hire stede, and there hath founde	
	A chambre derk withoute liht,	
	And goth to bedde to this knyht.	
2605	And he, to kepe his observance,	*dutiful worship*
	To love doth his obeissance,	
	And weneth it be Glodeside;	*thinks*
	And sche thanne after lay aside,	
	And axeth him what he hath do,	
2610	And who sche was sche tolde him tho,	*then*
	And seide: "Helmege, I am thi qwene,	
	Now schal thi love wel be sene	
	Of that thou hast thi wille wroght:	
	Or it schal sore ben aboght,	*Either; paid for*
2615	Or thou schalt worche as I thee seie.	*tell you*
	And if thou wolt be such a weie	

Do my plesance and holde it stille,
For evere I schal ben at thi wille,
Bothe I and al myn heritage."
2620 Anon the wylde loves rage,   *passion*
In which no man him can governe,   *can govern himself*
Hath mad him that he can noght werne,   *refuse*
Bot fell al hol to hire assent: *completely*
And thus the whiel is al miswent,   *awry*
2625 The which Fortune hath upon honde;
For how that evere it after stonde,
Thei schope among hem such a wyle,   *deceit*
The king was ded withinne a whyle.
So slihly cam it noght aboute
2630 That thei ne ben descoevered oute,   *But that they were discovered*
So that it thoghte hem for the beste   *it seemed best to them*
To fle, for there was no reste:
And thus the tresor of the king
Thei trusse and mochel other thing,   *load up*
2635 And with a certein felaschipe   *company*
Thei fledde and wente awey be schipe,
And hielde here rihte cours fro thenne,   *their straight*
Til that thei come to Ravenne,
Wher thei the dukes helpe soghte.
2640 And he, so as thei him besoghte,
A place granteth for to duelle;   *dwell*
Bot after, whan he herde telle
Of the manere how thei have do,
This duk let schape for hem so,
2645 That of a puison which thei drunke
Thei hadden that thei have beswunke.   *what they; labored for [i.e., reste, line 2632]*
    And al this made avant of Pride:
Good is therfore a man to hide
His oghne pris, for if he speke,   *praise (fame)*
2650 He mai lihtliche his thonk tobreke.   *easily his reward destroy*
In armes lith non avantance   *lies no advantage*
To him which thenkth his name avance   *who intends*
And be renomed of his dede.
And also who that thenkth to spede   *succeed*
2655 Of love, he mai him noght avaunte;
For what man thilke vice haunte,   *practices*
His pourpos schal ful ofte faile.
In armes he that wol travaile
Or elles loves grace atteigne,
2660 His lose tunge he mot restreigne,   *must*
Which berth of his honour the keie.   *guards (bears the key)*
Confessor Forthi, my sone, in alle weie
Tak riht good hiede of this matiere."

Amans	"I thonke you, my fader diere,	
2665	This scole is of a gentil lore;	
	And if ther be oght elles more	
	Of Pride, which I schal eschuie,	
	Now axeth forth, and I wol suie	*follow (pursue)*
	What thing that ye me wole enforme."	
Confessor	"Mi sone, yit in other forme	
	Ther is a vice of Prides lore,	*instruction*
	Which lich an hauk whan he wol sore,	*soar*
	Fleith upon heihte in his delices	*delight*
	After the likynge of his vices,	
2675	And wol no mannes resoun knowe,	
	Til he doun falle and overthrowe.	
	This vice veine gloire is hote,	*is called*
	Wherof, my sone, I thee behote	*promise*
	To trete and speke in such a wise,	
2680	That thou thee myht the betre avise."	*understand*

[VAINGLORY]

x.   *Gloria perpetuos pregnat mundana dolores,*
        Qui tamen est vanus gaudia vana cupit.
    Eius amiciciam, quem gloria tollit inanis,
        Non sine blandiciis planus habebit homo:
    Verbis compositis qui scit strigilare fauellum,
        Scandere sellata iura valebit eques.
    Sic in amore magis qui blanda subornat in ore
        Verba, per hoc brauium quod nequit alter habet.
    Et tamen ornatos cantus variosque paratus
        Letaque corda suis legibus optat amor.[1]

[Confessor]	"The proude vice of veine gloire	
☞	Remembreth noght of purgatoire;	*Thinks not of (see note)*
	Hise worldes joyes ben so grete,	*intense*
	Him thenkth of hevene no beyete:	*Heaven seems no profit to him*
2685	This lives pompe is al his pes.	*peace*
	Yit schal he deie natheles,	
	And therof thenkth he bot a lite,	*little*
	For al his lust is to delite	
	In newe thinges, proude and veine,	
2690	Als ferforth as he mai atteigne.	

---

[1] *Worldly glory engenders continual sorrows, but he who is vain desires vain joys. A plain and simple man will not gain without flattery the friendship of a man whom empty glory has raised up. He who knows how to curry Favel with carefully composed words will succeed in mounting up the saddled laws as a knight. Thus in love, the one who more greatly prepares flattering words in his mouth takes by this the prize that another cannot. And nonetheless elaborate songs and varied adornments and cheerful hearts — these love selects for its laws.*

	I trowe, if that he myhte make	*believe*
	His body newe, he wolde take	
	A newe forme and leve his olde!	
	For what thing that he mai beholde,	
2695	The which to comun us is strange,	*common use*
	Anon his olde guise change	*Soon; ways (fashion)*
	He wole and falle therupon,	
	Lich unto the camelion,	*(see note)*
	Which upon every sondri hewe	
2700	That he beholt he moste newe	*change*
	His colour, and thus unavised	*unwisely*
	Ful ofte time he stant desguised.	*in newfangled clothing*
	Mor jolif than the brid in Maii	*bird in May*
	He makth him evere freissh and gay,	*himself*
2705	And doth al his array desguise,	
☞	So that of him the newe guise	*from him; latest fashion (see note)*
	Of lusti folk alle othre take;	*Of people of pleasure*
	And ek he can carolles make,	*also; compose*
	Rondeal, balade and virelai.	
2710	And with al this, if that he may	
	Of love gete him avantage,	
	Anon he wext of his corage	
	So overglad, that of his ende	
	Him thenkth ther is no deth comende:	*death coming*
2715	For he hath thanne at alle tide	*time*
	Of love such a maner pride,	
	Him thenkth his joie is endeles.	
Confessor	Now schrif thee, sone, in Godes pes,	*confess yourself; peace*
	And of thi love tell me plein	*openly*
2720	If that thi gloire hath be so vein."	
Amans	"Mi fader, as touchinge of al	
	I may noght wel ne noght ne schal	
	Of veine gloire excuse me,	
	That I ne have for love be	
2725	The betre adresced and arraied;	*arranged and adorned*
	And also I have ofte assaied	*attempted*
	Rondeal, balade, and virelai	
	For hire on whom myn herte lai	
	To make, and also for to peinte	*devise; embellish*
2730	Caroles with my wordes qweinte,	*clever*
	To sette my pourpos alofte;	
	And thus I sang hem forth ful ofte	
	In halle and ek in chambre aboute,	
	And made merie among the route,	*company*
2735	Bot yit ne ferde I noght the bet.	*better*
	Thus was my gloire in vein beset	
	Of al the joie that I made;	

	For whanne I wolde with hire glade,	*rejoice*
	And of hire love songes make,	
2740	Sche saide it was noght for hir sake,	
	And liste noght my songes hiere	*wished not; to hear*
	Ne witen what the wordes were.	*Nor to know*
	So for to speke of myn arrai,	*dress*
	Yit couthe I nevere be so gay	
2745	Ne so wel make a songe of love,	
	Wherof I myhte ben above	
	And have encheson to be glad;	*reason*
	Bot rathere I am ofte adrad	*afraid*
	For sorwe that sche seith me nay.	*[may] say no to me*
2750	And natheles I wol noght say,	
	That I nam glad on other side;	*am not*
	For fame, that can nothing hide,	
	Alday wol bringe unto myn ere	*ear*
	Of that men speken hier and there,	
2755	How that my ladi berth the pris,	*bears the prize*
	How sche is fair, how sche is wis,	
	How sche is wommanlich of chiere;	*countenance*
	Of al this thing whanne I mai hiere,	
	What wonder is thogh I be fain?	*glad*
2760	And ek whanne I may hiere sain	*said*
	Tidinges of my ladi hele,	*News of my lady's health*
	Althogh I may noght with hir dele,	*associate*
	Yit am I wonder glad of that;	
	For whanne I wot hire good astat,	
2765	As for that time I dar wel swere,	
	Non other sorwe mai me dere,	*harm*
	Thus am I gladed in this wise.	
	Bot, fader, of youre lores wise,	*[drawing] from your wise teachings*
	Of whiche ye be fully tawht,	
2770	Now tell me if yow thenketh awht	*if anything occurs to you*
	That I therof am for to wyte."	*to blame*
Confessor	"Of that ther is I thee acquite,	
	Mi sone, he seide, and for thi goode	
	I wolde that thou understode:	*should ponder [this]*
2775	For I thenke upon this matiere	
	To telle a tale, as thou schalt hiere,	
	How that agein this proude vice	
	The hihe God of his justice	
	Is wroth and gret vengance doth.	
2780	Now herkne a tale that is soth:	*true*
	Thogh it be noght of loves kinde,	
	A gret ensample thou schalt finde	*love's nature*
	This veine gloire for to fle,	
	Which is so full of vanité."	

[NEBUCHADNEZZAR'S PUNISHMENT]

xi. *Humani generis cum sit sibi gloria maior,*
  Sepe subesse solet proximus ille dolor:
 Mens elata graues descensus sepe subibit,
  Mens humilis stabile molleque firmat iter.
 Motibus innumeris volutat fortuna per orbem;
  Cum magis alta petis, inferiora time.[1]

[Confessor]	"Ther was a king that mochel myhte,	*could wield great power*
	Which Nabugodonosor hihte,	*was called*
	Of whom that I spak hier tofore.	
☞	Yit in the Bible his name is bore,	*Even; fame is upheld (see note)*
	For al the world in orient	
2790	Was hol at his comandement:	*completely*
	As thanne of kinges to his liche	*compared to him*
	Was non so myhty ne so riche;	
	To his empire and to his lawes,	
	As who seith, alle in thilke dawes	*So to speak; those days*
2795	Were obeissant and tribut bere,	*paid*
	As thogh he godd of erthe were.	
	With strengthe he putte kinges under,	*subdued empires*
	And wroghte of Pride many a wonder;	
	He was so full of veine gloire,	
2800	That he ne hadde no memoire	
	That ther was eny good bot he,	*except himself*
	For pride of his prosperité;	
	Til that the hihe king of kinges,	*high*
	Which seth and knoweth alle thinges,	*sees*
2805	Whos yhe mai nothing asterte —	*eye; escape*
	The privetés of mannes herte	*secrets*
	Thei speke and sounen in his ere	*resound; ear*
	As thogh thei lowde wyndes were —	
	He tok vengance upon this pride.	
2810	Bot for He wolde awhile abide	
	To loke if he him wolde amende,	
	To him a foretokne He sende,	*warning*
	And that was in his slep be nyhte.	
	This proude kyng a wonder syhte	
2815	Hadde in his swevene, ther he lay:	*dream*
	Him thoghte, upon a merie day	

---

[1] *Even when the human race possesses a greater glory, sorrow often is likely to lie very near by. An exalted spirit will often drop down dangerous descents; a humble spirit establishes a reliable and gentle path. Fortune turns with innumerable movements through the world-wheel; when you seek the greater heights, fear the places that are all the lower.*

	As he behield the world aboute,	
	A tree fulgrowe he syh theroute,	
	Which stod the world amiddes evene,	*directly in the center*
2820	Whos heihte straghte up to the hevene;	*stretched up*
	The leves weren faire and large,	
	Of fruit it bar so ripe a charge,	*crop*
	That alle men it myhte fede:	
	He sih also the bowes spriede	
2825	Above al erthe, in whiche were	
	The kinde of alle briddes there;	*birds*
	And ek him thoghte he syh also	
	The kinde of alle bestes go	
	Under this tree aboute round	
2830	And fedden hem upon the ground.	
	As he this wonder stod and syh,	
	Him thoghte he herde a vois on hih	*up high*
	Criende, and seide aboven alle:	*louder than*
	"Hew doun this tree and lett it falle,	
2835	The leves let defoule in haste	
	And do the fruit destruie and waste,	
	And let of schreden every braunche,	*allow every branch to be hacked off*
	Bot ate rote let it staunche.	*root; be left intact*
	Whan al his Pride is cast to grounde,	
2840	The rote schal be faste bounde,	
	And schal no mannes herte bere,	
	Bot every lust he schal forbere	*relinquish*
	Of man, and lich an oxe his mete	*food*
	Of gras he schal pourchace and ete,	*gather and eat*
2845	Til that the water of the hevene	
	Have waisshen him be times sevene,	
	So that he be thurghknowe ariht	*be made to know absolutely correctly*
	What is the heveneliche myht,	
	And be mad humble to the wille	
2850	Of Him which al mai save and spille."	*destroy*
	This king out of his swefne abreide,	*dream awoke*
	And he upon the morwe it seide	*told*
	Unto the clerkes whiche he hadde:	*scholars*
	Bot non of hem the sothe aradde,	*truth interpreted*
2855	Was non his swevene cowthe undo.	*dream knew how to explicate*
	And it stod thilke time so,	*it happened at that time*
	This king hadde in subjeccioun	
	Judee, and of affeccioun	*Judea; friendship*
	Above alle othre on Daniel	
2860	He loveth, for he cowthe wel	*knew well how*
	Divine that non other cowthe:	*To elucidate as no others knew how to*
	To him were alle thinges cowthe,	*known*
	As he it hadde of Goddes grace.	*Since he it (understanding) had by*

He was before the kinges face
2865   Asent, and bode that he scholde   *Sent for; commanded*
Upon the point the king of tolde   *Upon matter the king would speak of*
The fortune of his swevene expounde,   *future destiny in his dream expound*
As it scholde afterward be founde.
Whan Daniel this swevene herde,
2870   He stod long time er he ansuerde,
And made a wonder hevy chiere.   *an extraordinarily dire expression*
The king tok hiede of his manere,
And bad him telle that he wiste,   *what he knew*
As he to whom he mochel triste,   *As if to someone he greatly trusted*
2875   And seide he wolde noght be wroth.   *angry*
Bot Daniel was wonder loth,   *reluctant [to reply]*
And seide: "Upon thi fomen alle,   *all your enemies*
Sire king, thi swevene mote falle;   *[if only] your dream would befall*
And natheles touchende of this   *But*
2880   I wol thee tellen how it is,   *how it is [for you]*
And what desese is to thee schape: *discomfort is fashioned for you*
God wot if thou it schalt ascape.
   The hihe tree, which thou hast sein
With lef and fruit so wel besein,   *furnished*
2885   The which stod in the world amiddes,
So that the bestes and the briddes
Governed were of him alone,
Sire king, betokneth thi persone,   *signifies*
Which stant above all erthli thinges.
2890   Thus regnen under thee the kinges,   *under you the [other] kings*
And al the poeple unto thee louteth,   *bow*
And al the world thi pouer doubteth,   *fears*
So that with vein honour deceived   *empty honor*
Thou hast the reverence weyved   *dismissed*
2895   Fro Him which is thi king above,
That thou for drede ne for love   *for neither fear nor*
Wolt nothing knowen of thi Godd,
Which now for thee hath mad a rodd   *made a [chastening] rod*
Thi veine gloire and thi folie
2900   With grete peines to chastie.   *pains to chastise*
And of the vois thou herdest speke,
Which bad the bowes for to breke   *boughs to be broken*
And hewe and felle doun the tree,
That word belongeth unto thee:
2905   Thi regne schal ben overthrowe,
And thou despuiled for a throwe,   *despoiled for a time*
Bot that the rote scholde stonde.   *Except that the root*
Be that thou schalt wel understonde,   *By*
Ther schal abyden of thi regne
2910   A time agein whan thou schalt regne.

	And ek of that thou herdest seie —	*heard said*
	To take a mannes herte aweie	*[Namely]*
	And sette there a bestial,	*bestial [heart]*
	So that he lich an oxe schal	
2915	Pasture, and that he be bereined	*Feed; rained upon*
	Be times sefne and sore peined,	*For seven times; sorely afflicted*
	Til that he knowe his Goddes mihtes,	
	Than scholde he stonde agein uprihtes —	
	Al this betokneth thin astat,	*condition*
2920	Which now with God is in debat:	*in conflict*
	Thi mannes forme schal be lassed,	*human shape shall be diminished*
	Til sevene yer ben overpassed,	
	And in the liknesse of a beste	*beast*
	Of gras schal be thi real feste.	*royal feast*
2925	The weder schal upon thee reine,	*weather; rain*
	And understond that al this peine,	
	Which thou schalt soffre thilke tide,	
	Is schape al only for thi pride	*fashioned entirely*
	Of veine gloire, and of the sinne,	
2930	Which thou hast longe stonden inne.	
	So upon this condicioun	
	Thi swevene hath exposicioun.	
	Bot er this thing befalle in dede,	*before; should occur indeed*
	Amende thee, this wolde I rede:	*Change your ways; advise*
2935	Gif and departe thin almesse,	*Give and distribute; alms*
	Do mercy forth with rihtwisnesse,	*along with righteousness*
	Besech and prei the hihe grace,	*high*
	For so thou myht thi pes pourchace	*obtain*
	With Godd, and stonde in good acord."	
2940	Bot Pride is loth to leve his lord,	
	And wol noght soffre humilité	
	With him to stonde in no degree;	
	And whan a schip hath lost his stiere,	*rudder*
	Is non so wys that mai him stiere	*guide*
2945	Agein the wawes in a rage.	*waves*
	This proude king in his corage	*heart*
	Humilité hath so forlore,	*completely lost*
	That, for no swevene he sih tofore,	*dream he saw beforehand*
	Ne yit for al that Daniel	
2950	Him hath conseiled everydel,	*had instructed him in every point*
	He let it passe out of his mynde,	
	Thurgh veine gloire, and as the blinde,	
	He seth no weie, er him be wo.	*before he have disaster*
	And fell withinne a time so,	*[it] befell*
2955	As he in Babiloine wente,	
	The vanité of Pride him hente;	*seized*
	His herte aros of veine gloire,	

	So that he drowh into memoire	
	His lordschipe and his regalie	
2960	With wordes of Surquiderie.	*presumption*
	And whan that he him most avaunteth,	*most boasts of himself*
	That lord which veine gloire daunteth,	*whom; conquers*
	Al sodeinliche, as who seith treis,	*quick as one, two, three*
	Wher that he stod in his paleis,	*palace*
2965	He tok him fro the mennes sihte.	*withdrew himself*
	Was non of hem so war that mihte	*none of them so shrewd who might*
	Sette yhe wher that he becom.	*eye*
	And thus was he from his kingdom	
	Into the wilde forest drawe,	*drawn (taken)*
2970	Wher that the myhti Goddes lawe	
	Thurgh His pouer dede him transforme	*caused him to change*
	Fro man into a bestes forme;	
	And lich an oxe under the fot	
	He graseth, as he nedes mot,	*grazes; must*
2975	To geten him his lives fode.	
	Tho thoghte him colde grases goode,	*Then seemed to him*
	That whilom eet the hote spices.	*[He] who once ate*
	Thus was he torned fro delices:	*delights*
	The wyn which he was wont to drinke	
2980	He tok thanne of the welles brinke	
	Or of the pet or of the slowh,	*Either; pit; slough*
	It thoghte him thanne good ynowh.	*enough*
	In stede of chambres wel arraied	
	He was thanne of a buissh wel paied,	*bush well pleased*
2985	The harde ground he lay upon,	
	For othre pilwes hath he non;	
	The stormes and the reines falle,	
	The wyndes blowe upon him alle,	
	He was tormented day and nyht,	
2990	Such was the hihe Goddes myht,	
	Til sevene yer an ende toke.	*came to an end*
	Upon himself tho gan he loke;	
	In stede of mete, gras, and stres,	*prepared food; straw*
	In stede of handes, longe cles,	*claws*
2995	In stede of man a bestes lyke	*beast's likeness*
	He syh; and thanne he gan to syke	*saw; sigh*
	For cloth of gold and for perrie,	*precious stones (OF pierre, "stone")*
	Which him was wont to magnefie.	
	Whan he behield his cote of heres,	*coat of hair*
3000	He wepte and with ful woful teres	*tears*
	Up to the hevene he caste his chiere	*countenance*
	Wepende, and thoghte in this manere;	
	Thogh he no wordes myhte winne,	*convey*
	Thus seide his herte and spak withinne:	

3005   "O mihti Godd, that al hast wroght   *created*
      And al myht bringe agein to noght,
      Now knowe I wel, bot al of Thee,   *except for You alone*
      This world hath no prosperité:
      In Thin aspect ben alle liche,   *all are the same*
3010   The povere man and ek the riche;   *also*
      Withoute Thee ther mai no wight,   *creature [be]*
      And Thou above alle othre miht.   *have power*
      O mihti lord, toward my vice
      Thi merci medle with justice;   *mingle*
3015   And I woll make a covenant,
      That of my lif the remenant   *remaining days*
      I schal it be Thi grace amende,   *by Your*
      And in Thi lawe so despende   *proceed*
      That veine gloire I schal eschuie,   *avoid*
3020   And bowe unto thin heste and suie   *command; follow*
      Humilité, and that I vowe."
      And so thenkende he gan doun bowe,
      And thogh him lacke vois and speche,
      He gan up with his feet areche,   *began upward; reach up*
3025   And wailende in his bestly stevene   *voice*
      He made his pleignte unto the hevene.
      He kneleth in his wise and braieth,   *manner and brays*
      To seche merci and assaieth   *appeals to*
      His God, which made him nothing strange,   *who did not ignore him*
3030   Whan that he sih his pride change.
      Anon as he was humble and tame,
      He fond toward his God the same,
      And in a twinklinge of a lok
      His mannes forme agein he tok,
3035   And was reformed to the regne   *restored; dominion*
      In which that he was wont to regne;   *reign*
      So that the Pride of veine gloire
      Evere afterward out of memoire
      He let it passe. And thus is schewed
3040   What is to ben of Pride unthewed   *uncivilized*
      Agein the hihe Goddes lawe,
      To whom no man mai be felawe.
Confessor   Forthi, my sone, tak good hiede
      So for to lede thi manhiede,   *govern*
3045   That thou ne be noght lich a beste.
      Bot if thi lif schal ben honeste,   *honorable*
      Thou most humblesce take on honde,
      For thanne myht thou siker stonde.   *securely*
      And for to speke it otherwise,
3050   A proud man can no love assise;   *satisfy*
      For thogh a womman wolde him plese,

His Pride can noght ben at ese.
   Ther mai no man to mochel blame
A vice which is for to blame;   *blameworthy*
3055   Forthi men scholde nothing hide
That mihte falle in blame of Pride,
Which is the werste vice of alle: *worst*
Wherof, so as it was befalle,
The tale I thenke of a cronique
3060   To telle, if that it mai thee like,
So that thou myht humblesce suie   *follow*
And ek the vice of Pride eschuie,
Wherof the gloire is fals and vein;
Which God Himself hath in desdeign,
3065   That thogh it mounte for a throwe,   *time*
It schal doun falle and overthrowe."

[HUMILITY AND THE TALE OF THREE QUESTIONS]

xii.   *Est virtus humilis, per quam deus altus ad yma*
      Se tulit et nostre viscera carnis habet.
    Sic humilis superest, et amor sibi subditur omnis,
      Cuius habet nulla sorte superbus opem:
    Odit eum terra, celum deiecit et ipsum,
      Sedibus inferni statque receptus ibi.[1]

[Confessor] "A king whilom was yong and wys,
☞   The which sette of his wit gret pris.   *value (see note)*
Of depe ymaginaciouns
3070   And strange interpretaciouns,
Problemes and demandes eke,   *questions also*
His wisdom was to finde and seke;
Wherof he wolde in sondri wise
Opposen hem that weren wise.   *Question those who were learned*
3075   Bot non of hem it myhte bere   *accomplish*
Upon his word to geve answere,   *To his statement; give*
Outaken on, which was a knyht.   *Except one*
To him was every thing so liht,   *easy*
That also sone as he hem herde,
3080   The kinges wordes he answerde;
What thing the king him axe wolde,
Therof anon the trowthe he tolde.
The king somdiel hadde an envie,   *became somewhat envious*

---

[1] *It is a humble power by which high God carried himself to the depths, and possessed the bowels of our flesh. Thus the humble is exalted, and love subdues all to itself, whose power the proud by no chance possesses. The earth hates the proud, even heaven itself expels him, and he remains in the regions of hell where he has been received.*

	And thoghte he wolde his wittes plie	*apply*
3085	To sette som conclusioun,	*proposition*
	Which scholde be confusioun	*humiliation*
	Unto this knyht, so that the name	
	And of wisdom the hihe fame	
	Toward himself he wolde winne.	
3090	And thus of al his wit withinne	
	This king began to studie and muse,	
	What strange matiere he myhte use	
	The knyhtes wittes to confounde;	
	And ate laste he hath it founde,	
3095	And for the knyht anon he sente,	
	That he schal telle what he mente.	*[So] that*
	Upon thre pointz stod the matiere	
	Of questions, as thou schalt hiere.	
	The ferste point of alle thre	
3100	Was this: "What thing in his degré	*its*
	Of al this world hath nede lest,	*least need [of help]*
	And yet men helpe it althermest?"	*most of all*
	The secounde is: "What most is worth,	*worth most*
	And of costage is lest put forth?"	*expense; least of all*
3105	The thridde is: "Which is of most cost,	*greatest cost*
	And lest is worth and goth to lost?"	*of least value; goes to ruin*
	The king thes thre demandes axeth,	*questions asks*
	And to the knyht this lawe he taxeth,	*prescribed duty he imposes*
	That he schal gon and come agein	
3110	The thridde weke, and telle him plein	*third week*
	To every point, what it amonteth.	*means*
	And if so be that he misconteth,	*misconstrues*
	To make in his answere a faile,	*And fails in his answer*
	Ther schal non other thing availe,	
3115	The king seith, bot he schal be ded	*executed*
	And lese hise goodes and his hed.	*lose; head*
	The knyht was sori of this thing	
	And wolde excuse him to the king,	*himself*
	Bot he ne wolde him noght forbere,	*reprieve*
3120	And thus the knyht of his ansuere	
	Goth hom to take avisement:	*think it over*
	Bot after his entendement	*purpose*
	The more he caste his wit aboute,	
	The more he stant therof in doute.	
3125	Tho wiste he wel the kinges herte,	*Then knew*
	That he the deth ne scholde asterte,	*should not escape*
	And such a sorwe hath to him take,	
	That gladschipe he hath al forsake.	
	He thoghte ferst upon his lif,	
3130	And after that upon his wif,	

Upon his children ek also,
Of whiche he hadde dowhtres tuo;
The yongest of hem hadde of age   *them*
Fóurtiene yer, and of visage
3135   Sche was riht fair, and of stature
Lich to an hevenely figure,
And of manere and goodli speche,
Thogh men wolde alle londes seche,   *might seek throughout the world*
Thei scholden noght have founde hir like.   *one who could compare to her*
3140   Sche sih hire fader sorwe and sike,   *saw; sigh*
And wiste noght the cause why;   *knew*
So cam sche to him prively,   *secretly*
And that was where he made his mone   *lament*
Withinne a gardin al him one;   *all by himself*
3145   Upon hire knes sche gan doun falle
With humble herte and to him calle,
And seide: "O goode fader diere,
Why make ye thus hevy chiere,   *mourning*
And I wot nothing how it is?
3150   And wel ye knowen, fader, this,
What aventure that you felle   *chance event*
Ye myhte it saufly to me telle,
For I have ofte herd you seid,
That ye such trust have on me leid,   *placed*
3155   That to my soster ne my brother,
In al this world ne to non other,
Ye dorste telle a privité   *private confidence*
So wel, my fader, as to me.
Forthi, my fader, I you preie,
3160   Ne casteth noght that herte aweie,   *love and trust away*
For I am sche that wolde kepe
Youre honour." And with that to wepe
Hire yhe mai noght be forbore,   *eyes; restrained*
Sche wissheth for to ben unbore,   *unborn*
3165   Er that hire fader so mistriste   *mistrust*
To tellen hire of that he wiste: *knew*
And evere among merci sche cride,   *again and again*
That he ne scholde his conseil hide
From hire that so wolde him good   *desired good for him*
3170   And was so nyh his fleissh and blod.   *near*
So that with wepinge ate laste
His chiere upon his child he caste,
And sorwfulli to that sche preide
He tolde his tale and thus he seide:
3175   "The sorwe, dowhter, which I make
Is noght al only for my sake,
Bot for thee bothe and for you alle:

For such a chance is me befalle,
That I schal er this thridde day

3180   Lese al that evere I lese may,   *Lose*
Mi lif and al my good therto:
Therfore it is I sorwe so."
"What is the cause, helas!" quod sche,
"Mi fader, that ye scholden be

3185   Ded and destruid in such a wise?"
And he began the pointz devise,
Whiche as the king told him be mowthe,   *by mouth*
And seid hir pleinly that he cowthe   *told her; could*
Ansuere unto no point of this.

3190   And sche, that hiereth how it is,
Hire conseil gaf and seide tho: *gave; then*
"Mi fader, sithen it is so,
That ye can se non other weie,
Bot that ye moste nedes deie,   *Except*

3195   I wolde preie of you a thing:
Let me go with you to the king,
And ye schull make him understonde
How ye, my wittes for to fonde,   *in order to test (discover)*
Have leid your ansuere upon me;

3200   And telleth him, in such degré
Upon my word ye wole abide   *You will abide by my word*
To lif or deth, what so betide.
For yit par chaunce I may pourchace   *yet perchance; obtain*
With som good word the kinges grace,

3205   Your lif and ek your good to save.
For ofte schal a womman have
Thing which a man mai noght areche."   *attain*
The fader herde his dowhter speche,   *daughter's*
And thoghte ther was resoun inne,

3210   And sih his oghne lif to winne   *saw [that]; gain*
He cowthe don himself no cure;
So betre him thoghte in aventure   *in a gamble*
To put his lif and al his good,
Than in the maner as it stod

3215   His lif in certein for to lese.   *lose*
And thus thenkende he gan to chese
To do the conseil of this maide,
And tok the pourpos which sche saide.
    The dai was come and forth thei gon,

3220   Unto the court thei come anon,
Wher as the king in juggement
Was set and hath this knyht assent.   *sent for*
Arraied in hire beste wise
This maiden with hire wordes wise

3225 Hire fader ladde be the hond
Into the place, wher he fond
The king with othre whiche he wolde, *others whom he wanted*
And to the king knelende he tolde
As he enformed was tofore,
3230 And preith the king that he therfore
His dowhtres wordes wolde take,
And seith that he wol undertake
Upon hire wordes for to stonde.
Tho was ther gret merveile on honde,
3235 That he, which was so wys a knyht,
His lif upon so yong a wyht *creature*
Besette wolde in jeupartie, *jeopardy*
And manye it hielden for folie:
Bot ate laste natheles
3240 The king comandeth ben in pes,
And to this maide he caste his chiere,
And seide he wolde hire tale hiere, *response hear*
He bad hire speke, and sche began:
"Mi liege lord, so as I can,"
3245 Quod sche, "the pointz of whiche I herde,
Thei schul of reson ben ansuerde. *shall be answered reasonably*
    The ferste I understonde is this,
What thing of al the world it is,
Which men most helpe and hath lest nede.
3250 Mi liege lord, this wolde I rede: *declare*
The erthe it is, which everemo
With mannes labour is bego; *worked upon*
Als wel in wynter as in Maii
The mannes hond doth what he mai
3255 To helpe it forth and make it riche,
And forthi men it delve and dyche *dig*
And eren it with strengthe of plowh, *cultivate; plow*
Wher it hath of himself ynowh, *itself*
So that his nede is ate leste. *its need [of him] is least of all*
3260 For every man and bridd and beste,
And flour and gras and rote and rinde, *root and bark*
And every thing be weie of kynde *nature*
Schal sterve, and erthe it schal become; *earth; die*
As it was out of erthe nome, *taken*
3265 It schal to th'erthe torne agein:
And thus I mai be resoun sein *say*
That erthe is the most nedeles, *without need*
And most men helpe it natheles.
So that, my lord, touchende of this
3270 I have ansuerd hou that it is.

That other point I understod,   *second point*
Which most is worth and most is good,
And costeth lest a man to kepe:
Mi lord, if ye woll take kepe,   *take heed*
3275   I seie it is humilité,
Thurgh which the hihe Trinité
As for decerte of pure love   *meritoriousness*
Unto Marie from above,
Of that He knew hire humble entente,   *From [the fact] that*
3280   His oghne sone adoun He sente,
Above alle othre and hire He ches   *chose*
For that vertu which bodeth pes.   *signifies peace*
So that I may be resoun calle   *by*
Humilité most worth of alle.
3285   And lest it costeth to maintiene,   *least*
In al the world as it is sene;
For who that hath humblesce on honde,   *humility*
He bringth no werres into londe,   *strife*
For he desireth for the beste
3290   To setten every man in reste.
Thus with your hihe reverence
Me thenketh that this evidence   *It seems to me*
As to this point is sufficant.
   And touchende of the remenant,
3295   Which is the thridde of youre axinges,   *questions*
What leste is worth of alle thinges,   *least*
And costeth most, I telle it, Pride;
Which mai noght in the hevene abide,
For Lucifer with hem that felle   *those who fell*
3300   Bar Pride with him into helle.   *Bore*
Ther was Pride of to gret a cost,
Whan he for Pride hath hevene lost;
And after that in paradis
Adam for Pride loste his pris: *prize*
3305   In midelerthe and ek also
Pride is the cause of alle wo,
That al the world ne mai suffise
To stanche of Pride the reprise: *To pay the cost of Pride*
Pride is the heved of alle sinne,   *head*
3310   Which wasteth al and mai noght winne;
Pride is of every mis the pricke,   *of every wrong the sting*
Pride is the werste of alle wicke,   *wickedness*
And costneth most and lest is worth
In place where he hath his forth.   *course*
3315   Thus have I seid that I wol seie
Of myn answere, and to you preie,
Mi liege lord, of youre office

That ye such grace and such justice
Ordeigne for mi fader hiere,
3320   That after this, whan men it hiere,
The world therof mai speke good."
    The king, which reson understod
And hath al herd how sche hath said,
Was inly glad and so wel paid   *pleased*
3325   That al his wraththe is overgo:
And he began to loke tho
Upon this maiden in the face,
In which he fond so mochel grace,
That al his pris on hire he leide,   *reward (praise); laid*
3330   In audience and thus he seide:
"Mi faire maide, wel thee be!
Of thin ansuere and ek of thee
Me liketh wel, and as thou wilt,
Forgive be thi fader gilt.
3335   And if thou were of such lignage,   *lineage*
That thou to me were of parage,   *equal rank*
And that thi fader were a pier,   *peer*
As he is now a bachilier,   *commoner*
So seker as I have a lif,   *As certainly as*
3340   Thou scholdest thanne be my wif.   *would in that case*
Bot this I seie natheles,
That I wol schape thin encress;   *fashion your prosperity*
What worldes good that thou wolt crave,
Axe of my gifte and thou schalt have."   *Ask from my gift*
3345   And sche the king with wordes wise
Knelende thonketh in this wise:
"Mi liege lord, God mot you quite!   *may God requite you*
Mi fader hier hath bot a lite
Of warison, and that he wende   *property; thought*
3350   Hadde al be lost; bot now amende
He mai wel thurgh your noble grace."
With that the king riht in his place
Anon forth in that freisshe hete   *fresh passion*
An erldom, which thanne of eschete   *escheat (forfeiture)*
3355   Was late falle into his hond,
Unto this knyht with rente and lond
Hath gove and with his chartre sesed;   *given; endowed*
And thus was al the noise appesed.   *quarrel reconciled*
    This maiden, which sat on hire knes
3360   Tofore the king, hise charitees   *Before*
Comendeth, and seide overmore: *moreover*
"Mi liege lord, riht now tofore
Ye seide, as it is of record,
That if my fader were a lord

3365	And pier unto these othre grete,	*great men*
	Ye wolden for noght elles lete	*prevent*
	That I ne scholde be your wif;	*But that I should be*
	And this wot every worthi lif,	
	A kinges word it mot ben holde.	*must*
3370	Forthi, my lord, if that ye wolde	
	So gret a charité fulfille,	
	God wot it were wel my wille.	*knows; desire*
	For he which was a bacheler,	
	Mi fader, is now mad a pier;	
3375	So whenne as evere that I cam,	*however I arrived formerly*
	An erles dowhter now I am."	*nobleman's*
	This yonge king, which peised al,	*weighed (assessed)*
	Hire beauté and hir wit withal,	
	As he that was with love hent,	*seized*
3380	Anon therto gaf his assent.	
	He myhte noght the maide asterte,	*escape [the cleverness of] the maiden*
	That sche nis ladi of his herte;	*[Such] that she is not*
	So that he tok hire to his wif,	
	To holde whyl that he hath lif:	
3385	And thus the king toward his knyht	
	Acordeth him, as it is riht.	
	And over this good is to wite,	*moreover it is good to know*
	In the cronique as it is write,	
	This noble king of whom I tolde	
3390	Of Spaine be tho daies olde	
	The kingdom hadde in governance,	
	And as the bok makth remembrance,	
	Alphonse was his propre name:	
	The knyht also, if I schal name,	
3395	Danz Petro hihte, and as men telle,	*was called*
	His dowhter wyse Peronelle	
	Was cleped, which was full of grace:	*Was called, who*
	And that was sene in thilke place,	
	Wher sche hir fader out of teene	*sorrow*
3400	Hath broght and mad hirself a qweene,	
	Of that sche hath so wel desclosed	
	The pointz wherof sche was opposed.	*questioned*
Confessor	"Lo now, my sone, as thou myht hiere,	
	Of al this thing to my matiere	*for my concern*
3405	Bot on I take, and that is Pride,	*Only one*
	To whom no grace mai betide:	*await*
	In hevene he fell out of his stede,	*place*
	And paradis him was forbede,	*forbidden*
	The goode men in erthe him hate,	
3410	So that to helle he mot algate,	*must assuredly go*
	Where every vertu schal be weyved	*rejected*

And every vice be received.
Bot Humblesce is al otherwise,
Which most is worth, and no reprise   *financial charge*
3415 It takth agein, bot softe and faire,   *takes back; quiet*
If eny thing stond in contraire,
With humble speche it is redresced.
Thus was this yonge maiden blessed,
The which I spak of now tofore.
3420 Hire fader lif sche gat therfore,
And wan with al the kinges love.
Forthi, my sone, if thou wolt love,
It sit thee wel to leve Pride   *leave*
And take Humblesce upon thi side;
3425 The more of grace thou schalt gete."
Amans "Mi fader, I woll noght forgete
Of this that ye have told me hiere,
And if that eny such manere
Of humble port mai love appaie,   *satisfy*
3430 Hierafterward I thenke assaie: *plan to try*
Bot now forth over I beseche
That ye more of my schrifte seche."   *confession*
Confessor "Mi goode sone, it schal be do: *done*
Now herkne and ley an ere to;
3435 For as touchende of Prides fare,
Als ferforth as I can declare
In cause of vice, in cause of love,
That hast thou pleinly herd above,
So that ther is no mor to seie
3440 Touchende of that; bot other weie
Touchende Envie I thenke telle,
Which hath the propre kinde of helle: *characteristic nature*
Withoute cause to misdo
Toward himself and othre also,
3445 Hierafterward as understonde   *As hereafter; recognize*
Thou schalt the spieces, as thei stonde."   *categories*

EXPLICIT LIBER PRIMUS

CONFESSIO AMANTIS: BOOK 8 (LECHERY)

INCIPIT LIBER OCTAVUS

i	*Qve fauet ad vicium vetus hec modo regula confert,*	*(see note)*
	Nec nouus econtra qui docet ordo placet.	
	Cecus amor dudum nondum sua lumina cepit,	
	Quo Venus impositum deuia fallit iter.[1]	*(see note)*

[ON MARRIAGE AND INCEST]

[Confessor]	"The myhti God, which unbegunne	*who without beginning*
	Stant of Himself and hath begunne	
☞	Alle othre thinges at His wille,	*(see note)*
	The hevene Him liste to fulfille	*it pleases Him; fill completely*
5	Of alle joie, where as He	*With*
	Sit inthronized in His see,	*throne (seat)*
	And hath Hise angles Him to serve,	*angels*
	Suche as Him liketh to preserve,	*it pleases Him*
	So that thei mowe noght forsueie:	*might not go astray*
10	Bot Lucifer He putte aweie,	
	With al the route apostazied	*mob*
	Of hem that ben to him allied,	*those who*
	Whiche out of hevene into the helle	
	From angles into fendes felle;	
15	Wher that ther is no joie of lyht,	
	Bot more derk than eny nyht	
	The peine schal ben endeles;	
	And yit of fyres natheles	*fires*
	Ther is plenté, bot thei ben blake,	
20	Wherof no syhte mai be take.	
	Thus whan the thinges ben befalle,	
	That Luciferes court was falle	
	Wher dedly Pride hem hath conveied,	
	Anon forthwith it was pourveied	*it [hell] was established*

---

[1] *This rule that favors the old vice is useful at the present time, nor does the new order please which teaches contrarily to that. Love long blind has not yet received its eyes, wherefore devious Venus warps with deception the affixed path.*

25   Thurgh Him which alle thinges may;   *who has power [to do] all things*
      He made Adam the sexte day
      In Paradis, and to his make   *as his mate*
      Him liketh Eve also to make,
      And bad hem cresce and multiplie.   *them increase*
30   For of the mannes progenie,
      Which of the womman schal be bore,
      The nombre of angles which was lore,   *was lost*
      Whan thei out fro the blisse felle,
      He thoghte to restore, and felle   *and to fill*
35   In hevene thilke holy place
      Which stod tho voide upon His grace.   *stood then empty*
      Bot as it is wel wiste and knowe,   *known; known*
      Adam and Eve bot a throwe,   *a moment*
      So as it scholde of hem betyde,   *Just as it had for them come to pass*
40   In Paradis at thilke tyde   *that time*
      Ne duelten, and the cause why,   *Dwelt not [but a moment]*
      Write in the bok of Genesi,
      As who seith, alle men have herd,   *So to speak*
      Hou Raphael the fyri swerd
45   In honde tok and drof hem oute,
      To gete here lyves fode aboute   *get their*
      Upon this wofull erthe hiere.
      Metodre seith to this matiere,   *Methodius*
      As he be revelacion
50   It hadde upon avision,   *by visionary experience*
      Hou that Adam and Eve also
      Virgines comen bothe tuo
      Into the world and were aschamed,
      Til that nature hem hath reclamed   *recalled*
55   To love, and tauht hem thilke lore,   *taught them this wisdom*
      That ferst thei keste, and overmore   *[So] that; kissed; thereafter*
      Thei don that is to kinde due,   *nature*
      Wherof thei hadden fair issue.
      A sone was the ferste of alle,
60   And Chain be name thei him calle;   *Cain by name*
      Abel was after the secounde,
      And in the geste as it is founde,   *story*
      Nature so the cause ladde,
      Tuo douhtres ek Dame Eve hadde,
65   The ferste cleped Calmana
      Was, and that other Delbora.
      Thus was mankinde to beginne;
      Forthi that time it was no sinne
      The soster for to take hire brother,
70   Whan that ther was of chois non other:
      To Chain was Calmana betake,   *Cain*

	And Delboram hath Abel take,	
	In whom was gete natheles	
	Of worldes folk the ferste encres.	*increase*
75	Men sein that nede hath no lawe,	*necessity has no law*
	And so it was be thilke dawe	*in that day*
	And laste into the Secounde Age,	
	Til that the grete water rage,	*storm*
	Of Noe, which was seid the flod,	*Noah; called the flood*
80	The world, which thanne in senne stod,	*sin*
	Hath dreint, outake lyves eyhte.	*drowned except for; eight*
	Tho was mankinde of litel weyhte;	*little force (quantity, importance)*
	Sem, Cham, Japhet, of these thre,	
	That ben the sones of Noe,	
85	The world of mannes nacion	
	Into multiplicacion	
	Was tho restored newe agein	
	So ferforth, as the bokes sein,	*To such a degree*
	That of hem thre and here issue	*those three; their*
90	Ther was so large a retenue,	
	Of naciouns seventy and tuo,	
	In sondri place ech on of tho	*[That] in; each one of those*
	The wyde world have enhabited.	
	Bot as nature hem hath excited,	
95	Thei token thanne litel hiede,	*took; heed*
	The brother of the sosterhiede	*from among*
	To wedde wyves, til it cam	
	Into the time of Habraham.	*Abraham*
	Whan the thridde Age was begunne,	
100	The nede tho was overrunne,	*necessity then was past*
	For ther was poeple ynouh in londe.	*enough*
	Thanne ate ferste it cam to honde,	
	That sosterhode of mariage	*circumstance of marrying sisters*
	Was torned into cousinage,	*marrying blood-relatives*
105	So that after the rihte lyne	
	The cousin weddeth the cousine.	*male relative; female relative*
	For Habraham, er that he deide,	*before he died*
	This charge upon his servant leide,	*duty; laid (placed)*
	To him and in this wise spak,	
110	That he his sone Isaac	
	Do wedde for no worldes good,	*Cause to wed; worldly goods*
	Bot only to his oghne blod:	*own*
	Wherof this servant, as he bad,	*commanded*
	Whan he was ded, his sone hath lad	
115	To Bathuel, wher he Rebecke	
	Hath wedded with the whyte necke;	
	For sche, he wiste wel and syh,	*knew; saw*
	Was to the child cousine nyh.	*near blood-relative*

	And thus as Habraham hath tawht,	
120	Whan Isaac was God betawht,	*in the hands of God (i.e., dead)*
	His sone Jacob dede also,	
	And of Laban the dowhtres tuo,	
	Which was his em, he tok to wyve,	*Who; uncle*
	And gat upon hem in his lyve,	*begot; them during his lifetime*
125	Of hire ferst which hihte Lie,	*was called Leah*
	Sex sones of his progenie,	*Six*
	And of Rachel tuo sones eke:	*two; also*
	The remenant was for to seke,	
	That is to sein of foure mo,	
130	Wherof he gat on Bala tuo,	*begat upon Beulah two*
	And of Zelpha he hadde ek tweie.	*two*
	And these tuelve, as I thee seie,	
	Thurgh providence of God Himselve	
	Ben seid the Patriarkes tuelve;	*Are called*
135	Of whom, as afterward befell,	
	The tribes tuelve of Irahel	
	Engendred were, and ben the same	
	That of Hebreus tho hadden name,	*then had the name*
	Which of sibrede in alliance	*kinship*
140	For evere kepten thilke usance	*that same custom*
	Most comunly, til Crist was bore.	*born*
	Bot afterward it was forbore	*abandoned*
	Amonges ous that ben baptized;	
	For of the lawe canonized	*canon law*
145	The Pope hath bede to the men,	*ordained*
	That non schal wedden of his ken	
	Ne the seconde ne the thridde.	
	Bot thogh that holy cherche it bidde,	
	So to restreigne mariage,	
150	Ther ben yit upon loves rage	*from love's passion*
	Full manye of suche nou aday	*nowadays*
	That taken wher thei take may.	
	For love, which is unbesein	*unendowed*
	Of alle reson, as men sein,	*any reason*
155	Thurgh sotie and thurgh nyceté,	*folly; stupidity*
	Of his voluptuosité	
	He spareth no condicion	*distinguishes no social circumstance*
	Of ken ne yit religion,	*kin nor*
	Bot as a cock among the hennes,	
160	Or as a stalon in the fennes,	*stallion; marshlands*
	Which goth amonges al the stod,	*all the horses*
	Riht so can he no more good,	*he knows no more*
	Bot takth what thing comth next to honde.	
Confessor	Mi sone, thou schalt understonde,	
165	That such delit is for to blame.	

Forthi if thou hast be the same
To love in eny such manere,
Tell forth therof and schrif thee hiere."   *confess yourself here*

Amans   "Mi fader, nay, God wot the sothe,
170   Mi feire is noght of such a bothe,   *commerce; booth*
So wylde a man yit was I nevere,
That of mi ken or lief or levere   *kin; dear or more dear*
Me liste love in such a wise: *It pleases me*
And ek I not for what emprise   *do not know; purpose*
175   I scholde assote upon a nonne,   *become besotted; nun*
For thogh I hadde hir love wonne,
It myhte into no pris amonte,   *amount of anything valuable*
So therof sette I non acompte.   *no value*
Ye mai wel axe of this and that,
180   Bot sothli for to telle plat,   *truly to speak plainly*
In al this world ther is bot on   *one*
The which myn herte hath overgon;   *Who was overcome*
I am toward alle othre fre."   *unattached*

Confessor   "Full wel, mi sone, nou I see
185   Thi word stant evere upon o place.   *(i.e., you still have not reformed)*
Bot yit therof thou hast a grace,
That thou thee myht so wel excuse   *exculpate yourself*
Of love suche as som men use,
So as I spak of now tofore.
190   For al such time of love is lore,   *lost*
And lich unto the bitterswete;
For thogh it thenke a man ferst swete,   *it seems to a person at first*
He schal wel fielen ate laste   *perceive*
That it is sour and may noght laste.
195   For as a morsell envenimed,   *poisoned*
So hath such love his lust mistimed,   *misled*
And grete ensamples manyon
A man mai finde therupon.

[EXAMPLES OF INCEST]

At Rome ferst if we beginne,
200   Ther schal I finde hou of this sinne
☞   An emperour was for to blame,   *(see note)*
Gayus Caligula be name,   *by name*
Which of his oghne sostres thre
Berefte the virginité: *Stolen*
205   And whanne he hadde hem so forlein,   *raped*
As he the which was al vilein,
He dede hem out of londe exile.
Bot afterward withinne a while
God hath beraft him in his ire

210	His lif and ek his large empire:	
	And thus for likinge of a throwe	*pleasure of a moment*
	Forevere his lust was overthrowe.	
	Of this sotie also I finde,	*folly*
	Amon his soster agein kinde,	*against nature*
215	Which hihte Thamar, he forlay;	*Who was called; violated*
	Bot he that lust an other day	*later*
	Aboghte, whan that Absolon	*Paid for*
	His oghne brother therupon,	
	Of that he hadde his soster schent,	*disgraced*
220	Tok of that senne vengement	*sin vengeance*
	And slowh him with his oghne hond:	
	And thus th'unkinde unkinde fond.	*unnatural one*
	And for to se more of this thing,	
☞	The Bible makth a knowleching,	*(see note)*
225	Wherof thou miht take evidence	
	Upon the sothe experience.	*true*
	Whan Lothes wif was overgon	*overwhelmed*
	And schape into the salte ston,	
	As it is spoke into this day,	
230	Be bothe hise dowhtres thanne he lay,	*By*
	With childe and made hem bothe grete,	
	Til that nature hem wolde lete,	*them; release*
	And so the cause aboute ladde	*thus [nature] managed the matter*
	That ech of hem a sone hadde,	*[So] that*
235	Moab the ferste, and the seconde	
	Amon, of whiche, as it is founde,	
	Cam afterward to grete encres	
	Tuo nacions: and natheles,	
	For that the stockes were ungoode,	*trunks [of the genealogical tree]*
240	The branches mihten noght be goode;	
	For of the false Moabites	
	Forth with the strengthe of Amonites,	
	Of that thei weren ferst misgete,	*misbegotten*
	The poeple of God was ofte upsete	
245	In Irahel and in Judee,	*Israel; Judah*
	As in the Bible a man mai se.	
Confessor	Lo thus, my sone, as I thee seie,	
	Thou miht thiselve be beseie	*furnished*
	Of that thou hast of othre herd.	*From what*
250	For evere yit it hath so ferd,	
	Of loves lust if so befalle	
	That it in other place falle	
	Than it is of the lawe set,	
	He which his love hath so beset	*fixed*
255	Mote afterward repente him sore.	
	And every man is othres lore;	*counsel*

	Of that befell in time er this	
	The present time which now is	
	Mai ben enformed hou it stod,	
260	And take that him thenketh good,	*that which seems to him*
	And leve that which is noght so.	
	Bot for to loke of time go,	*time passed*
	Hou lust of love excedeth lawe,	
	It oghte for to be withdrawe;	
265	For every man it scholde drede,	
	And nameliche in his sibrede,	*kindred*
	Which torneth ofte to vengance:	
	Wherof a tale in remembrance,	
	Which is a long process to hiere,	*narrative (drama)*
270	I thenke for to tellen hiere."	

[TALE OF APOLLONIUS OF TYRE]

ii.   *Omnibus est communis amor, set et immoderatos*
           Qui facit excessus, non reputatur amans.
       Sors tamen vnde Venus attractat corda, videre
           Que racionis erunt, non racione sinit.[1]

	Of a cronique in daies gon,	*chronicle*
☞	The which is cleped *Pantheon*,	*(see note)*
	In loves cause I rede thus,	
	Hou that the grete Antiochus,	
275	Of whom that Antioche tok	
	His ferste name, as seith the bok,	
	Was coupled to a noble queene,	
	And hadde a dowhter hem betwene:	
	Bot such fortune cam to honde,	
280	That deth, which no king mai withstonde,	
	Bot every lif it mote obeie,	
	This worthi queene tok aweie.	
	The king, which made mochel mone,	*lament*
	Tho stod, as who seith, al him one	*so to speak, alone by himself*
285	Withoute wif, bot natheles	
	His doghter, which was piereles	*beyond compare*
	Of beauté, duelte aboute him stille.	
	Bot whanne a man hath welthe at wille,	
	The fleissh is frele and falleth ofte,	*frail*
290	And that this maide tendre and softe,	*that [truth]*
	Which in hire fadres chambres duelte,	

---

[1] *Love belongs to all the community; but let he who carries out immoderate excesses not be thought a lover. Yet the fate by which Venus attracts hearts does not allow [us] by means of reason to see the things of reason.*

	Withinne a time wiste and felte.	*knew; experienced*
	For likinge and concupiscence	*desire; carnal lust*
	Withoute insihte of conscience	
295	The fader so with lustes blente,	*desires blinded*
	That he caste al his hole entente	
	His oghne doghter for to spille.	*destroy*
	This king hath leisir at his wille	*leisure for*
	With strengthe, and whanne he time sih,	*saw*
300	This yonge maiden he forlih.	*raped*
	And sche was tendre and full of drede,	
	Sche couthe noght hir maidenhede	*knew not how her*
	Defende, and thus sche hath forlore	*To protect; lost*
	The flour which sche hath longe bore.	*flower; carried*
305	It helpeth noght althogh sche wepe,	
	For thei that scholde hir bodi kepe	*protect*
	Of wommen were absent as thanne,	
	And thus this maiden goth to manne.	*is taken by a man*
	The wylde fader thus devoureth	
310	His oghne fleissh, which non socoureth,	*whom no one helps*
	And that was cause of mochel care.	
	Bot after this unkinde fare	*unnatural business*
	Out of the chambre goth the king,	
	And sche lay stille, and of this thing,	
315	Withinne hirself such sorghe made,	*sorrow*
	Ther was no wiht that mihte hir glade,	*person; console*
	For feere of thilke horrible vice.	*fear of that same*
	With that cam inne the norrice	*nurse*
	Which fro childhode hire hadde kept,	
320	And axeth if sche hadde slept,	
	And why hire chiere was unglad.	*countenance*
	Bot sche, which hath ben overlad	*compelled*
	Of that sche myhte noght be wreke,	*avenged*
	For schame couthe unethes speke;	*could scarcely*
325	And natheles mercy sche preide	*prayed*
	With wepende yhe and thus sche seide:	*weeping eyes*
	"Helas, mi soster, waileway,	*Alas*
	That evere I sih this ilke day!	*saw; same*
	Thing which mi bodi ferst begat	*first begat my body*
330	Into this world, onliche that	
	Mi worldes worschipe hath bereft."	*honor; stolen*
	With that sche swouneth now and eft,	*fainted; again*
	And evere wissheth after deth,	
	So that wel nyh hire lacketh breth.	*breath failed her*
335	That other, which hire wordes herde,	*heard*
	In confortinge of hire ansuerde,	
	To lette hire fadres fol desir	*obstruct; foolish passion*
	Sche wiste no recoverir.	*knew; helper*

	Whan thing is do, ther is no bote,	*done; remedy*
340	So suffren thei that suffre mote;	*must*
	Ther was non other which it wiste.	*knew*
	Thus hath this king al that him liste	*pleased him*
	Of his likinge and his plesance,	*desire; pleasure*
	And laste in such continuance,	*persisted in*
345	And such delit he tok therinne,	
	Him thoghte that it was no sinne;	
	And sche dorste him nothing withseie.	*oppose*
	Bot fame, which goth every weie,	
	To sondry regnes al aboute	
350	The grete beauté telleth oute	
	Of such a maide of hih parage:	*noble lineage*
	So that for love of mariage	
	The worthi princes come and sende,	*arrive and send [messages]*
	As thei the whiche al honour wende,	*expect*
355	And knewe nothing hou it stod.	
	The fader, whanne he understod,	
	That thei his dowhter thus besoghte,	
	With al his wit he caste and thoghte	
	Hou that he myhte finde a lette;	*invent an obstruction*
360	And such a statut thanne he sette,	*statute; established*
	And in this wise his lawe he taxeth,	*imposes*
	That what man that his doghter axeth,	
	Bot if he couthe his question	*Unless*
	Assoile upon suggestion	*Solve*
365	Of certein thinges that befelle,	
	The whiche he wolde unto him telle,	
	He scholde in certein lese his hed.	*certainly lose; head*
	And thus ther weren manye ded,	
	Here hevedes stondende on the gate,	*Their heads piked*
370	Til ate laste longe and late,	
	For lacke of ansuere in the wise,	*according to the rules*
	The remenant that weren wise	*remainder*
	Eschuieden to make assay.	*Avoided making the attempt*
☞	Til it befell upon a day	*(see note)*
375	Appolinus the Prince of Tyr,	
	Which hath to love a gret desir,	
	As he which in his hihe mod	*high spirits*
	Was likende of his hote blod,	*Was amorously disposed because of his passion*
	A yong, a freissh, a lusti knyht,	
380	As he lai musende on a nyht	*musing*
	Of the tidinges whiche he herde,	
	He thoghte assaie hou that it ferde.	*to ascertain; would fare*
	He was with worthi compainie	
	Arraied, and with good navie	
385	To schipe he goth, the wynd him dryveth,	

	And seileth, til that he arryveth.	
	Sauf in the port of Antioche	*Safe*
	He londeth, and goth to aproche	
	The kinges court and his presence.	
390	Of every naturel science,	
	Which eny clerk him couthe teche,	*could*
	He couthe ynowh, and in his speche	*knew enough*
	Of wordes he was eloquent;	
	And whanne he sih the king present,	
395	He preith he moste his dowhter have.	*[that] he might*
	The king agein began to crave,	*demand (asserted his privilege)*
	And tolde him the condicion,	
	Hou ferst unto his question	
	He mote ansuere and faile noght,	*must*
400	Or with his heved it schal be boght.	*head*
	And he him axeth what it was.	*(Apollonius) asked; (the question)*
☞	The king declareth him the cas	*(see note)*
	With sturne lok and sturdi chiere,	*harsh expression*
☞	To him and seide in this manere:	*(see note)*
405	"With felonie I am upbore,	*sustained (see note)*
	I ete and have it noght forbore	*have not desisted from doing it*
	Mi modres fleissh, whos housebonde	
	Mi fader for to seche I fonde,	*try*
	Which is the sone ek of my wif.	*also*
410	Hierof I am inquisitif;	
	And who that can mi tale save,	*riddle solve*
	Al quyt he schal my doghter have;	*By rights (Freely)*
	Of his ansuere and if he faile,	
	He schal be ded withoute faile.	
415	Forthi my sone," quod the king,	
	"Be wel avised of this thing,	
	Which hath thi lif in jeupartie."	*jeopardy*
☞	Appolinus for his partie,	
	Whan he this question hath herd,	
420	Unto the king he hath ansuerd	
	And hath rehersed on and on	*one by one*
	The pointz, and seide therupon:	
	"The question which thou hast spoke,	
	If thou wolt that it be unloke,	*elucidated (unlocked)*
425	It toucheth al the priveté	*secret matters*
	Betwen thin oghne child and thee,	
	And stant al hol upon you tuo."	*pertains entirely to*
☞	The king was wonder sory tho,	*vexed then (see note)*
	And thoghte, if that he seide it oute,	
430	Than were he schamed al aboute.	
	With slihe wordes and with felle	*sly; treacherous [words]*
	He seith, "Mi sone, I schal thee telle,	

Though that thou be of litel wit,
It is no gret merveile as yit,
435   Thin age mai it noght suffise:
Bot loke wel thou noght despise
Thin oghne lif, for of my grace
Of thretty daies fulle a space
I grante thee, to ben avised."   *be advised (beware)*
☞   And thus with leve and time assised   *permission; established (see note)*
441   This yonge prince forth he wente,
And understod wel what it mente,
Withinne his herte as he was lered,   *taught*
That for to maken him afered   *afraid*
445   The king his time hath so deslaied.   *delayed*
Wherof he dradde and was esmaied,   *afraid (dismayed)*
Of treson that he deie scholde,
For he the king his sothe tolde;   *secret (truth) revealed*
And sodeinly the nyhtes tyde,
450   That more wolde he noght abide,
Al prively his barge he hente   *took*
And hom agein to Tyr he wente;
And in his oghne wit he seide   *own*
For drede, if he the king bewreide,   *betrayed (exposed)*
455   He knew so wel the kinges herte,
That deth ne scholde he noght asterte,   *escape*
The king him wolde so poursuie.   *pursue*
Bot he, that wolde his deth eschuie,   *avoid*
And knew al this tofor the hond,
460   Forsake he thoghte his oghne lond,
That there wolde he noght abyde;   *remain*
For wel he knew that on som syde   *occasion*
This tirant of his felonie
Be som manere of tricherie
465   To grieve his bodi wol noght leve.   *aggrieve; leave off*
☞   Forthi withoute take leve,   *(see note)*
Als priveliche as evere he myhte,   *secretly*
He goth him to the see be nyhte   *sea at night*
In schipes that be whete laden: *were laden with grain*
470   Here takel redy tho thei maden
And hale up seil and forth thei fare.   *hauled up the sail*
Bot for to tellen of the care   *anxiety*
That thei of Tyr begonne tho,   *experienced then*
Whan that thei wiste he was ago,   *knew; gone*
475   It is a pité for to hiere.
Thei losten lust, thei losten chiere,   *pleasure; cheerfulness*
Thei toke upon hem such penaunce,   *themselves*
Ther was no song, ther was no daunce,
Bot every merthe and melodie

480   To hem was thanne a maladie;
       For unlust of that aventure   *sorrow*
       Ther was no man which tok tonsure;   *got a shave and a haircut*
       In doelful clothes thei hem clothe,
       The bathes and the stwes bothe   *brothels (stews)*
485   Thei schetten in be every weie;   *closed up*
       Ther was no lif which leste pleie   *who preferred to seek pleasure*
       Ne take of eny joie kepe,
       Bot for here liege lord to wepe;   *Except to lament their*
       And every wyht seide as he couthe,
490   "Helas, the lusti flour of youthe,
       Oure prince, oure heved, our governour,   *head*
       Thurgh whom we stoden in honour,
       Withoute the comun assent
       Thus sodeinliche is fro ous went!"
495   Such was the clamour of hem alle.
☞   Bot se we now what is befalle   *(see note)*
       Upon the ferste tale plein,
       And torne we therto agein.
       Antiochus the grete sire,   *powerful ruler*
500   Which full of rancour and of ire
       His herte berth, so as ye herde,
       Of that this Prince of Tyr ansuerde,   *Concerning that which*
       He hadde a feloun bacheler,   *villainous*
       Which was his privé consailer,
505   And Taliart be name he hihte: *was called*
       The king a strong puison him dihte   *prepared*
       Withinne a buiste and gold therto,   *box*
       In alle haste and bad him go
       Strawht unto Tyr, and for no cost   *Directly*
510   Ne spare he, til he hadde lost   *gotten rid of*
       The Prince which he wolde spille.   *destroy*
       And whan the king hath seid his wille,
       This Taliart in a galeie   *boat*
       With alle haste he tok his weie:
515   The wynd was good, he saileth blyve,   *swiftly*
       Til he tok lond upon the ryve   *shore*
       Of Tyr, and forthwithal anon   *speedily*
       Into the burgh he gan to gon,   *city; went*
       And tok his in and bod a throwe.   *lodging and waited a bit*
520   Bot for he wolde noght be knowe,   *so that*
       Desguised thanne he goth him oute;
       He sih the wepinge al aboute,   *saw*
       And axeth what the cause was,   *asked*
       And thei him tolden al the cas,   *situation*
525   How sodeinli the prince is go.   *has gone*
       And whan he sih that it was so,

And that his labour was in vein, — *vain*
Anon he torneth hom agein,
And to the king, whan he cam nyh,
530 He tolde of that he herde and syh,
Hou that the Prince of Tyr is fled,
So was he come agein unsped. — *without success*
The king was sori for a while, — *vexed*
Bot whan he sih that with no wyle — *deceit*
535 He myhte achieve his crualté,
He stinte his wraththe and let him be. — *controlled; anger*
☞   Bot over this now for to telle — *(see note)*
Of aventures that befelle
Unto this prince of whom I tolde,
540 He hath his rihte cours forth holde
Be ston and nedle, til he cam — *compass*
To Tharse, and there his lond he nam. — *made his landfall*
A burgeis riche of gold and fee — *citizen; landed income*
Was thilke time in that cité, — *at that (the same)*
545 Which cleped was Strangulio, — *Who was called*
His wif was Dionise also:
This yonge prince, as seith the bok,
With hem his herbergage tok; — *lodging*
And it befell that cité so
550 Before time and thanne also, — *Previously; then*
Thurgh strong famyne which hem ladde — *burdened them*
Was non that eny whete hadde. — *any grain*
Appolinus, whanne that he herde
The meschief, hou the cité ferde, — *misfortune; fared*
555 Al freliche of his oghne gifte
His whete, among hem for to schifte, — *distribute*
The which be schipe he hadde broght, — *by ship*
He gaf, and tok of hem riht noght. — *from them nothing in return*
Bot sithen ferst this world began,
560 Was nevere yit to such a man
Mor joie mad than thei him made.
For thei were alle of him so glade,
That thei for evere in remembrance
Made a figure in resemblance — *statue*
565 Of him, and in the comun place
Thei sette him up, so that his face
Mihte every maner man beholde,
So as the cité was beholde; — *Just as; beholden*
It was of latoun overgilt: — *latten (copper-tin alloy)*
570 Thus hath he noght his gifte spilt. — *wasted*
☞   Upon a time with his route — *company (see note)*
This lord to pleie goth him oute,
And in his weie of Tyr he mette — *from Tyre*

	A man, the which on knees him grette,	*greeted*
575	And Hellican be name he hihte,	*was called*
	Which preide his lord to have insihte	*concern*
	Upon himself, and seide him thus,	*For himself (his safety)*
	Hou that the grete Antiochus	
	Awaiteth if he mihte him spille.	*Lay in ambush so that; destroy*
580	That other thoghte and hield him stille,	
	And thonked him of his warnynge,	
	And bad him telle no tidinge,	
	Whan he to Tyr cam hom agein,	
	That he in Tharse him hadde sein.	
☞	Fortune hath evere be muable	*changeable (see note)*
586	And mai no while stonde stable,	
	For now it hiheth, now it loweth,	*rises; falls*
	Now stant upriht, now overthroweth,	
	Now full of blisse and now of bale,	*happiness; sorrow*
590	As in the tellinge of mi tale	
	Hierafterward a man mai liere,	*learn*
	Which is gret routhe for to hiere.	*pity; hear*
	This lord, which wolde don his beste,	
	Withinne himself hath litel reste,	
595	And thoghte he wolde his place change	
	And seche a contré more strange.	*remote*
	Of Tharsiens his leve anon	
	He tok, and is to schipe gon.	
	His cours he nam with seil updrawe,	*took; sail unfurled*
600	Where as Fortune doth the lawe,	*To where Fortune determines [he should go]*
	And scheweth, as I schal reherse,	*explain*
	How sche was to this lord diverse,	*adverse*
	The which upon the see sche ferketh.	*sea; swiftly conveys*
	The wynd aros, the weder derketh,	*weather grew dark*
605	It blew and made such tempeste,	
	Non ancher mai the schip areste,	*keep secure*
	Which hath tobroken al his gere;	*broken asunder; its rigging*
	The schipmen stode in such a feere,	
	Was non that myhte himself bestere,	*make a movement*
610	Bot evere awaite upon the lere,	*destruction*
	Whan that thei scholde drenche at ones.	*drown*
	Ther was ynowh withinne wones	*within the chambers (cabins)*
	Of wepinge and of sorghe tho;	*then*
	This yonge king makth mochel wo	
615	So for to se the schip travaile:	*suffer*
	Bot al that myhte him noght availe;	
	The mast tobrak, the seil torof,	*ripped in shreds*
	The schip upon the wawes drof,	*waves was driven*
	Til that thei sihe a londes cooste.	
620	Tho made avou the leste and moste,	*made vow(s); least; greatest*

	Be so thei myhten come alonde;	*Provided that*
	Bot he which hath the see on honde,	
	Neptunus, wolde noght acorde,	
	Bot al tobroke cable and corde,	*shattered utterly*
625	Er thei to londe myhte aproche,	
	The schip toclef upon a roche,	*split apart*
	And al goth doun into the depe.	
	Bot he that alle thing mai kepe	
	Unto this lord was merciable,	
630	And broghte him sauf upon a table,	*plank*
	Which to the lond him hath upbore;	
	The remenant was al forlore,	*lost*
	Wherof he made mochel mone.	*lament (moan)*
☞	Thus was this yonge lord him one,	*by himself alone (see note)*
635	Al naked in a povere plit:	*wretched condition*
	His colour, which whilom was whyt,	*formerly; fair*
	Was thanne of water fade and pale,	
	And ek he was so sore acale	*chilled*
	That he wiste of himself no bote,	*remedy*
640	It halp him nothing for to mote	*complain*
	To gete agein that he hath lore.	*lost*
	Bot sche which hath his deth forbore,	*held off*
	Fortune, thogh sche wol noght yelpe,	*boast*
	Al sodeinly hath sent him helpe,	
645	Whanne him thoghte alle grace aweie;	
	Ther cam a fisshere in the weie,	*fisherman*
	And sih a man ther naked stonde,	
	And whan that he hath understonde	
	The cause, he hath of him gret routhe,	*pity*
650	And onliche of his povere trouthe	*purely; loyalty [even as a poor man]*
	Of suche clothes as he hadde	
	With gret pité this lord he cladde.	
	And he him thonketh as he scholde,	
	And seith him that it schal be yolde,	*repaid*
655	If evere he gete his stat agein,	*social position*
	And preide that he wolde him sein	*tell him*
	If nyh were eny toun for him.	*nearby; any*
	He seide, "Yee, Pentapolim,	
	Wher bothe king and queene duellen."	
660	Whanne he this tale herde tellen,	
	He gladeth him and gan beseche	*entreated*
	That he the weie him wolde teche.	
	And he him taghte, and forth he wente	
	And preide God with good entente	
665	To sende him joie after his sorwe.	
☞	It was noght passed yit midmorwe,	*mid-day (see note)*
	Whan thiderward his weie he nam,	*took*

	Wher sone upon the non he cam.	*noon*
	He eet such as he myhte gete,	
670	And forth anon, whan he hadde ete,	
	He goth to se the toun aboute,	
	And cam ther as he fond a route	*crowd*
	Of yonge lusti men withalle.	
	And as it scholde tho befalle,	
675	That day was set of such assise,	*appointment*
	That thei scholde in the londes guise,	*custom of the land*
	As he herde of the poeple seie,	
	Here comun game thanne pleie;	
	And crid was that thei scholden come	
680	Unto the gamen alle and some	
	Of hem that ben delivere and wyhte,	*agile; strong*
	To do such maistrie as thei myhte.	
	Thei made hem naked as thei scholde,	
	For so that ilke game wolde,	
685	As it was tho custume and us,	*then; use*
	Amonges hem was no refus.	*[being naked] was no disgrace*
	The flour of al the toun was there	
	And of the court also ther were,	
	And that was in a large place	
690	Riht evene afore the kinges face,	
	Which Artestrathes thanne hihte.	*was called*
	The pley was pleid riht in his sihte,	
	And who most worthi was of dede	*valiant; in combat*
	Receive he scholde a certein mede	*reward*
695	And in the cité bere a pris.	*gain distinction*
☞	Appolinus, which war and wys	*savvy; wise (see note)*
	Of every game couthe an ende,	*knew a bit*
	He thoghte assaie, hou so it wende,	*to try his luck*
	And fell among hem into game.	
700	And there he wan him such a name,	
	So as the king himself acompteth	*took note*
	That he alle othre men surmonteth,	
	And bar the pris above hem alle.	*had excellence*
	The king bad that into his halle	
705	At souper time he schal be broght;	
	And he cam thanne and lefte it noght,	*did not leave [his meal]*
	Withoute compaignie al one.	*all alone*
	Was non so semlich of persone,	
	Of visage and of limes bothe,	
710	If that he hadde what to clothe.	*If [only]; something [appropriate]*
	At soupertime natheles	
	The king amiddes al the pres	*crowd*
	Let clepe him up among hem alle,	*invite*
	And bad his mareschall of halle	

715 To setten him in such degré
    That he upon him myhte se.
    The king was sone set and served,
    And he, which hath his pris deserved   *distinction*
    After the kinges oghne word,   *According to*
720 Was mad beginne a middel bord,   *table [above the general table]*
    That bothe king and queene him sihe.   *[So] that; might see him*
    He sat and caste aboute his yhe   *eye*
    And sih the lordes in astat,
    And with himself wax in debat   *grew conflicted*
725 Thenkende what he hadde lore,   *lost*
    And such a sorwe he tok therfore,
    That he sat evere stille and thoghte,
    As he which of no mete roghte.   *food was concerned*
☞   The king behield his hevynesse,   *(see note)*
730 And of his grete gentillesse
    His doghter, which was fair and good
    And ate bord before him stod,
    As it was thilke time usage,   *at that time customary*
    He bad to gon on his message   *told [her] to go at his request*
735 And fonde for to make him glad.   *attempt*
    And sche dede as hire fader bad,
    And goth to him the softe pas   *gently*
    And axeth whenne and what he was,
    And preith he scholde his thoghtes leve.   *put aside*
740 He seith, "Ma dame, be youre leve,
    Mi name is hote Appolinus,   *called*
    And of mi richesse it is thus,
    Upon the see I have it lore.   *sea; lost*
    The contré wher as I was bore,
745 Wher that my lond is and mi rente,   *income*
    I lefte at Tyr, whan that I wente.   *departed*
    The worschipe of this worldes aghte,   *honor; possessions*
    Unto the god ther I betaghte."   *god I commended there (left behind)*
    And thus togedre as thei tuo speeke,
750 The teres runne be his cheeke.   *tears*
    The king, which therof tok good kepe,   *paid careful attention*
    Hath gret pité to sen him wepe,
    And for his doghter sende agein,
    And preide hir faire and gan to sein   *courteously; proceeded to say*
755 That sche no lengere wolde drecche,   *hesitate*
    Bot that sche wolde anon forth fecche
    Hire harpe and don al that sche can
    To glade with that sory man.   *find enjoyment; unhappy*
    And sche to don hir fader heste   *father's command*
760 Hire harpe fette, and in the feste   *fetched; feast*
    Upon a chaier which thei fette

       Hirself next to this man sche sette:

       With harpe bothe and ek with mouthe

       To him sche dede al that sche couthe

765   To make him chiere, and evere he siketh,   *sighs*

       And sche him axeth hou him liketh.   *asks; it pleases him*

       "Ma dame, certes wel," he seide,

       "Bot if ye the mesure pleide   *ratios (metrics) played (see note)*

       Which, if you list, I schal you liere,   *teach*

770   It were a glad thing for to hiere."

       "Ha, lieve sire," tho quod sche,   *dear sir*

       "Now tak the harpe and let me se

       Of what mesure that ye mene."

       Tho preith the king, tho preith the queene,   *Then pray*

775   Forth with the lordes alle arewe,   *together*

       That he som merthe wolde schewe;

       He takth the harpe and in his wise   *in his [own] style*

       He tempreth, and of such assise   *tunes; manner*

       Singende he harpeth forth withal,

780   That as a vois celestial

       Hem thoghte it souneth in here ere,   *It seemed to them*

       As thogh that he an angel were.

       Thei gladen of his melodie,

       Bot most of all the compainie

785   The kinges doghter, which it herde,

       And thoghte ek hou that he ansuerde,

       Whan that he was of hire opposed,   *questioned*

       Withinne hir herte hath wel supposed

       That he is of gret gentilesse.

790   Hise dedes ben therof witnesse

       Forth with the wisdom of his lore;   *teaching*

       It nedeth noght to seche more,

       He myhte noght have such manere,

       Of gentil blod bot if he were.   *unless he were*

795   Whanne he hath harped al his fille,

       The kinges heste to fulfille,   *command*

       Awey goth dissh, awey goth cuppe,

       Doun goth the bord, the cloth was uppe,

       Thei risen and gon out of halle.

800   The king his chamberlein let calle,

☞   And bad that he be alle weie   *in every fashion (see note)*

       A chambre for this man pourveie,   *prepare*

       Which nyh his oghne chambre be.

       "It schal be do, mi lord," quod he.

805   Appolinus of whom I mene

       Tho tok his leve of king and queene

       And of the worthi maide also,

       Which preide unto hir fader tho,

That sche myhte of that yonge man   *from that*
810 Of tho sciences whiche he can   *Of the kinds of learning he had knowledge of*
His lore have; and in this wise
The king hir granteth his aprise,   *instruction*
So that himself therto assente.   *Provided that [Apollonius]*
Thus was acorded er thei wente,
815 That he with al that evere he may
This yonge faire freisshe may   *maiden*
Of that he couthe scholde enforme;
And full assented in this forme   *on these terms*
Thei token leve as for that nyht.
☞   And whanne it was amorwe lyht,   *(see note)*
821 Unto this yonge man of Tyr,
Of clothes and of good atir
With gold and selver to despende
This worthi yonge lady sende:
825 And thus sche made him wel at ese,
And he with al that he can plese
Hire serveth wel and faire agein.   *in turn*
He tawhte hir til sche was certein   *accomplished*
Of harpe, of citole, and of rote,   *(see note)*
830 With many a tun and many a note   *tune*
Upon musique, upon mesure,
And of hire harpe the temprure   *tuning*
He tawhte hire ek, as he wel couthe.
Bot as men sein that frele is youthe,
835 With leisir and continuance   *persistence*
This mayde fell upon a chance,   *change of fortune*
That love hath mad him a querele   *made himself quarrel*
Agein hire youthe freissh and frele,
That malgré wher sche wole or noght,   *despite whether*
840 Sche mot with al hire hertes thoght   *must*
To love and to his lawe obeie;
And that sche schal ful sore abeie.   *sorely pay for*
For sche wot nevere what it is,
Bot evere among sche fieleth this: *continually*
845 Thenkende upon this man of Tyr,
Hire herte is hot as eny fyr,
And otherwhile it is acale;   *chilled (a-cold)*
Now is sche red, nou is sche pale
Riht after the condicion
850 Of hire ymaginacion.
Bot evere among hire thoghtes alle,   *continually*
Sche thoghte, what so mai befalle,
Or that sche lawhe, or that sche wepe,   *Whether; laugh*
Sche wolde hire goode name kepe
855 For feere of wommannysshe schame.

Bot what in ernest and in game,
Sche stant for love in such a plit,
That sche hath lost al appetit
Of mete, of drinke, of nyhtes reste,   *For food*
860   As sche that not what is the beste;   *who knows not what*
Bot for to thenken al hir fille
Sche hield hire ofte times stille   *kept herself*
Withinne hir chambre, and goth noght oute:
The king was of hire lif in doute,
865   Which wiste nothing what it mente.   *Who knew*
☞   Bot fell a time, as he out wente   *(see note)*
To walke, of princes sones thre
Ther come and felle to his kne;
And ech of hem in sondri wise
870   Besoghte and profreth his servise,
So that he myhte his doghter have.
The king, which wolde his honour save,
Seith sche is siek, and of that speche   *Says; sick; matter*
Tho was no time to beseche;   *implore*
875   Bot ech of hem do make a bille   *declaration [of wealth and position]*
He bad, and wryte his oghne wille,
His name, his fader, and his good;   *possessions*
And whan sche wiste hou that it stod,
And hadde here billes oversein,   *their inventories perused*
880   Thei scholden have ansuere agein.
Of this conseil thei weren glad,
And writen as the king hem bad,
And every man his oghne bok   *petition*
Into the kinges hond betok,
885   And he it to his dowhter sende,
And preide hir for to make an ende
And wryte agein hire oghne hond,
Riht as sche in hire herte fond.
☞   The billes weren wel received,   *(see note)*
890   Bot sche hath alle here loves weyved,   *their; rejected*
And thoghte tho was time and space
To put hire in hir fader grace,
And wrot agein and thus sche saide:
"The schame which is in a maide
895   With speche dar noght ben unloke,
Bot in writinge it mai be spoke;
So wryte I to you, fader, thus:
Bot if I have Appolinus,   *Unless*
Of al this world, what so betyde,   *whatever happens*
900   I wol non other man abide.   *tolerate*
And certes if I of him faile,   *fail [to have] him*
I wot riht wel withoute faile

Ye schull for me be dowhterles."
This lettre cam, and ther was press | *a crowd*
905 Tofore the king, ther as he stod; | *Before*
And whan that he it understod,
He gaf hem ansuer by and by, | *them*
Bot that was do so prively, | *secretly*
That non of othres conseil wiste. | *[So] that*
910 Thei toke her leve, and wher hem liste | *their; it pleased them*
Thei wente forth upon here weie. | *their*
    The king ne wolde noght bewreie | *reveal*
The conseil for no maner hihe, | *haste*
☞ Bot soffreth til he time sihe: | *saw (see note)*
915 And whan that he to chambre is come,
He hath unto his conseil nome | *taken*
This man of Tyr, and let him se
The lettre and al the priveté, | *secret contents*
The which his dowhter to him sente.
920 And he his kne to grounde bente
And thonketh him and hire also,
And er thei wenten thanne atuo, | *before; separated*
With good herte and with good corage
Of full love and full mariage
925 The king and he ben hol acorded.
And after, whanne it was recorded
Unto the dowhter hou it stod,
The gifte of al this worldes good
Ne scholde have mad hir half so blythe: | *joyous*
930 And forth withal the king als swithe, | *swiftly*
For he wol have hire good assent,
Hath for the queene hir moder sent.
The queene is come, and whan sche herde
Of this matiere hou that it ferde,
935 Sche syh debat, sche syh desese, | *conflict; distress*
Bot if sche wolde hir dowhter plese, | *Unless*
And is therto assented full.
Which is a dede wonderfull,
For no man knew the sothe cas | *true situation*
940 Bot he himself, what man he was; | *Except*
And natheles, so as hem thoghte, | *it seems to them*
Hise dedes to the sothe wroghte | *pointed to the truth*
That he was come of gentil blod.
Him lacketh noght bot worldes good,
945 And as therof is no despeir,
For sche schal ben hire fader heir,
And he was able to governe.
Thus wol thei noght the love werne | *forbid*
Of him and hire in none wise,

950	Bot ther acorded thei divise	*agreed upon a plan for*
☞	The day and time of mariage.	*(see note)*
	Wher love is lord of the corage,	*heart*
	Him thenketh longe er that he spede;	*It seems to him; succeed*
	Bot ate laste unto the dede	
955	The time is come, and in her wise	*according to their custom*
	With gret offrende and sacrifise	
	Thei wedde and make a riche feste,	
	And every thing which was honeste	*honorable*
	Withinnen house and ek withoute	
960	It was so don, that al aboute	
	Of gret worschipe, of gret noblesse	
	Ther cride many a man largesse	*cried out for (gave thanks for) almsgiving*
	Unto the lordes hihe and loude;	
	The knyhtes that ben yonge and proude,	
965	Thei jouste ferst and after daunce.	
	The day is go, the nyhtes chaunce	
	Hath derked al the bryhte sonne;	
	This lord, which hath his love wonne,	
	Is go to bedde with his wif,	
970	Wher as thei ladde a lusti lif,	
	And that was after somdel sene,	*somewhat revealed*
	For as thei pleiden hem betwene,	
	Thei gete a child betwen hem tuo,	
	To whom fell after mochel wo.	
☞	Now have I told of the spousailes.	*wedding (see note)*
976	Bot for to speke of the mervailes	
	Whiche afterward to hem befelle,	
	It is a wonder for to telle.	
	It fell adai thei riden oute,	
980	The king and queene and al the route,	*company*
	To pleien hem upon the stronde,	*shore*
	Wher as thei sen toward the londe	
	A schip sailende of gret array.	
	To knowe what it mene may,	
985	Til it be come thei abide;	*awaited*
	Than sen thei stonde on every side,	
	Endlong the schipes bord to schewe,	*ship's side*
	Of penonceals a riche rewe.	*banners; display (row)*
	Thei axen when the schip is come.	*whence*
990	Fro Tyr, anon ansuerde some,	
	And over this thei seiden more	
	The cause why thei comen fore	
	Was for to seche and for to finde	
	Appolinus, which was of kinde	*by birth right*
995	Her liege lord: and he appiereth,	*Their*
	And of the tale which he hiereth	

He was riht glad; for thei him tolde,
That for vengance, as God it wolde,
Antiochus, as men mai wite,   *know*
1000   With thondre and lyhthnynge is forsmite;
His doghter hath the same chaunce,
So be thei bothe in o balance.
"Forthi, oure liege lord, we seie
In name of al the lond, and preie,
1005   That left al other thing to done,
It like you to come sone   *[That] it please you*
And se youre oghne liege men   *own*
With othre that ben of youre ken,   *kin (quality)*
That live in longinge and desir
1010   Til ye be come agein to Tyr."
This tale after the king it hadde   *heard it*
Pentapolim al overspradde,
Ther was no joie for to seche;   *seek*
For every man it hadde in speche
1015   And seiden alle of on acord,   *one*
"A worthi king schal ben oure lord:
That thoghte ous ferst an hevinesse   *What seemed to us; burdensome*
Is schape ous now to gret gladnesse."   *Has become for us*
Thus goth the tidinge overal.
☞   Bot nede he mot, that nede schal: *(see note)*
1021   Appolinus his leve tok,
To God and al the lond betok   *commended (said farewell to)*
With al the poeple long and brod,   *far and wide*
That he no lenger there abod.
1025   The king and queene sorwe made,
Bot yit somdiel thei weren glade
Of such thing as thei herden tho.   *then*
And thus betwen the wel and wo   *gladness; woe*
To schipe he goth, his wif with childe,   *pregnant wife*
1030   The which was evere meke and mylde   *Who*
And wolde noght departe him fro,
Such love was betwen hem tuo.
Lichorida for hire office
Was take, which was a norrice,   *nurse*
1035   To wende with this yonge wif,   *travel*
To whom was schape a woful lif.   *For whom was destined*
Withinne a time, as it betidde,   *happened*
Whan thei were in the see amidde,   *sea amidst*
Out of the north thei sihe a cloude;
1040   The storm aros, the wyndes loude
Thei blewen many a dredful blast,
The welkne was al overcast,   *heaven*
The derke nyht the sonne hath under,

Ther was a gret tempeste of thunder;
1045   The mone and ek the sterres bothe   *moon; also*
In blake cloudes thei hem clothe,
Wherof here brihte lok thei hyde.   *their; appearance*
This yonge ladi wepte and cride,
To whom no confort myhte availe;
1050   Of childe sche began travaile,   *entered into labor*
Wher sche lay in a caban clos.
Hire woful lord fro hire aros,
And that was longe er eny morwe,   *before any*
So that in anguisse and in sorwe
1055   Sche was delivered al be nyhte   *by*
And ded in every mannes syhte;   *[was] dead*
Bot natheles for al this wo
A maide child was bore tho.
    Appolinus whan he this knew,   *(see note)*
1060   For sorwe a swoune he overthrew,   *he was overthrown in a faint*
That no man wiste in him no lif.   *knew*
And whanne he wok, he seide, "Ha, wif,
Mi lust, mi joie, my desir,
Mi welthe and my recoverir,   *helper*
1065   Why schal I live, and thou schalt dye?
Ha, thou Fortune, I thee deffie,
Nou hast thou do to me thi werste.
Ha, herte, why ne wolt thou berste,   *burst*
That forth with hire I myhte passe?
1070   Mi peines weren wel the lasse."   *agonies would be; less*
In such wepinge and in such cry
His dede wif, which lay him by,
A thousend sithes he hire kiste;   *times*
Was nevere man that sih ne wiste   *saw nor knew*
1075   A sorwe unto his sorwe lich.   *alike*
For evere among upon the lich   *corpse*
He fell swounende, as he that soghte   *one who*
His oghne deth, which he besoghte   *own; prayed for*
Unto the goddes alle above
1080   With many a pitous word of love.
Bot suche wordes as tho were   *those*
Yit herde nevere mannes ere,
Bot only thilke whiche he seide.   *Except for those [present]*
The maister schipman cam and preide   *prayed*
1085   With othre suche as be therinne,
And sein that he mai nothing winne
Agein the deth, bot thei him rede,   *unless they advise him*
He be wel war and take hiede,
The see be weie of his nature
1090   Receive mai no creature

Withinne himself as for to holde   *in order to carry*
The which is ded: forthi thei wolde,   *The [one] who*
As thei conseilen al aboute,
The dede body casten oute.
1095 For betre it is, thei seiden alle,
That it of hire so befalle,
Than if thei scholden alle spille.   *perish*
☞   The king, which understod here wille   *their intention (see note)*
And knew here conseil that was trewe,
1100 Began agein his sorwe newe
With pitous herte, and thus to seie:
"It is al reson that ye preie.
I am," quod he, "bot on alone,   *one*
So wolde I noght for mi persone
1105 Ther felle such adversité.
Bot whan it mai no betre be,
Doth thanne thus upon my word,
Let make a cofre strong of bord,
That it be ferm with led and pich."   *[Such] that; strengthened*
1110 Anon was mad a cofre sich,   *Soon; such a coffin*
Al redy broght unto his hond;
And whanne he sih and redy fond
This cofre mad and wel enclowed,   *nailed shut*
The dede bodi was besowed   *sewed up*
1115 In cloth of gold and leid therinne.
And for he wolde unto hire winne   *gain for her*
Upon som cooste a sepulture,
Under hire heved in aventure   *head as a gamble [with Fortune]*
Of gold he leide sommes grete   *great quantities*
1120 And of jeueals a strong beyete   *jewels a great possession*
Forth with a lettre, and seide thus:
☞   "I, king of Tyr Appollinus,   *(see note)*
Do alle maner men to wite,   *Cause; know*
That hiere and se this lettre write,   *Who hear; written*
1125 That helpeles withoute red   *help (a cure)*
Hier lith a kinges doghter ded: *Here lies*
And who that happeth hir to finde,
For charité tak in his mynde,   *let him take thought*
And do so that sche be begrave   *buried*
1130 With this tresor, which he schal have."
Thus whanne the lettre was full spoke,
Thei have anon the cofre stoke,   *coffin nailed shut*
And bounden it with yren faste,   *iron*
That it may with the wawes laste,   *waves endure*
1135 And stoppen it be such a weie,   *sealed*
That it schal be withinne dreie,   *dry*
So that no water myhte it grieve.   *harm*

And thus in hope and good believe
Of that the corps schal wel aryve,
1140   Thei caste it over bord als blyve.   *quickly*
☞   The schip forth on the wawes wente;   *(see note)*
The prince hath changed his entente,
And seith he wol noght come at Tyr
As thanne, bot al his desir
1145   Is ferst to seilen unto Tharse.
The wyndy storm began to skarse,   *diminish*
The sonne arist, the weder cliereth,   *arose; weather clears*
The schipman which behinde stiereth,
Whan that he sih the wyndes saghte,   *at peace*
1150   Towardes Tharse his cours he straghte.   *made straight*
☞   Bot now to mi matiere agein,   *(see note)*
To telle as olde bokes sein,
This dede corps of which ye knowe
With wynd and water was forthrowe   *tossed about*
1155   Now hier, now ther, til ate laste
At Ephesim the see upcaste   *sea cast ashore*
The cofre and al that was therinne.
Of gret merveile nou beginne
Mai hiere who that sitteth stille;
1160   That God wol save mai noght spille.   *What; perish*
Riht as the corps was throwe alonde,
Ther cam walkende upon the stronde   *shore*
A worthi clerc, a surgien,   *scholar; surgeon*
And ek a gret phisicien,
1165   Of al that lond the wisest on,   *one*
Which hihte Maister Cerymon;   *Who was called*
Ther were of his disciples some.   *several of his students*
This maister to the cofre is come,
He peiseth ther was somwhat in,   *feels by weight*
1170   And bad hem bere it to his in,   *them bear; residence*
And goth himselve forth withal.
Al that schal falle, falle schal;
Thei comen hom and tarie noght;
This cofre is into chambre broght,
1175   Which that thei finde faste stoke,   *tightly nailed shut*
Bot thei with craft it have unloke.
Thei loken in, where as thei founde   *look*
A bodi ded, which was bewounde
In cloth of gold, as I seide er,   *said before*
1180   The tresor ek thei founden ther
Forth with the lettre, which thei rede.
And tho thei token betre hiede;   *heed*
Unsowed was the bodi sone,   *Unsewn*
And he, which knew what is to done,

1185	This noble clerk, with alle haste	
	Began the veines for to taste,	*veins; probe*
	And sih hire age was of youthe,	*saw*
	And with the craftes whiche he couthe	*knew*
	He soghte and fond a signe of lif.	
1190	With that this worthi kinges wif	
	Honestely thei token oute,	*Honorably*
	And maden fyres al aboute;	
	Thei leide hire on a couche softe,	
	And with a scheete warmed ofte	
1195	Hire colde brest began to hete,	
	Hire herte also to flacke and bete.	*flutter*
	This maister hath hire every joignt	
	With certein oile and balsme enoignt,	*anointed*
	And putte a liquour in hire mouth,	
1200	Which is to fewe clerkes couth,	*known*
	So that sche coevereth ate laste:	*recovers*
	And ferst hire yhen up sche caste,	*eyes*
	And whan sche more of strengthe cawhte,	
	Hire armes bothe forth sche strawhte,	*stretched*
1205	Hield up hire hond and pitously	
	Sche spak and seide, "Ha, wher am I?	
	Where is my lord, what world is this?"	
	As sche that wot noght hou it is.	
	Bot Cerymon the worthi leche	*physician (leech)*
1210	Ansuerde anon upon hire speche	
	And seith, "Ma dame, yee ben hiere	
	Wher yee be sauf, as yee schal hiere	
	Hierafterward; forthi as nou	
	Mi conseil is, conforteth you:	*take comfort*
1215	For trusteth wel withoute faile,	
	Ther is nothing which schal you faile,	*be lacking for you*
	That oghte of reson to be do."	
	Thus passen thei a day or tuo;	
	Thei speke of noght as for an ende,	*not of a final resolution [to the situation]*
1220	Til sche began somdiel amende,	
	And wiste hireselven what sche mente.	*knew herself what she intended*
☞	Tho for to knowe hire hol entente,	*(see note)*
	This maister axeth al the cas,	
	Hou sche cam there and what sche was.	*who*
1225	"Hou I cam hiere wot I noght,"	
	Quod sche, "bot wel I am bethoght	*I am well aware*
	Of othre thinges al aboute":	
	Fro point to point and tolde him oute	
	Als ferforthli as sche it wiste.	*straightforwardly; knew*
1230	And he hire tolde hou in a kiste	*coffin (chest)*
	The see hire threw upon the lond,	*sea*

And what tresor with hire he fond,
Which was al redy at hire wille,
As he that schop him to fulfille   *prepared himself to*
1235   With al his myht what thing he scholde.
Sche thonketh him that he so wolde,
And al hire herte sche discloseth,
And seith him wel that sche supposeth
Hire lord be dreint, hir child also;   *drowned*
1240   So sih sche noght bot alle wo.
Wherof as to the world no more
Ne wol sche torne, and preith therfore
That in som temple of the cité
To kepe and holde hir chasteté,
1245   Sche mihte among the wommen duelle.
Whan he this tale hir herde telle,
He was riht glad, and made hire knowen
That he a dowhter of his owen
Hath, which he wol unto hir give
1250   To serve, whil thei bothe live,
In stede of that which sche hath lost;
Al only at his oghne cost
Sche schal be rendred forth with hire.   *delivered*
Sche seith, "Grant mercy, lieve sire,   *dear*
1255   God quite it you, ther I ne may."   *May God repay*
And thus thei drive forth the day,
Til time com that sche was hol;   *well*
And tho thei take her conseil hol,   *whole*
To schape upon good ordinance
1260   And make a worthi pourveance
Agein the day whan thei be veiled.
And thus, whan that thei be conseiled,
In blake clothes thei hem clothe,
This lady and the dowhter bothe,
1265   And yolde hem to religion.   *submitted (surrendered) themselves*
The feste and the profession
After the reule of that degré
Was mad with gret solempneté,
Where as Diane is seintefied;   *sanctified*
1270   Thus stant this lady justefied   *made righteous*
In ordre wher sche thenkth to duelle.
☞   Bot now ageinward for to telle   *(see note)*
In what plit that hire lord stod inne:
He seileth, til that he may winne   *reach*
1275   The havene of Tharse, as I seide er;   *before*
And whanne he was aryved ther,
And it was thurgh the cité knowe,
Men myhte se withinne a throwe,   *in a short time*

As who seith, al the toun at ones, *So to speak; at once*
1280 That come agein him for the nones, *towards him*
To given him the reverence,
So glad thei were of his presence:
And thogh he were in his corage
Desesed, yit with glad visage *Distressed*
1285 He made hem chiere, and to his in, *dwelling (inn)*
Wher he whilom sojourned in,
He goth him straght and was resceived.
And whan the presse of poeple is weived, *crowd; expelled*
He takth his hoste unto him tho,
1290 And seith, "Mi frend Strangulio,
Lo, thus and thus it is befalle,
And thou thiself art on of alle, *one*
Forth with thi wif, whiche I most triste. *trust*
Forthi, if it you bothe liste, *pleases*
1295 Mi doghter Thaise be youre leve *with your permission*
I thenke schal with you beleve *remain*
As for a time; and thus I preie,
That sche be kept be alle weie, *in every way [appropriate]*
And whan sche hath of age more,
1300 That sche be set to bokes lore. *learning*
And this avou to God I make,
That I schal nevere for hir sake
Mi berd for no likinge schave, *in spite of any preference*
Til it befalle that I have
1305 In covenable time of age *opportune moment*
Beset hire unto mariage."
Thus thei acorde, and al is wel, *agree*
And for to resten him somdel, *somewhat*
As for a while he ther sojorneth,
1310 And thanne he takth his leve and torneth
To schipe, and goth him hom to Tyr,
Wher every man with gret desir
Awaiteth upon his comynge.
Bot whan the schip com in seilinge,
1315 And thei perceiven it is he,
Was nevere yit in no cité
Such joie mad as thei tho made; *then*
His herte also began to glade *be joyful*
Of that he sih the poeple glad.
1320 Lo, thus fortune his hap hath lad; *circumstance has determined*
In sondri wise he was travailed, *afflicted*
Bot hou so evere he be assailed,
His latere ende schal be good.
☞ And for to speke hou that it stod *(see note)*
1325 Of Thaise his doghter, wher sche duelleth,

	In Tharse, as the cronique telleth,	*chronicle*
	Sche was wel kept, sche was wel loked,	*watched over*
	Sche was wel tawht, sche was wel boked,	
	So wel sche spedde hir in hire youthe	*succeeded*
1330	That sche of every wisdom couthe,	*knew*
	That for to seche in every lond	*seek*
	So wys another no man fond,	
	Ne so wel tawht at mannes yhe.	*to the human eye*
	Bot wo worthe evere fals envie!	
1335	For it befell that time so,	
	A dowhter hath Strangulio,	
	The which was cleped Philotenne.	*called*
	Bot fame, which wole evere renne,	*travel*
	Cam al day to hir moder ere,	*ear*
1340	And seith, wher evere hir doghter were	
	With Thayse set in eny place,	
	The comun vois, the comun grace	
	Was al upon that other maide,	
	And of hir doghter no man saide.	
1345	Who wroth but Dionise thanne?	*became angry*
	Hire thoghte a thousend yer til whanne	*It seemed to her*
	Sche myhte ben of Thaise wreke	*avenged*
	Of that sche herde folk so speke.	*For what*
	And fell that ilke same tyde,	*very same time*
1350	That ded was trewe Lychoride,	
	Which hadde be servant to Thaise,	
	So that sche was the worse at aise,	*ease*
	For sche hath thanne no servise	
	Bot only thurgh this Dionise,	
1355	Which was hire dedlich anemie	*enemy*
	Thurgh pure treson and envie.	
	Sche, that of alle sorwe can,	*who; knows*
	Tho spak unto hire bondeman,	
	Which cleped was Theophilus,	
1360	And made him swere in conseil thus,	
	That he such time as sche him sette	
	Schal come Thaise for to fette,	*fetch*
	And lede hire oute of alle sihte,	*lead; sight*
	Wher as no man hire helpe myhte,	
1365	Upon the stronde nyh the see,	*shore near; sea*
	And there he schal this maiden sle.	*slay*
	This cherles herte is in a traunce,	*daze*
	As he which drad him of vengance	*feared vengeance for himself*
	Whan time comth an other day;	
1370	Bot yit dorste he noght seie nay,	*dared*
	Bot swor and seide he schal fulfille	
	Hire hestes at hire oghne wille.	*orders; own*

☞   The treson and the time is schape,   *arranged (see note)*
            So fell it that this cherles knape   *churlish attendant*
1375   Hath lad this maiden ther he wolde   *where*
            Upon the stronde, and what sche scholde   *should [endure]*
            Sche was adrad; and he out breide   *drew*
            A rusti swerd and to hir seide,
            "Thou schalt be ded." "Helas!" quod sche,
1380   "Why schal I so?" "Lo thus," quod he,
            "Mi ladi Dionise hath bede,   *commanded*
            Thou schalt be moerdred in this stede."   *place*
            This maiden tho for feere schryhte,   *fear screamed*
            And for the love of God almyhte
1385   Sche preith that for a litel stounde   *time*
            Sche myhte knele upon the grounde,
            Toward the hevene for to crave,   *beseech*
            Hire wofull soule if sche mai save.
            And with this noise and with this cry,
1390   Out of a barge faste by,
            Which hidd was ther on scomerfare,   *piracy*
            Men sterten out and weren ware
            Of this feloun, and he to go,   *he [Theophilus] fled*
            And sche began to crie tho,   *then*
1395   "Ha, mercy, help for Goddes sake!
            Into the barge thei hire take,
            As thieves scholde, and forth thei wente.
            Upon the see the wynd hem hente,   *took*
            And malgré wher thei wolde or non,   *despite*
1400   Tofor the weder forth thei gon,   *Before the [bad] weather*
            Ther halp no seil, ther halp non ore,
            Forstormed and forblowen sore
            In gret peril so forth thei dryve,
            Til ate laste thei aryve
1405   At Mitelene the cité.
            In havene sauf and whan thei be,
            The maister schipman made him boun,   *prepared a plan for himself*
            And goth him out into the toun,
            And profreth Thaise for to selle.
1410   On Leonin it herde telle,   *A certain Leonin*
            Which maister of the bordel was,   *Who; brothel*
            And bad him gon a redy pas   *quick pace*
            To fetten hire, and forth he wente,
            And Thaise out of his barge he hente,   *seized*
1415   And to this bordeller hir solde.   *brothel-keeper*
            And he, that be hire body wolde
            Take avantage, let do crye,
            That what man wolde his lecherie
            Attempte upon hire maidenhede,

1420   Lei doun the gold and he schal spede.   *succeed*
       And thus whan he hath crid it oute
       In syhte of al the poeple aboute,
☞   He ladde hire to the bordel tho.   *brothel (see note)*
          No wonder is thogh sche be wo:
1425   Clos in a chambre be hireselve,
       Ech after other ten or tuelve
       Of yonge men to hire in wente;
       Bot such a grace God hire sente,
       That for the sorwe which sche made
1430   Was non of hem which pouer hade
       To don hire eny vileinie.
       This Leonin let evere aspie,
       And waiteth after gret beyete;   *profit*
       Bot al for noght, sche was forlete,   *abandoned*
1435   That mo men wolde ther noght come.   *[Such] that*
       Whan he therof hath hiede nome,   *taken heed*
       And knew that sche was yit a maide,
       Unto his oghne man he saide,
       That he with strengthe agein hire leve   *without her permission*
1440   Tho scholde hir maidenhod bereve.   *rob*
       This man goth in, bot so it ferde,
       Whan he hire wofull pleintes herde
       And he therof hath take kepe,
       Him liste betre for to wepe   *It pleased him*
1445   Than don oght elles to the game.
       And thus sche kepte hirself fro schame,
       And kneleth doun to th'erthe and preide
       Unto this man, and thus sche seide:
       "If so be that thi maister wolde
1450   That I his gold encresce scholde,
       It mai noght falle be this weie: *come about by this means*
       Bot soffre me to go mi weie
       Out of this hous wher I am inne,
       And I schal make him for to winne
1455   In som place elles of the toun,
       Be so it be religioun,   *Provided that it be a religious house*
       Wher that honeste wommen duelle.
       And thus thou myht thi maister telle,
       That whanne I have a chambre there,
1460   Let him do crie ay wyde where,
       What lord that hath his doghter diere,
       And is in will that sche schal liere   *learn*
       Of such a scole that is trewe,
       I schal hire teche of thinges newe,
1465   Which as non other womman can
       In al this lond." And tho this man   *as soon as*

Hire tale hath herd, he goth agein,
And tolde unto his maister plein
That sche hath seid; and therupon, *What*
1470 Whan than he sih beyete non *saw no gain*
At the bordel because of hire,
He bad his man to gon and spire *seek*
A place wher sche myhte abyde,
That he mai winne upon som side
1475 Be that sche can: bot ate leste *By what she knew*
Thus was sche sauf fro this tempeste.
☞   He hath hire fro the bordel take, *(see note)*
Bot that was noght for Goddes sake,
Bot for the lucre, as sche him tolde. *for gain*
1480 Now comen tho that come wolde
Of wommen in her lusty youthe,
To hiere and se what thing sche couthe: *knew*
Sche can the wisdom of a clerk, *knew*
Sche can of every lusti werk *knew; desirable skill*
1485 Which to a gentil womman longeth, *belongs*
And some of hem sche underfongeth *took in [as students]*
To the citole and to the harpe,
And whom it liketh for to carpe *to tell*
Proverbes and demandes slyhe, *cunning riddles*
1490 An other such thei nevere syhe,
Which that science so wel tawhte:
Wherof sche grete giftes cawhte, *received*
That sche to Leonin hath wonne; *gained*
And thus hire name is so begonne *established*
1495 Of sondri thinges that sche techeth,
That al the lond unto hir secheth
Of yonge wommen for to liere.
☞   Nou lete we this maiden hiere, *(see note)*
And speke of Dionise agein
1500 And of Theophile the vilein, *scoundrel*
Of whiche I spak of nou tofore.
Whan Thaise scholde have be forlore, *utterly destroyed*
This false cherl to his lady
Whan he cam hom, al prively
1505 He seith, "Ma dame, slain I have
This maide Thaise, and is begrave *buried*
In privé place, as ye me biede. *secret; commanded*
Forthi, ma dame, taketh hiede
And kep conseil, hou so it stonde." *keep it secret, however things should go*
1510 This fend, which this hath understonde,
Was glad, and weneth it be soth:
Now herkne, hierafter hou sche doth.
Sche wepth, sche sorweth, sche compleigneth,

And of sieknesse which sche feigneth
1515 Sche seith that Taise sodeinly
Be nyhte is ded, "as sche and I
Togedre lyhen nyh my lord."
Sche was a womman of record,   *good repute*
And al is lieved that sche seith;   *believed*
1520 And for to give a more feith,   *greater credibility*
Hire housebonde and ek sche bothe
In blake clothes thei hem clothe,
And made a gret enterrement;   *funeral*
And for the poeple schal be blent,   *blinded*
1525 Of Thaise as for the remembrance,
After the real olde usance   *ancient royal custom*
A tumbe of latoun noble and riche   *tomb; latten (tin and copper alloy)*
With an ymage unto hir liche   *statue in her likeness*
Liggende above therupon
1530 Thei made and sette it up anon.
Hire epitaffe of good assisse   *in a proper manner*
Was write aboute, and in this wise
It spak: "O yee that this beholde,
Lo, hier lith sche, the which was holde   *here lies; considered*
1535 The faireste and the flour of alle,
Whos name Thaisis men calle.
The king of Tyr Appolinus
Hire fader was: now lith sche thus.
Fourtiene yer sche was of age,
1540 Whan deth hir tok to his viage."   *journey*
☞   Thus was this false treson hidd,   *(see note)*
Which afterward was wyde kidd,   *widely known*
As be the tale a man schal hiere.
Bot for to clare mi matiere,   *declare*
1545 To Tyr I thenke torne agein,
And telle as the croniqes sein.
Whan that the king was comen hom,
And hath left in the salte fom   *foam (i.e., sea)*
His wif, which he mai noght forgete,
1550 For he som confort wolde gete,
He let somoune a parlement,
To which the lordes were asent;
And of the time he hath ben oute,
He seth the thinges al aboute,
1555 And told hem ek hou he hath fare,
Whil he was out of londe fare;   *traveling*
And preide hem alle to abyde,   *wait*
For he wolde at the same tyde   *time*
Do schape for his wyves mynde,   *Have arrangements made; wife's memory*
1560 As he that wol noght ben unkinde.   *disloyal (ungrateful)*

Solempne was that ilke office,
And riche was the sacrifice;
The feste reali was holde.   *feast royally*
And therto was he wel beholde;   *entirely duty-bound*
1565   For such a wif as he hadde on   *one*
In thilke daies was ther non.
☞   Whan this was do, thanne he him thoghte   *(see note)*
Upon his doghter, and besoghte
Suche of his lordes as he wolde,
1570   That thei with him to Tharse scholde,
To fette his doghter Taise there.
And thei anon al redy were,
To schip thei gon and forth thei wente,
Til thei the havene of Tharse hente.   *reached*
1575   Thei londe and faile of that thei seche   *cannot acquire what; seek*
Be coverture and sleyhte of speche.   *By concealment; trickery*
This false man Strangulio,
And Dionise his wif also,
That he the betre trowe myhte,   *trust (believe)*
1580   Thei ladden him to have a sihte
Wher that hir tombe was arraied.
The lasse yit he was mispaied,   *displeased*
And natheles, so as he dorste,   *dared*
He curseth and seith al the worste
1585   Unto Fortune, as to the blinde,
Which can no seker weie finde;   *secure*
For sche him neweth evere among,   *changes*
And medleth sorwe with his song.   *intermixes*
1589   Bot sithe it mai no betre be,   *since*
☞   He thonketh God and forth goth he   *(see note)*
Seilende toward Tyr agein.
Bot sodeinly the wynd and reyn
Begonne upon the see debate,   *sea churn*
So that he soffre mot algate   *in any case*
1595   The lawe which Neptune ordeigneth;
Wherof ful ofte time he pleigneth,   *laments*
And hield him wel the more esmaied   *dismayed*
Of that he hath tofore assaied.   *before endured*
So that for pure sorwe and care,
1600   Of that he seth his world so fare,   *Since he sees; go*
The reste he lefte of his caban,
That for the conseil of no man
Agein therinne he nolde come,   *would not*
Bot hath benethe his place nome,   *in the hold; taken*
1605   Wher he wepende alone lay,
Ther as he sih no lyht of day.
And thus tofor the wynd thei dryve,

Til longe and late thei aryve
With gret distresce, as it was sene,
1610 Upon this toun of Mitelene,
Which was a noble cité tho.
And hapneth thilke time so,
The lordes bothe and the comune
The hihe festes of Neptune
1615 Upon the stronde at the rivage,   *shore at the coast*
As it was custumme and usage,
Sollempneliche thei besihe.   *Solemnly they celebrated*
☞   Whan thei this strange vessel syhe   *(see note)*
Come in, and hath his seil avaled,   *lowered*
1620 The toun therof hath spoke and taled.   *argued (gossiped)*
The lord which of the cité was,
Whos name is Athenagoras,
Was there, and seide he wolde se
What schip it is, and who thei be
1625 That ben therinne: and after sone,
Whan that he sih it was to done,
His barge was for him arraied,
And he goth forth and hath assaied.   *investigated*
He fond the schip of gret array,
1630 Bot what thing it amonte may,   *whatever it signified*
He seth thei maden hevy chiere,   *sees they were lamenting*
Bot wel him thenkth be the manere
That thei be worthi men of blod,
And axeth of hem hou it stod;
1635 And thei him tellen al the cas,
Hou that here lord fordrive was,   *desperately driven*
And what a sorwe that he made,
Of which ther mai no man him glade.   *cheer up*
He preith that he here lord mai se,   *their*
1640 Bot thei him tolde it mai noght be,
For he lith in so derk a place,
That ther may no wiht sen his face.   *person see*
Bot for al that, thogh hem be loth,   *But despite; it displeased them*
He fond the ladre and doun he goth,
1645 And to him spak, bot non ansuere
Agein of him ne mihte he bere   *Back from him*
For oght that he can don or sein;   *do or say*
And thus he goth him up agein.
Tho was ther spoke in many wise
1650 Amonges hem that were wise,
Now this, now that, bot ate laste
☞ The wisdom of the toun this caste,   *determined (see note)*
That yonge Taise were asent.   *would be sent for*
For if ther be amendement

1655	To glade with this woful king,
	Sche can so moche of every thing,
	That sche schal gladen him anon.
	A messager for hire is gon,
	And sche cam with hire harpe on honde,
1660	And seide hem that sche wolde fonde
	Be alle weies that sche can,
	To glade with this sory man.
	Bot what he was sche wiste noght,
	Bot al the schip hire hath besoght
1665	That sche hire wit on him despende,
	In aunter if he myhte amende,
	And sein it schal be wel aquit.
	Whan sche hath understonden it,
	Sche goth hir doun, ther as he lay,
1670	Wher that sche harpeth many a lay
	And lich an angel sang withal;
	Bot he no more than the wal
	Tok hiede of eny thing he herde.
	And whan sche sih that he so ferde,
1675	Sche falleth with him into wordes,
	And telleth him of sondri bordes,
	And axeth him demandes strange,
	Wherof sche made his herte change,
	And to hire speche his ere he leide
1680	And hath merveile of that sche seide.
	For in proverbe and in probleme
	Sche spak, and bad he scholde deme
	In many soubtil question:
	Bot he for no suggestioun
1685	Which toward him sche couthe stere,
	He wolde noght o word ansuere,
	Bot as a madd man ate laste
	His heved wepende awey he caste,
	And half in wraththe he bad hire go.
1690	Bot yit sche wolde noght do so,
	And in the derke forth sche goth,
	Til sche him toucheth, and he wroth,
	And after hire with his hond
	He smot: and thus whan sche him fond
1695	Desesed, courtaisly sche saide,
	"Avoi, mi lord, I am a maide;
	And if ye wiste what I am,
	And out of what lignage I cam,
	Ye wolde noght be so salvage."
☞	With that he sobreth his corage
1701	And put awey his hevy chiere.

Glosses (right margin):

- *knows* (1656)
- *attempt* (1660)
- *every means that she is able* (1661)
- *who; knew* (1663)
- *Except; crew had begged her* (1664)
- *employ* (1665)
- *On the chance that; improve* (1666)
- *[had] said; well worth her effort* (1667)
- *grasped this* (1668)
- *where* (1669)
- *like* (1671)
- *wall (i.e., source of strength)* (1672)
- *saw; fared so* (1674)
- *various tales (jests)* (1676)
- *unusual riddles* (1677)
- *puzzle (riddle)* (1681)
- *asked; judge* (1682)
- *prompting* (1684)
- *That in respect to him; could stir up* (1685)
- *He, weeping, quickly turned his head away* (1688)
- *recoiled* (1692)
- *struck* (1694)
- *Desist!* (1696)
- *knew how* (1697)
- *savage* (1699)
- *mood (see note)* (1700)
- *morose behavior* (1701)

	Bot of hem tuo a man mai liere	*of those two one may learn*
	What is to be so sibb of blod.	*akin by blood*
	Non wiste of other hou it stod,	*Neither knew*
1705	And yit the fader ate laste	
	His herte upon this maide caste,	
	That he hire loveth kindely,	*[Such] that; warmly (naturally)*
	And yit he wiste nevere why.	
	Bot al was knowe er that thei wente;	*discovered before*
1710	For God, which wot here hol entente,	*who knew their whole*
	Here hertes bothe anon descloseth.	*Their; soon*
	This king unto this maide opposeth,	*questioned*
	And axeth ferst what was hire name,	
	And wher sche lerned al this game,	
1715	And of what ken that sche was come.	*parentage*
	And sche, that hath hise wordes nome,	*understood*
	Ansuerth and seith, "My name is Thaise,	
	That was som time wel at aise.	*ease*
	In Tharse I was forthdrawe and fed;	*brought up*
1720	Ther lerned I til I was sped	*successful*
	Of that I can. Mi fader eke	*what I know*
	I not wher that I scholde him seke;	*know not*
	He was a king, men tolde me.	
	Mi moder dreint was in the see."	*drowned*
1725	Fro point to point al sche him tolde,	
	That sche hath longe in herte holde,	*held*
	And nevere dorste make hir mone	*dared; complaint*
	Bot only to this lord alone,	
	To whom hire herte can noght hele,	*stay concealed*
1730	Torne it to wo, torne it to wele,	*Whether it may turn*
	Torne it to good, torne it to harm.	
	And he tho toke hire in his arm,	*then*
	Bot such a joie as he tho made	
	Was nevere sen; thus be thei glade,	
1735	That sory hadden be toforn.	
	Fro this day forth Fortune hath sworn	
	To sette him upward on the whiel;	
	So goth the world, now wo, now wel:	
	This king hath founde newe grace,	
1740	So that out of his derke place	
	He goth him up into the liht,	
	And with him cam that swete wiht,	*creature*
	His doghter Thaise, and forth anon	
	Thei bothe into the caban gon	
1745	Which was ordeigned for the king,	
	And ther he dede of al his thing,	*carried out all his business*
	And was arraied realy.	*royally*
☞	And out he cam al openly,	*(see note)*

Wher Athenagoras he fond,
1750   The which was lord of al the lond.
He preith the king to come and se
His castell bothe and his cité,
And thus thei gon forth alle in fiere,   *all together*
This king, this lord, this maiden diere.
1755   This lord tho made hem riche feste   *celebration*
With every thing which was honeste,   *honorable*
To plese with this worthi king.
Ther lacketh him no maner thing.
Bot yit for al his noble array,
1760   Wifles he was into that day,   *he (Athenagoras); up to this point*
As he that yit was of yong age.
So fell ther into his corage   *heart*
The lusti wo, the glade peine
Of love, which no man restreigne
1765   Yit nevere myhte as nou tofore.
This lord thenkth al his world forlore,   *lost*
Bot if the king wol don him grace;   *king (Apollonius)*
He waiteth time, he waiteth place,
Him thoghte his herte wol tobreke,   *burst asunder*
1770   Til he mai to this maide speke
And to hir fader ek also
For mariage. And it fell so,
That al was do riht as he thoghte,   *hoped*
His pourpos to an ende he broghte,
1775   Sche weddeth him as for hire lord.
Thus be thei alle of on acord.
☞   Whan al was do riht as thei wolde,   *wished (see note)*
The king unto his sone tolde   *son-in-law (Athenagoras)*
Of Tharse thilke traiterie,
1780   And seide hou in his compaignie
His doghter and himselven eke
Schull go vengance for to seke.
The schipes were redy sone,
And whan thei sihe it was to done,
1785   Withoute lette of eny wente   *hindrance of any plan*
With seil updrawe forth thei wente
Towardes Tharse upon the tyde.
Bot he that wot what schal betide,
The hihe God, which wolde him kepe,   *protect*
1790   Whan that this king was faste aslepe,
Be nyhtes time he hath him bede   *ordered*
To seile into an other stede: *place*
To Ephesim he bad him drawe,
And as it was that time lawe,
1795   He schal do there his sacrifise;

And ek he bad in alle wise
That in the temple amonges alle
His fortune, as it is befalle,   *The events of his life*
Touchende his doghter and his wif
1800 He schal beknowe upon his lif.   *declare*
The king of this avisioun
Hath gret ymaginacioun,
What thing it signefie may;
And natheles, whan it was day,
1805 He bad caste ancher and abod;   *waited*
And whil that he on ancher rod,
The wynd, which was tofore strange,   *unfavorable*
Upon the point began to change,
And torneth thider as it scholde.
1810 Tho knew he wel that God it wolde,   *Then*
And bad the maister make him yare,   *ship captain; ready*
Tofor the wynd for he wol fare
To Ephesim, and so he dede.
And whanne he cam unto the stede   *place*
1815 Where as he scholde londe, he londeth
With al the haste he may, and fondeth   *strives*
To schapen him be such a wise,   *To prepare himself*
That he may be the morwe arise
And don after the mandement   *mandate*
1820 Of Him which hath him thider sent.
And in the wise that he thoghte,
Upon the morwe so he wroghte;
His doghter and his sone he nom,   *took*
And forth unto the temple he com
1825 With a gret route in compaignie,
Hise giftes for to sacrifie.
The citezeins tho herden seie
Of such a king that cam to preie
Unto Diane the godesse,
1830 And left al other besinesse,
Thei comen thider for to se
The king and the solempneté.
☞   With worthi knyhtes environed   *surrounded (see note)*
The king himself hath abandoned   *humbly gone*
1835 Into the temple in good entente.
The dore is up, and he in wente,
Wher as with gret devocioun
Of holi contemplacioun
Withinne his herte he made his schrifte;   *confession*
1840 And after that a riche gifte
He offreth with gret reverence,
And there in open audience

	Of hem that stoden thanne aboute,	
	He tolde hem and declareth oute	
1845	His hap, such as him is befalle,	*circumstances*
	Ther was nothing forgete of alle.	*omitted at all*
	His wif, as it was Goddes grace,	
	Which was professed in the place,	
	As sche that was abbesse there,	
1850	Unto his tale hath leid hire ere:	*laid her ear*
	Sche knew the vois and the visage,	
	For pure joie as in a rage	*passion*
	Sche strawhte unto him al at ones,	*went straight*
	And fell aswoune upon the stones,	
1855	Wherof the temple flor was paved.	
	Sche was anon with water laved,	*washed*
	Til sche cam to hirself agein,	
	And thanne sche began to sein,	*say*
	"Ha, blessed be the hihe sonde,	*decree*
1860	That I mai se myn housebonde,	
	That whilom he and I were on!"	
	The king with that knew hire anon,	
	And tok hire in his arm and kiste.	
	And al the toun thus sone it wiste.	*knew*
1865	Tho was ther joie manyfold,	
	For every man this tale hath told	
	As for miracle, and were glade,	
	Bot nevere man such joie made	
	As doth the king, which hath his wif.	
1870	And whan men herde hou that hir lif	
	Was saved, and be whom it was,	*by*
	Thei wondren alle of such a cas.	
	Thurgh al the lond aros the speche	
	Of Maister Cerymon the leche	*physician*
1875	And of the cure which he dede.	*healing; performed*
	The king himself tho hath him bede,	*summoned*
	And ek this queene forth with him,	
	That he the toun of Ephesim	
	Wol leve and go wher as thei be,	
1880	For nevere man of his degré	
	Hath do to hem so mochel good;	
	And he his profit understod,	
	And granteth with hem for to wende.	*them to go*
	And thus thei maden there an ende,	
1885	And token leve and gon to schipe	
	With al the hole felaschipe.	
☞	This king, which nou hath his desir,	*(see note)*
	Seith he wol holde his cours to Tyr.	
	Thei hadden wynd at wille tho,	

1890   With topseilcole and forth thei go,   *topsail-wind (i.e., wind on the topsail)*
        And striken nevere, til thei come   *never with sails lowered (stricken)*
        To Tyr, where as thei havene nome,   *took haven*
        And londen hem with mochel blisse.
        Tho was ther many a mowth to kisse,
1895   Echon welcometh other hom,
        Bot whan the queen to londe com,
        And Thaise hir doghter be hir side,
        The joie which was thilke tyde
        Ther mai no mannes tunge telle:
1900   Thei seiden alle, "Hier comth the welle
        Of alle wommannysshe grace."
        The king hath take his real place,   *royal*
        The queene is into chambre go:
        Ther was gret feste arraied tho;
1905   Whan time was, thei gon to mete,   *dinner*
        Alle olde sorwes ben forgete,
        And gladen hem with joies newe.
        The descoloured pale hewe
        Is now become a rody cheke,
1910   Ther was no merthe for to seke,
        Bot every man hath that he wolde.   *what he wanted*
☞   The king, as he wel couthe and scholde,   *was able and ought to (see note)*
        Makth to his poeple riht good chiere;
        And after sone, as thou schalt hiere,
1915   A parlement he hath sommoned,
        Wher he his doghter hath coroned
        Forth with the lord of Mitelene,
        That on is king, that other queene.
        And thus the fadres ordinance
1920   This lond hath set in governance,
        And seide thanne he wolde wende
        To Tharse, for to make an ende
        Of that his doghter was betraied.
        Therof were alle men wel paied,   *pleased*
1925   And seide hou it was for to done.
        The schipes weren redi sone,
        And strong pouer with him he tok;
        Up to the sky he caste his lok,
        And syh the wynd was covenable.   *favorable*
☞   Thei hale up ancher with the cable,   *(see note)*
1931   The seil on hih, the stiere in honde,
        And seilen, til thei come alonde
        At Tharse nyh to the cité;
        And whan thei wisten it was he,
1935   The toun hath don him reverence,
        He telleth hem the violence,

Which the tretour Strangulio
And Dionise him hadde do
Touchende his dowhter, as yee herde.
1940   And whan thei wiste hou that it ferde,
As he which pes and love soghte,
Unto the toun this he besoghte,
To don him riht in juggement.
Anon thei were bothe asent
1945 With strengthe of men, and comen sone,
And as hem thoghte it was to done,
Atteint thei were be the lawe   *Convicted*
And diemed for to honge and drawe,   *sentenced*
And brent and with the wynd toblowe,   *burned; blown in all directions*
1950 That al the world it myhte knowe.   *[So] that*
And upon this condicion
The dom in execucion   *judgment*
Was put anon withoute faile.
And every man hath gret mervaile,
1955 Which herde tellen of this chance,
And thonketh Goddes pourveance,   *providence*
Which doth mercy forth with justice.
Slain is the moerdrer and moerdrice
Thurgh verray trowthe of rihtwisnesse,
1960 And thurgh mercy sauf is simplesse   *saved is the innocence*
Of hire whom mercy preserveth;
Thus hath he wel that wel deserveth.   *goodness who goodness*
☞   Whan al this thing is don and ended, *(see note)*
This king, which loved was and frended,
1965 A lettre hath, which cam to him
Be schipe fro Pentapolim,
Be which the lond hath to him write,
That he wolde understonde and wite
Hou in good mynde and in good pes   *good memory*
1970 Ded is the king Artestrates,
Wherof thei alle of on acord   *one*
Him preiden, as here liege lord,   *beseeched; their*
That he the lettre wel conceive   *consider*
And come his regne to receive,
1975 Which God hath gove him and fortune;
And thus besoghte the commune   *commons*
Forth with the grete lordes alle.
This king sih how it was befalle,   *saw*
Fro Tharse and in prosperité
1980 He tok his leve of that cité
And goth him into schipe agein:
The wynd was good, the see was plein, *calm*
Hem nedeth noght a riff to slake,   *reef sail; let out*

	Til thei Pentapolim have take.	
1985	The lond, which herde of that tidinge,	
	Was wonder glad of his cominge;	
	He resteth him a day or tuo	
	And tok his conseil to him tho,	
	And sette a time of Parlement,	
1990	Wher al the lond of on assent	
	Forth with his wif hath him corouned,	
	Wher alle goode him was fuisouned.	*abundantly supplied*
	Lo, what it is to be wel grounded:	
	For he hath ferst his love founded	
1995	Honesteliche as for to wedde,	*Honorably*
	Honesteliche his love he spedde	*Honorably; fulfilled*
	And hadde children with his wif,	
	And as him liste he ladde his lif;	*it pleased him*
	And in ensample as it is write,	*written*
2000	That alle lovers myhten wite	*know*
	How ate laste it schal be sene	
	Of love what thei wolden mene.	*intend*
	For se now on that other side,	
	Antiochus with al his pride,	
2005	Which sette his love unkindely,	*unnaturally*
	His ende he hadde al sodeinly,	
	Set agein kinde upon vengance,	*against nature*
	And for his lust hath his penance.	

[THE CONFESSOR'S FINAL COUNSEL]

Confessor ad Amantem	"Lo thus, mi sone, myht thou liere	
	What is to love in good manere,	
	And what to love in other wise.	
	The mede arist of the servise;	*reward arises out of*
	Fortune, thogh sche be noght stable,	
	Yit at som time is favorable	
2015	To hem that ben of love trewe.	
	Bot certes it is for to rewe	
	To se love agein kinde falle,	*nature oppose*
	For that makth sore a man to falle,	
	As thou myht of tofore rede.	
2020	Forthi, my sone, I wolde rede	*advise*
	To lete al other love aweie,	
	Bot if it be thurgh such a weie	
	As love and reson wolde acorde.	
	For elles, if that thou descorde,	
2025	And take lust as doth a beste,	*beast*
	Thi love mai noght ben honeste;	

        For be no skile that I finde   *reason*
        Such lust is noght of loves kinde."   *love's nature*

[THE LOVER'S ADMISSION AND REQUEST]

[Amans]   "Mi fader, hou so that it stonde,
☞   Youre tale is herd and understonde,   *(see note)*
          As thing which worthi is to hiere,
          Of gret ensample and gret matiere,
          Wherof, my fader, God you quyte.   *repay*
          Bot if this point miself aquite   *But if I might quit myself on this point*   *acquit*
2035   I mai riht wel, that nevere yit
          I was assoted in my wit,
          Bot only in that worthi place
          Wher alle lust and alle grace
          Is set, if that Danger ne were.   *frustration in love*
2040   Bot that is al my moste fere.   *greatest fear*
          I not what ye fortune acompte,   *know not; will render accountable*
          Bot what thing danger mai amonte   *love's aloofness may add up to*
          I wot wel, for I have assaied;   *attempted [it]*
          For whan myn herte is best arraied
2045   And I have al my wit thurghsoght   *scoured*
          Of love to beseche hire oght,
          For al that evere I skile may,   *may argue*
          I am concluded with a nay.   *refuted; "no"*
          That o sillable hath overthrowe
2050   A thousend wordes on a rowe
          Of suche as I best speke can;
          Thus am I bot a lewed man.
          Bot, fader, for ye ben a clerk
          Of love, and this matiere is derk,
2055   And I can evere leng the lasse,   *know; the longer the less*
          Bot yit I mai noght let it passe,
          Youre hole conseil I beseche,   *whole*
          That ye me be som weie teche
          What is my beste, as for an ende."

[THE CONFESSOR'S REPLY]

[Confessor]   "Mi sone, unto the trouthe wende   *turn*
          Now wol I for the love of thee,
          And lete alle othre truffles be.   *frivolities*
            The more that the nede is hyh,
          The more it nedeth to be slyh   *skillfully contrived*
2065   To him which hath the nede on honde.
          I have wel herd and understonde,
          Mi sone, al that thou hast me seid,

☞   And ek of that thou hast me preid,   *(see note)*
          Nou at this time that I schal
2070   As for conclusioun final
          Conseile upon thi nede sette.
          So thenke I finaly to knette   *knit*
          This cause, where it is tobroke,   *broken*
          And make an ende of that is spoke.
2075   For I behihte thee that gifte   *promised you*
          Ferst whan thou come under my schrifte,
          That thogh I toward Venus were,   *under the control of*
          Yit spak I suche wordes there,
          That for the presthod which I have,
2080   Min ordre and min astat to save,
          I seide I wolde of myn office
          To vertu more than to vice
          Encline, and teche thee mi lore.
          Forthi to speken overmore
2085   Of love, which thee mai availe,
          Tak love where it mai noght faile.
          For as of this which thou art inne,
          Be that thou seist it is a sinne,   *By what*
          And sinne mai no pris deserve;   *prize*
2090   Withoute pris and who schal serve,   *Without reward; whoever should deserve*
          I not what profit myhte availe.   *do not know*
          Thus folweth it, if thou travaile   *labor*
          Wher thou no profit hast ne pris,   *reward*
          Thou art toward thiself unwis.
2095   And sett thou myhtest lust atteigne,   *And assume [for the sake of the argument] that*
          Of every lust th'ende is a peine,
          And every peine is good to fle;
          So it is wonder thing to se,
          Why such a thing schal be desired.
2100   The more that a stock is fyred,   *stick is burned*
          The rathere into aisshe it torneth;   *sooner; ashes*
          The fot which in the weie sporneth   *foot; trips (spurns)*
          Ful ofte his heved hath overthrowe.   *head*
          Thus love is blind and can noght knowe
2105   Wher that he goth, til he be falle.   *fallen*
          Forthi, bot if it so befalle   *unless it should so happen*
          With good conseil that he be lad,
          Him oghte for to ben adrad.   *afraid (cautious)*
          For conseil passeth alle thing
2110   To him which thenkth to ben a king;
          And every man for his partie
          A kingdom hath to justefie,
          That is to sein his oghne dom.   *domain (judgment, head)*
          If he misreule that kingdom,

2115	He lest himself, and that is more	*loses*
	Than if he loste schip and ore	*oar*
	And al the worldes good withal:	
	For what man that in special	
	Hath noght himself, he hath noght elles,	
2120	No mor the perles than the schelles;	*pearls; shells*
	Al is to him of o value.	*one [indiscriminate] value*
	Thogh he hadde at his retenue	*in his command*
	The wyde world riht as he wolde,	
	Whan he his herte hath noght withholde	
2125	Toward himself, al is in vein.	
	And thus, my sone, I wolde sein,	
	As I seide er, that thou aryse,	*before*
	Er that thou falle in such a wise	
	That thou ne myht thiself rekevere;	*recover*
2130	For love, which that blind was evere,	
	Makth alle his servantz blinde also.	
	My sone, and if thou have be so,	
	Yit is it time to withdrawe,	
	And set thin herte under that lawe,	
2135	The which of reson is governed	
	And noght of will. And to be lerned,	*instructed*
	Ensamples thou hast many on	*many a one*
	Of now and ek of time gon,	
	That every lust is bot a while;	*passing moment*
2140	And who that wole himself beguile,	
	He may the rathere be deceived.	*sooner*
	Mi sone, now thou hast conceived	
	Somwhat of that I wolde mene.	
	Hierafterward it schal be sene	
2145	If that thou lieve upon mi lore;	*believe; instruction*
	For I can do to thee no more	
	Bot teche thee the rihte weie:	
	Now ches if thou wolt live or deie."	

[DEBATE BETWEEN THE CONFESSOR AND THE LOVER]

[Amans]	"Mi fader, so as I have herd	
2150	Your tale, bot it were ansuerd,	
☞	I were mochel for to blame.	*(see note)*
	Mi wo to you is bot a game,	
	That fielen noght of that I fiele.	*feel*
	The fielinge of a mannes hiele	*heel*
2155	Mai noght be likned to the herte:	*heart*
	I mai noght, thogh I wolde, asterte,	*escape*
	And ye be fre from al the peine	*Even if you*
	Of love, wherof I me pleigne.	*complain*

	It is riht esi to comaunde;	*give orders*
2160	The hert which fre goth on the launde	*hart*
	Not of an oxe what him eileth;	*Knows nothing; ox; ails*
	It falleth ofte a man merveileth	*It often happens that*
	Of that he seth an other fare,	*About what he sees*
	Bot if he knewe himself the fare,	*condition*
2165	And felt it as it is in soth,	*truth*
	He scholde don riht as he doth,	*do the same as he does*
	Or elles werse in his degré:	
	For wel I wot, and so do ye,	*you*
	That love hath evere yit ben used,	
2170	So mot I nedes ben excused.	
	Bot, fader, if ye wolde thus	
	Unto Cupide and to Venus	
	Be frendlich toward mi querele,	
	So that myn herte were in hele	*health*
2175	Of love which is in mi briest,	*With regard to love*
	I wot wel thanne a betre prest	
	Was nevere mad to my behove.	*advantage*
	Bot al the whiles that I hove	*linger (hover)*
	In noncertein betwen the tuo,	*uncertainty*
2180	And not if I to wel or wo	*know not whether; gladness; woe*
	Schal torne, that is al my drede,	
	So that I not what is to rede.	*know not; best to do*
	Bot for final conclusion	
	I thenke a supplicacion	
2185	With pleine wordes and expresse	*clear and open words*
	Wryte unto Venus the goddesse,	
	The which I preie you to bere	
	And bringe agein a good ansuere."	*back*
[Amans to reader]	Tho was betwen mi prest and me	
2190	Debat and gret perplexeté:	*Conflict*
	Mi resoun understod him wel,	
	And knew it was soth everydel	*altogether true*
	That he hath seid, bot noght forthi	*What; not even so*
	Mi will hath nothing set therby.	*will (desire)*
2195	For techinge of so wis a port	*wise a bearing*
	Is unto love of no desport;	*delight*
	Yit myhte nevere man beholde	
	Reson, wher love was withholde;	
	Thei be noght of o governance.	*the same (one)*
2200	And thus we fellen in distance,	
	Mi prest and I, bot I spak faire,	
	And thurgh mi wordes debonaire	
	Thanne ate laste we acorden,	*agreed*
	So that he seith he wol recorden	*remember*
2205	To speke and stonde upon mi syde	

To Venus bothe and to Cupide;
And bad me wryte what I wolde,
And seith me trewly that he scholde
Mi lettre bere unto the queene.

2210   And I sat doun upon the grene
Fulfilt of loves fantasie,
And with the teres of myn ye
In stede of enke I gan to wryte   *ink; began*
The wordes whiche I wolde endite   *to express*

2215 Unto Cupide and to Venus.
And in mi lettre I seide thus:

[THE LOVER'S POETIC SUPPLICATION] *Venus: Goddess of Love*
Genius: Venus's Priest

[Amans] "The wofull peine of loves maladie,
Agein the which mai no phisique availe,   *medicine (see note)*
Min herte hath so bewhaped with sotie,   *overwhelmed; dotage*

2220 That wher so that I reste or I travaile,   *whether I*
I finde it evere redy to assaile
Mi resoun, which that can him noght defende. *himself not protect*
Thus seche I help, wherof I mihte amende.

Ferst to Nature if that I me compleigne,
2225 Ther finde I hou that every creature
Som time ayer hath love in his demeine,   *in the year*
So that the litel wrenne in his mesure   *wren in its music*
Hath yit of kinde a love under his cure; *by nature; its jurisdiction*
And I bot on desire, of which I misse: *only one*
2230 And thus, bot I, hath every kinde his blisse. *except; species*

The resoun of my wit it overpasseth,
Of that Nature techeth me the weie
To love, and yit no certein sche compasseth
Hou I schal spede, and thus betwen the tweie   *succeed*
2235 I stonde, and not if I schal live or deie.   *do not know*
For thogh reson agein my will debate,   *be in conflict*
I mai noght fle, that I ne love algate. *[so] that I do not love anyway*

Upon miself is thilke tale come,
Hou whilom Pan, which is the god of kinde,   *nature*
2240 With love wrastlede and was overcome:
For evere I wrastle and evere I am behinde,
That I no strengthe in al min herte finde,
Wherof that I mai stonden eny throwe;   *tumble (event)*
So fer mi wit with love is overthrowe.

2245   Whom nedeth help, he mot his helpe crave,
         Or helpeles he schal his nede spille:
         Pleinly thurghsoght my wittes alle I have,   *thoroughly searched*
         Bot non of hem can helpe after mi wille;
         And als so wel I mihte sitte stille,
2250   As preie unto mi lady eny helpe:
         Thus wot I noght wherof miself to helpe.

         Unto the grete Jove and if I bidde,   *pray*
         To do me grace of thilke swete tunne,   *that sweet cup*
         Which under keie in his celier amidde   *key; wine cellar*
2255   Lith couched, that fortune is overrunne,   *Lies*
         Bot of the bitter cuppe I have begunne,
         I not hou ofte, and thus finde I no game;
         For evere I axe and evere it is the same.

         I se the world stonde evere upon eschange,   *change*
2260   Nou wyndes loude, and nou the weder softe;   *weather still*
         I mai sen ek the grete mone change,   *full moon*
         And thing which nou is lowe is eft alofte;
         The dredfull werres into pes ful ofte
         Thei torne; and evere is Danger in o place,   *(see note)*
2265   Which wol noght change his will to do me grace.

         Bot upon this the grete clerc Ovide,
         Of love whan he makth his remembrance,
         He seith ther is the blinde god Cupide,
         The which hath love under his governance,
2270   And in his hond with many a fyri lance
         He woundeth ofte, ther he wol noght hele;   *heal*
         And that somdiel is cause of mi querele.

         Ovide ek seith that love to parforne   *fulfill*
         Stant in the hond of Venus the goddesse;
2275   Bot whan sche takth hir conseil with Satorne,   *(melancholic god of destruction)*
         Ther is no grace, and in that time, I gesse,
         Began mi love, of which myn hevynesse
         Is now and evere schal, bot if I spede:
         So wot I noght miself what is to rede.   *to follow as a course of action*

2280   Forthi to you, Cupide and Venus bothe,
         With al myn hertes obeissance I preie,
         If ye were ate ferste time wrothe,
         Whan I began to love, as I you seie,
         Nou stynt, and do thilke infortune aweie,   *stop; do away with*
2285   So that Danger, which stant of retenue
         With my ladi, his place mai remue.   *remove*

O thou Cupide, god of loves lawe,
That with thi dart brennende hast set afyre   *burning*
Min herte, do that wounde be withdrawe,   *cause; to be taken away*
2290   Or gif me salve such as I desire.   *love balm (salve)*
For service in thi court withouten hyre   *payment*
To me, which evere yit have kept thin heste,   *who; obeyed your commands*
Mai nevere be to loves lawe honeste.

O thou, gentile Venus, loves queene,
2295   Withoute gult thou dost on me thi wreche;   *Without [my being] guilty; vengeance*
Thou wost my peine is evere aliche grene   *fresh*
For love, and yit I mai it noght areche: *attain*
This wold I for my laste word beseche,   *pray*
That thou mi love aquite as I deserve,
2300   Or elles do me pleinly for to sterve."   *cause me fully to die*

[VENUS' REPLY]

[**Amans to reader**]   Whanne I this supplicacioun
With good deliberacioun,
☞   In such a wise as ye nou wite,   *(see note)*
Hadde after min entente write   *written*
2305   Unto Cupide and to Venus,
This prest which hihte Genius   *who was called*
It tok on honde to presente,
On my message and forth he wente
To Venus, for to wite hire wille.   *know*
2310   And I bod in the place stille,   *waited*
And was there bot a litel while,
Noght full the montance of a mile,   *duration of a mile's walk*
Whan I behield and sodeinly
I sih wher Venus stod me by.
2315   So as I myhte, under a tre
To grounde I fell upon mi kne,
And preide hire for to do me grace:
Sche caste hire chiere upon mi face,
And as it were halvinge a game   *half in jest*
2320   Sche axeth me what is mi name.
"Ma dame," I seide, "John Gower."
[**Venus**]   "Now John," quod sche, "in my pouer
Thou most as of thi love stonde;
For I thi bille have understonde,   *epistle (petition)*
2325   In which to Cupide and to me
Somdiel thou hast compleigned thee,   *Somewhat*
And somdiel to Nature also.
Bot that schal stonde among you tuo,
For therof have I noght to done;

2330	For Nature is under the mone	*moon*
	Maistresse of every lives kinde,	*species of life*
	Bot if so be that sche mai finde	*Unless*
	Som holy man that wol withdrawe	
	His kindly lust agein hir lawe;	*natural desire*
2335	Bot sielde whanne it falleth so,	*seldom*
	For fewe men ther ben of tho,	
	Bot of these othre ynowe be,	
	Whiche of here oghne nyceté	*wantonness*
	Agein Nature and hire office	
2340	Deliten hem in sondri vice,	
	Wherof that sche ful ofte hath pleigned,	
	And ek my court it hath desdeigned	
	And evere schal; for it receiveth	
	Non such that kinde so deceiveth.	*nature*
2345	For al onliche of gentil love	
	Mi court stant alle courtz above	
	And takth noght into retenue	*under its command*
	Bot thing which is to kinde due,	
	For elles it schal be refused.	
2350	Wherof I holde thee excused,	
	For it is manye daies gon,	
	That thou amonges hem were on	
	Which of my court hast ben withholde;	
	So that the more I am beholde	*obliged*
2355	Of thi desese to commune,	*discomfort to discuss*
	And to remue that fortune,	*change*
	Which manye daies hath thee grieved.	
	Bot if my conseil mai be lieved,	*believed*
	Thou schalt ben esed er thou go	
2360	Of thilke unsely jolif wo,	*unhappy*
	Wherof thou seist thin herte is fyred.	
	Bot as of that thou hast desired	
	After the sentence of thi bille,	
	Thou most therof don at my wille,	
2365	And I therof me wole avise.	*take thought*
	For be thou hol, it schal suffise.	
	Mi medicine is noght to sieke	*seek*
	For thee and for suche olde sieke,	*sick [men]*
	Noght al per chance as ye it wolden,	
2370	Bot so as ye be reson scholden,	
	Acordant unto loves kinde.	
	For in the plit which I thee finde,	
	So as mi court it hath awarded,	
	Thou schalt be duely rewarded;	
2375	And if thou woldest more crave,	
	It is no riht that thou it have."	

[OLD AGE]

iii.   *Qvi cupit id quod habere nequit, sua tempora perdit,*
       Est vbi non posse, velle salute caret.
     Non estatis opus gelidis hirsuta capillis,
       Cum calor abcessit, equiperabit hiems;
     Sicut habet Mayus non dat natura Decembri,
       Nec poterit compar floribus esse lutum;
     Sic neque decrepita senium iuvenile voluptas
       Floret in obsequium, quod Venus ipsa petit.
     Conveniens igitur foret, vt quos cana senectus
       Attigit, vlterius corpora casta colant.[1]

	Venus, which stant withoute lawe	
☞	In noncertein, bot as men drawe	*(see note)*
	Of Rageman upon the chance,	*(see note)*
2380	Sche leith no peis in the balance,	*lays no weight*
	Bot as hir lyketh for to weie;	*weigh*
	The trewe man ful ofte aweie	
	Sche put, which hath hir grace bede,	*who has prayed to her for grace*
	And set an untrewe in his stede.	
2385	Lo, thus blindly the world sche diemeth	*judges*
	In loves cause, as to me siemeth:	*as it seems to me*
	I not what othre men wol sein,	*know not; say*
	Bot I algate am so besein,	*assuredly; so circumstanced*
	And stonde as on amonges alle	
2390	Which am out of hir grace falle,	
	It nedeth take no witnesse:	
	For sche which seid is the goddesse,	*called*
	To whether part of love it wende,	*whichever; turns*
	Hath sett me for a final ende	
2395	The point wherto that I schal holde.	
	For whan sche hath me wel beholde,	
	Halvynge of scorn, sche seide thus:	*Half in scorn*
	"Thou wost wel that I am Venus,	
	Which al only my lustes seche;	
2400	And wel I wot, thogh thou beseche	
	Mi love, lustes ben ther none,	
	Whiche I mai take in thi persone;	
	For loves lust and lockes hore	*love's desire; gray hair*
	In chambre acorden neveremore,	

---

[1] *Whoever desires what he cannot have, wastes his time; where "I'm able" is absent, "I want" is unhealthy. Winter, hairy with icy locks, is not equal to summer's work, when its heat has receded. Nature does not give to December just as May has, nor can clay compare to flowers; and thus old men's lust does not flower in youthful compliance, as Venus herself demands. It would be appropriate, therefore, for those whom white old age touches henceforth to cultivate chaste bodies.*

2405	And thogh thou feigne a yong corage,	
	It scheweth wel be the visage	
	That olde grisel is no fole:	*old gray nag; foal*
	There ben ful manye yeeres stole	
	With thee and with suche othre mo,	
2410	That outward feignen youthe so	
	And ben withinne of pore assay.	*i.e., likely to fail the test*
	'Min herte wolde and I ne may'	
	Is noght beloved nou adayes;	
	Er thou make eny suche assaies	*attempts*
2415	To love, and faile upon the fet,	*event*
	Betre is to make a beau retret;	*graceful exit*
	For thogh thou myhtest love atteigne,	
	Yit were it bot an ydel peine,	
	Whan that thou art noght sufficant	
2420	To holde love his covenant.	*uphold love's*
	Forthi tak hom thin herte agein,	
	That thou travaile noght in vein,	*[So] that you labor*
	Wherof my court may be deceived.	
	I wot and have it wel conceived,	
2425	Hou that thi will is good ynowh;	
	Bot mor behoveth to the plowh,	
	Wherof thee lacketh, as I trowe:	*you are deficient*
	So sitte it wel that thou beknowe	*So let it be suitable; knowledge*
	Thi fieble astat, er thou beginne	
2430	Thing wher thou miht non ende winne.	*accomplish nothing*
	What bargain scholde a man assaie,	*attempt*
	Whan that him lacketh for to paie?	*lacks means of payment*
	Mi sone, if thou be wel bethoght,	
	This toucheth thee; forget it noght:	
2435	The thing is torned into was;	*i.e., is past*
	That which was whilom grene gras,	
	Is welked hey at time now.	*sun-dried hay*
	Forthi mi conseil is that thou	
	Remembre wel hou thou art old."	

[PARLIAMENT OF EXEMPLARY LOVERS]

2440	Whan Venus hath hir tale told,	
	And I bethoght was al aboute,	
☞	Tho wiste I wel withoute doute,	*(see note)*
	That ther was no recoverir;	*treatment*
	And as a man the blase of fyr	
2445	With water quencheth, so ferd I;	
	A cold me cawhte sodeinly,	
	For sorwe that myn herte made	
	Mi dedly face pale and fade	

Becam, and swoune I fell to grounde.

2450 And as I lay the same stounde, *time*
Ne fully quik ne fully ded, *Neither; alive nor*
Me thoghte I sih tofor myn hed *head*
Cupide with his bowe bent,
And lich unto a Parlement,

2455 Which were ordeigned for the nones,
With him cam al the world at ones
Of gentil folk that whilom were *once*
Lovers, I sih hem alle there
Forth with Cupide in sondri routes. *diverse groups*

2460 Min yhe and as I caste aboutes, *And as I cast my eye around*
To knowe among hem who was who,
I sih wher lusti youthe tho,
As he which was a capitein,
Tofore alle othre upon the plein

2465 Stod with his route wel begon, *endowed*
Here hevedes kempt, and therupon
Garlandes noght of o colour,
Some of the lef, some of the flour, *leaf*
And some of grete perles were;

2470 The newe guise of Beawme there, *Bohemia*
With sondri thinges wel devised,
I sih, wherof thei ben queintised. *adorned*
It was al lust that thei with ferde,
Ther was no song that I ne herde,

2475 Which unto love was touchende;
Of Pan and al that was likende
As in pipinge of melodie
Was herd in thilke compaignie
So lowde, that on every side

2480 It thoghte as al the hevene cride
In such acord and such a soon *sound*
Of bombard and of clarion
With cornemuse and schallemele, *bagpipe; shawm*
That it was half a mannes hele *health*

2485 So glad a noise for to hiere.
And as me thoghte, in this manere
Al freissh I syh hem springe and dance,
And do to love her entendance
After the lust of youthes heste. *youth's ordinance*

2490 Ther was ynowh of joie and feste,
For evere among thei laghe and pleie,
And putten care out of the weie,
That he with hem ne sat ne stod.
And over this I understod,

2495 So as myn ere it myhte areche, *extend to*

	The moste matiere of her speche	
	Was al of knyhthod and of armes,	
	And what it is to ligge in armes	
	With love, whanne it is achieved.	
2500	Ther was Tristram, which was believed	*who was accepted as a lover*
☞	With bele Ysolde, and Lancelot	*By the beautiful (see note)*
	Stod with Gunnore, and Galahot	*Guinevere*
	With his ladi, and as me thoghte,	
	I syh wher Jason with him broghte	
2505	His love, which that Creusa hihte,	*was called*
	And Hercules, which mochel myhte,	
	Was ther berende his grete mace,	*carrying*
	And most of alle in thilke place	
	He peyneth him to make chiere	
2510	With Eolen, which was him diere.	
	Theseus, thogh he were untrewe	
	To love, as alle wommen knewe,	
	Yit was he there natheles	
	With Phedra, whom to love he ches.	
2515	Of Grece ek ther was Thelamon,	
	Which fro the king Lamenedon	
	At Troie his doghter refte aweie,	*snatched away*
	Eseonen, as for his preie,	*prey*
	Which take was whan Jason cam	
2520	Fro Colchos, and the cité nam	*took*
	In vengance of the ferste hate;	
	That made hem after to debate,	*to enter conflict*
	Whan Priamus the newe toun	
	Hath mad. And in avisioun	
2525	Me thoghte that I sih also	
	Ector forth with his brethren tuo;	
	Himself stod with Pantaselee,	
	And next to him I myhte se,	
	Wher Paris stod with faire Eleine,	*Helen*
2530	Which was his joie sovereine;	*highest joy*
	And Troilus stod with Criseide,	
	Bot evere among, althogh he pleide,	
	Be semblant he was hevy chiered,	*sad*
	For Diomede, as him was liered,	*taught*
2535	Cleymeth to ben his parconner.	*partner [in love with Criseyde]*
	And thus full many a bacheler,	
	A thousend mo than I can sein,	
	With yowthe I sih ther wel besein	*endowed*
	Forth with here loves glade and blithe.	*their*
2540	And some I sih whiche ofte sithe	*saw; often times*
	Compleignen hem in other wise;	
	Among the whiche I syh Narcise	

        And Piramus, that sory were.
        The worthi Grek also was there,
2545   Achilles, which for love deide.
        Agamenon ek, as men seide,
        And Menelay the king also
        I syh, with many an other mo,
        Which hadden be fortuned sore   *Who had been unfortunate*
2550   In loves cause.
                        And overmore
        Of wommen in the same cas,
        With hem I sih wher Dido was,
        Forsake which was with Enee;   *by Aeneas*
        And Phillis ek I myhte see,
2555   Whom Demephon deceived hadde;
        And Adriagne hir sorwe ladde,   *Ariadne*
        For Theseus hir soster tok
        And hire unkindely forsok.   *unnaturally*
        I sih ther ek among the press   *crowd*
2560   Compleignende upon Hercules
        His ferste love Deyanire,
        Which sette him afterward afyre.
        Medea was there ek and pleigneth
        Upon Jason, for that he feigneth,   *deceived*
2565   Withoute cause and tok a newe;
        Sche seide, "Fy on alle untrewe!"
        I sih there ek Deydamie,
        Which hadde lost the compaignie
        Of Achilles, whan Diomede
2570   To Troie him fette upon the nede.   *fetched*
           Among these othre upon the grene
        I syh also the wofull queene
        Cleopatras, which in a cave
        With serpentz hath hirself begrave   *buried*
2575   Al quik, and so sche was totore,   *Quite alive; torn to pieces*
        For sorwe of that sche hadde lore   *lost*
        Antonye, which hir love hath be.
        And forth with hire I sih Tisbee,
        Which on the scharpe swerdes point
2580   For love deide in sory point;   *at a sad moment*
        And as myn ere it myhte knowe,
        Sche seide, "Wo worthe alle slowe!"
        The pleignte of Progne and Philomene
        Ther herde I what it wolde mene,
2585   How Tereus of his untrouthe
        Undede hem bothe, and that was routhe;   *Destroyed; pity*
        And next to hem I sih Canace,
        Which for Machaire hir fader grace   *father's*

Hath lost, and deide in wofull plit.
2590 And as I sih in my spirit,
Me thoghte amonges othre thus
The doghter of king Priamus,
Polixena, whom Pirrus slowh,   *killed*
Was there and made sorwe ynowh,   *enough*
2595 As sche which deide gulteles
For love, and yit was loveles.
       And for to take the desport,
I sih there some of other port,   *of another bearing*
And that was Circes and Calipse,
2600 That cowthen do the mone eclipse,   *cause eclipses of the moon*
Of men and change the liknesses,   *And change the shapes of men*
Of art magique sorceresses;
Thei hielde in honde many on,   *many a one*
To love wher thei wolde or non.   *whether they would or not*
2605   Bot above alle that ther were
Of wommen I sih foure there,
Whos name I herde most comended:
Be hem the court stod al amended;
For wher thei comen in presence,
2610 Men deden hem the reverence,
As thogh thei hadden be goddesses,
Of al this world or emperesses.
And as me thoghte, an ere I leide,   *ear*
And herde hou that these othre seide,
2615 "Lo, these ben the foure wyves,   *Behold*
Whos feith was proeved in her lyves:
For in essample of alle goode
With mariage so thei stode
That fame, which no gret thing hydeth,
2620 Yit in cronique of hem abydeth."
       Penolope that on was hote,   *[first] one was called*
Whom many a knyht hath loved hote,   *passionately*
Whil that hire lord Ulixes lay   *Ulysses*
Full many a yer and many a day
2625 Upon the grete siege of Troie.
Bot sche, which hath no worldes joie
Bot only of hire housebonde,
Whil that hir lord was out of londe,
So wel hath kept hir wommanhiede,
2630 That al the world therof tok hiede,
And nameliche of hem in Grece.
       That other womman was Lucrece,   *second*
Wif to the Romain Collatin;
And sche constreigned of Tarquin
2635 To thing which was agein hir wille,

Sche wolde noght hirselven stille,   *keep silent*
Bot deide only for drede of schame   *died*
In keping of hire goode name,
As sche which was on of the beste.   *one*
2640   The thridde wif was hote Alceste,   *called*
Which whanne Ametus scholde dye
Upon his grete maladye,   *Because of*
Sche preide unto the goddes so,
That sche receyveth al the wo
2645   And deide hirself to give him lif:
Lo, if this were a noble wif.
      The ferthe wif which I ther sih,
I herde of hem that were nyh
Hou sche was cleped Alcione,
2650   Which to Seyix hir lord al one
And to no mo hir body kepte;
And whan sche sih him dreynt, sche lepte
Into the wawes where he swam,
And there a sefoul sche becam,   *seafowl*
2655   And with hire wenges him bespradde   *embraced*
For love which to him sche hadde.
      Lo, these foure were tho   *those*
Whiche I sih, as me thoghte tho,   *saw; then*
Among the grete compaignie
2660   Which Love hadde for to guye.   *lead*
Bot Youthe, which in special
Of Loves court was mareschal,
So besy was upon his lay,   *law*
That he non hiede where I lay
2665   Hath take. And thanne, as I behield,
Me thoghte I sih upon the field,
Wher Elde cam a softe pas   *quietly*
Toward Venus, ther as sche was.
With him gret compaignie he ladde,
2670   Bot noght so manye as Youthe hadde:
The moste part were of gret age,
And that was sene in the visage,
And noght forthi, so as thei myhte,
Thei made hem yongly to the sihte:
2675   Bot yit herde I no pipe there
To make noise in mannes ere,
Bot the musette I myhte knowe,   *musette (a kind of bagpipe)*
For olde men which souneth lowe,
With harpe and lute and with citole.
2680   The hovedance and the carole,   *court dance*
In such a wise as love hath bede,
A softe pas thei dance and trede;

And with the wommen otherwhile
With sobre chier among thei smyle,
2685   For laghtre was ther non on hyh.
And natheles full wel I syh
That thei the more queinte it made   *graciously they behaved*
For love, in whom thei weren glade.
     And there me thoghte I myhte se
2690   The king David with Bersabee,
And Salomon was noght withoute:
Passende an hundred on a route
Of wyves and of concubines,
Juesses bothe and Sarazines,   *Jewesses*
2695   To him I sih alle entendant.
I not if he was sufficant,   *do not know; up to [so many women]*
Bot natheles for al his wit
He was attached with that writ   *arrested by*
Which love with his hond enseleth,   *had sealed*
2700   Fro whom non erthly man appeleth.   *might appeal*
And over this, as for a wonder,
With his leon which he put under,   *conquered*
With Dalida Sampson I knew,
Whos love his strengthe al overthrew.
2705   I syh there Aristotle also,
Whom that the queene of Grece so
Hath bridled, that in thilke time
Sche made him such a silogime,   *syllogism*
That he forgat al his logique;
2710   Ther was non art of his practique,
Thurgh which it mihte ben excluded
That he ne was fully concluded   *determined*
To love, and dede his obeissance.
And ek Virgile of aqueintance
2715   I sih, wher he the maiden preide,   *saw*
Which was the doghter, as men seide,
Of th'emperour whilom of Rome;
Sortes and Plato with him come,   *Socrates (see note)*
So dede Ovide the poete.
2720   I thoghte thanne how love is swete,
Which hath so wise men reclamed,
And was miself the lasse aschamed,
Or for to lese or for to winne   *Either to lose or*
In the meschief that I was inne:
2725   And thus I lay in hope of grace.
     And whan thei comen to the place
Wher Venus stod and I was falle,
These olde men with o vois alle   *one*
To Venus preiden for my sake.

2730 And sche, that myhte noght forsake
     So gret a clamour as was there,
     Let pité come into hire ere;
     And forth withal unto Cupide
     Sche preith that he upon his side
2735 Me wolde thurgh his grace sende
     Som confort, that I myhte amende,   *improve*
     Upon the cas which is befalle.
     And thus for me thei preiden alle
     Of hem that weren olde aboute,
2740 And ek some of the yonge route,   *crowd*
     Of gentilesse and pure trouthe
     I herde hem telle it was gret routhe,   *pity*
     That I withouten help so ferde.
     And thus me thoghte I lay and herde.

[CUPID RETURNS]

2745   Cupido, which may hurte and hele
     In loves cause, as for myn hele   *health*
     Upon the point which him was preid
     Cam with Venus, wher I was leid
☞   Swounende upon the grene gras.   *(see note)*
2750 And, as me thoghte, anon ther was
     On every side so gret presse,   *crowd*
     That every lif began to presse,   *began to feel the pressure*
     I wot noght wel hou many score,
     Suche as I spak of now tofore,
2755 Lovers, that comen to beholde,
     Bot most of hem that weren olde.
     Thei stoden there at thilke tyde,
     To se what ende schal betyde
     Upon the cure of my sotie.   *foolishness*
2760 Tho myhte I hiere gret partie
     Spekende, and ech his oghne avis   *own advice*
     Hath told, on that, another this: *one that*
     Bot among alle this I herde,
     Thei weren wo that I so ferde,
2765 And seiden that for no riote   *love disorder*
     An old man scholde noght assote;   *be foolish*
     For as thei tolden redely,
     Ther is in him no cause why,
     Bot if he wolde himself benyce;   *Except; make foolish*
2770 So were he wel the more nyce.   *foolish*
     And thus desputen some of tho,
     And some seiden nothing so,
     Bot that the wylde loves rage   *passion*

	In mannes lif forberth non age;	*does not spare age*
2775	Whil ther is oyle for to fyre,	*burn*
	The lampe is lyhtly set afyre,	*easily*
	And is ful hard er it be queynt	*before it be quenched*
	Bot only if it be som seint,	*saint*
	Which God preserveth of his grace.	
2780	And thus me thoghte, in sondri place	
	Of hem that walken up and doun	
	Ther was diverse opinioun,	
	And for a while so it laste,	
	Til that Cupide to the laste,	
2785	Forth with his moder full avised,	
	Hath determined and devised	
	Unto what point he wol descende.	
	And al this time I was liggende	*lying*
	Upon the ground tofore his yhen,	*before; eyes*
2790	And thei that my desese syhen	*saw*
	Supposen noght I scholde live;	
	Bot he, which wolde thanne give	
	His grace, so as it mai be,	
	This blinde god which mai noght se,	
2795	Hath groped til that he me fond;	
	And as he pitte forth his hond	
	Upon my body, wher I lay,	
	Me thoghte a fyri lancegay,	*dart*
	Which whilom thurgh myn herte he caste,	
2800	He pulleth oute, and also faste	*immediately*
	As this was do, Cupide nam	*took*
	His weie, I not where he becam,	
	And so dede al the remenant	
	Which unto him was entendant,	
2805	Of hem that in avision	
	I hadde a revelacion,	
	So as I tolde now tofore.	

[HEALING LOVE'S WOUND]

	Bot Venus wente noght therfore,	
	Ne Genius, whiche thilke time	
2810	Abiden bothe faste byme.	*by me*
	And sche which mai the hertes bynde	
	In loves cause and ek unbinde,	
	Er I out of mi trance aros,	
	Venus, which hield a boiste clos,	*closed box*
2815	And wolde noght I scholde deie,	
	Tok out mor cold than eny keie	
	An oignement, and in such point	

Sche hath my wounded herte enoignt,
My temples and mi reins also.   *kidneys (L. renes)*
2820   And forth withal sche tok me tho   *then*
A wonder mirour for to holde,
In which sche bad me to beholde
And taken hiede of that I syhe;   *should see*
Wherinne anon myn hertes yhe   *eye*
2825   I caste, and sih my colour fade,   *saw; pale*
Myn yhen dymme and al unglade,   *eyes*
Mi chiekes thinne, and al my face
With elde I myhte se deface,   *old age; defaced*
So riveled and so wo besein,   *wrinkled; woebegone*
2830   That ther was nothing full ne plein,
I syh also myn heres hore.   *hair turned gray*
Mi will was tho to se no more
Outwith, for ther was no plesance;
And thanne into my remembrance
2835   I drowh myn olde daies passed,
And as reson it hath compassed,
☞   I made a liknesse of miselve   *(see note)*
Unto the sondri monthes twelve,
Wherof the yeer in his astat   *its*
2840   Is mad, and stant upon debat,   *Made*
That lich til other non acordeth.
For who the times wel recordeth,
And thanne at Marche if he beginne,
Whan that the lusti yeer comth inne,
2845   Til Augst be passed and Septembre,
The myhty youthe he may remembre
In which the yeer hath his deduit   *delight*
Of gras, of lef, of flour, of fruit,
Of corn and of the wyny grape.
2850   And afterward the time is schape
To frost, to snow, to wynd, to rein,   *rain*
Til eft that Mars be come agein:
The wynter wol no somer knowe,
The grene lef is overthrowe,
2855   The clothed erthe is thanne bare,
Despuiled is the somerfare,
That erst was hete is thanne chele.   *once was hot*
And thus thenkende thoghtes fele,   *many*
I was out of mi swoune affraied,   *affrighted*
2860   Wherof I sih my wittes straied,
And gan to clepe hem hom agein.
And whan Resoun it herde sein
That loves rage was aweie,
He cam to me the rihte weie,

2865   And hath remued the sotie   removed; folly
        Of thilke unwise fantasie,
        Wherof that I was wont to pleigne,   complain
        So that of thilke fyri peine
        I was mad sobre and hol ynowh.
2870   Venus behield me than and lowh,   laughed
        And axeth, as it were in game,
        What love was. And I for schame
        Ne wiste what I scholde ansuere;
        And natheles I gan to swere
2875   That be my trouthe I knew him noght;
        So ferr it was out of mi thoght,
        Riht as it hadde nevere be.
        "Mi goode sone," tho quod sche,
        "Now at this time I lieve it wel,   believe
2880   So goth the fortune of my whiel;
        Forthi mi conseil is thou leve."
            "Ma dame," I seide, "be your leve,
        Ye witen wel, and so wot I,
        That I am unbehovely   unfit
2885   Your court fro this day forth to serve.
        And for I may no thonk deserve,
        And also for I am refused,
        I preie you to ben excused.
        And natheles as for the laste,
2890   Whil that my wittes with me laste,
        Touchende mi confession
        I axe an absolucion
        Of Genius, er that I go."   From; before
        The prest anon was redy tho,
2895   And seide, "Sone, as of thi schrifte
        Thou hast ful pardoun and forgifte;
        Forget it thou, and so wol I."
            "Min holi fader, grant mercy,"
        Quod I to him, and to the queene
2900   I fell on knes upon the grene,
        And tok my leve for to wende.   depart
        Bot sche, that wolde make an ende,
        As therto which I was most able,
        A peire of bedes blak as sable   set of identical beads
2905   Sche tok and heng my necke aboute;
        Upon the gaudes al withoute   ornamental beads
        Was write of gold, Por reposer.   For repose
        "Lo," thus sche seide, "John Gower,
        Now thou art ate laste cast,   determined (thrown)
2910   This have I for thin ese cast,   ordained (shaped)
        That thou no more of love sieche.   seek

Bot my will is that thou besieche
And preie hierafter for the pes,   *peace*
And that thou make a plein reles
2915 To love, which takth litel hiede
Of olde men upon the nede,
Whan that the lustes ben aweie:
Forthi to thee nys bot o weie,   *one way*
In which let reson be thi guide;
2920 For he may sone himself misguide,
That seth noght the peril tofore.
Mi sone, be wel war therfore,   *well advised*
And kep the sentence of my lore   *teaching*
And tarie thou mi court no more,
2925 Bot go ther vertu moral duelleth,   *where*
Wher ben thi bokes, as men telleth,
Whiche of long time thou hast write.
For this I do thee wel to wite,   *order you*
If thou thin hele wolt pourchace,   *health; obtain*
2930 Thou miht noght make suite and chace,   *chase (hunt)*
Wher that the game is noght pernable;   *suitable to be taken*
It were a thing unresonable,
A man to be so overseie.   *imprudent*
Forthi tak hiede of that I seie;
2935 For in the lawe of my comune   *fellowship*
We be noght schape to comune,   *discourse together*
Thiself and I, nevere after this.
Now have y seid al that ther is
Of love as for thi final ende.
2940 Adieu, for y mot fro thee wende."

[LEAVE-TAKING OF VENUS]

And with that word al sodeinly,
Enclosid in a sterred sky,
Venus, which is the qweene of love,
Was take into hire place above,
2945 More wist y nought wher sche becam.
And thus my leve of here y nam,   *her; took*

[The first recension of the poem reads as follows (lines *2941–*3114):]

[Venus] . . . "And gret wel Chaucer whan ye mete,   *greet; meet [him]*
As mi disciple and mi poete:
For in the floures of his youthe
In sondri wise, as he wel couthe,   *knows how*
*2945 Of ditees and of songes glade,
The whiche he for mi sake made,

     And forth with al the same tide
     Hire prest, which wolde nought abide,
     Or be me lief or be me loth,   *Whether it was pleasing or displeasing to me*
2950 Out of my sighte forth he goth,
     And y was left withouten helpe.
     So wiste I nought wher of to yelpe,   *boast*
     Bot only that y hadde lore   *lost*
     My time, and was sori therfore.
2955 And thus bewhapid in my thought,   *overwhelmed*
     Whan al was turnyd into nought,
     I stod amasid for a while,
     And in myself y gan to smyle
     Thenkende uppon the bedis blake,   *beads*
2960 And how they weren me betake,   *given to me*
     For that y schulde bidde and preie.   *ask for mercy; pray*
     And whanne y sigh non othre weie   *saw*
     Bot only that y was refusid,
     Unto the lif which y hadde usid
2965 I thoughte nevere torne agein:
     And in this wise, soth to seyn,
     Homward a softe pas y wente,
     Wher that with al myn hol entente

     The lond fulfild is overal:
     Wherof to him in special
     Above alle othre I am most holde.   *loyal (beholden)*
*2950 For thi now in hise daies olde
     Thow schalt him telle this message,
     That he upon his latere age,
     To sette an ende of alle his werk,
     As he which is myn owne clerk,
*2955 Do make his testament of love,
     As thou hast do thi schrifte above,
     So that mi court it mai recorde."
[Amans]   "Madame, I can me wel acord,"
     Quod I, "to telle as ye me bidde."
*2960 And with that word it so betidde,   *happened*
     Out of my sihte al sodeynly,
     Enclosed in a sterred sky,
     Up to the hevene Venus straghte,
     And I my rihte weie cawhte,
*2965 Hoom fro the wode and forth I wente,   *wood*
     Wher as with al myn hoole entente,
     Thus with mi bedes upon honde,   *beads*
     For hem that trewe love foonde

Uppon the poynt that y am schryve   *confessed (absolved)*
2970   I thenke bidde whil y live.   *pray*

[PRAYER FOR ENGLAND]

iv   *Parce precor, Criste, populus quo gaudeat iste;*
        Anglia ne triste subeat, rex summe, resiste.
        Corrige quosque status, fragiles absolue reatus;
        Vnde deo gratus vigeat locus iste beatus.[1]

        He which withinne daies sevene
        This large world forth with the hevene
☞   Of his eternal providence   *(see note)*
        Hath mad, and thilke intelligence
2975   In mannys soule resonable
        Hath schape to be perdurable,   *eternal*
        Wherof the man of his feture
        Above alle erthli creature

        I thenke bidde whil I lyve   *intend to pray*
*2970   Uppon the poynt which I am schryve.

[PRAYER FOR RICHARD]

iv   *Ad laudem Cristi, quem tu, virgo, peperisti,*
        Sit laus Ricardi, quem sceptra colunt leopardi.
        Ad sua precepta compleui carmina cepta,
        Que Bruti nata legat Anglia perpetuata.[2]

        He which withinne dayes sevene
        This large world forth with the hevene
☞   Of His eternal providence
        Hath maad, and thilke intelligence
*2975   In mannes soule resonable
        Enspired to himself semblable,
        Wherof the man of his feture
        Above alle erthly creature

---

[1] *Spare I pray, O Christ, the people in order that they may rejoice; stand in opposition, highest king, lest England should sadly go down. Correct each estate, absolve frail defendants. May this blessed place thereupon thrive, grateful [or pleasing] to God.*

[2] *For the praise of Christ which you, O Virgin, gave birth to, let there be praise of Richard, whom the leopard's scepters honor. At his orders I have completed the songs that were undertaken; let England, born of Brutus, read them, thus made perpetual.*

Aftir the soule is immortal,
2980   To thilke lord in special,
As He which is of alle thinges
The creatour, and of the kynges
Hath the fortunes uppon honde,
His grace and mercy for to fonde   *discover*
2985   Uppon my bare knes y preie,
That He this lond in siker weie   *certain*
Wol sette uppon good governance.
For if men takyn remembrance   *take notice*
What is to live in unité,
2990   Ther ys no staat in his degree
That noughte to desire pes,
Withouten which, it is no les,   *lie*
To seche and loke into the laste,
Ther may no worldes joye laste.
2995   Ferst for to loke the clergie,
Hem oughte wel to justefie
Thing which belongith to here cure,   *their jurisdiction*
As for to praie and to procure
Oure pes toward the hevene above,
3000   And ek to sette reste and love

After the soule is immortal,
*2980   To thilke Lord in special,
As He which is of alle thinges
The creatour, and of the kinges
Hath the fortunes upon hoonde,
His grace and mercy for to foonde   *discover*
*2985   Upon mi bare knees I preye,
That he my worthi king conveye,
Richard by name the Secounde,
In whom hath evere yit be founde
Justice medled with pité,
*2990   Largesce forth with charité.
In his persone it mai be schewed
What is a king to be wel thewed,   *of good disposition*
Touching of pité namely:
For he yit nevere unpitously
*2995   Agein the liges of his loond,   *vassals*
For no defaute which he foond,
Thurgh crualté vengaunce soghte;
And thogh the worldes chaunce in broghte
Of infortune gret debat,
*3000   Yit was he not infortunat,

Among ous on this erthe hiere.
For if they wroughte in this manere
Aftir the reule of charité,
I hope that men schuldyn se
3005   This lond amende.
                And ovyr this,
To seche and loke how that it is
Touchende of the chevalerie,   *knighthood*
Which for to loke, in som partie
Is worthi for to be comendid,
3010   And in som part to ben amendid,   *improved*
That of here large retenue
The lond is ful of maintenue,   *maintenance (i.e., private armies)*
Which causith that the comune right
In fewe contrees stant upright.
3015   Extorcioun, contekt, ravine   *assault, pillaging*
Withholde ben of that covyne,   *Are loyal to that conspiracy*
Aldai men hierin gret compleignte   *hear*
Of the desease, of the constreignte,
Wherof the poeple is sore oppressid:
3020   God graunte it mote be redressid.
For of knyghthode th'ordre wolde
That thei defende and kepe scholde

For he which the fortune ladde,
The hihe God, him overspradde
Of His Justice, and kepte him so,   *With*
That his astat stood evere mo
*3005   Sauf, as it oghte wel to bee;
Lich to the sonne in his degree,   *its*
Which with the clowdes up alofte
Is derked and bischadewed ofte,
But hou so that it trowble in th'eir,
*3010   The sonne is evere briht and feir,
Withinne himself and noght empeired:
Althogh the weder be despeired,
The heed planete is not to wite.   *principal; not to blame*
Mi worthi prince, of whom I write,
*3015   Thus stant he with himselve cleer,
And dooth what lith in his poweer
Not oonly heer at hoom to seeke
Love and acorde, but outward eeke,
As he that save his poeple wolde.
*3020   So been we alle wel byholde
To do service and obeyssaunce
To him, which of his heyh suffraunce

	The comun right and the fraunchise	
	Of holy cherche in alle wise,	
3025	So that no wikke man it dere,	*injure*
	And therfore servith scheld and spere.	
	Bot for it goth now other weie,	
	Oure grace goth the more aweie.	
	And for to lokyn ovyrmore,	
3030	Wherof the poeple pleigneth sore,	
	Toward the lawis of oure lond,	
	Men sein that trouthe hath broke his bond	
	And with brocage is goon aweie,	*clandestine business dealings*
	So that no man can se the weie	
3035	Wher for to fynde rightwisnesse.	
	And if men sechin sikernesse	*certitude*
	Uppon the lucre of marchandie,	*wealth of worldly goods*
	Compassement and tricherie	*Scheming*
	Of singuler profit to wynne,	
3040	Men seyn, is cause of mochil synne,	
	And namely of divisioun,	
	Which many a noble worthi toun	
	Fro welthe and fro prosperité	
	Hath brought to gret adversité.	

	Hath many a grete debat appesed,	*great conflict settled*
	To make his lige men been esed;	
*3025	Wherfore that his croniqe schal	
	For evere be memorial	
	To the loenge of that he dooth.	*praise*
	For this wot every man in sooth,	*truly*
	What king that so desireth pees,	
*3030	He takth the weie which Crist chees:	*chose*
	And who that Cristes weies sueth,	*follows*
	It proveth wel that he eschueth	
	The vices and is vertuous,	
	Wherof he mot be gracious	
*3035	Toward his God and acceptable.	
	And so to maake his regne stable,	
	With al the wil that I mai give	
	I preie and schal whil that I live,	
	As I which in subjeccioun	
*3040	Stonde under the proteccioun,	
	And mai miselven not bewelde,	*wield control over myself*
	What for seknesse and what for elde,	*sickness*
	Which I receyve of Goddes grace.	
	But thoght me lacke to purchace	*obtain*

3045 So were it good to ben al on,   *united*
      For mechil grace ther uppon
      Unto the citees schulde falle,
      Which myghte availle to ous alle,
      If these astatz amendid were,
3050 So that the vertus stodyn there
      And that the vices were aweie,
      Me thenkth y dorste thanne seie,   *dare*
      This londis grace schulde arise.

[ON KINGSHIP]

         Bot yit to loke in othre wise,
3055 Ther is a stat, as ye schul hiere,
      Above alle othre on erthe hiere,
      Which hath the lond in his balance.
         To him belongith the leiance   *allegiance*
      Of clerk, of knyght, of man of lawe;
3060 Undir his hond al is forth drawe
      The marchant and the laborer;
      So stant it al in his power
      Or for to spille or for to save.   *Either to destroy or save*
      Bot though that he such power have,
3065 And that his myghtes ben so large,

---

*3045 Mi kinges thonk as by decerte,   *merit*
       Yit the simplesce of mi poverte
       Unto the love of my ligance
       Desireth for to do plesance:
       And for this cause in myn entente
*3050 This povere book heer I presente
       Unto his hihe worthinesse,
       Write of my simple bisinesse,   *occupation*
       So as seeknesse it suffre wolde.   *To the extent that illness would allow*
       And in such wise as I ferst tolde,
*3055 Whan I this book began to maake,
       In som partie it mai by taake
       As for to lawhe and for to pleye;   *laugh*
       And for to looke in other weye,
       It mai be wisdom to the wise,
*3060 So that somdel for good aprise   *learning*
       And eek somdel for lust and game
       I have it mad, as thilke same
       Which axe for to been excused,
       That I no rethoriqe have used
*3065 Upon the forme of eloquence,

	He hath hem nought withouten charge,	*responsibilities*
	To which that every kyng ys swore.	*sworn*
	So were it good that he therfore	
	First unto rightwisnesse entende,	
3070	Wherof that he hymself amende	*improve*
	Toward his God and leve vice,	*leave*
	Which is the chief of his office;	
	And aftir al the remenant	
	He schal uppon his covenant	
3075	Governe and lede in such a wise,	
	So that ther be no tirandise,	
	Wherof that he his poeple grieve,	
	Or ellis may he nought achieve	
	That longith to his regalie.	
3080	For if a kyng wol justifie	*make righteous*
	His lond and hem that beth withynne,	
	First at hymself he mot begynne,	
	To kepe and reule his owne astat,	
	That in hymself be no debat	*conflict*
3085	Toward his God: for othre wise	
	Ther may non erthly kyng suffise	
	Of his kyngdom the folk to lede,	

	For that is not of mi science;	
	But I have do my trewe peyne	
	With rude wordes and with pleyne	
	To speke of thing which I have toold.	
*3070	But now that I am feble and oold,	
	And to the worschipe of mi king	
	In love above alle other thing	
	That I this book have mad and write,	
	Mi muse dooth me for to wite	*causes me to know*
*3075	That it is to me for the beste	*What*
	Fro this day forth to taake reste,	
	That I no moore of love maake.	
	But he which hath of love his maake	
	It sit him wel to singe and daunce,	
*3080	And do to love his entendance	
	In songes bothe and in seyinges	
	After the lust of his pleyinges,	
	For he hath that he wolde have:	
	But where a man schal love crave	
*3085	And faile, it stant al ootherwise.	
	In his proverbe seith the wise,	
	Whan game is beste, is best to leve:	

	Bot he the kyng of hevene drede.	*Unless he*
	For what kyng sett hym uppon pride	
3090	And takth his lust on every side	
	And wil nought go the righte weie,	
	Though God his grace caste aweie	
	No wondir is, for ate laste	
	He schal wel wite it mai nought laste,	*know*
3095	The pompe which he secheth here.	
	Bot what kyng that with humble chere	
	Aftir the lawe of God eschuieth	*avoids*
	The vices, and the vertus suieth,	*follows*
	His grace schal be suffisant	
3100	To governe al the remenant	
	Which longith to his duité;	*appertains*
	So that in his prosperité	
	The poeple schal nought ben oppressid,	
	Wherof his name schal be blessid,	
3105	For evere and be memorial.	

[FAREWELL TO THE BOOK]

	And now to speke as in final,	
	Touchende that y undirtok	
☞	In Englesch for to make a book	*(see note)*

	And thus forthi my fynal leve,	
	Withoute makyng eny moore,	*writing*
*3090	I take now for evere moore	
	Of love and of his dedly heele,	
	Which no phisicien can heele.	
	For his nature is so divers,	
	That it hath evere som travers	
*3095	Or of to moche or of to lite,	
	That fully mai no man delyte,	
	But if him lacke or that or this.	
	But thilke love which that is	
	Withinne a mannes herte affermed,	
*3100	And stant of charité confermed,	
	That love is of no repentaile;	*has no remorse*
	For it ne berth no contretaile,	*reckoning of debt*
	Which mai the conscience charge,	
	But it is rather of descharge,	*freedom of debt*
*3105	And meedful heer and overal.	
	Forthi this love in special	
	Is good for every man to hoolde,	
	And who that resoun wol byholde,	

Which stant betwene ernest and game,

3110   I have it maad as thilke same

Which axe for to ben excusid,   *Who asks*

And that my bok be nought refusid

Of lered men, whanne thei it se,   *learned*

For lak of curiosité: *subtle learning [in my book]*

3115   For thilke scole of eloquence

Belongith nought to my science,

Uppon the forme of rethoriqe

My wordis for to peinte and pike,   *embellish; polish*

As Tullius som tyme wrot.   *Cicero*

3120   Bot this y knowe and this y wot,

That y have do my trewe peyne

With rude wordis and with pleyne,   *unsophisticated words*

In al that evere y couthe and myghte,

This bok to write as y behighte,   *promised*

3125   So as siknesse it soffre wolde;   *To the extent that illness would allow it*

And also for my daies olde,

That y am feble and impotent,   *feeble; powerless*

I wot nought how the world ys went.   *know not*

So preye y to my lordis alle

3130   Now in myn age, how so befalle,

That y mote stonden in here grace;   *their*

For though me lacke to purchace   *obtain*

Here worthi thonk as by decerte,   *merit*

Yit the symplesse of my poverte

3135   Desireth for to do plesance

To hem undir whos governance

I hope siker to abide.   *secure*

[FAREWELL TO EARTHLY LOVE]

But now uppon my laste tide

That y this book have maad and write,

3140   My muse doth me for to wite,   *causes me to know firsthand*

And seith it schal be for my beste

Fro this day forth to take reste,

That y no more of love make,   *write about*

Al oother lust is good to daunte: *pleasure*

*3110   Which thing the hihe God us graunte

Forth with the remenant of grace

So that of hevene in thilke place

Wher resteth love and alle pees,

Our joye mai been endelees.

[Here ends the poem in the First Recension.]

	Which many an herte hath overtake,	
3145	And ovyrturnyd as the blynde	
	Fro reson into lawe of kynde;	*nature*
	Wher as the wisdom goth aweie	
	And can nought se the ryhte weie	
	How to governe his oghne estat,	*own*
3150	Bot everydai stant in debat	*conflict*
	Withinne himself, and can nought leve.	
	And thus forthy my final leve	
	I take now for evere more,	
	Withoute makynge any more	*waiting*
3155	Of love and of his dedly hele,	*its deadly remedy*
	Which no phisicien can hele.	
	For his nature is so divers,	
	That it hath evere som travers	*obstacle*
	Or of to moche or of to lite,	*Either*
3160	That pleinly mai no man delite,	
	Bot if him faile or that or this.	*Unless is lost to him either*
	Bot thilke love which that is	
	Withinne a mannes herte affermed,	
	And stant of charité confermed:	
3165	Such love is goodly for to have,	
	Such love mai the bodi save,	
	Such love mai the soule amende.	
	The hyhe God such love ous sende	
	Forthwith the remenant of grace,	*Along with*
3170	So that above in thilke place	
	Wher resteth love and alle pes,	
	Oure joie mai ben endeles.	

Explicit iste liber, qui transeat, obsecro liber
Vt sine liuore vigeat lectoris in ore.
Qui sedet in scannis celi det vt ista Iohannis
Perpetuis annis stet pagina grata Britannis.
Derbeie Comiti, recolunt quem laude periti,
Vade liber purus, sub eo requiesce futurus.

[Here ends this book, and may it, I implore, travel free so that without a bruise it may thrive in the reader's ear. May He who sits in the throne of heaven grant that this page of John remain for all time pleasing to the Britains. Go, spotless book, to the Count of Derby,[1] whom the learned honor with praise, and take repose when you will be in his keeping.]

[Here ends the poem in the Lancastrian Recension.]

---

[1] That is, Henry Bolingbroke, who ascended to the throne in 1400. Gower shifted his endorsement from Richard to Henry well before that time, at the latest by 1392. See Prologue, lines 24–92, and the note to Prologue, lines 22ff.

EXIT GOWER

**Epistola super huius opusculi sui complementum
Iohanni Gower a quodam philosopho transmissa:**

*Qvam cinxere freta, Gower, tua carmina leta
Per loca discreta canit Anglia laude repleta.
Carminis Athleta, satirus, tibi, siue Poeta,
Sit laus completa quo gloria stat sine meta.*

[An epistle on the completion of this work of John Gower, conveyed by a certain philosopher:

In diverse regions, O Gower, England, which the waters girdle around, full of praise sings your happy songs.[1] Champion of song, satirist, or poet — to you may praise be full by which glory stands without limit.]

---

[1] Whether the songs are "full of praise" for England, or England "full of praise" for Gower's poetry is grammatically ambiguous (*laude repleta*). For a similar grammatically possible, hyperbolic praise of Gower's poem, see the Latin verses after *2971, along with the note. That the verse here too allows that meaning by the same technique, along with metrical and other features of the Latin here, suggests either that Gower himself wrote these words of the "certain philosopher," or that a Latinist very much in his "school" of Latin poetry constructed them. The very existence of marginal glosses written by the author for his own work somewhat supports the former possibility. At the least, he had no modesty about including them.

THE COLOPHONS

John Fisher notes that at least fifteen of the earliest versions of *Vox Clamantis* and *Confessio Amantis* conclude with a colophon.[1] These are basically alike, consisting of four short paragraphs: 1) In the first John Gower acknowledges the intellectual gifts that God has given him and asserts that in the time allotted him on earth he has composed three books of instructive material for the benefit of others. 2) The first book, written in French (i.e., the *Mirour de l'Omme*), is in ten parts, treats of the vices and virtues, and would teach the right path for the sinner's return to God. He then names the book — *Speculum Hominis*, in the first recension manuscripts, and *Speculum Meditantes* in the later ones. 3) The second book, written in Latin, tells of the peasants rebellion in the fourth year of young King Richard II and the outrages that fell upon men. This book was titled *Vox Clamantis*. 4) The third book, written in English, is in eight parts, made at the request of Richard II. It follows the prophecy of Daniel on the mutability of earthly kingdoms and treats of the education of King Alexander. The subject is love and includes many exempla. The book is called *Confessio Amantis*.

But although the colophons in the several manuscripts are essentially the same, there are some noteworthy variations — enough to warrant printing all three examples: St. John's 34 (a revised version of the first recension); Bodley 294 (a second recension manuscript of the early fifteenth century); and Bodley Fairfax 3 (a third recension manuscript, end of the fourteenth century, which is the base text of the present edition). Fisher includes the colophon to Bodley 902 rather than St. John's 34, for which he provides a translation on pp. 88–89. He prints it along with the colophons to Bodley 294 and Fairfax 3 as Appendix B, pp. 311–12.

FIRST RECENSION (St. John's 34, fols. 214r–214v)

> *Quia vnusquisque prout a deo accepit aliis impartiri tenetur, Iohannes Gower super hiis que deus sibi intellectualiter donauit, villicacionis sue racionem,[2] dum tempus instat, secundum aliquid alleuiare cupiens, inter labores et ocia ad aliorum noticiam tres libros doctrine causa forma subsequenti propterea composuit.[3]*

---

[1] The colophons generally appear at the end of the manuscripts. Thus in St. John's 34 the colophon appears directly following *CA*, while in Fairfax 3 the colophon is separated from *CA* by *Traitié* and *Carmen super multiplici viciorum pestilencia*. See Fisher, *John Gower*, pp. 88–91.

[2] There is an allusion and a pun here: in Luke 16:2, the parable of the unjust steward, the lord asks the steward to "render an account of your stewardship"; but the Latin word for "account" is *ratio*, which also means "reason, rational ability." In Gower's passage God has endowed Gower's reason with many things, as well as "his account of his stewardship."

[3] Possibly because the third recension was originally added to a copy containing the first rather than the second recension, the initial two paragraphs of those recensions are the same, apart from

Primus liber Gallico sermone editus in x diuiditur partes, et tractans de viciis et virtutibus, necnon et de variis huius seculi gradibus, viam qua peccator transgressus ad sui creatoris agnicionem redire debet, recto tramite docere conatur. Titulusque libelli istius Speculum Hominis nuncupatus est.

Secundus enim liber, sermone Latino versibus exametri et pentametri[4] compositus, tractat super illo mirabili euentu qui in Anglica tempore domini Regis Ricardi secundi anno regni sui quarto contigit, quando seruiles rustici impetuose contra nobiles et ingenuos regni insurexerunt. Innocenciam tamen dicti domini Regis tunc minoris etatis causa inde excusabilem pronuncians, culpas aliunde, ex quibus et non a fortuna talia inter homines contingunt enormia, euidencius declarat. Titulusque voluminis huius, cuius ordo vii continet paginas, Vox Clamantis nominatur.

Tercius liber iste Anglico sermone in viii partes diuisus, qui ad instanciam serenissimi principis dicti domini Regis Anglie Ricardi secundi conficitur, secundum Danielis propheciam super huius mundi regnorum mutacione a tempore Regis Nabugodonosor usque nunc tempora distinguit. Tractat eciam secundum Nectanabum et Aristotilem super hiis quibus Rex Alexander tam in sui regimen quam aliter eorum disciplina edoctus fuit. Principalis tamen huius libri materia super amorem et amantum condiciones fundamentum habet. Ubi variarum cronicarum historiarumque sentencie necnon Poetarum Philosophorumque scripture ad exemplum distinccius inseruntur. Nomenque presentis opusculi Confessio Amantis specialiter intitulatur.

[Since each man is obliged to impart to others as he has received from God, John Gower, desiring, while time allows, to mitigate somewhat the account of his stewardship concerning those things with which God has intellectually endowed him, has composed between labors and leisure for the notice of others three books, for the sake of doctrine, in the following form:

The first book, produced in the French language, is divided into ten parts and, discoursing about vices and virtues as well as about the various social degrees of this world, it strives to teach by the straight path the way by which a sinner, having transgressed, ought to return to a recognition of his Creator. The title of this book is declared to be the *Mirror of Man*.

The second book, composed in Latin hexameter and pentameter verses, discourses about that astonishing event that occurred in England in the time of the lord King Richard II, in the fourth year of his reign, when rustic bondsmen impetuously rebelled against the nobles and magnates of the kingdom. Noting the excusable innocence, however, of the said lord king then on the grounds that he was underage, it declares the blame for these things to fall more clearly elsewhere, from which, and not by mere fortune, such terrible things happen among human beings. And the title of this volume, whose structure contains eight pieces of writing, is named the *Vox Clamantis* (*Voice of One Crying*).

---

the Latin title of the *Mirour de l'Omme*, and the change of "intellectually" to "materially" to describe the advantages with which God had endowed the poet. The second recension, which introduces those changes, also differs in various other details in those paragraphs. Apart from those parallels or traces of some direct connection in the opening paragraphs, the first and third recensions otherwise differ more widely than the second and third. The three colophons alter the comments on King Richard II most visibly, and they alter the descriptions of Gower's French and Latin poems somewhat. Only one small change was made in the description of the *Confessio Amantis* in later recensions: the omission of the next to last sentence describing its various kinds of sources and materials.

[4] That is, elegiac couplets. The third recension of the colophon simplifies this notice about the meter of the *Vox Clamantis*.

The third book, which is fashioned in the English language on account of reverence to the most vigorous lord, his lord Henry of Lancaster, then count of Derby, differentiated historical times according to the prophecy of Daniel concerning the transformation of the kingdoms of this world, from the time of King Nebuchadnezzar up until now. It also discourses about those things in which King Alexander was tutored in accord with Nectabanus and Aristotle, as much in his governance as in other matters of his instruction. But the principal subject of this work has its basis in love and lovers' infatuated passions. There, the essences of various chronicles and histories as well as the writings of poets and philosophers are inserted more particularly by way of example. And the name specifically designated for it was chosen to be the *Confessio Amantis* (*Confession of a Lover*).]

SECOND RECENSION (Bodley 294, fol. 199v)

Quia vnusquisque prout a deo accepit aliis impartiri tenetur, Iohannes Gower, super hiis que deus sibi sensualiter[5] donauit villicacionis sue racionem secundum aliquid alleuiare cupiens, tres precipue libros per ipsum, dum vixit, doctrine causa compositos ad aliorum noticiam in lucem seriose produxit.

Primus liber Gallico sermone editus in decem diuiditur partes, et tractans de viciis et virtutibus viam precipue qua peccator in penitendo Cristi misericordiam assequi poterit, tota mentis deuocione finaliter contemplatur. Titulusque libelli istius Speculum Meditantis nuncupatus est.

Secundus liber versibus exametri et pentametre sermone latino componitur. Tractat de variis infortuniis tempore Regis Ricardi secundi in Anglia multiplicitur contingentibus, vbi pro statu regni compositor deuocius exorat. Nomenque volumina huius, quod in septem diuiditur partes, Vox Clamantis intitulat.

Tercius iste liber qui in octo partes ob reuerencia serenissimi domini sui domini Henrici de Lancastria tunc Derbie Comitis Anglico sermone conficitur secundum Danielis propheciam super huius mundi regnorum mutacione a tempore Regis Nabugodonosor usque nunc tempora distinguit. Tractat eciam secundum Aristotilem super hiis quibus Rex Alexander tam in sui regimen quam aliter eius disciplina edoctus fuit. Principalis tamen huius operis materia super amorem et infatuatas amantum passiones fundamentum habet. Nomenque sibi appropriatum Confessio Amantis specialiter sortitus est.

[Since each man is obliged to impart to others as he has received from God, John Gower, desiring, while he lives, to mitigate somewhat the account of his stewardship concerning those things with which God has materially endowed him, has in particular brought forth into the light three books by him, fashioned for the sake of doctrine for the notice of others.

The first book, produced in the French language, is divided into ten parts, and, discoursing about vices and virtues, it contemplates at the end the path especially by which a penitent sinner with total devotion of mind might be able to follow Christ's mercy, and the title of this book is declared to be the *Mirror of the Contemplator*.

The second book is composed in the Latin language in hexameter and pentameter. It treats about the various misfortunes occurring in England in the time of King Richard II,

---

[5] Fisher observes that the first recension *intellectualiter* is replaced in the later recensions by *sensualiter*, "perhaps in recognition of the fortunate physical endowment which carried the poet through nearly eight decades" (*John Gower*, p. 89). Possibly also he was recording his gratitude for his increasing material wealth as he matured.

where the maker devoutly prays on behalf of the realm's condition. And the name of this book, which is divided into seven parts, is entitled *Vox Clamantis* (*Voice of One Crying*).

The third book, which is fashioned in the English language on account of reverence to the most vigorous lord, his lord Henry of Lancaster, then count of Derby, differentiated historical times according to the prophecy of Daniel concerning the transformation of the kingdoms of this world, from the time of King Nebuchadnezzar up until now. It also discourses about those things in which King Alexander was tutored in accord with Aristotle, as much in his governance as in other matters of his instruction. But the principal subject of this work has its basis in love and lovers' infatuated passions. And the name specifically designated for it was chosen to be the *Confessio Amantis* (*Confession of a Lover*).]

THIRD RECENSION (Fairfax 3, fol. 194v)

Quia vnusquisque, prout a deo accepit, aliis impartiri tenetur, Iohannes Gower super hiis que deus sibi sensualiter donauit villicacionis sue racionem, dum tempus instat, secundum aliquid alleuiare cupiens, inter labores et ocia ad aliorum noticiam tres libros doctrine causa forma subsequenti propterea composuit.

Primus liber Gallico sermone editus in decem diuiditur partes, et tractans de viciis et virtutibus, necnon et de variis huius seculi gradibus,[6] viam qua peccator transgressus ad sui creatoris agnicionem redire debet, recto tramite docere conatur. Titulusque libelli istius Speculum Meditantis nuncupatus est.

Secundus enim liber sermone latino metrice compositus tractat de variis infortuniis tempore Regis Ricardi Secundi in Anglia contingentibus. Vnde non solum regni proceres et communes tormenta passi sunt, set et ipse crudelissimus rex suis ex demeritis ab alto corruens in foueam quam fecit finaliter proiectus est.[7] Nomenque voluminis huius Vox Clamantis intitulatur.

Tercius iste liber qui ob reuerenciam strenuissimi domini sui domini Henrici de Lancastria, tunc Derbeie Comitis, Anglico sermone conficitur, secundum Danielis propheciam super huius mundi regnorum mutacione a tempore regis Nabugodonosor vsque nunc tempora distinguit. Tractat eciam secundum Aristotilem super hiis quibus rex Alexander tam in sui regimen quam aliter eius disciplina edoctus fuit. Principalis tamen huius operis materia super amorem et infatuatas amantum passiones fundamentum habet. Nomenque sibi appropriatum Confessio Amantis specialiter sortitus est.

[Since each man is obliged to impart to others as he has received from God, John Gower, desiring, while time allows, to mitigate somewhat the account of his stewardship concerning those things with which God has materially endowed him, has composed, between labors and leisure for the notice of others three books, for the sake of doctrine, in the following form:

---

[6] The phrase, "as well as about the various social degrees of this world," appearing in the first and third recension but dropped from the second, reflects the turn in the later part of the *Mirour de l'Omme* toward estates satire.

[7] The scathing denunciation of the ruin during Richard II's reign in the final recension of this passage in the colophon treats the general disruption of society depicted in the survey of estates in the *Vox Clamantis* as if it were an analysis specifically of the ills of Richard's reign. The view extends and even hardens the anti-Ricardian revised Prologue of the *Confessio Amantis* and the changed dedication at beginning and ending of that poem; the three colophons chart the progress of the poet's condemnation of Richard.

The first book, produced in the French language, is divided into ten parts and, discoursing about vices and virtues as well as about the various social degrees of this world, it strives to teach by the straight path the way by which a sinner, having transgressed, ought to return to a recognition of his Creator. The title of this book is declared to be the *Mirror of the Contemplator*.

The second book, composed metrically in Latin, discourses about the various misfortunes occurring in England in the time of King Richard II. Wherefore not only the nobility of the kingdom and the commons suffered torments, but even the most unfit king himself, because of his own shortcomings rushing down from on high, was thrown into the pit that he had made; and this volume is entitled the *Vox Clamantis* (*Voice of One Crying*).

The third book, which is fashioned in the English language on account of reverence to the most vigorous lord, his lord Henry of Lancaster, then count of Derby, differentiated historical times according to the prophecy of Daniel concerning the transformation of the kingdoms of this world, from the time of King Nebuchadnezzar up until now. It also discourses about those things in which King Alexander was tutored in accord with Aristotle, as much in his governance as in other matters of his instruction. But the principal subject of this work has its basis in love and lovers' infatuated passions. And the name specifically designated for it was chosen to be the *Confessio Amantis* (*Confession of a Lover*).]

Illustration 4: MS Bodl. 294, fol. 4v. Bodleian Library, Oxford University. Nebuchadnez-zar's dream of the Monster of Time.

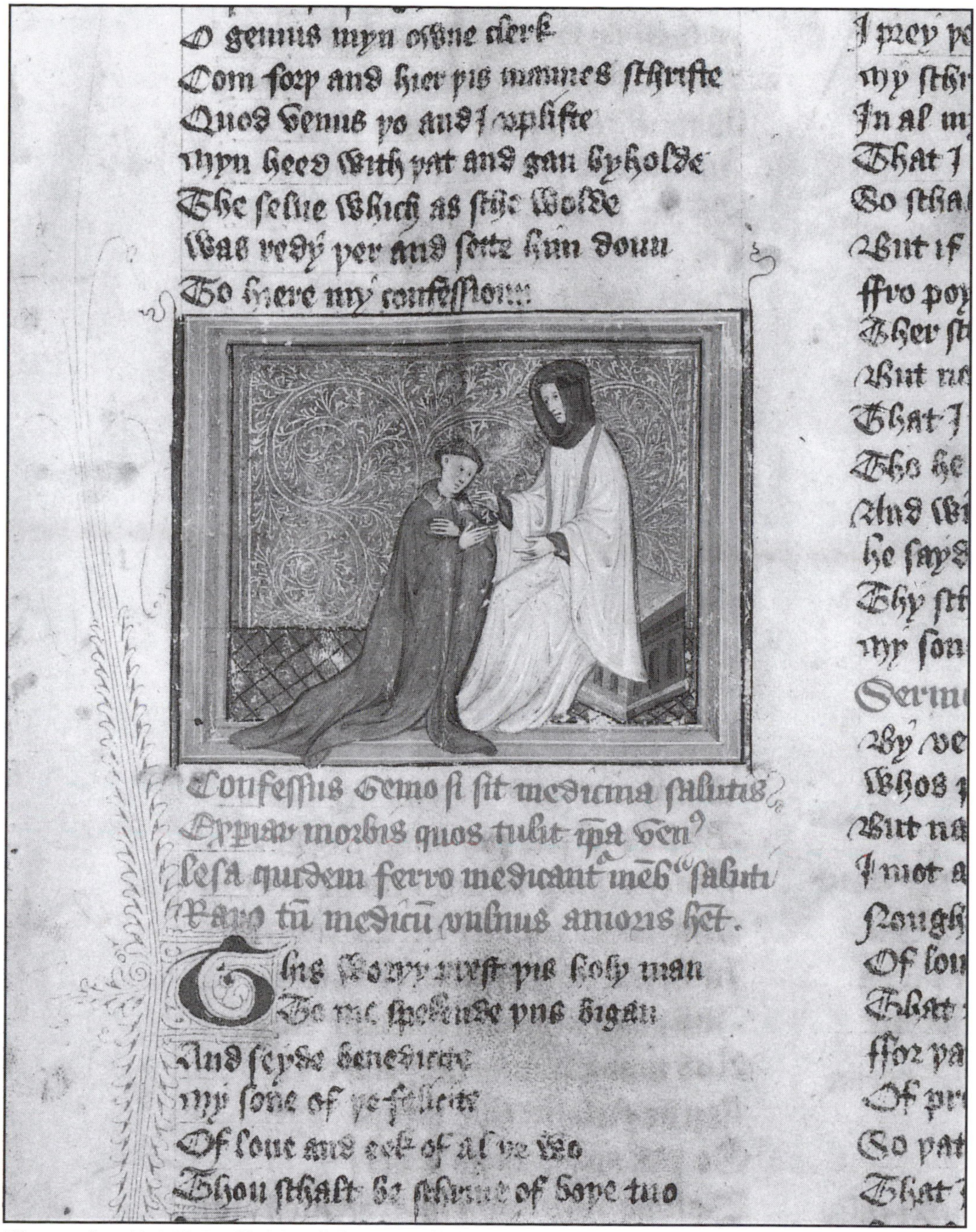
O genius myn owne clerk
Com forþ and hier þis mannes schrifte
Quod Venus þo and I vplifte
Myn heed with þat and gan byholde
The selue which as sche wolde
Was redy þer and sette him doun
To here my confessioun
Confessus Genio si sit medicina salutis
Experiar morbis quos tulit ipsa Venus
Lesa quidem ferro medicantur membra saluti
Raro tamen medicum vulnus amoris habet.
This worþi prest þis holy man
To me spekende þus bigan
And seyde benedicite
My sone of þe felicite
Of loue and ek of al þe wo
Thou schalt be schriue of boþe tuo

Illustration 5: MS Bodl. 294, fol. 9r. Bodleian Library, Oxford University. The Lover confesses to Genius.

EXPLANATORY NOTES

ABBREVIATIONS: ***Anel.***: Chaucer, *Anelida and Arcite*; ***BD***: Chaucer, *Book of the Duchess*; ***CA***: Gower, *Confessio Amantis*; ***CT***: Chaucer, *Canterbury Tales*; ***HF***: Chaucer, *House of Fame*; ***LGW***: Chaucer, *Legend of Good Women*; **Mac**: Macaulay (4 vol. *Complete Works*); ***MED***: *Middle English Dictionary*; ***Met.***: Ovid, *Metamorphoses*; ***MO***: Gower, *Mirour de l'Omme*; **MS(S)**: manuscript(s); ***OED***: *Oxford English Dictionary*; ***PF***: Chaucer, *Parliament of Fowls*; ***PL***: *Patrologia Latina*; ***RR***: Lorris and de Meun, *Roman de la Rose*; ***TC***: Chaucer, *Troilus and Criseyde*; **Tilley**: Tilley, *Dictionary of Proverbs in England*; **Vat. Myth.**: Vatican Mythographer I, II, or III; ***VC***: Gower, *Vox Clamantis*; **Whiting**: Whiting, *Proverbs, Sentences, and Proverbial Phrases*. For manuscript abbreviations, see p. 303.

EXPLANATORY NOTES TO PROLOGUE

Illustration 2: Fairfax 3, fol. 2r. Nebuchadnezzar's Dream of the Monster of Time. This is the most recurrent subject for illustration in the Gower MSS. The drawings are always unique, but all include two basic components, namely the sleeping king and the monster. See Illustration 4 to compare the Bodley 294 illustrator's representation with that of the Fairfax illustrator. In some MSS, such as Bodley 902, the first page is missing; in others, such as the Stafford MS, the picture has been cut out; in others still, a blank has been left for the picture to be drawn in. See Griffiths, "Poem and Its Pictures," for discussion of the placement of the illustrations and Emmerson, "Reading Gower," on the relationship of the illustration to the *mise en page*. N.b. note to Latin verse v below (p. 248).

Latin verses i (before line 1). **Lines 1–2:** Opening protestations of literary modesty were legion in medieval Latin poetry. This verse parallels in brief outline the longer, preliminary sections of the popular twelfth-century school-text, Johannes de Hauvilla's *Architrenius*, which inveighs against Sloth, Lechery, Sleep, Detraction, Mockery, Error, etc. (lines 1–40), asserts the poet's modest abilities yet confidence in success (lines 55–56), and exhorts envious detractors to remain far off (lines 213–15). Behind the modesty trope, Gower challenges his audience to read his work sympathetically, even though it is written in English. The implication is that English, Hengist's language (**line 3**), is inferior as a literary language. To counteract its insularity he alludes to the history of the peoples of the island and the heroic origins of the nation founded by Brutus, the great-grandson of Aeneas. See Geoffrey of Monmouth's *History of the Kings of Britain* for the full account of the Trojan descendant's winning of the island from giants, founding his kingdom, and siring a line of kings that culminates with King Arthur, despite the treachery of Hengist. Hengist was the first Saxon on the

237

island. One anecdote in this mythical history recounts that Hengist's daughter greeted the reigning British king, Vortiger, with the drinking toast "Wassail!" ("Be healthy!"); according to the fourteenth- and fifteenth-century prose *Brut*, a popular French and English adaptation and continuation of Geoffrey's history, this was the first "Englisshe" word spoken in Britain (*Brut*, ch. 57; ed. Brie, 1.52). **Line 4**: *Carmentis* is said by Isidore of Seville to have first brought Latin script to the speakers of ancient Italy (*Etymologies* 1.4.1). Gower will "utter" but also write his English verses, an event implicitly as foundational as Hengist's and Carmentis' founding contributions to linguistic history. See Echard, "With Carmen's Help," pp. 3–10, on Carmen as Gower's muse and one who makes tongues. **Line 5**: The tongue, whose lack of bones yet had "bone-breaking" power, was the subject of many Latin proverbs (ed. Echard and Fanger, pp. xxxvii and 3). See also *VC* 5.921–22: "Res mala lingua loquax, res peior, pessima res est, / Que quamuis careat ossibus, ossa terit" ("An evil thing is a talkative tongue . . . / which although it lack bones, destroys bones"); and *CA* 3.462–65: "the harde bon . . . [a] tunge brekth it al to pieces." **Line 6**: The *Architrenius* also concludes its introductory sections with the same ritual apotropaicism: "Let the slanderous razor of envy, keen only in treachery, remain far off, and far off too be that viper whose venom is harmful only to noteworthy achievements" (lines 213–15).

On the subject of *CA* as a bilingual poem with distinct functions for each language, see Yeager, "'*Oure englisshe*' and Everyone's Latin"; Minnis, *Medieval Theory of Authorship*, pp. 274–75n45; and Olsen, "*Betwene Ernest and Game*," pp. 5–18 (on likenesses between its bilingual structure and that of Dante's *Vita Nuova*). Pearsall suggests that the vernacular author who nearest approaches Gower in his extensive use of Latin in diverse ways (vatic verse headings, scholastic apparatus of prose commentaries, Latin speech prefixes, and elaborate Latin apparatus at the end of the poem including a long colophon and various Latin poems) is Boccaccio ("Gower's Latin in the *Confessio Amantis*," p. 15). For further discussion of Gower's Latin verses see Echard and Fanger, *Latin Verses*, especially pp. xiii–lviii, and sundry notes. On Gower's shorter Latin poems see the edition by Yeager (*Minor Latin Works*). On tensions between Latin and English texts see Batchelor, "Feigned Truth and Exemplary Method."

2   *bokes duelle*. Gower positions books as the repository of moral values and history, against which he encourages the reader to judge present behavior. Books provide examples from "olde wyse" (line 7); that wisdom of the past enables people to see what is new, whether in method, topic, or circumstance.

7   *Essampled*. For discussion of Gower's use of narrative exempla see Yeager, "John Gower and the *Exemplum* Form"; Shaw, "Gower's Illustrative Tales"; Simpson, *Sciences and the Self*; Runacres, "Art and Ethics"; and Mitchell, *Ethics and Exemplary Narrative*. For his use of Ovid see Harbert, "Lessons from the Great Clerk." See also note to Book 1, line 79.

7–8   *wyse . . . wyse*. Gower's verse thrives on *rime riche*, the rhyming of homophones (words with the same sound but different meanings or functions). The device catches the ear off-guard and provokes double, more careful reading, the way riddles do. Single glosses (e.g., *wyse* as both "wise" [men or books] and "manner") can scarcely do justice to the device which, like puns, flourishes on multiplicity of meanings and function, such as adjective versus noun, etc. The device reminds us that glosses are starting points only, not simple equations or "facts." See note to Prol.237–38.

11–18   An inkblot in the middle of the first column obliterates a portion of the text. The blot apparently was made sometime after the page had been copied and bound, for two streaks extend toward the center, as if running down the page. A corresponding blot occurs on the facing page, a mirror image of the first blot. If this MS was in fact corrected by Gower, as Macaulay suggested, the poet himself could be the culprit (2:cxxx). More likely, the accident occurred at some later date after the presentation of the copy.

17   The *middel weie* is both a rhetorical and an ethical proposition. Gower would see his poem as a mediator between social issues and personal moral choices. See Middleton ("Idea of Public Poetry," pp. 101–02) on the public dimensions of Gower's methodological agenda. By striking a medial position between wisdom and delight, with English as his medium, the poet would make fictive paradigms from which moral therapy might be achieved. See Introduction, pp. 13–15.

19   *Somwhat of lust, somwhat of lore.* See Zeeman on Gower's appropriation of "Amans, his love, his text and all texts of courtly love into an exemplum of worldly uncertainty and deceit" ("Framing Narrative," p. 223). *Lust*, she suggests, denotes desire, the feeling of pleasure and delight, but also the object of desire and something causing pleasure. The shift of the narrator from *auctor* to Amans engages the reader in the pleasure of narrative, while the conversion of the lover into the old man in Book 8 brutally subverts the courtly narrative as a deceit from which there is no "recoverir" (pp. 231–32, with reference to 8.2443).

22 ff.   ☞ **Latin marginalia**: *Hic in principio declarat qualiter in anno Regis Ricardi secundi sexto decimo Iohannes Gower presentem libellum composuit et finaliter compleuit, quem strenuissimo domino suo domino Henrico de Lancastria tunc Derbeie Comiti cum omni reuerencia specialiter destinauit.* [Here in the beginning he declares how in the sixteenth year of King Richard II John Gower composed and ultimately completed the present little book, which he especially designated with all reverence for the most vigorous lord, his lord Henry of Lancaster, at that time Earl of Derby.] This Latin inscription is found in only five MSS, and appears to be a late addition, after the establishing of the third recension, though not necessarily in third recension copies. It does *not* occur, however, in Fairfax 3. Olsson points out that what is important here is the fact that the note replaces a gloss at Prol.34 of the first recension, which read: "John Gower . . . most zealously compiled the present little book, like a honeycomb gathered from various flowers" (see full text of the gloss below, at the end of the following note). Olsson suggests that the shift from *compilauit* to *compleuit* (from compilation to composition) may indicate a shift in Gower's conception of his work as he puts aside the earlier sense of himself as a *compilator* gathering flowers of wisdom from the past to consider himself more confidently in the role of *auctor* (*Structures of Conversion*, pp. 5–11). Nicholson ("Dedications," pp. 171–74),

on the other hand, suggests that the Latin note was added by Gower or a scribe long after the original presentation to Henry, and thus the gloss gives a misleading account of the history of *CA*.

24   *A bok for Engelondes sake.* Aers ("Reflections on Gower as '*Sapiens* in Ethics and Politics'") sees in the phrase an epitome of Gower's attack on ecclesiastical failure. Aers suggests that Gower is attempting to persuade lay power, especially that of the sovereign (line 25), that what was destructive of the church was also subversive of royal power, and that "the sovereign needed the wholehearted support of the church. . . . The *auctor* of the Prologue and Genius in Book II [with his attack on the papacy] develop a radical critique of the actually existing church combined with a defence of the secular sovereign's role in challenging the ecclesiastical hierarchy when it is judged to be in serious error" (p. 196).

24–92   These lines are found only in third recension MSS. That is, they must have been written c. 1392 when Gower rededicated the poem to Henry of Lancaster, count of Derby. Nicholson ("Dedications") argues that the change in text represents the honoring of a patron, not some disenchanted transfer of allegiance from Richard to the count of Derby; others have seen evidences of disappointment in Richard (e.g., Peck, *Kingship and Common Profit*, pp. 7–9; "Politics and Psychology," pp. 224–38; Ferster, *Fictions of Advice*, pp. 109–10; and Simpson, *Sciences and the Self*, pp. 297–99). The majority of the MSS include the Richard citation here marked as *24–*92, rather than the dedication to Henry that was introduced in 1392 as in the carefully corrected Fairfax 3 MS. But the earlier dedication continued to be copied after 1392, almost certainly with Gower's approval. Thus I have placed the first dedication as a parallel text in this edition. For further comment see note to Prol.25, below. On Gower as a Lancastrian advocate, see Staley, *Languages of Power*, pp. 351–55.

*24–*25   *book . . . bilongeth.* N.b. spelling differences here as juxtaposed to the spelling of the Fairfax scribe. Macaulay uses Bodley 294 as the text for the Ricardian version, as do I. He allows that the spelling in his edition has been "slightly normalized" (2:457), which is an understatement. I have followed the spelling of Bodley 294 as an antidote to any notion that the spelling of the Fairfax 3 scribe necessarily equates with Gower's.

25   *The yer sextenthe of Kyng Richard.* Gower completed his first version of *CA* during or prior to the fourteenth year of Richard's reign. Although some portions of the poem may have been written four or five years or perhaps even seven years earlier, when Chaucer was working on *TC* and beginning *LGW*, the Prologue of *CA* may have been completed later. In that first version, lines *24–*92 tell of Gower's boarding of the royal barge and the king's requesting that he write the poem, which the poet agrees to do despite ill health (*79–*80), out of "ligeance" and "obeissance" (lines *25–*26) to his king. By 1392, the sixteenth year of Richard's reign, Gower rewrote this beginning and conclusion of the poem, deleting the king's commission here and the ending of the poem in praise of Richard's worthiness, and dedicated the poem to Henry of Lancaster (see Prol. 81–92 and the Latin postscript to Book 8), even as much as seven years before Henry would become king. (See Mac 2:cxxvii–clxx, for a description of most of

the known MSS and an account of the revisions; see Fisher, *John Gower*, pp. 116–17, for discussion of the revisions in their historical setting.) The politics underlying the revision are not known. Perhaps Gower became disenchanted with Richard's behavior as king at the time of the king's harsh treatment of London officials earlier in 1392. That he sees hope for England in a man like Henry of Lancaster so long before he would return from exile to "save" England seems clairvoyant, though it is quite possible that Gower meant only for the Fairfax 3 version of *CA* to be a compliment to Henry and that recopying of the earlier recensions continued with the poet's approval.

*33   *That his corone longe stonde.* This line, especially, resonates in its omission from the third recension, where Gower speaks of time reversing itself as it yearns for the good rule of one like Henry of Lancaster. In the *Tripartite Chronicle*, Gower, perhaps anachronistically, sees Richard's misbehavior reaching back to 1392 and earlier as he quite boldly speaks of not only shortening but ending Richard's reign.

*34–*35   ☞ **Latin marginalia**: Inserted between lines *34–*35 in MS Bodley 294, a second recension MS which has been my copy-text for lines *24–*92, is a Latin summary: *Hic declarat in primis qualiter ob reuerenciam serenissimi principis domini sui [Regis Anglie Ricardi secundi] totus suus humilis Iohannes Gower, licet graui infirmitate a diu multipliciter fatigatus, huius opusculi labores suscipere non recusauit, sed tanquam fauum ex variis floribus recollectum, presentem libellum ex variis cronicis, historiis, poetarum philosophorumque dictis, quatenus sibi infirmitas permisit, studiosissime compilauit.* [Here he declares particularly how, because of reverence of the most serene prince, his lord king of England Richard II, his own and humble John Gower, although long wearied in many ways by grave illness, did not refuse to take up the labors of this little work, but instead has most zealously compiled the present little book from various chronicles, histories, and sayings of poets and philosophers, like a honeycomb gathered from various flowers, to the extent that his infirmity allowed him.] In some first and second recension MSS, e.g., Cambridge University Library Mm 2.21, the Latin note appears in the margin, though the practice of inserting marginal prose summaries into the text itself, just as the Latin verse epigrams appear in the text, is common in many of the later MSS, even though the insertion disrupts the sense and syntax of the English verse. Usually the Latin insertions are written in a different colored ink, as here. On the *variis floribus* trope as evidence of Gower's initial regard for his work as *compilatio*, a sort of anthology of purposeful writing from former days, see Olsson, *Structures of Conversion*, pp. 5–11.

*37   *newe Troye.* Gower flatters Richard and the kingdom with the allusion to London as the "new Troye," as if to identify a renaissance of ancient culture of which they are the heart. The designation was encouraged by Edward III and Richard II, as part of the celebration of the new vernacular culture surpassing that of France or even Italy. The term evolves from the mythography of Geoffrey of Monmouth, since the Trojan descendant Brutus founded his kingdom on the happy island. Contemporary romances based on Geoffrey, such as *The Alliterative Morte Arthure*, impress their audience with the superiority of Arthur's culture to that of Rome or France. See note to Latin verses i, above.

*45   *He bad me come into his barge.* For speculation against the historicity of the meeting on the Thames, see Grady, "Gower's Boat." But see Staley, *Languages of Power*, pp. 16–17.

52   *burel clerk.* Literally, one dressed in coarse clothing — hence common or ignorant; possibly a lay clerk, though more likely an oxymoron (secular-religious). See Galloway, "Gower in His Most Learned Role," on the unusual posture of secular learnedness that Gower cultivates.

59   *neweth every dai.* See Olsson, *Structures of Conversion*, pp. 10 ff., on Gower's concept of the value of reading and of the past as new ideas come out of old works. The idea is intimately linked to his technique of *compilatio*, which becomes a means of invention rather than encyclopedic accumulation. The retelling converts dead ideas to living ones for the audience as well as for Amans. Olsson goes on to suggest that this process of perpetual renewal provides an interconnectedness between Gower's earlier writings and *CA* (pp. 16 ff.). Compare Chaucer's "For out of olde feldes, as men seyth, / Cometh al this newe corn from yer to yere" (*PF* lines 22–23).

60   *So as I can, so as I mai.* Proverbial: "As I am able, so will I do." Not in Whiting, though Tilley, *Dictionary of Proverbs*, offers the variant: "Men must do as they may (can), not as they would" (M554).

61–62   Although the allusion to the poet's illness enhances the Prologue's theme of the degenerating world and thus anticipates the conclusion to the poem where the poet rejects mundane love because of his decrepitude, biographers generally agree that Gower was in fact in ill health during his later years. He had retired from public life some fifteen years earlier and was now over sixty years old. It is noteworthy that this couplet alone is found in both the first and third recensions (compare *79–*80). Gower changed the dedication, but not the reference to his illness.

67   *to wisdom al belongeth.* Simpson argues that the branch of wisdom to which Gower is referring is that of the stoic and moral philosophers (Socrates, Seneca, and Boethius), who, according to Robert Holcot's third kind of *sapientia* in his *Commentum super librum sapientiae*, define *sapientia* as "the collection of intellectual and moral powers" ("Ironic Incongruence," pp. 618–19).

72   *bot the god alone.* Conceivably the sense might be "God alone." But Macaulay (2:459) notes the preeminence of locutions such as "the god" (i.e., the good) in 2:594, and "the vertu" (Prol.116), "the manhode" (Prol.260), "the man" (Prol.546, 582), and "[t]he charité" (Prol.319), etc. See also "the vertu and the vice" (Prol.79). The placement of the article reflects a French affectation. The implication seems deterministic, as if the good know by virtue of their goodness. See Mark 4:11–12, where the good see and hear the mysteries of God, but to others (those outside the faith) things happen in parables.

77 ff.   Macaulay suggests that in lines 77 ff. Gower alludes to Book 7, which deals with the instruction of great men. He glosses the lines to read: "I shall make a discourse also with regard to those who are in power, marking the distinction

between the virtues and the vices which belong to their office" (2:459). Certainly the sense of the lines is complex with respect to authority and submission (see marginal gloss to lines 77–80). Book 7 provides one context; but the lines might also be understood in terms of *CA* 8.2109–20, where the focus shifts from great men as power figures now to kingship as a psychological phenomenon. That is, in writing about love which has upset so many men he will in this "wise" (that is, in the mode of courtly romance) consider virtues and vices which have general significance to "great" men of all times. See Peck's discussion of 8.2109 ff. in *Kingship and Common Profit*, pp. 173–74, and his earlier edition (1967), pp. xxi–xxii.

81–87   *Bot for my wittes . . . amendement . . . is Henri named*. The modesty trope with deference to the patron is common in late fourteenth- and early fifteenth-century literature, as the author presents his work as receptive to criticism.

*86–88   *in proverbe*. See Whiting W646.

Latin verses ii (before line 93). **Line 2**: *vertit in orbe* has punning implications difficult to translate in brief: *vertit* may mean "has overturned, destroyed," but also in context the rotation of Fortune's orb; *in orbe* may mean "on [Fortune's] wheel" or "in the world." The association between Fortune's *orbis* and the world's *orbis* is increasingly clear in the verse (as throughout Gower's poetry). "World-wheel" makes an effort to capture both the global sense and the pun on Fortune's inexorably turning wheel. Compare Chaucer's "Lak of Stedfastnesse" and "Fortune: Balade de Visage sanz Peinture." The idea of a "golden age" is a commonplace of ancient and medieval poetry; for Gower's likeliest models see Boethius, *Consolation* 2.m.5, and Jean de Meun, *RR*, lines 8381–9668. Compare Chaucer's "The Former Age." **Line 9**: For a different comparison to the chameleon, see *CA* 1.2698–2702.

94   *The tyme passed*. On Gower's nostalgic feel for the ancients and former days as an *ubi sunt* golden age, see Peter, *Complaint and Satire*, p. 70.

     ☞ **Latin marginalia**: *De statu regnorum, vt dicunt, secundum temporalia, videlicet tempore regis Ricardi secundi anno regni sui sexto decimo*. [Concerning the status of kingdoms, as they say, in regard to worldly matters, in the time of King Richard II in the sixteenth year of his reign.]

113   *The word was lich to the conceite*. A phrase equivalent to Chaucer's "The wordes moote be cosyn to the dede" (*CT* I[A]742), which Chaucer attributes to Plato. The phrase is proverbial. See Whiting W645.

120   *in special*. "In its specifics, or singularities," or "in its details, or particularities." Gower frequently uses the term with philosophical precision, as if it marks features of the minor premise from which causation might be deduced. See Prol.165, 281, 383, 432, 572, 946. Boethius speaks of the confusion of humankind in terms of knowing and not knowing simultaneously: "while the soule is hidd in the cloude and in the derknesse of the membres of the body, it ne hath nat al foryeten itself, but it withholdeth the somme of thinges and lesith the *singularites*. Thanne who so that sekith sothnesse, he nis in neyther nother

habite, for he not nat al, ne he ne hath nat al foryeten; but yit hym remembreth the somme of thinges that he withholdeth, and axeth conseile, and retretith deepliche thinges iseyn byforne (that is to seyn, the grete somme in his mynde) so that he mowe *adden the parties* that he hath foryeten to thilke that he hath withholden" (Chaucer's *Boece*, 5.m.3.43–56; emphasis mine).

124   *comune vois*. Macaulay emends to *comun vois*. His emendation improves the meter. In his idealism, Gower imagines an innate voice of truth lying within the people of every society, like a God-given conscience which might be sounded in hard times despite the almost universal corruptions of sin and oppression. See Peck, *Kingship and Common Profit* (especially pp. xi–xxv), for discussion of the people and the common voice. Compare the proverb *vox populi vox dei*, which recurs in *MO* and *VC*. See Whiting V52–V54.

143   *Stonde in this world upon a weer*. *Weer* derives from Old Germanic **warra*, meaning "conflict," "doubt," "uncertainty." N.b. OHG *werra*, MDu, MLG *werre*, ONF *wiere*, and OE and ME *wer(e)*. In ME its homonym *weir*, for a bog or stagnant water, provides a rich pun, as one who *stonde* in doubt is akin to one who stands on unstable ground or is "bogged down." A second homonym, *were* (the past tense of the verb *to be*), provides a further pun, as if the newness of an idea passes, becomes lost, and the mind falls back into a forgetting. See Chaucer's *HF*, lines 970–82, for a similar use of the term. This wordplay is highly Boethian in its sense of place versus lack of steadfastness, a sensibility commonly implicit in the often-repeated main verb *to stand*, which is used philosophically several hundred times in *CA* (e.g., "evere stant . . . in doute" [Prol.562] or "stant evere upon debat" [Prol.567]). On uncertainty and mutability as philosophical concepts within the Prologue and Book 1, see Simpson, *Sciences and the Self*.

152–53   ☞ **Latin marginalia**: *Apostolus. Regem honorificate* [The Apostle: "Honor the king" — 1 Peter 2:17]

155   *With al his herte and make hem chiere*. "And welcome them with all his heart." Gower commonly places the conjunction in a medial position where we would require its position at the head of the clause. See also Prol.521, 756, and 1014. Macaulay cites Prol.759 as well, which is possible, though I have punctuated the sentence as if the first clause were an instance of enjambment and "wroghte" a transitive verb.

156 ff.   ☞ **Latin marginalia**: *Salomon. Omnia fac cum consilio* [Solomon: "Do all things with counsel"] *Fili sine consilio nihil facias, et post factum non paeniteberis* [My son, do nothing without counsel, and thou shalt not repent when thou hast done — Vulgate/Douai, Ecclesiasticus 32:24]. Macaulay (2:460) notes that Gower often cites Ecclesiasticus in *MO*, but the proverb is very common. Compare Chaucer's Miller's Tale (I[A]3529–30): "For thus seith Salomon, that was ful trewe: / 'Werk al by conseil, and thou shalt nat rewe'"; and Merchant's Tale (IV[E]1485–86): "Wirk alle thyng by conseil . . . And thanne shaltow nat repente thee." See Whiting C470. The proverb also occurs in The Tale of Melibee (VII[B²]1003) which Benson suggests is due to Albertanus of Brescia, *Lib.*

consolationis et consilii, a source for The Tale of Melibee.

167   *Among the men to geve pes*. Gower is alluding to the recurrent wars with France, Spain, and Scotland. A three-year truce had been made with France and Scotland in 1389, but, because of profiteering, it was not maintained. An attempt for a truce with Spain in the same year failed. Not until 1396, when Richard married the daughter of the king of France, was a firm truce established with the French.

Latin verses iii (before line 193). **Line 4**: Macaulay suggests the double virtue to be charity and chastity (2:460).

194–99   ☞ **Latin marginalia**: *De statu cleri, vt dicunt, secundum spiritualia, videlicet tempore Roberti Gibbonensis, qui nomen Clementis sibi sortitus est, tunc antipape*. [Concerning the status of the clergy, as they call them, in regard to spiritual matters, in the time of Robert of Geneva, who took to himself the name Clement, at that time the antipope.] In 1378 the Great Schism began, in which both Pope Urban VI (supported by the English) and Clement VII (supported by the French) were elected popes, in Rome and Avignon respectively; the schism did not end until 1418. Gower attacks the Avignon pope Clement also in *VC* 3.955–56. It may be a sign of his different anticipated audiences or different kinds of linguistic decorum that, although Gower discusses in English the moral point of the schism (below, lines 360–77), he names names only in Latin.

196   *Ensample*. The term is a favorite of Gower in defining "a fitting vehicle for his personal philosophy by mirroring the complexities and interrelatedness of the microcosm and the macrocosm in its multileveled construction" (Shaw, "Gower's Illustrative Tales," p. 447). See Simpson, *Sciences and the Self*; Runacres, "Art and Ethics"; and Mitchell, *Ethics and Exemplary Narrative*, on the diversity of rhetorical functions of "ensamples" in *CA* as Gower effects the transformation of sources for judiciously particularized situations.

204   *Simon*. Simon Magus, a Samaritan sorcerer mentioned in Acts 8:18–24. Simon offers money for purchasing the power of the Holy Spirit, but Peter rebukes him, condemning his iniquity. Hence, *simony*, the practice of buying or selling ecclesiastical preferment, benefices, emoluments, or sacred objects for personal gain. Simon's name became synonymous with ecclesiastical corruption. See also line 241.

207–11   *Lumbard . . . withoute cure*. Lombardy, especially Milan and Lucca, was the banking center of Europe in the fourteenth century. The Lombards were so notorious as bankers, moneylenders, and pawnbrokers that their name came to denote such behavior in both Old French and Middle English (*OED*). Langland links Lombards and Jews to exemplify avarice in *Piers Plowman* B 5.238, and in C 4.193–94 he yokes merchants, "mytrede bysshopes," Lombards, and Jews as enemies of Conscience. Lombard bankers were often employed as intermediaries in church and state transactions, which sometimes became confused. The Lombard's refusal to make *exchange* alludes to King Richard's dispute with London when city officials would not lend revenue to the king but would lend to the Lombards. Macaulay notes that "the 'letter' referred to [in line 209] is the papal provision, or perhaps the letter of request addressed to the pope in favour of a particular person" (2:461). Gower makes a similar complaint in *VC* 3.1375 ff. (See also *CA* 2.2093 ff.) For full discussion of the relationship of the Lombard bankers to English kings in the previous century, see Kaeuper, *Bankers to the Crown*.

237–38   *goode . . . goode*. *Rime équivoque*, where the poet repeats words or portions of words with punning effect (compare *rime riche*), and metonymic structures are preeminent features of Gower's rhetoric and the basis of much of its wit and innuendo. For discussion of the devices and their effects upon the poem's texture see Olsen, *"Betwene Ernest and Game,"* pp. 33–69. For a *tour de force* example of the device see 5.79–90.

247   *lawe positif*. Positive law refers to any law which is arbitrarily instituted; it is customarily classified as distinct from divine law and natural law. Gower's point is that the church has departed from its own regulation. It is perhaps noteworthy that under positive law fell the selling of indulgences, pardons, trentals, and the like, a jurisdiction that was much abused. Chaucer satirizes the manipulations of such laws in The Friar's Tale, The Summoner's Tale, and The Pardoner's Tale. See also *Piers Plowman* B 7.168–95 and *VC* 3.227 ff.

266–77   "The allusion is to the circumstances of the campaign of the Bishop of Norwich in 1385; cf. *Vox Clam*. iii. 373 (margin), and see Froissart (ed. Lettenhove [Brussels, 1879]), vol. x. p. 207" (Mac 2:461–62).

284   *Gregoire*. The allusion is to Gregory I's *Pastoral Care* 1.8, 9. (See *PL* 76.1128.)

298–305   ☞ **Latin marginalia**: *Gregorius. Terrenis lucris inhiant, honore prelacie gaudent, et non vt prosint, set vt presint, episcopatum desiderant*. [Gregory: "They gulp down worldly riches, rejoice in the honor of the prelacy and desire a bishopric, not to be a help but to be the head."] Macaulay observes that the passage is taken loosely from Gregory's *Homilies on the Gospel*, printed in *PL* 76:1128 and *Regula Pastoralis* 2.6. See his note (2:462).

329   *Ethna*. Mt. Etna, the Sicilian volcano (the highest in Europe, over 10,000 feet), frequently cited in classical sources from Thucydides to Lucretius and repeatedly used in Gower as a metaphor of the explosive fires of Envy. See *CA* 2.20, 163, 2337, 5.1289, and so on. Perhaps Gower takes the figure from Ovid, *Met*. 8.868, though references abound in all mythographers.

331   Gower refers to the papal dispute between Clement VII at Avignon and Boniface IX at Rome, both of whom claimed the allegiance of Christendom. He sees the schism in the head of the church as responsible for schismatic heresies such as Lollardry throughout the clergy.

349   *Lollardie*. A derogatory term implicating Christian fundamentalists who, following the views of Wyclif and promulgating the first straight translation of the Bible into English since the Norman Conquest, challenged the authority of the priesthood and the efficacy of the sacraments.

369   *For trowthe mot stonde ate laste*. Proverbial. See Whiting T509.

389   *ther I love, ther I holde*. Proverbial. See Whiting L571. The sense is that one is loyal to what one loves and that that may be the best "defence" (line 388).

434–36   ☞ **Latin marginalia**: *Qui vocatur a deo tanquam Aaron*. ["Who is called by God, like Aaron" — Hebrews 5:4]. Aaron was the articulate priest, chosen by God to assist his brother Moses in guiding the children of Israel out of Egypt and through the desert. The full passage (Hebrews 5:1–6) refers to those who choose themselves for the priesthood versus those chosen by God. See Exodus 4:14. In Gower's day, Hebrews was thought to have been written by St. Paul.

462 ff.   *betwen ernest and game*. Gower's objection is to evasiveness by ecclesiasts who turn moral issues into word games with which to advantage their worldly estates. They use fiction ("holy tales") for harm rather than common profit.

484   *made ferst the mone*. I.e., created the first sphere, beneath which is the chaos of the world (see line 142), the sublunar realm of shadows, doubts, sloth, greed, and such confusions that so afflict the church these days.

491–92   *For every man hise oghne werkes / Schal bere*. Proverbial. See Whiting M79.

496   *mirour of ensamplerie*. Good "clerkes" (line 492) reflect the "goodnesse" of "the hyhe God" (line 485), and, thus, though in the realm of sublunar chaos, provide good example of ordinances between "the men and the Godhiede" (line 498).

Latin verses iv (before line 499). **Line 1**: *Vulgaris populus . . . .* The tone of these verses is akin to that of the first book of *VC*, where Gower assails the people for becoming destructively willful during the Rising of 1381.

504–07   ☞ **Latin marginalia**: *De statu plebis ut dicunt, secundum accidencium mutabilia.* [Concerning the status of the people, as they say, in regard to the changeability of events.]

511   *Wher lawe lacketh, errour groweth*. Proverbial. See Whiting L109.

518–19   *And therupon his jugement / Gifth every man in sondry wise.* "And thereupon every man gives his judgment in diverse ways."

529–43   ☞ **Latin marginalia**: *Nota contra hoc, quod aliqui sortem fortune, aliqui influenciam planetarum ponunt, per quod, vt dicitur, rerum euentus necessario contingit. Set pocius dicendum est, quod ea que nos prospera et aduersa in hoc mundo vocamus, secundum merita et demerita hominum digno dei iudicio proveniunt.* [Note against this, that some posit the chance of fortune, some the influence of planets, as the means by which, as is said, the outcome of things is contingent on necessity. But it should rather be said that those things we call prosperity and adversity in this world devolve according to the merit or demerits of human beings, by the worthy judgment of God.]

567–71   ☞ **Latin marginalia**: *Boicius. O quam dulcendo humane vite multa amaritudine aspersa est.* [Boethius: "O how the sweetness of human life is stained by much bitterness."] See *Consolation* 2.pr.4. Gower's rendition simplifies the wording.

Latin verses v (before line 585). **Line 1**: *Prosper et . . .* The vision of Nebuchadnezzar is frequently depicted at this point in MSS which have miniatures at or near the beginning of *CA* (see illustrations 2 and 4). Gower's account of the vision is based on Daniel 2:19–45, though Gower expands Daniel's commentary anachronistically (lines 633–821) in order to comment on the decadence of contemporary history. See *VC* 7, where he uses the same biblical device. For discussion see Introduction, pp. 11–13, and Peck, "John Gower and the Book of Daniel."

591–608   ☞ **Latin marginalia**: *Hic in prologo tractat de Statua illa, quam Rex Nabugodonosor viderat in sompnis, cuius caput aureum, pectus argenteum, venter eneus, tibie ferree, pedum vero quedam pars ferrea, quedam fictilis videbatur, sub qua membrorum diuersitate secundum Danielis exposicionem huius mundi variacio figurabatur.* [Here in the Prologue he discourses about that Statue that King Nebuchadnezzar had seen in dreams, whose head was gold, chest silver, stomach brass, legs iron, but whose feet were some part iron, some part clay, through which diversity of members, according to Daniel's exposition, the variation of this world is figured.] See Daniel 2:31–45. The passage was a common locus for medieval historical allegory.

617–24   ☞ **Latin marginalia**: *Hic narrat vlterius de quodam lapide grandi, qui, vt in dicto sompnio videbatur, ab excelso monte super statuam corruens ipsam quasi in nichilum penitus contruit.* [Here he narrates further concerning the certain great stone, which, as appeared in the said dream, rushed from a high mountain onto the statue and utterly crushed it almost to nothing.]

619   *of sodein aventure.* Gower treats fortune (*aventure*) as a demonstrative component of God's will, an important counterforce to the classical notion of the degeneration of time.

626–30   ☞ **Latin marginalia**: *Hic loquitur de interpretacione sompnii, et primo dicit de significacione capitis aurei.* [Here he speaks concerning the interpretation of the dream, and first he speaks concerning the interpretation of the head of gold.]

635–39   ☞ **Latin marginalia**. Brief Latin directors at the appropriate lines: line 635: *De pectore argenteo* [Concerning the silver chest]; line 637: *De ventre eneo* [Concerning the brass stomach]; line 639: *De tibeis ferreis* [Concerning the iron legs].

641 ff.   ☞ **Latin marginalia**: *De significacione pedum, qui ex duabus materiis discordantibus adinuicem diuisi extiterant.* [Concerning the significance of the feet, which exist in division because of the two mutually discordant materials.]

641–42   *the werste of everydel / Is last.* Proverbial. See variants in Tilley W918 and W911. The saying is congruent with an entropic theory of history, one which Daniel counters with his theory of divine purpose that he proceeds to explicate.

651–54   ☞ **Latin marginalia**: *De lapidis statuam confringentis significacione.* [Concerning the significance of the stone shattering the statue.]

658   *the laste.* Gower projects an apocalyptic conclusion to the old world, after which the new age of the Parousia shall begin.

661–69   ☞ **Latin marginalia**: *Hic consequenter scribit qualiter huius seculi regna variis muta-cionibus, prout in dicta statua figurabatur, secundum temporum distincciones senci-biliter hactenus diminuuntur.* [Here consequently he writes how the kingdoms of this world, because of various mutations, just as they are figured in the said statue, are perceptibly diminished in accord with each distinction of historical times right up to the present.]

663   *thus expondeth Daniel.* Daniel's explication satisfies Nebuchadnezzar's concern by providing meaning to the king's otherwise depressing vision of the degeneration of time, where worse moves to worst.

670–76   ☞ **Latin marginalia**: *De seculo aureo, quod in capite statue designatum est, a tempore ipsius Nabugodonosor Regis Caldee vsque in regnum Ciri Regis Persarum.* [Concerning the golden age, which is designated in the statue's head, from the time of that Nebuchadnezzar, King of Chaldea, up to the kingdom of Cyrus, King of the Persians.]

688–94   ☞ **Latin marginalia**: *De seculo argenteo, quod in pectore designatum est, a tempore ipsius Regis Ciri vsque in regnum Alexandri Regis Macedonie.* [Concerning the silver age, which is designated in the chest from the time of King Cyrus up to the kingdom of Alexander, King of Macedonia.]

698   *soffre thei that nedes mote.* Proverbial. Variant of Whiting N61. See 1.1714 and 8.1020.

699–705   ☞ **Latin marginalia**: *De seculo eneo, quod in ventre designatum est, a tempore ipsius Alexandri vsque in regnum Iulii Romanorum Imparatoris.* [Concerning the age of brass, which is designated in the belly, from the time of that Alexander up to the kingdom of Julius, Emperor of the Romans.]

731–37   ☞ **Latin marginalia**: *De seculo ferreo, quod in tibeis designatum est, a tempore Iulii vsque in regnum Karoli magni Regis Francorum.* [Concerning the age of iron, which is designated in the legs, from the time of Julius up to the kingdom of Charles the Great, King of the Franks.]

745 ff.   "It is hardly necessary to point out that our author's history is here incorrect. Charlemagne was not called in against the Emperor Leo, who died in the year before he was born, but against the Lombards by Adrian I, and then against the rebellious citizens of Rome by Leo III, on which latter occasion he received the imperial crown" (Mac 2:464). Gower is following Brunetto Latini's account in the *Trésor*.

759   *wise; and.* See note to line 155.

772 ff.   Macaulay notes (2:464) that "Here again the story is historically inaccurate, but it is not worthwhile to set it straight." Gower's historicist/ethical point is plainly evident, despite the deficiency of historical accuracy.

779–806   ☞ **Latin marginalia**: *De seculo nouissimis iam temporibus ad similitudinem pedum in discordiam lapso et diuiso, quod post decessum ipsius Karoli, cum imperium Romanorum in manus Longobardorum peruenerat, tempore Alberti et Berengarii incepit: nam ob eorum diuisionem contigit, vt Almanni imperatoriam adepti sunt maiestatem. In* *cuius solium quendam principem theotonicum Othonem nomine sublimari primitus constituerunt. Et ab illo regno incipiente diuisio per vniuersum orbem in posteros concreuit, vnde nos ad alterutrum diuisi huius seculi consummacionem iam vltimi expectamus.* [Concerning the age of the most recent times, in the likeness of the feet, fallen and divided in discord, which began after the passing of that Charles, when the Roman Empire fell to the hands of the Lombards, in the time of Albert and Berengar: for on their account division occurred as the Germans seized the imperial majesty. In this throne they caused to be raised up a certain Teutonic prince, Otto by name. And from the inception of this kingdom, division hardened through the whole world for subsequent generations, whence we expect from one or the other of the divisions the end of this present, last age.]

851–52   *divisioun . . . moder of confusioun.* On *divisioun* as a moral crux in *CA* see Introduction, pp. 11–13. Also see White, "Division and Failure," p. 600, and Peck, *Kingship and Common Profit*, pp. 14–22 and 32–35. Right use of memory is the best remedy for division, which is, ultimately, a kind of forgetting. See Chandler on three types of remembering — confession, tales, and spiritual memory — that "work to reunite Amans' divided self" ("Memory and Unity," p. 18).

881–83   *Th'apostel writ . . . Th'ende of the world.* Macaulay (2:465) sees an allusion here to St. Paul, 1 Corinthians 10:11–12: "These things . . . are written for our correction, upon whom the ends of the world are come . . . let him take heed lest he fall."

881–85   ☞ **Latin marginalia**: *Hic dicit secundum apostolum, quod nos sumus in quos fines seculi deuenerunt.* [Here he speaks in accord with the Apostle, that we are "those upon whom the end of the world has come."] See 1 Corinthians 10:11–12: "these things . . . are written for our correction, upon whom the ends of the world are come. . . . [L]et him take heed lest he fall." N.b. the apocalyptic overtones of the various references to the world divided against itself in wars, especially lines 883–904 and 1029–44.

904   *Wher dedly werre is take on honde.* The first of Gower's antiwar assertions, which remain prominent to the end of his life. See his last English poem *In Praise of Peace* (ed. Livingston).

910 ff.   See *MO*, lines 26605 ff. and *VC* 7.509 ff. on the corruption of all creation due to man's fall.

918–23   ☞ **Latin marginalia**: *Hic scribit quod ex diuisionis passione singula creata detrimentum corruptibile paciuntur.* [Here he writes that from the suffering of and desire for division, all created things suffer a corrupting diminishment.] "Suffering of and desire for division" seeks to translate *divisionis passione.* "Suffering" is the routine sense of *passio* elsewhere to mean, like ME "passioun," both "desire to sin" as well as "suffering" (see, e.g., the marginal Latin at line 9). Thus it is likely that an ambiguous sense of "sinful desire for" as well as "suffering of" obtains in the Latin as in the corresponding English here: "man hath passioun / Of seknesse" (Prol.915–16). This ambiguity, however, is absent from the verb for the second Latin clause, *paciuntur,* as from the corresponding English: "So soffren othre creatures" (Prol.917).

945 ff.   *Gregoire in his Moral. Moralia* VI.16 (*PL* 75.740). Macaulay (2:465) notes that this idea of man as a microcosm is one of Gower's favorite citations. Gregory is commenting on Job 5:10 ("Who giveth rain upon the earth, and sendeth waters upon the fields" — Douai), where he gives the *sensus mysticus* of *universa* as "man." See *MO*, lines 26869 ff., which attributes the "man as a microcosm" idea to Aristotle (see especially line 26929), and *VC* 7.639 ff. Gregory's passage is also quoted in *RR*, lines 19246 ff. See Fox, *Mediaeval Sciences*, pp. 18–19.

949 ff.   Following Gregory's elaboration of Job 5:10 (see note to lines 945 ff., above), Gower delineates the medieval concept of a tripartite soul, with intelligence akin to the divine, feeling akin to that of the animal, and growth to that of the vegetable.

967–70   ☞ **Latin marginalia**: *Hic dicit secundum euangelium, quod omne regnum in se diuisum desolabitur.* [Here he speaks in accord with the Evangelist, that "every kingdom divided against itself will be devastated."] See Luke 11:17, with the present tense changed to future.

971–72   *Division aboven alle / . . . makth the world to falle.* On division as the primary effect of the Fall that leaves the psyche stranded amidst contingencies, see Introduction, pp. 11–13, and White ("Division and Failure," pp. 601–03, 607 ff.) on such bifurcations as soul and body, reason and its antagonists (sex, desire, appetite, complexion, need, etc.), and other forms of fragmentation both social and personal.

974–77   ☞ **Latin marginalia**: *Quod ex sue complexionis materia diuisus homo mortalis existat.* [That, divided because of the components of his constitution, every human being is mortal.]

975–79   *complexioun / Is mad upon divisioun . . . the contraire of his astat.* Macaulay: "That is, the opposite elements in his constitution ('complexioun') are so much at variance with one another" (2:465).

978   *He mot be verray kynde dye.* Gower's theory of death and the corruptibility of mixed elements is in agreement with medical theories of his day. Averroës, following Aristotle's thesis that all living things consist of mixtures of the primal elements, argues that if bodies were one and the same there would be no contrariety corrupting them. But unlike stones, which have one nature and are permanent, the body is composed of various natures and thus decays (*Avicennae Cantica cum Averrois Commentariis*, I.19. See Fox, *Mediaeval Sciences*, p. 34.) Plato explains this idea of corruptibility fully in *Timaeus* 81c–82b. The *Timaeus* was the one Platonic dialogue that was well known and honored in the Latin West during the Middle Ages. Although Gower probably did not know the *Timaeus* firsthand, he certainly knew of it.

982   *no final pes be nome.* The line anticipates Gower's conclusion where Venus gives Amans a "peire of bedes" upon which is written "*Por reposer*" (8.2904–07), putting to rest his internal conflict, giving him back his true name "John Gower," and restoring his quiet vision of "pes" (see below, 8.2913 ff.).

989–90   *he may noght laste, / That he ne deieth ate laste*. "He may not survive / But that he dies in the end." The *noght . . . That . . . ne* idiom occurs repeatedly in Gower, where *ne* functions not as a negative but as a calque with *That* to form a relative conjunction "But that," "Than that." See *MED that* conj. 2c on *that ne* constructions that the *MED* glosses as "lest." Gower's additional *noght* alters the sense somewhat. See notes to 1.786–88, 1.2046–47, and 1.2091–93.

991–96   ☞ **Latin marginalia**: *Quod homo ex corporis et anime condicione diuisus, sicut saluacionis ita et dampnacionis aptitudinem ingreditur.* [That every human being, divided because of the condition of body and soul, is capable of salvation as much as of damnation.]

1001   *The fieble hath wonne the victoire*. In sin, beginning with the fall from Paradise (Prol.1005), the proverb "the weaker has the worse" becomes inverted (so it seems). See Whiting W131 and F110.

1002–06   ☞ **Latin marginalia**: *Qualiter Adam a statu innocencie diuisus a paradiso voluptatis in terram laboris peccator proiectus est.* [How Adam, divided from a state of innocence as a sinner, was cast from a paradise of pleasure into a world of labor.]

1005   *ferst began in Paradis*. Sin began in Paradise, but it is noteworthy that Gower does not place the blame for divisiveness on Eve. The Latin marginalia at 1002 mentions Adam's division from innocence, but the Fall is not otherwise linked to gender problems.

1011–17   ☞ **Latin marginalia**: *Qualiter populi per vniuersum orbem a cultura dei diuisi, Noe cum sua sequela dumtaxat exceptis, diluuio interierunt.* [How the populace of the entire earth, divided from the worship of God, were destroyed in the flood, except for Noah with his following.]

1013   *sende*. A preterit form. Macaulay cites 1.851, 992, 1452, etc., as parallel examples (2:466).

1018–26   ☞ **Latin marginalia**: *Qualiter in edificacione turris Babel, quam in dei contemptum Nembrot erexit, lingua prius hebraica in varias linguas celica vindicta diuidebatur.* [How in the building of the Tower of Babel, which Nembrot erected in contempt of God, language, at first Hebrew, was divided by heavenly retribution into various languages.]

1022–25   On the "poetic Babel" that Gower, a master at multiple voicing, introduces in this passage — a babel of voices that oppose and even contradict, so that the mind can scarcely contain the contradictions — see Echard, "With Carmen's Help," p. 30. Elsewhere in her essay Echard stresses Gower's awareness of "the uncontrollable nature of text, in both its intellectual complexities and physical manifestations" (p. 10). Throughout the *Confessio* "language — all language — is shown to be radically unreliable" (p. 9).

1031–41   ☞ **Latin marginalia**: *Qualiter mundus, qui in statu diuisionis quasi cotidianis presenti tempore vexatur flagellis, a lapide superueniente, id est a diuina potencia vsque ad resolucionem omnis carnis subito conterentur.* [How the world, which is almost daily in a state of division at the present time and is ravaged by punishments, will, by the stone coming down on it (that is, by divine power), be suddenly crushed, destroying all flesh.]

1045–52   One reason love is so powerful in Gower's scheme is that it has the capacity, when experienced wholesomely, to heal division. See lines 967–1044.

1047   *loveday*. A day set for making peaceful settlement of deadlocked disputes.

1053–54   *wolde God . . . An other such as Arion*. Echard, "With Carmen's Help," pp. 29–30, notes the conditional tense as part of her argument that Gower is keenly aware of the inability of language, even that of the poet, to contain authority in any stable way. Echard agrees with Yeager (*John Gower's Poetic*) that Gower may be in search of a new Arion, but that Gower knows how difficult it will be to find him. The story of Arion first appears in Herodotus 1.24. Also see Ovid, *Fasti*, 2.79–118 ff., Hyginus, *Fables* 194, and Solinus, cap. 11, for a third-century account of Arion as a dolphin. The story is well known in the later Middle Ages and appears in collections of Latin moralized tales such as those described in the *British Museum Catalogue of Romances* and in some versions of the *Gesta Romanorum* (for example, see Oesterley, cap. 148). Gower ignores that part of the story which deals with the dolphin and concentrates on Arion the peacemaker to create an effect appropriately reminiscent of the peaceable kingdom in Isaias 11:1–10. See *VC* 1.i.1–124, for a description of what England might be like if it were to find its Arion. The figure of Arion, with his harp and sense of good measure, becomes a metaphor for the poet himself. See Yeager (*John Gower's Poetic*) for an extended analysis of Gower's Arion poetic. See also Peck, *Kingship and Common Profit*, pp. 22–23; and Simpson, *Sciences and the Self*, p. 289.

1053–72   ☞ **Latin marginalia**: *Hic narrat exemplum de concordia et vnitate inter homines prouocanda; et dicit qualiter quidam Arion nuper Citharista ex sui cantus cithareque consona melodia tante virtutis extiterat, ut ipse non solum virum cum viro, set eciam leonem cum cerua, lupum cum agno, canem cum lepore, ipsum audientes vnanimiter absque vlla discordia adinvicem pacificauit.* [Here he tells a story about the stimulating of concord and unity among human beings: and he says how a certain Arion, a harper in recent times, was of such power and virtue because of the harmonious melody of his song and his harp that he pacified unanimously and without any discord those hearing him, not only mutually pacifying man with man, but even lion with deer, wolf with sheep, and hound with hare.]

1056   *good mesure*. The idea is Pythagorean and could allude to the harmonic ratio of sounds to each other in a well-tempered instrument, though more likely the sense is that the performer kept good rhythm.

1088   In his revisions of the first recension, Gower may have added ten lines. Macaulay (2:466) notes that Sidney College MS concludes the Prologue as follows:

> So were it gode at þis tide
> Þat eueri man vpon his side
> besowt and preied for þe pes
> wiche is þe cause of al encres
> of worschep and of werldis welþe

of hertis rest of soule helþe
withouten pes stant no þing gode
forthi to crist wiche sched his blode
for pes beseketh alle men
Amen amen amen amen.

Macaulay observes that the Sidney College MS is related to the Stafford MS, which is missing the conclusion to the Prologue. Had they been found in the Stafford MS, Macaulay suggests, "the authority of S would be conclusive in their favour." The lines were printed by Caxton and Berthelet, with some variation in spelling.

EXPLANATORY NOTES TO BOOK 1

Illustration 3: Fairfax 3, fol. 8r. The Lover confesses to Genius. Variations on this drawing of Amans confessing to Genius are found in more than half the *CA* MSS. Only in Fairfax 3 and Harley 3869 does it appear at the head of Book 1. Usually it is placed after 1.202, as in Bodley 902 (Illustration 1), where the illumination depicts "Amans" as an old man that some have thought might represent the elderly poet. Macaulay (2:cxxxviii) sees a likeness between the portrait and the effigy on Gower's tomb. See Griffiths, "*Confessio Amantis*: The Poem and Its Pictures," p. 177, for a short account of twenty-seven MSS that contain or left space for pictures, especially the Dream of Precious Metals drawings and/or Amans and his confessor drawings. For comparison with Bodley 294, see illustration 5. The Fairfax 3 reproduction provides a good image of the placement of marginal glosses in our base text.

Latin verses i (before line 1). **Line 1**: *Naturatus amor*. The translation presented for the enigmatic and crucial phrase *naturatus amor* is informed by Winthrop Wetherbee's discussion of this phrase ("Latin Structure and Vernacular Space") in terms of the self-conflicting presentations of human love in Boethius, Alanus de Insulis, and Jean de Meun that Gower mines throughout the *CA*. Wetherbee remarks that Gower's phrase "conveys a sense of scholastic authority that is belied by close scrutiny" (p. 7). Yet the translation here is also informed by an analogous phrase from medieval Latin discussions of Aristotle, *natura naturata*, which may be understood as "nature instantiated in specific forms of life," or in a broader sense as the means by which nature has furthered its inherent purpose of creating life, as shown by twelfth-century Latin translations of Averroës' Arabic commentary on Aristotle, the means by which Aristotle's works were known in the West: "for this is the end of Nature, namely that it does not act except on account of something, just as artifice does not act except on account of something. Then [Aristotle] has declared that that on account of which, having been [specifically] instantiated [*naturata*], Nature acts, is seen to be the soul [or: life force, *anima*] in living things [*animalibus*]" (*Averrois Cordubensis Commentarium Magnum in Aristotelis De Anima Libros*, ed. Crawford, p. 187). The teleological and instantiating freight of the medieval Aristotelian tradition of *natura naturata* has at least indirectly influenced Gower's Latin, and perhaps more pervasively his historical and ethical outlook on nature and love, available to Gower in the works of the thirteenth-century popular pur-

veyers of medieval Aristotelianism, Brunetto Latini, Giles of Rome, and Bar-
tholomaeus Anglicus, although none of these uses the phrase *natura naturata*
or, less surprisingly, *naturatus amor* (Brunetto Latini comes close to the former
when he defines Nature as "double: that which gives birth, and that which is
born" [*une ki fet naistre, et une de ce ki est net*] — *Li Livres dou tresor* 3.52, ed.
Carmody, p. 360). Significantly, elsewhere Gower novelly adapted the Latin
verb *naturare* to English, evidently to mean "to give a species specific traits":
"He which natureth every kinde, / The myhti God" (*CA* 7.393–94). He is the
only writer attested before the sixteenth century to have used this word in
English. **Line 2**: *vnanimes concitat esse feras*. The syntax is perfectly ambiguous,
so the diametrically opposed alternate meanings have been printed in the
translation itself. **Line 3**: *Huius enim mundi Princeps*. White (*Nature, Sex, and
Goodness*, p. 219) notes that *huius princeps mundi* is also the title of the Devil.

   Translation of the epigram is also assisted by the marginal gloss (see the
next note), where Gower states that he is discussing "that love by which not
only the human species but indeed every living thing is naturally subjected."
Yet an inherent contradiction and instability lies in the phrase, as Wetherbee
correctly emphasizes: human love, in Gower's and the medieval Christian per-
ception of the post-lapsarian world, is the very thing that most resists harmony
with Nature's positive, pristine purposes. In the context of the *CA*, the two
terms of the phrase resist reconciliation as few other pairings might. The radi-
cal ambiguity of the rest of Gower's sentence emphasizes this irreconcilability.

9 ff.   ☞ **Latin marginalia**: *Postquam in Prologo tractatum hactenus existit, qualiter hodi-*
          erne condicionis diuisio caritatis dileccionem superauit, intendit auctor ad presens suum
          libellum, cuius nomen Confessio Amantis nuncupatur, componere de illo amore, a quo
          non solum humanum genus, sed eciam cuncta animancia naturaliter subiciuntur. Et
          quia nonnulli amantes ultra quam expedit desiderii passionibus crebro stimulantur,
          materia libri per totum super hiis specialius diffunditur. [After he has set forth to
          this point the treatment in the Prologue of how the division of today's condi-
          tion has overcome the love of charity, the author presently intends to compose
          his little book, whose name is "The Confession of a Lover," concerning that
          love by which not only the human species but indeed every living thing is
          naturally subjected. And since some lovers are often goaded by the passions
          of desire beyond what is appropriate, the matter of the book throughout is set
          forth for these especially.] For a picture of this gloss in the manuscript itself,
          see Illustration 3.

18–24   *loves lawe is out of reule . . . ther is no man . . . that can / Of love tempre the mesure.*
          See White, *Nature, Sex, and Goodness*, pp. 218–19, on the potency of desire that
          affects all people in defiance of Aristotelian ideas of balance and measure.
          Loves lawe (line 18) here equates with that *cupiditas* that Boethius says is born
          into all creatures that could lead to the true good but seldom does (*De cons.*
          3.p2).

35   *love is maister wher he wile*. Proverbial. See Whiting L518.

59 ff.   ☞ **Latin marginalia**: *Hic quasi in persona aliorum, quos amor alligat, fingens se auctor*
          esse Amantem, varias eorum passiones variis huius libri distinccionibus per singula

scribere proponit. [Here the author, fashioning himself to be the Lover as if in the role of those others whom love binds, proposes to write about their various passions one by one in the various sections of this book.] For discussion of this passage as Gower projects a persona and an epistemology of make-believe for his narrative, see Peck, "Phenomenology of Make Believe," pp. 257 ff.

62   *I am miselven on of tho.* N.b., the Latin marginal gloss (above). From this point on, Gower projects a persona who is not simply a moral commentator on society but an embodiment of human stresses, a dramatic component of his "proof" (see line 61). In the Prologue he had announced that he would pro- vide a "Mirour of ensamplerie" (Prol.496); henceforth the "ensample" will be complicated through a first-person drama as well as a textual one — an empirical mean between the abstract and the personal. See Spitzer, "Note on the Poetic and Empirical 'I' in Medieval Authors"; and Strohm, "Note on Gower's Personas," pp. 293–95. For discussion of the narrative of *CA* in terms of its framing devices, see Pearsall, "Gower's Narrative Art": "The poem as a whole gains enormously from the dramatic scheme, just as Gower himself gained from the freedom it gave him" (p. 477).

72   *To hem that ben lovers.* In defining a new dramatic function for his persona Gower likewise provides a dramatic role for his audience. On this love trope Staley raises the question "was Richard's court during this period a place of love talk," talk that was not simply a matter of sexual practice but rather a "language that expressed relationships of power?" (*Languages of Power*, p. 51). Compare love tropes in Usk, Chaucer, and the *Gawain*-poet (pp. 42–59).

79   *That every man ensample take.* On the philosophical premises of Gower's use of examples for instruction, see notes to Prol.7, 196, and 1.1339–40. Simpson, *Sciences and the Self*, using Alan de Lille's *Anti-claudianus* as a text parallel in many ways with *CA*, explores Alan's notion that narrative images provide the soul with a means of picturing itself (pp. 244–48). Such "ensamples" function as a kind of inducted "'scientific' information by which the soul can place itself in the cosmos and society" (p. 230).

88   *jolif wo.* Compare *le jolif mal sanz cure* of Gower's *Cinkante Balades* 13, line 24. The courtly phrase is a favorite. See also *CA* 6.84 and 8.2360, with variants such as "jolif peine" in 7.1910.

Latin verses ii (before line 93). **Line 1**: *Non ego . . . .* Latin proverbs often list powerful or wise men deceived by women; see *Sir Gawain and the Green Knight*, lines 2416– 28, for a Middle English rendition of this tradition. Gower's passage resembles the longer discussion of lust's power in the *Architrenius*, where Hercules, rare in other Latin proverbs of this kind, appears along with Sampson, Solomon, and Ulysses as a victim of Venus (7.116–33).

98 ff.   ☞ **Latin marginalia**: *Hic declarat materiam, dicens qualiter Cupido quodam ignito iaculo sui cordis memoriam graui vlcere perforauit, quod Venus percipiens ipsum, vt dicit, quasi in mortis articulo spasmatum, ad confitendum se Genio sacerdoti super amoris causa sic semiviuum specialiter commendauit.* [Here he declares the substance of his story, saying how Cupid pierced through the memory of his heart by means of a cer-

tain burning missile, leaving a serious wound; whereby Venus, perceiving him, as he states, twitching as if in his death throes, particularly recommended that, half-alive, he confess to Genius the priest about the topic of love.]

100–39   *in the monthe of Maii . . . And with that word I sawh anon / The kyng of love and qweene bothe*. The poet imagines a characteristic dream vision situation when, in the month of May, the dreamer sets out into a wood, prays while listening to the birds, and sleeps to dream of the King and Queen of Love; except that here the "dreamer/lover" never goes to sleep. But this is not to say that he is "awake," either. As Olsson so aptly puts it, "The lover, though 'awake,' does not know he lives in a dream" (*Structures of Conversion*, p. 47).

124   [*Amans.*] The amanuensis of Fairfax 3 regularly places speech tags in the margin. The brackets indicate speech markers that do not appear in the MS but have been added to the edition for clarity.

   O thou Cupide, O thou Venus. For discussion of Gower's use of these amorous deities, see Tinkle, *Medieval Venuses and Cupids*, especially pp. 178–97, though her remarks throughout the book are germane.

138   *with that word I sawh anon*. The important thing to notice here is that ideas appear as visual personifications to the lover. On the prominence of visual imaginings in medieval thought processes see Kolve, *Chaucer and the Imagery of Narrative*, especially pp. 24–42. See the Latin gloss on sight and hearing as doors of the mind (preceding 1.289) and Genius' discussion of eyes and ears as the dominant intuitive senses. See also footnotes 29–31 in the Introduction.

140   *yhen wrothe*. The situation is similar in ways to Chaucer's Prol. to *LGW*, where Cupid, the God of Love, with his queen, comes upon Geoffrey near the daisy and looks upon him with angry, piercing eyes. Chaucer's queen is Alceste, rather than Venus, but in neither instance is Cupid presented as blind.

145   *herte rote*. *MED* glosses the term as the seat of the passions, or the vital center of life. Exactly what the anatomical designations might be is unclear. *MED* suggests the hollow of the heart or perhaps the "apex." The conclusion to Plato's *Timaeus* (91 a–e) describes a conduit that runs down the spine to the scrotum, from which living sperm, seeking egress, take their path. Conceivably the *herte rote* may extend even to that depth. In the *RR* (lines 1679–2008) Cupid shoots five arrows into the lover's heart, two (Beauty and Simplicity) through the eye, and three (Courtesy, Company, and Fair Seeming) through the side or below the breast. This pattern seems evident in *CA* 1.144–45, where "A firy dart me thoghte he [Cupid] hente / And threw it thurgh myn herte rote." If it enters through the side and lodges in the heart's inner chamber that would precipitate a sympathetic response in the lower region. Another organ linked to the concept of *herte rote* is the "reines," which are also regarded the seat of passions and can refer to the kidneys, heart, or the male generative organ (*MED* reine n.[2]. 2a and 2b). E.g., in the treatise *Sidrak and Bokkus* we learn that if a lecher overexerts his lechery, "Of his reynes he leseþ þe might. / Þan is þe seed feble and veyne / And to engendre haþ no mayne [strength]" (lines 6874–76 in Bodleian Laud MS 559). According to the Middle English version of *The*

Anatomy of Guy de Chauliae, "Þe sperme takeþ þe sauour off þe harte, of þe liuer, and þe Reynes, and bi þe nerues þe whiche, be cause of delectacioun, descenden fro þe braines to þe ballockes" (ed. Wallner, p. 73). Similarly *The Prose Salernitan Questions* (c. 1200) observes: "The natural heat is . . . aroused by the psychic virtue, and by their combined action, the blood contained in the liver moves and in moving emits heat; from it there evaporates a smoky cloud which, when it has been made subtle, spreads from the liver to the heart. From the heart the spirit moves to the penis by means of the arteries and makes it stiffen" (see Jacquart and Thomasset, *Sexuality and Medicine in the Middle Ages*, p. 83). That is, Cupid's arrow piercing the side and lodging in the heart might thus be thought to affect the whole emotional system, from the chambers of the heart to the kidneys and male organs, the *herte rote*.

148–49   *source and welle / Of wel or wo.* Traditionally, Venus carries two cups, one sweet, the other bitter, from which the lover drinks; thus, in medieval courtly poetry she is the *source and welle* of the lover's joy and/or pain.

161   *caitif.* It is noteworthy that two early MSS, Bodley 294 and Egerton 1991, identify the speaker here as *Iohn Gowere*, rather than *caitif*.

178   *Mi world stod on an other whiel.* Proverbial. See Whiting W208.

196   *O Genius myn oghne clerk.* The originals behind Gower's Genius may be found in Jean de Meun's portion of *RR* and Alanus de Insulis' *De Planctu Naturae*. Gower's Genius defines several voices in the poem. He is presented as an agent of memory who can compile and relate afresh the stories and materials of history; he is a creative agent, capable of formulating propositions according to nature and moral concepts as well; he is a priest of both the emotional and rational capacities of the individual, though his capacities as a philosopher are limited by the circumstances of the occasion; and he is usually benevolent in his role as intermediary between Amans, momentary situations, and Nature. See the Introduction, pp. 5–6, 7–10, 17, 18, 34. For further discussion of Genius, see Economou, "Character *Genius*"; Schueler, "Gower's Characterization of Genius"; Nitzsche, *Genius Figure*; Baker, "Priesthood of Genius"; Wetherbee, "Theme of Imagination" and "Genius and Interpretation"; Peck, *Kingship and Common Profit* and "Problematics of Irony," pp. 212–24; Olsson, *Structures of Conversion*, pp. 52–62; and Simpson, *Sciences and the Self*, pp. 148–97.

Latin verses iii (before line 203). The "wound" of love (**line 4**) is a topos reaching far back in medieval and classical writing. A widely influential classical instance is Dido in *Aeneid* 4.1–2, and much French poetry elaborated the metaphor. Boethius' *Consolation*, whose dialogue form was a direct model for *CA*, invokes throughout its first book the metaphor of the narrator's "illness" of false love for the goods of Fortune, and Philosophy's "cure" by means of the "medicine" of her teachings. At the end of *CA*, Gower revisits the same issues in English (8.3152–56). Simpson (*Sciences and the Self*, pp. 200–01) links this passage to Ovid's *Remedia amoris* as a warning against love's catastrophes.

203   *This worthi prest, this holy man*. On Genius as confessor to Amans, see Simpson, *Sciences and the Self*, especially pp. 148–66 ("Genius, praeceptor amoris"). Simpson sees Genius and Amans as two aspects of a single person, with Genius as a figure of imagination and Amans as the will in an unstable relationship richly informed with Ovidian irony and what Gower calls elsewhere "double speche" (7.1733).

205   *Benedicité*. "Bless you." The standard form of address of the priest to the one confessing, answered by the penitent with *Dominus*, "Lord [Father, I have sinned]."

209 ff.   ☞ **Latin marginalia**: *Hic dicit qualiter Genio pro Confessore sedenti prouolutus Amans ad confitendum se flexis genibus incuruatur, supplicans tamen, vt ad sui sensus informacionem confessor ille in dicendis opponere sibi benignius dignaretur.* [Here he tells how the Lover, bowled over, kneels on bent knees to confess to Genius seated as a confessor, beseeching nonetheless that, to inform his understanding, the Confessor would graciously deign to question him in matters that ought to be said.] For graphic representations of the idea see illustrations 1, 3, and 5. Pearsall ("Gower's Latin," pp. 22–24) reads this marginal commentary as a means to establish a clerical code that underlies much of the poem. See also Craun on Gower's methodology in querying the deviant speaker (*Lies, Slander, and Obscenity*, pp. 131 ff.).

236   ☞ **Latin marginalia**: *Sermo Genii sacerdotis super confessione ad Amantem.* [The sermon of Genius·the priest to the Lover about confession.]

275–76   See note to 1.1339–40.

284   *trowthe hise wordes wol noght peinte*. Proverbial. See Whiting T515.

Latin verses iv (before line 289). The buried coin, *fossa talenta* (**line 4**), recalls the Gospel parable of the talents, where the sinful servant takes the talent his lord has given him and buries it in the earth (Matthew 25:14–30).

294 ff.   ☞ **Latin marginalia**: *Hic incipit confessio Amantis, cui de duobus precipue quinque sensuum, hoc est de visu et auditu, confessor pre ceteris opponit.* [Here begins the confession of the Lover, to whom the Confessor particularly inquires concerning two of the five senses, that is concerning sight and sound.]

299–308   This passage begins in the third person, then, by line 304, modulates into the voice of the confessor as he addresses Amans as "mi sone." It is not until line 530 that the MS starts using marginal speech tags, though beside line 236 the marginal Latin gloss identifies the speakers, along with their activities.

304–08   See *Timaeus* 45b–47e for Plato's explanation of why the eye is man's principal sense organ and the ear next in importance. These two senses enable man to perceive the numbers, motions, harmonies, and rhythms of the universe, whereby the soul is illuminated. Plato ignores the other three senses entirely as agencies for illuminating the soul, although later (61d–68d) he discusses all five senses as part of man's physical mechanism for understanding material phenomena. Plato's premises constitute one basis for medieval preoccupations with vision and harmony (see the Latin verses after *CA* 1.288). They also explain why Genius exorcises only these two of the Lover's five senses. They are the doors to his soul, which Genius hopes to restore. See Introduction, notes 25 and 26, for citation of medieval medical treatises linking the eye to the frontal lobe of the brain, where Imagination and Fantasy reside.

333 ff.   Compare Ovid, *Met.* 3.130–259. Genius omits from the story Acteon's companions and his friendly gesture of giving them the rest of the day off, the account of Diana's disrobing, the efforts of the nymphs to hide their mistress from the eyes of the intruder, the throwing of water on Acteon to distract him, the catalog of hounds, Acteon's efforts to speak, and the debate of the gods on the justice of Diana's revenge. Genius adds the detail of Acteon's pride (1.341). Ovid puts the blame on Fortune, but Genius implies that Acteon might have turned his eye away had he chosen to do so (1.366). The conventional romance description of his entering the forest (1.352–60) suggests why he did not: he turns the enclosed garden (*hortus conclusus*) into a garden of delight and does not get out. Amans fares better, thanks to Genius, and, ultimately, accepts the trials of old age.

334   *touchende of mislok.* See Schutz's discussion of the issues of seeing in her analysis of the stories of Acteon and Medusa as mirror images of each other ("Absent and Present Images," pp. 108–15).

334 ff.   ☞ **Latin marginalia**: *Hic narrat Confessor exemplum de visu ab illicitis preseruando, dicens qualiter Acteon Cadmi Regis Thebarum nepos, dum in quadam Foresta venacionis causa spaciaretur, accidit vt ipse quendam fontem nemorosa arborum pulcritudine circumventum superveniens, vidit ibi Dianam cum suis Nimphis nudam in flumine balneantem; quam diligencius intuens oculos suos a muliebri nuditate nullatenus auertere volebat. Vnde indignata Diana ipsum in cerui figuram transformauit; quem canes proprii apprehendentes mortiferis dentibus penitus dilaniarunt.* [Here the Confessor relates an instructive example concerning the guarding of sight from illicit things, saying how Acteon the nephew of Cadmus the King of the Thebans, while he was walking in a certain forest to go hunting, happened to come upon a certain stream surrounded by the woodsy beauty of trees where he saw Diana nude with her nymphs bathing in the river, whom he carefully examined, not at all wishing to turn away his eyes from her womanly nudity. Wherefore Diana, indignant, transformed him into the form of a stag, whom his own dogs caught and tore to pieces with their deadly teeth.]

384   *Betre is to winke than to loke.* Proverbial. See Whiting W366.

389 ff.   Compare Ovid, *Met.* 4.772–803. Gower is apparently using additional sources, however. Genius names Medusa's sisters, as Ovid does, though he calls Stheno, "Stellibon," and Euryale, "Suriale." Moreover, he combines the story of the Graeae, who share one tooth and one eye, with the story of the Gorgons. Macaulay (2:468) notes that this confusion appears in Boccaccio, *Genealogiae Deorum Gentilium* 10.10, which Gower may have known. Whether Gower follows Boccaccio or not, the mingling of the two stories is fortuitous for Genius' purpose in demonstrating the evil of "misloke" and the wisdom of looking well.

391 ff.   ☞ **Latin marginalia**: *Hic ponit aliud exemplum de eodem, vbi dicit quod quidam princeps nomine Phorceus tres progenuit filias, Gorgones a vulgo nuncupatas, que vno partu exorte deformitatem monstrorum serpentinam obtinuerunt; quibus, cum in etatem peruenerant, talis destinata fuerat natura, quod quicumque in eas aspiceret in lapidem subito mutabatur. Et sic quam plures incaute respicientes visis illis perierunt. Set Perseus miles clipeo Palladis gladioque Mercurii munitus eas extra montem Athlantis conhabitantes animo audaci absque sui periculo interfecit.* [Here he presents another instructive example about the same thing, where he says that a certain prince, Phorceus by name, bore three daughters, commonly called the Gorgons, who acquired the serpentine deformity of monsters from one aspect of their birth. For these, when they had come to maturity, nature had been destined in such ways that whoever should look at them was suddenly turned into a stone. And thus all those who incautiously glanced at them died at the sight. But Perseus, a knight furnished with the shield of Pallas and the sword of Mercury, with a bold spirit and without any danger to himself killed them as they were dwelling beyond Mount Athlans.]

423   *Lente him a swerd.* Macaulay notes that "Mercury's sword is not mentioned either by Ovid or Boccaccio" (2:468).

463 ff.   The legend of Aspidis derives from Psalm 57:5–6, which speaks of "the deaf asp that stoppeth her ears." In his commentary on the psalm Augustine explains how the serpent can stop two ears with one tail; his suggestion is followed by Isidore in *Etymologies* 12.4, though neither mentions the carbuncle (see also *MO*, lines 15253–64). That detail may come from the legendary jewel in the toad's head, or perhaps from Brunetto Latini's *Trésor*. Compare the jewel-bearing serpent in the Tale of Adrian and Bardus (*CA* 5.5060 ff.), or the serpent who carries a jewel of health in his mouth in the English *Gesta Romanorum* (cap. 7). For discussion of the ambiguity of the asp as an *in bono* (prudence) and *in malo* (obstinence) figure of the senses, see Olsson, *Structures of Conversion*, pp. 63–72.

465–67   *The ston noblest of alle / . . . carbuncle calle / Berth in his hed.* On the folk-type of the serpent with a crown or precious jewel in/on/about his head, see Aarne-Thompson, *Types of the Folktale* 672 (the serpent's crown), 672A (a man who steals a serpent's crown), 672B (a little girl takes away the serpent's gold crown), 672C (serpent at wedding leaves crown), and, especially, 672D (the stone of the snake). See also Stith Thompson, *Motif-Index of Folk-Literature*, vol.1, B103.42 (serpent with jewel in his mouth), B103.4.2.1 (grateful snake spits out lump of gold for his rescuer), B103.4.2.2 (snake vomits jewels), B108.1 (serpent as patron of wealth), B112 (treasure-producing serpent's crown); and vol. 2 D1011.3.1 (magic serpent's crown). The *Epistola Alexandri ad Aristotelem de Mirabilibus Indiae* speaks of serpents with emeralds around their necks who, in the spring, sometimes fight, leaving behind "emeralds of enormous size" (Katz, *Romances of Alexander*, p. 123).

466 ff.   ☞ **Latin marginalia**: *Hic narrat Confessor exemplum, vt non ab auris exaudicione fatua animus deceptus inuoluatur. Et dicit qualiter ille serpens, qui aspis vocatur, quendam preciosissimum lapidem nomine Carbunculum in sue frontis medio gestans,*

contra verba incantantis aurem vnam terre affigendo premit, et aliam sue caude stimulo firmissime obturat. [Here the Confessor recounts an instructive example in order that a deceived soul might not be assailed by the ear's foolish overhearing. And he says how the serpent who is called Aspis, carrying a certain most pre-cious stone, Carbuncle by name, in the middle of its forehead, protected him-self against the words of an enchanter by pressing down one ear and fixing it to the ground, and closing off the other most firmly with the point of its tail.]

481 ff.   Gower follows Guido delle Colonne, *Hist. Troiae* III (*Gest Historiale* lib. 32), in presenting his Tale of the Sirens. Benoît tells the story in *Roman de Troie*, but he does not include all the details that Gower includes, though Vat. Myth. II (101) does.

483 ff.   ☞ **Latin marginalia**: *Aliud exemplum super eodem, qualiter rex Vluxes cum a bello Troiano versus Greciam nauigio remearet, et prope illa Monstra marina, Sirenes nun-cupata, angelica voce canoras, ipsum ventorum aduersitate nauigare oporteret, om-nium nautarum suorum aures obturari coegit. Et sic salutari prouidencia prefultus abs-que periculo saluus cum sua classe Vluxes pertransiit.* [Another instructive example about the same thing: how king Ulysses, when he was returning toward Greece from the Trojan war traveled back on a ship. When approaching those seaside monsters called the Sirens, singers with angelic voices, he was forced to sail against the winds, and he ordered the ears of all his sailors to be stopped up. And thus assisted by a saving providence and safe from danger, Ulysses with his vessel passed through.]

576 ff.   ☞ **Latin marginalia**: *Hic loquitur quod septem sunt peccata mortalia, quorum caput Superbia varias species habet, et earum prima Ypocrisis dicitur, cuius proprietatem secundum vicium simpliciter Confessor Amanti declarat.* [Here he says that there are seven mortal sins, whose head, Pride, has various species, and the first of these is called Hypocrisy, whose properties as a vice the Confessor declares to the Lover in simple terms.]

608   *Ipocrisis Religiosa.* [Religious Hypocrisy.]

627–28   *Ipocrisis Ecclesiastica.* [Ecclesiastic Hypocrisy.]

648   *Ipocrisis Secularis.* [Secular Hypocrisy.]

674 ff.   ☞ **Latin marginalia**: *Hic tractat Confessor cum Amante super illa presertim Ipocri-sia, que sub amoris facie fraudulenter latitando mulieres ipsius ficticiis credulas sepis-sime decipit innocentes.* [Here the Confessor discourses with the Lover partic-ularly about that Hypocrisy that, fraudulently hiding under a face of love, very often deceives innocent, credulous women with his fictions.]

704–06   *berth lowest the seil . . . to beguile / The womman.* Proverbial. See Whiting S14.

708   *Opponit Confessor.* [The Confessor inquires.]

712   *Respondet Amans.* [The Lover replies.]

752   *To love is every herte fre.* Proverbial. See Whiting L516. See also *CA* 1.1929–30. Compare Chaucer, *CT* I(A)1606 and *CT* V(F)767.

759 *a croniqe*. Precisely what chronicle Genius alludes to is unclear. The story of Mundus and Paulina is said to be historical by Josephus, *Antiquitatum Judaicarum* 18. Hegesippus, 2.4, follows Josephus, who in turn is followed by Vincent of Beauvais, *Speculum Historiale* 7.4, any of which may have been Gower's source. The story is told in verse by Godfrey of Viterbo, *Pantheon* 15, but Macaulay says this version was certainly not Gower's source (2:470).

763 ff. ☞ **Latin marginalia**: *Quod Ipocrisia sit in amore periculosa, narrat exemplum qualiter sub regno Tiberii Imperatoris quidam miles nomine Mundus, qui Romanorum dux milicie tunc prefuit, dominam Paulinam pulcherrimam castitatisque famosissimam mediantibus duobus falsis presbiteris in templo Ysis deum se esse fingens sub ficte sanctitatis ypocrisi nocturno tempore viciauit. Vnde idem dux in exilium, presbiteri in mortem ob sui criminis enormitatem dampnati extiterant, ymagoque dee Ysis a templo euulsa vniuerso conclamante populo in flumen Tiberiadis proiecta mergebatur.* [Showing that Hypocrisy is most dangerous in love, he presents an instructive example how under the reign of Tiberius the Emperor a certain knight, Mundus by name, who then was preeminent before all others as a duke of the army of the Romans, defiled the most beautiful and most famously chaste lady Paulina, with two false priests as go-betweens in the temple of Isis, fashioning himself to be a god under the hypocrisy of a feigned sanctity at nighttime. Wherefore the same duke was condemned to exile, and the priests to death on account of the enormity of their crime, while the image of the goddess, pulled from the temple with universal approval by the people, was thrown into the Tiber river and sunk.]

767 *of al the cité the faireste*. An analogue to the Tale of Mundus and Paulina may be found in the Hebrew *Tales of Alexander the Macedonian* (אלכסנדרוס מוקדון ספר) found in a compilation of the eleventh-century *Chronicles of Jerahmeel*. The surviving MS, now in the Bodleian Library, dates from about 1325. A very beautiful woman, the fairest on earth, goes once a month to the temple of the god Atzilin to offer sacrifice. The priest, Matan, smitten by her beauty, tells her that the god would beget a son upon her, "for there is no other woman in the entire world worthy to be with him" (Reich, ed., *Tales of Alexander the Macedonian*, p. 75). She gets permission from her husband, who sends pillows, coverings, mattresses, and silken garments to adorn the occasion. Matan accepts the gifts and sends the woman's maid away. At midnight he enters to perform his rites, but the maid slips into the room to watch. Matan has intercourse with the woman nine times. After he has exhausted his strength and rises to leave, the maid strikes him on the head with a statue of Atzilin, killing him. The beautiful woman is scandalized by the deception and insists on telling her husband, who goes to the king. He takes the case to Alexander who says the temple should be destroyed, since it has been defiled. He then asks to see the woman himself, and, amazed at her beauty, demands that she be given to him. The king would protect the woman and her husband, but is overwhelmed by Alexander, who locks the woman in a portable temple where he has his way with her night and day. She gives birth to a son whom he names Alexander. But the child dies at the age of nine months on the same day that Alexander's horse Bucephalus dies. Alexander builds a mausoleum for his

horse and son, then consoles his wife, who conceives a second child. She dies in childbirth. See Reich, ed., *Tales of Alexander the Macedonian*, pp. 73–79. This analogue ties in as well with Gower's Tale of Nectanabus, *CA* 6.1789–2366. Gower's knowledge of Alexander lore is extensive, though it is doubtful that he could have known the Hebrew manuscript directly, which was still in Italy during his lifetime.

773   *Of thilke bore frele kinde*. Macaulay observes: "Human nature is described as frail from birth, and by its weakness causing blindness of the heart" (2:470).

775   Just as the eye is the most important sense organ for human revelation (see note to lines 1.304–08 above), so too it is the principal sense organ for guiding reason. Augustine's three steps toward virtue (*visio, contemplatio, actio*) mark also the three steps toward sin. In both instances the process begins with the eye's response to beauty or the desirable, which in turn stimulates the will and desire. The process is one, though the ends are different. All cupidinous lovers are first struck through the eye by Cupid's first arrow — beauty; see *RR*, lines 1681 ff.

786–88   *noght . . . That . . . ne*. See notes to Prol. 989–90, 1.1295–96, 1.2046–47, 1.2091–93, 1.2629–30, 1.2722–24, 1.3366–67. Gower's construction here and in the other cited examples is unusual in Middle English, where the *ne* following *that* serves as a calque rather than a simple negative. Andrew Galloway (correspondence May 2, 2005) suggests that the construction is parallel to the Old French construction "pres (que) ne," "por poi (que) ne," etc., where *ne* denotes not a negative but instead "an action that has/had almost occurred" (see Kibler, *Introduction to Old French*, pp. 264–65). The Old French analogy is insightful, it seems to me, in that it takes what might otherwise be regarded as a medial negative conjunction and binds it to the relative conjunction ("but that," "than that"). The sense of "almost," however, does not hold precisely. We could translate: "But yet he was not of such strength / To withstand the power of love / But that he was almost reined in [by love], / Despite whether he would or not," though the *so* in line 788 displaces the adverbial sense of *almost*. I.e., the sense is more likely "But he was so reined in [by love] / That despite whether he would or not" (lines 788–89). Compare 1.1296, where the *algate* likewise obliterates any sense of *almost*. In some instances the preceding "noght" is not required, though the sense is still "But that": e.g., 1.1321. In other instances, instead of "noght," Gower uses "non": e.g., 1.1465, 1.1778–79; or a neither/nor construction as in 1.2470–71. And there are several instances when the *ne* simply functions as a negative after *That*, as in 1.1379, where the *for* cancels the conjunctive function of *ne*; or 1.2800 and 1.3045, where it is part of a double negative. But there are instances in which it simply functions as a negative adverb: 1.3168 and 1.3307.

852   *Glad was hire innocence tho*. Gower's Paulina "which in hire lustes grene / Was fair and freissch and tendre of age" (1.778–79) is innocent in her youth and of "humble cheire" (1.854). As Olsson observes, Gower presents Paulina in an entirely positive light: "Genius has left out the boasts of her counterparts in tradition: the Paulina of Josephus' *Antiquities* (18.3.4), the foolish Madonna

Lisetta da Ca' Quirino of Boccaccio's *Decameron* (4.2), and the Olympias of Gower's later story of Nectanabus (6.1789–2366) all, to some degree, have an exaggerated sense of self-worth, and they easily succumb to the blandishments of a pretender-god or angel" (*Structures of Conversion*, p. 74).

966   *Hire faire face and al desteigneth*. N.b. the medial coordinating conjunction: "And stains her face all over."

975   *honeste*. Of persons or their hearts, honest signifies virtuousness or chastity (*MED*). A wife is said to be chaste if she has to do only with her husband in a seemly manner. When Pauline learns "Now I defouled am of tuo" (line 977), she fears that she can no longer claim that honor. See Chaucer's Parson's Tale (X[I]940). On tensions between communal honor and manipulative deceit, see Craun, *Lies, Slander, and Obscenity*, pp. 129–31.

1003   *til that sche was somdiel amended*. See Rytting, "In Search of the Perfect Spouse," p. 119, on the importance of compassion and appropriate displays of affection in Gower's perception of what constitutes a good marriage like that epitomized in the relationship of Paulina and her spouse.

1077 ff.   The story of the Trojan Horse is found in Dictys, *De Bello Trojano* V.II,12; Benoît, *Roman de Troie* 25620 ff.; and Guido, *Hist. Troiae* III (*Gest Historiale* 29.11846 ff.), all of which Gower may have known. Guido and his translators (not Dictys or Benoît) describe the horse as made of brass.

1081 ff.   ☞ **Latin marginalia**: *Hic vlterius ponit exemplum de illa eciam Ypocrisia, que inter virum et virum decipiens periculosissima consistit. Et narrat, qualiter Greci in obsidione ciuitatis Troie, cum ipsam vi comprehendere nullatenus potuerunt, fallaci animo cum Troianis pacem vt dicunt pro perpetuo statuebant: et super hoc quendam equum mire grossitudinis de ere fabricatum ad sacrificandum in templo Minerue confingentes, sub tali sanctitatis ypocrisi dictam Ciuitatem intrarunt, et ipsam cum inhabitantibus gladio et igne comminuentes pro perpetuo penitus deuastarunt.* [Here he presents a further instructive example concerning that same Hypocrisy, who stands as most dangerous when bringing deceit between man and man. And he tells how the Greeks in the siege of the city of Troy, although they were not able to take it by any means of force, with a false spirit established peace with the Trojans, in perpetuity, as they say. And in addition to this, fashioning a certain horse of miraculous size made from brass for sacrificing in the temple of Minerva, under such hypocrisy of sanctity they entered the said city, and threatening it along with its inhabitants with fire and the sword they utterly and permanently destroyed it.]

1085   The treachery *of Calcas and of Crise* is part of the medieval invention that ultimately culminated in Chaucer's *TC*. In Homer he is the son of Thestor, a diviner who accompanies the Greek army to Troy (*Iliad* 1.69 ff.), and in Virgil he helps build the wooden horse (*Aeneid* 2.185). But once he is made a Trojan who betrays the city and claims the return of his daughter in exchange for Antenor, his treachery becomes a key component of all retellings.

1087   *hors of bras.* An unusual detail, given the prominence of the wooden horse
            myth in Virgil. Perhaps Gower found the forging of a brass horse, as in Guido
            (see note to lines 1077 ff.), rather than the building of a wooden horse, as in
            Dares and Dictys and Benoît, to be more compatible with the machinations of
            hypocrisy. Hypocrites are forgers (lines 1087–88), not carpenters. Brass horses
            are not unknown in romance literature. See Chaucer's Squire's Tale.

1091   *Epius.* The name *Epius* (i.e., Epeius) appears to come from Virgil through
            Benoît (as opposed to *Apius* in Guido), as does the account of the destruction
            of Neptune's gates (lines 1151–55). In Homer's *Odyssey* 8.493, Epeius is the
            maker of the wooden horse, with the help of Athena.

1095   *Anthenor . . . Enee.* The treachery of Antenor and Aeneas is scarcely mentioned
            in Virgil, but it is much emphasized in Dictys, Benoît, and Guido. On Ante-
            nor's deceit see Chaucer's *TC* 4.197–205.

Latin verses vi (before line 1235). The reference in **line 2** is to Ecclesiasticus 13:3.

1241 ff.   ☞ **Latin marginalia**: *Hic loquitur de secunda specie Superbie, que Inobediencia dici-
            tur: et primo illius vicii naturam simpliciter declarat, et tractat consequenter super illa
            precipue Inobediencia, que in curia Cupidinis exosa amoris causam ex sua imbecillitate
            sepissime retardat. In cuius materia Confessor Amanti specialius opponit.* [Here he
            speaks concerning a second species of Pride, which is called Disobedience; and
            first he declares in general terms the nature of that vice, and consequently
            discourses about that Disobedience in particular, which, despising the cause
            of love in the court of Cupid, is very often impeded because of its stupidity. In
            this matter the Confessor particularly questions the Lover.]

1273   *Opponit Confessor.* [The Confessor inquires.]

1274   *Respondet Amans.* [The Lover replies.]

1293   *For specheles may no man spede.* Proverbial. Macaulay compares *CA* 6.447, "For
            selden get a domb man lond" (2:472). See Whiting S554. See also *CA* 4.439–40.

1295–96   See note to 1.786–88.

1328   *retenue.* The gloss "engagement of service" is Macaulay's, who compares *Bal-
            ades* 8.17: "Q'a vous servir j'ai fait ma retenue" (2:472).

1339–40   *forme . . . enforme.* See Simpson, *Sciences and the Self,* pp. 1–10, on Gower's use
            of "information" as a component of self-formation in *CA.* (Compare 1.275–76,
            1973–74, 2669–70 and 8.817–18.) Simpson reads *CA* as a fable of the soul "in
            which the impetus of the soul to reach its own perfection, or form, determines
            the narrative form" (*Sciences and the Self,* p. 230). Form informing form is a
            reciprocal inside-outside paradigm in which exemplary matter provides peda-
            gogical information that impresses the heart as text "follows the soul's con-
            tours" (p. 7). "The pedagogic sense lies in wait behind the artistic" (p. 8), a
            paradigm that makes possible an "information" of the reader by the simul-
            taneous processes of understanding backwards and forwards (inwards and
            outwards) required in any creative process. Simpson presents the argument in
            terms of twelfth- and fourteenth-century philosophical/empirical theory.

1344 ff.   ☞ **Latin marginalia**: *Hic loquitur de Murmure et Planctu, qui super omnes alios In-obediencie secreciores vt ministri illi deseruiunt.* [Here he speaks about Grumbling and Complaint, which above all others serve Disobedience very intimately as his ministers.]

1345 ff.   See Echard, "With Carmen's Help," pp. 32–34, on the ambiguous relationships between the Latin marginal gloss and the English text as Genius shifts the topic from murmur and complaint to truth and obedience in the exemplary Tale of Florent.

1403–06   Unique to third recension manuscripts. See textual note. Hahn cites the first recension couplet, where, instead of Fairfax's "In a cronique as it is write" (1.1404), we get: "And in ensample of this matiere / A tale I fynde, as thou shalt hiere." Hahn concludes: "This revision transforms the pedigree of Gower's retelling from a popular *tale* — perhaps *Ragnelle*, in its surviving form, or some other performative text — to literate narrative" ("Old Wives Tales," p. 100).

1407 ff.   The Tale of Florent is apparently based on the same source as Chaucer's Wife of Bath's Tale; or, more likely, Chaucer drew upon Gower's story as he put together the marriage group of *CT* in the 1390s. See Peck, "Folklore and Powerful Women." The tale joins two folk motifs, the loathly lady transformed through love and the answering of a riddle to save one's life. See Thompson, *Motif-Index of Folk-Literature*, D732, and Whiting's discussion in Bryan and Dempster, eds., *Sources and Analogues of Chaucer's Canterbury Tales*, pp. 223–68. A similar story is found in *The Wedding of Sir Gawain and Dame Ragnelle*; see Hahn, ed., *Sir Gawain*, pp. 41–80. Macaulay (2:473) notes Shakespeare's allusion to Gower's version of the story in *Taming of the Shrew*, I.ii.69. For comparison of the three Middle English versions of the tale and the possibility that The Wife of Bath's tale is a playful inversion of Gower's more sober narrative, see Lindahl, "Oral Undertones," pp. 72–75. Dimmick notes that Florent is the only one of the analogues that does not use an Arthurian setting ("'Redinge of Romance,'" p. 135).

1408 ff.   ☞ **Latin marginalia**: *Hic contra amori inobedientes ad commendacionem Obediencie Confessor super eodem exemplum ponit; vbi dicit quod, cum quedam Regis Cizilie filia in sue iuuentutis floribus pulcherrima ex eius Nouerce incantacionibus in vetulam turpissimam transformata extitit, Florencius tunc Imparatoris Claudi Nepos, miles in armis strenuissimus amorosisque legibus intendens, ipsam ex sua obediencia in pulcritudinem pristinam mirabiliter reformauit.* [Here against those disobedient to love and as commendation to Obedience, the Confessor presents an instructive example on the same thing, where he tells that, when a certain daughter of the King of Sicily who was most beautiful in the bloom of her youth but transformed into a most ugly old woman by her stepmother's incantation, Florent, then the nephew of the Emperor Claudius, a knight most strenuous in fighting and committed to the laws of love, miraculously refashioned her, because of his obedience, into her original beauty.] For discussion of the juxtaposition of this Latin text with the vernacular Tale of Florent to create a dynamic ambiguity, a kind of *mise-en-page disputatio* between the two texts, see Batchelor, "Feigned Truth and Exemplary Method," pp. 3–10.

1409   *nevoeu to th'emperour*. Gower has shifted the location of some portions of the story from the Celtic Arthurian world found in Irish loathly lady narratives to the continent with its *emperour*. See the Latin marginal gloss where *Florencius* (Florent) is identified with his uncle, the Roman Emperor Claudius (*Imparatoris Claudi*). When the grantdame tells Florent to seek the answer to her question "in th'empire / Wher as thou hast most nowlechinge" (1.1482–83), she, in effect, sends him home to the familiar patriarchial terrain of his uncle, in whom Florent confides, but also whom he cautions against retaliation when he fails to obtain the answer. The grantdame's strategy misleads the youth by returning him to the patriarchal ignorance of his roots, while, at the same time, co-opting the emperor's revenge. That the hag (the wild card against the grantdame's scheme) comes from "Cizile" (1.1841) also locates the story on the continent as do Florent's learned but futile attempts to find the answer "be constellacion [and] kinde" (1.1508); such academic schemes help him no more than does Aurelius' trip to the "tregetour" of Orleans in Chaucer's Franklin's Tale.

1413 ff.   See Dimmick, "'Redinge of Romance,'" pp. 128–30, on Florent as a tale of "wish-fulfilment disguised as an *exemplum*" (p. 128).

1417   *marches*. "Borderlands," i.e., marginal areas where Florent seeks adventures. They could be the western marches of England, though not necessariy, given the fact that their location is unspecified. Thomas Hahn has suggested to me that perhaps Florent, like Arveragus in Chaucer's Franklin's Tale, seeks to make his name "In Engelond, that cleped was eek Briteyne / To seke in armes worshipe and honour" (*CT* V[F]810–11).

1474   *under seales write*. On the precision of legal contracts and procedures throughout the tale, see Peck, "Folklore and Powerful Women."

1509   *is al shape unto the lere*. Macaulay glosses "'prepared for the loss' (OE. lyre)" (2:473). But see *MED leir* n.1b, meaning "burial place." I.e., Florent is "prepared for his death"; or, he is "all set (resigned) to be brought to his grave."

1533   *redely*. "Quickly" is an obvious gloss; but "carefully" perhaps makes better sense, based on *MED red* n.1a, 5a, or 6a, implying "advice, deliberation, prudence."

1634   *that olde mone*. "Consort" is perhaps too gentle a gloss. Clearly, the phrase is meant to be derogatory. Given the root of the word (*gemaene*: intercourse), "old fuck" might be more apt. See also *MED mon* n.2: "evil personified, the Devil," which is likewise an apt pejorative description.

1686   *a More*. Used here as a sign of ugliness. Compare Dunbar's disparaging wit in his short poem "Of a Black Moor," with its refrain "My lady with the mickle lips."

1714   *nede he mot that nede schal*. Proverbial. See Whiting N61. Compare Prol.698 and 8.1020.

1769   *go we*. See Green, "Speech Acts and the Art of the Exemplum," pp. 178–79, on Gower's use of subjunctive mood rather than imperative mood, which he uses very little.

Latin verses viii (before line 1883). On the importance of self-knowledge in Gower and its medieval tradition, see Simpson, *Sciences and the Self*, pp. 125–33, 203–211.

1887 ff.   ☞ **Latin marginalia**: *Hic loquitur de tercia specie Superbie, que Presumpcio dicitur, cuius naturam primo secundum vicium Confessor simpliciter declarat.* [Here he speaks about the third species of Pride, which is called Presumption, whose nature as a vice the Confessor first declares in simple terms.]

1911 ff.   ☞ **Latin marginalia**: *Hic tractat Confessor cum Amante super illa saltem presumpcione, ex cuius superbia quam plures fatui amantes, cum maioris certitudinis in amore spem sibi promittunt, inexpediti cicius destituuntur.* [Here the Confessor discourses with the Lover especially about that presumption from the pride of which very many foolish lovers, when they promise themselves hope of greater certainty in love, are suddenly and unpreparedly made destitute.]

1917   *heweth up so hihe*. Proverbial. See Whiting H221.

1977 ff.   The story of Capaneus' presumption was a favorite exemplum of pride among medieval writers. See Chaucer, *Anel.* line 59; *TC* 5.1504. His story is told in Statius, *Thebaid* 3.598 ff., 4.165 ff., 6.731 ff., and 10 *passim*, especially 738 to the end. Statius is probably Gower's main source, though the story is mentioned in varying degrees of completeness in Hyginus, *Fabularum Liber* LXVIII, LXX, LXXI; Boccaccio, *Genealogie deorum gentilium libri* 9.36; and Ovid, *Met.* 9.404. See Shaw ("Gower's Illustrative Tales," pp. 439–40) on the tale's service as an exemplum.

1978 ff.   ☞ **Latin marginalia**: *Hic ponit Confessor exemplum contra illos, qui de suis viribus presumentes debiliores efficiuntur. Et narrat qualiter ille Capaneus, miles in armis probatissimus, de sua presumens audacia inuocacionem ad superos tempore necessitatis ex vecordia tantum et non aliter primitus prouenisse asseruit. Vnde in obsidione Ciuitatis Thebarum, cum ipse quodam die coram suis hostibus ad debellandum se obtulit, ignis de celo subito superveniens ipsum armatum totaliter in cineres combussit.* [Here the Confessor presents an instructive example against those who, presuming on their own powers, are made weaker. And he tells how that Capaneus, a knight most tested in arms, presuming on his boldness, asserted that a vow to the gods at a time of need proceeded only from madness and nothing else. Wherefore in the siege of the city of the Thebans, when he himself on a certain day threw himself into fighting before his enemies, a fire descending from heaven suddenly burned him, fully armed, to ashes.]

2021 ff.   Versions of the *Trump of Death* occur in the Latin *Gesta Romanorum* (cap. 143), *Vita Barlaam et Josaphat*, cap. vi (*PL* 74.462), exemplum 42 of Jacques de Vitry's *Exempla* (ed. Crane, p. 151), and other sermon books, etc. Shaw ("Gower's Illustrative Tales," pp. 440–47) offers a detailed examination of Gower's adaptation of his sources in shaping his "ensample" (1.2019). See Schutz ("Absent and Present Images," pp. 115–18) on binary mirroring in the tale.

2031 ff.   ☞ **Latin marginalia**: *Hic loquitur Confessor contra illos, qui de sua sciencia presumentes aliorum condiciones diiudicantes indiscrete redarguunt. Et narrat exemplum de quodam principe Regis Hungarie germano, qui cum fratrem suum pauperibus in publico vidit humiliatum, ipsum redarguendo in contrarium edocere presumebat: set Rex omni sapiencia prepollens ipsum sic incaute presumentem ad humilitatis memoriam terribili prouidencia micius castigauit.* [Here the Confessor speaks against those who, presuming on their own knowledge and judging carelessly, rebuke the condition of others. And he offers an instructive example concerning a certain prince, the brother of the king of Hungary, who when he saw his brother abase himself in public to paupers, by rebuking him presumed to instruct him to the contrary. But the king, preeminent in every wisdom, punished more gently than terrible providence does the one presuming so incautiously, so that he would remember humility.]

2046–47   "There was such a small account of natural vitality left / That they seemed almost totally dead." See Galloway, "Middle English Poetics." Galloway explains the syntactic oddity of the "Bot a lite . . . That . . . ne" clause as a calque of the Old French "presque . . . ne" where the *ne* denotes not a negative but, instead, "an action that has almost occurred," citing examples in Chrétien's *Le Chevalier de la Charette*. See also the explanatory note to 1.786–88.

2091–93   *noght . . . That . . . ne.* The *ne* functions with *That* as a relative conjunction "Than that." See notes to Prol.989–90 and 1.786–88.

2214 ff.   Macaulay (2:474) cites *Vita Barlaam et Josephat*, cap. vi, here:

              O stulte ac demens, si fratris tui, cum quo idem tibi genus et par honos est, in quem nullius omnino sceleris tibi conscius es, praeconem ita extimuisti, quonam modo mihi reprehensionis notam idcirco inussisti, quod Dei mei praecones, qui mortem, ac Domini, in quem me multa et gravia scelera perpetrasse scio, pertimescendum adventum mihi quavis tuba vocalius altiusque denuntiant, humiliter ac demisse salutarim? ["O mad fool, if you are so terrified at the herald of your brother, with whom you are equal in family and rank, against whom you are aware of no crime at all of yours, might I pay respects humbly and meekly to the heralds of my God, who announce to me vocally and loudly, with whatever sort of trumpet, my death and the fearsome arrival of my lord, against whom I know I have committed many terrible crimes?"]

2247   *al schal deie.* Proverbial. See Whiting D101.

2274   *clerk Ovide.* See *Met.* 3.344–510, for the story of Narcissus; also Boccaccio's *Genealogie deorum gentilium libri* 7.59. Genius alters the conclusion to suit his heterosexual vision. Medieval writers commonly present Narcissism as a dangerous component of erotic love. Guillaume de Lorris' *RR*, lines 1439–1614, was an influential text in this regard. See Schutz ("Absent and Present Images," pp. 109, 118–20) on Gower's alteration of his source to use specular effects to create introspection.

2279 ff.   ☞ **Latin marginalia**: *Hic in speciali tractat Confessor cum Amante contra illos, qui de propria formositate presumentes amorem mulieris dedignantur. Et narrat exemplum* *qualiter cuiusdam Principis filius nomine Narcizus estiuo tempore, cum ipse venacionis causa quendam ceruum solus cum suis canibus exagitaret, in grauem sitim incurrens necessitate compulsus ad bibendum de quodam fonte pronus se inclinauit; vbi ipse faciem suam pulcherrimam in aqua percipiens, putabat se per hoc illam Nimpham, quam Poete Ekko vocant, in flumine coram suis oculis pocius conspexisse; de cuius amore confestim laqueatus, vt ipsam ad se de fonte extraheret, pluribus blandiciis adulabatur. Set cum illud perficere nullatenus potuit, pre nimio languore deficiens contra lapides ibidem adiacentes caput exuerberans cerebrum effudit. Et sic de propria pulcritudine qui fuerat presumptuosus, de propria pulcritudine fatuatus interiit.* [Here in particular the Confessor discourses with the Lover against those who, presuming on their own beauty, disdain the love of a woman. And he narrates an instructive example about how a son of a certain prince, Narcissus by name, during the springtime, when hunting alone with his hounds he pursued a certain stag, and running with severe thirst, compelled by necessity to drink from a certain stream, he lowered himself flat to the ground. There, perceiving in the water his own most beautiful face, he thought instead that he was regarding that nymph whom poets call Echo, in the river before his eyes. Instantly snared by love of her, in order that he might draw her out from the stream he wooed her with many seductions. But when he could not at all achieve that, growing weak from too great an illness, he struck his head against stones lying around in that same place, pouring out his brains. And thus he who had been presumptuous about his own beauty died infatuated by his own beauty.]

2304–21   Genius introduces a Celtic component of fairy magic to his version of Narcissus' downfall as he dismounts at heat of day and under a tree drinks from a well. Compare *Sir Orfeo*, in Laskaya and Salisbury, eds., *Middle English Breton Lays*, pp. 15–60, especially lines 65–174, where Herodis (Eurydice) sleeps under "a fair ympe-tre" (line 70) at the heat of day and is taken by the king of fairies. See Severs, "Antecedents of *Sir Orfeo*," for discussion of the Celtic/Irish tradition. Compare Celtic fairy motifs in the Tale of Florent.

2343–58   "This pretty passage is a late addition, appearing only in the third recension MSS and one other copy, so far as I know" (Mac 2:475). The application of the story to the fact that the narcissus blooms in early spring (1.2355–57) appears to be Gower's invention.

2406 ff.   ☞ **Latin marginalia**: *Hic loquitur de quarta specie Superbie, que Lactancia dicitur, ex cuius natura causatur, vt homo de seipso testimonium perhibens suarum virtutum merita de laude in culpam transfert, et suam famam cum ipse extollere vellet, illam proprio ore subuertit. Set et Venus in amoris causa de isto vicio maculatos a sua Curia super omnes alios abhorrens expellit, et eorum multiloquium verecunda detestatur. Vnde Confessor Amanti opponens materiam plenius declarat.* [Here he speaks concerning the fourth species of Pride, which is called Boasting, by whose nature it is brought about that a man, offering testimonial about himself, transforms the merits of his own virtues from praise to blame, and when he himself would wish to extol his own fame overturns it with his own mouth. But Venus, abhorring above all others those stained by this vice in the cause of love, expels them and, ashamed of their blabbing, execrates them. Whence the Confessor, querying the Lover, declares the matter more fully.]

2443   *daunger. Daunger* personifies the woman's aloofness in courtly relationships. In *RR* he is presented as a somewhat churlish figure who perpetually thwarts the aggressions of male desire.

2459 ff.   The popular story of Albinus and Rosemund is first told by Paulus Diaconus, *Historia Langobardorum* 2.28. See also Godfrey of Viterbo, *Pantheon*, 23.5–6.

2462 ff.   ☞ **Latin marginalia**: *Hic ponit Confessor exemplum contra istos, qui uel de sua in armis probitate, vel de suo in amoris causa desiderio completo se iactant. Et narrat qualiter Albinus primus Rex Longobardorum, cum ipse quendam alium Regem nomine Gurmvndum in bello morientem triumphasset, testam capitis defuncti auferens ciphum ex ea gemmis et auro circumligatum in sue victorie memoriam fabricari constituit: insuper et ipsius Gurmvndi filiam Rosemundam rapiens, maritali thoro in coniugem sibi copulauit. Vnde ipso Albino postea coram sui Regni nobilibus in suo regali conuiuio sedente, dicti Gurmvndi ciphum infuso vino ad se inter epulas afferri iussit; quem sumptum vxori sue Regine porrexit dicens, "Bibe cum patre tuo." Quod et ipsa huius-modi operis ignara fecit. Quo facto Rex statim super hiis que per prius gesta fuerant cunctis audientibus per singula se iactauit. Regina vero cum talia audisset, celato animo factum abhorrens in mortem domini sui Regis circumspecta industria conspir-auit; ipsumque auxiliantibus Glodesida et Helmege breui subsecuto tempore interfecit: cuius mortem Dux Ravenni tam in corpus dicte Regine quam suorum fautorum postea vindicauit. Set et huius tocius in infortunii sola superbie iactancia fomitem ministrabat.* [Here the Confessor presents an instructive example against those who boast either about their trials in war or about their fulfilled desires in the cause of love. And he narrates how Albinus, the first king of the Lombards, when he himself was triumphant over a certain other king dying in battle, Gurmund by name, carried away the top of the dead man's skull and caused a goblet, bound with gems and gold, to be fabricated from it, in memory of his victory. In addition to this, he captured the daughter of this same Gurmund, Rosemund, and coupled her to himself as a spouse in the marital bedchamber. Wherefore when this Albinus was later sitting before the nobles of his kingdom at his royal banquet, amidst the feasting he ordered the goblet of the said Gurmund to be brought filled with wine to him. When he had received it, he offered it to his wife the queen, saying, "Drink with your father," which indeed she, ig-norant of a piece of work of this kind, unknowingly did. Once done, the king immediately boasted to all those listening about those things that he had formerly accomplished, one by one. But when the queen had heard such things she, abhorring in her concealed thoughts his deed, conspired the death of her lord the king by a circumspect endeavor, and with Glodesida and Hel-mege helping her, she killed him a short while after. The duke of Ravenna later revenged his death on the bodies both of the said queen and of her help-ers. But indeed of this whole misfortune a single boasting of pride furnished the kindling-wood.] Macaulay notes that the wording *"Bibe cum patre tuo"* is exactly that of the prose account in Godfrey of Viterbo's *Pantheon* (2:477).

2565   *thilke unkynde Pride. MED unkinde* 4c cites this line in Gower with the meaning "lacking natural affection or concern for or loyalty to a spouse; of a wife: undutiful toward her husband, fractious; of a husband, husband's pride: lacking proper respect for his wife, indifferent to his wife's feelings." N.b. *CA* 3.2055, where Orestes condemns Clytemnestra: "O cruel beste unkinde" for the slaughter of her own lord. See also *MED unkynde* 6a and 4d. That the duke of Ravenna quietly poisons Rosemund (1.2644–46) would seem to be the result of an unspoken law: wives don't kill husbands, lest they be *unkynde*.

2629–30   *noght . . . That . . . ne.* See note to 1.786–88.

2642 ff.   Macaulay observes that Gower "winds up the story abruptly. According to the original story, Longinus the Prefect of Ravenna conspired with Rosemunda to poison Helmichis; and he, having received drink from her hand and feeling himself poisoned, compelled her to drink also of the same cup" (2:477).

Latin verses x (before line 2681). **Line 5**: *fauellum.* Favel, a medieval creation, is generally related to flattery (from Latin *fabella*) and is bodied forth as a horse to be "curried" by his followers (because *fauvel* is 'fawn colored' in Old French, hence a fawn-colored horse): see the fourteenth-century French *Roman de Fauvel* (ed. Langförs). In that poem Fauvel is acrostically defined as the progenitor of **f**lattery, **a**varice, **v**illainy, **v**ariety (changeability), **e**nvy, and **l**aziness; he seeks to marry Fortune but is denied because of Fortune's higher lineage and so must settle for Vaine Gloire. *Piers Plowman* introduces Favel to English literature, but not specifically as a horse (B.2.158 ff.). The "saddled laws" that Gower places on Favel's back could show some connection with the passage in *Piers Plowman*, where saddled sheriffs and professional jury members carry Meed and False (so Echard and Fanger, *Latin Verses in the Confessio Amantis*). More likely, however, Gower's saddling Favel with laws and climbing on Favel as a knight are simply elaborations of the allegory of the *Roman de Fauvel*, a connection confirmed by Gower's association of Favel with Vain Glory whom Favel marries in the *Roman.* Yet by the late fourteenth and early fifteenth century the dramatized idea of "currying favor" was very widespread in England and in more literal terms than our own cliché usually conveys; the chronicler Thomas Walsingham describes a public sermon in 1406 where a lord ordered his servant to present to the preacher a currying comb, "suggesting that he was fawning on the prelates of the church." The archbishop of Canterbury, less amused than the other spectators, ordered the servant to walk naked for several days as penance with a curry-comb in one hand and a candle in the other. Obviously the symbolism of the curry-comb in both events was clear to many without any specific literary source (see Walsingham, *St. Albans Chronicle*, ed. Galbraith, p. 2).

2657   *His pourpos schal ful ofte faile.* See Bakalian, *Aspects of Love*, pp. 12–20, on Albinus' avantance (boasting) and the swiftness of his demise once he "overreaches himself and is swept away by his pride" (p. 18).

2682 ff.   ☞ **Latin marginalia**: *Hic loquitur de quinta specie superbie, que Inanis gloria vocatur, et eiusdem vicii naturam primo describens super eodem in amoris causa Confessor*

Amanti consequenter opponit. [Here he speaks about the fifth species of Pride, which is called Empty (or Vain) Glory, and first describing the nature of this same vice, the Confessor consequently questions the Lover concerning it, in the cause of love.]

2698   *camelion.* Probably the lizard but not necessarily. The *MED* cites Gower's line here to signify a creature of diverse colors and notes various references in Gower's contemporary, John Trevisa, where the chameleon is "a litel beste of dyverse coloures" like a *stellio* (gecko) or the *lusardis*; or an evete (lizard, salamander, or newt); or "a flekked beste" like a leopard or basilisk. Trevisa also uses the word to indicate a giraffe, while Mandeville uses the word for "a lytill best as a Goot." See Whiting C137 for proverbial underpinning.

2706 ff.   ☞ **Latin marginalia**: *Salomon. Amictus eius annunciat de eo.* [Solomon: "His cloak declares what he is."] See Ecclesiasticus 19:27, which Gower abbreviates.

2722–24   *noght . . . That . . . ne.* See note to 1.786–88.

2727   *Rondeal, balade and virelai.* Burrow ("Portrayal of Amans," p. 21) notes that in Gower "these compositions are not incorporated in the text of the poem itself as we would expect in Machaut or Froissart."

2785 ff.   Based on Daniel 4:1–34 (Dan. 4:4–37, King James). The story was a popular exemplum of pride (e.g., *VC* 7; *MO*, lines 1885–95 and 21979–96; and Chaucer's Monk's Tale, *CT* VII[B²]2143–82). For detailed discussion of the passage, see Peck, "John Gower and the Book of Daniel."

2788 ff.   ☞ **Latin marginalia**: *Hic ponit Confessor exemplum contra vicium inanis glorie, narrans qualiter Nabugodonosor Rex Caldeorum, cum ipse in omni sue maiestatis gloria celsior extitisset, deus eius superbiam castigare volens ipsum extra formam hominis in bestiam fenum comedentem transmutauit. Et sic per septennium penitens, cum ipse potenciorem se agnouit, misertus deus ipsum in sui regni solium restituta sanitate emendatum graciosius collocauit.* [Here the Confessor presents an instructive example against the vice of Empty (or Vain) Glory, relating how Nebuchadnezzar, King of the Chaldeans, when he himself was established very high in all the glory of his majesty, God, wishing to chastise his pride, transmuted him into a grass-eating beast. And thus making penance for seven years, when this one acknowledged him to be more powerful, God took pity and graciously placed him again on the soil of his kingdom, freed from blemish and with his health restored.]

2925   *The weder schal upon thee reine.* "The weather shall rain upon you." But it also could mean, "The sheep shall rule over you."

3067 ff.   No specific source has been identified for the Tale of Three Questions.

3068 ff.   ☞ **Latin marginalia**: *Hic narrat Confessor exemplum simpliciter contra Superbiam; et dicit quod nuper quidam Rex famose prudencie cuidam militi suo super tribus questionibus, vt inde certitudinis responsionem daret, sub pena capitalis sentencie terminum prefixit. Primo, quid minoris indigencie ab inhabitantibus orbem auxilium maius obtinuit. Secundo, quid maioris valencie meritum continens minoris expense reprisas exiguit.*

*Tercio, quid omnia bona diminuens ex sui proprietate nichil penitus valuit. Quarum
vero questionum quedam virgo dicti militis filia sapientissima nomine patris sui solu-
cionem aggrediens taliter Regi respondit. Ad primam dixit, quod terra nullius indiget,
quam tamen adiuuare cotidianis laboribus omnes intendunt. Ad secundam dixit, quod
humilitas omnibus virtutibus prevalet, que tamen nullius prodegalitatis expensis men-
suram excedit. Ad terciam dixit, quod superbia omnia tam corporis quam anime bona
deuastans maiores expensarum excessus inducit. Et tamen nullius valoris, ymmo tocius
perdicionis, causam sua culpa ministrat.* [Here the Confessor narrates an instruc-
tive example against pride in general; and he says that in recent times a cer-
tain King, famous for his prudence, presented to a certain one of his knights
a logical challenge comprising three questions, to which he might give a cor-
rect response under pain of capital punishment: first, what having less need
has obtained greater help from inhabitants on earth; second, what having
merit of greater value demands less expense; third, what diminishes all good
things but is worth utterly nothing in itself. Of these questions, however, a
certain most wise virgin daughter of the said knight, advancing a solution in
the name of her father, responded thusly to the king. To the first, she said that
the earth has need of nothing, but all strive to help it with daily labors. To the
second, she said that humility is worth more than all virtues, but it does not
exceed any expense of prodigality. To the third, she said that pride devas-
tating all good things both of the body and the soul induces excessive ex-
penses. And nonetheless its guilt furnishes the source of no value but instead
of total loss.] In the phrase *minoris expense reprisas, reprisa* means "expenses lost,
cost," but, like its Old French and ME versions (both *reprise*), it is commonly
found in legal documents and normally with the technical legal sense of "a
fixed charge deducted annually from an estate's revenue" (Latham, *Revised
Medieval Latin Word-List*, and *MED*). Gower is the only writer attested as
broadening the meaning of the word in English to mean, as here, simply "cost"
(see explanatory notes to 1.3308 and 5.4708). His usage was not followed by
other writers.

3308   *To stanche . . . the reprise.* Macaulay glosses *reprise* as "trouble"; i.e., "To stop the
            trouble of Pride" (2:479). But the *MED* favors "To pay the cost of Pride" (see
            MED s.v. *reprise* b; and s.v. *staunchen* 3c). See also the comment on the Latin
            reprisa above.

3366–67   *noght . . . That . . . ne.* See note to 1.786–88.

3369 ff.   Macaulay (2:479) notes that Gower has heavily corrected these lines.

3397–3400   The MS is torn here, with line 3397 ending *gr;* line 3398 ending *plac;* and line
            3400 ending *qwee.*

EXPLANATORY NOTES TO BOOK 8

Notes to Latin verses i (before line 1). **Line 1:** *confert.* While unusual in other Latin writers,
            "is useful" is a regular sense of *confert* for Gower (e.g., in *VC*); as is also com-
            mon in Gower's Latin (but more striking here), the object of verbs of pleasure

and displeasure is omitted — "people at the present time" are implicitly those who find the rule of lechery useful, and the "new teaching" against it unpleasing. This grammatically understood object ("us") has been the implied target of much of the poem, in view from the first line on. **Line 4**: *impositum*. "Affixed" here translates *impositum*, which may mean the path was "imposed" either legitimately (like the proper order of a restrained life) or deceptively (compare "impostor"). "The impostured path" would be a possible although awkward rendition of the phrase.

1 ff.   Macaulay imagines that Gower "had some embarrassment as regards the subject [incest] of his eighth book" (3:536). But contrast Scanlon's perceptive juxtaposing of medieval attitudes toward the topic with those of the nineteenth and twentieth centuries ("Riddle of Incest," pp. 93–112).

3 ff.   ☞ **Latin marginalia**: *Postquam ad instanciam Amantis confessi Confessor Genius super hiis que Aristotiles Regem Alexandrum edocuit, vna cum aliarum Cronicarum exemplis seriose tractauit, iam vltimo in isto octauo volumine ad confessionem in amoris causa regrediens tractare proponit super hoc, quod nonnulli primordia nature ad libitum voluptuose consequentes, nullo humane racionis arbitrio seu ecclesie legum imposicione a suis excessibus debite refrenantur. Vnde quatenus amorem concernit Amantis conscienciam pro finali sue confessionis materia Genius rimari conatur.* [After the confessor Genius has discoursed at the urging of the confessing Lover about those things that Aristotle taught King Alexander along with instructive examples taken one by one from other chronicles, now finally in this eighth book he returns to confession in the cause of love. He proposes to discourse about that matter which some, voluptuously following at their will the initial order of nature, do not refrain from by any judgment of human reason or statute of ecclesiastical law. About this insofar as it pertains to love, as the final portion of his confession, Genius tries to probe the Lover's conscience.]

10   *Bot Lucifer He putte aweie*. Medieval popular histories of creation commonly begin with the fall of the angels, Lucifer being the brightest and second only to God. That fall makes way for the creation of humankind as replacement for the angelic failure. Compare the sequence of events in *Cursor Mundi* or in the mystery plays.

21–26   The N-Town plays place the fall of the angels on the fifth day of creation, followed by the creation of man on the sixth. Perhaps Gower has a similar scheme in mind as he speaks of the fall of Lucifer through deadly pride, then jumps to the sixth day and Adam's creation.

30–34   *of the mannes progenie . . . The nombre of angles . . . to restore*. That the numbers of creation, disrupted by the fallen angels, would be restored with the creation and redemption of mankind was commonplace in fourteenth-century thought. See, for example, *Cursor Mundi*, lines 514–16 ("Adam þer-for was wroght þan / Þe tent ordir for to fullfill, / Þat lucifer did for to spill" — ed. Morris, pp. 36–38); similarly in the York Cycle, at the end of the first play, "The Fall of the Angels," Deus announces that his "after-warkes" (line 152) will make up for the lack caused by the fall; then, in the second play, "Creation," that "syne þat þis world es ordand euyn"(line 29), Deus will begin creation to restore what has been lost. As a patristic source for the idea, see St. Augustine, *Enchiridion*, ch. 29, entitled: "The Restored Part of Humanity Shall, in Accordance with the Promises of God, Succeed to the Place Which the Rebellious Angels Lost." Augustine is uncertain about what the exact number is but is confident that God has such a number in mind since he ordered all things in "measure, and number, and weight" (in Schaff, *Nicene and Post-Nicene Fathers*, 3.247). See also Augustine's *De civitate Dei* Book 22, ch. 1.

48   *Metodre*. The reference is to Methodius, "in whose *Revelationes* it is written, 'Sciendum namque est, exeuntes Adam et Evam de Paradiso virgines fuisse' [For it should be known that Adam and Eve were virgins when they left Paradise], so that 'Into the world' in l.53 must mean from Paradise into the outer world" (Mac 2:536).

54   *nature hem hath reclamed*. The sexual drive of "nature" serves a positive function here. The issue of incest, soon to come, qualifies the regulation of desire. See the sinister consequences of Lot's daughters following "nature" in 8.230 ff., or the circumstances of Antiochus, who acts "[w]ithoute insihte of conscience" in following his "likinge and concupiscence" (8.293–94).

62 ff.   Methodius identifies the sisters of Cain and Abel as Calmana and Debora (Mac 2:536).

146   *non schal wedden of his ken*. On the history of Ecclesiastical Law regarding marriage of kin, see Donavin's discussion of the meaning of incest in the Middle Ages (*Incest Narratives*, pp. 9–19) and the sophisticated cultural psychoanalysis of incest in *CA* by Scanlon ("Riddle of Incest").

147   *Ne the seconde ne the thridde*. On Gower's scheme of the traditional first three ages and Gower's fourth where papal law rules against marriage of immediate kin or those twice or three times removed, see Scanlon, "Riddle of Incest," pp. 109–12.

158   *ne yit religion*. Macaulay notes: "The seduction of one who was a professed member of a religious order was usually accounted to be incest: cp. *Mirour*, lines 9085 ff. and line 175 below" (3:536).

163   *what thing comth next to honde*. See Olsson, "Love, Intimacy, and Gower," pp. 93–95, on the cost of betrayal of intimacy at home. Olsson draws interesting parallels between Antiochus' incestuous behavior and Amans' shortsightedness in love. See also Peck, *Kingship and Common Profit*, p. 164.

201 ff.   ☞ **Latin marginalia**: *Hic loquitur contra illos, quos Venus sui desiderii feruore inflammans ita incestuosos efficit, vt neque propriis Sororibus parcunt. Et narrat exemplum, qualiter pro eo quod Gayus Caligula tres sorores suas virgines coitu illicito oppressit, deus tanti sceleris peccatum impune non ferens ipsum non solum ab imperio set a vita iusticia vindice priuauit. Narrat eciam aliud exemplum super codem, qualiter Amon filius Dauid fatui amoris concupiscencia preuentus, sororem suam Thamar a sue virginitatis pudicicia inuitam defflorauit, propter quod et ipse a fratre suo Absolon postea interfectus, peccatum sue mortis precio inuitus redemit.* [Here he speaks against

those whom Venus has made so incestuously inflamed by the fervor of their desire that they do not spare even their own sisters. And he narrates an instructive example how, because Gaius Caligula assaulted his three virgin sisters in illicit coitus, God, not tolerating the sin of so great a crime to be unpunished, by just vindication not only deprived him of imperial rule, but of life. He narrates also another instructive example on the same matter, how Amon the son of David, overwhelmed by lust of fatuous love, sexually violated his unwilling sister Tamar, deflowering her modest virginity, on account of which he, later being killed by his brother Absolon, also unwilling, repaid his sin with the price of his death.]

202   *Caligula.* Gower's source is Suetonius, *Lives of the Caesars* 4.24. That Gower knew Suetonius directly is likely in that Chaucer cites "Swetonius" as source for his account of Nero in The Monk's Tale. Higden's *Polychronicon*, Bk. 4, ch. 7, also tells of Caligula's incest: he was "A swiþe wicked man. . . . he lay by his owne sustres, and gat a douȝter on þat oon, and lay by þat oþer afterward, and at þe laste he exiled his sustres þat he hadde i-lay by" (Trevisa's translation, pp. 363–65). Neither Suetonius nor Higden attribute the cause of his death to incest, however. That seems to be Genius' insight.

214–19   *Amon . . . Thamer . . . Absolon . . . his soster schent.* The story of Amon's incestuous rape of Tamar and Absolon's jealous revenge may be found in 2 Kings [2 Samuel] 13.

224 ff.   ☞ **Latin marginalia:** *Hic narrat, qualiter Loth duas filias suas ipsis consencientibus carnali copula cognouit, duosque ex eis filios, scilicet Moab et Amon, progenuit quorum postea generacio praua et exasperans contra populum dei in terra saltim promissionis vario grauamine quam sepius insultabat.* [Here he narrates how Lot knew in carnal copulation his two daughters, with them both consenting, and how he generated two sons from them, namely Moab and Amon, whose depraved and exasperating lineage was later very often abusive against the people of God, at least in the Land of Promise, by means of various kinds of trouble.] The story of Lot's fellowship with his daughters is found in Genesis 19:30–38.

232   As in the Tale of Canacee and Machaire, nature impels the incestuous desire and, in birth, provides a release, but with disastrous progeny. See Kelly, *Love and Marriage*, pp. 140–41.

256   *every man is othres lore.* Proverbial. See Whiting M170.

263   *excedeth lawe.* Diane Watt suggests that although Amans claims he is not guilty of incest (8.184–89), in a sense he *is* guilty "insofar as he seems to be engaged in an oedipal struggle with his own incestuous parents: Venus and Cupid, the queen and king of love" (*Amoral Gower*, p. 128).

269   *process.* Gower thinks of history as a process (L. *processus*); that is, a pageant or play, staged on "middelerthe." It is a narrative, a story that unfolds. See *MED proces* 3a, c, and f.

271 ff.   The "Tale of Apollonius" was popular and appears in English before Gower in an Old English translation. See Archibald, *Apollonius of Tyre*, Appendix 1: "Latin

and Vernacular Versions of *HA* to 1609," pp. 182–216. Appendix 2 deals with "Medieval and Renaissance Allusions to the Story of Apollonius." The tale occurs in Godfrey of Viterbo's *Pantheon*, which Gower used frequently, though his version includes many details not to be found in Godfrey, or in the Latin *Gesta Romanorum*, cap. 153. The eleventh-century Latin prose version, *Historia Apollonii Tyrii*, a version which Godfrey used as his source, was most likely known by Gower as well. It includes details found in Gower which do not occur in Godfrey. See Macaulay's useful discussion (3:536–38) and Singer's edition and discussion of *Apollonius von Tyrus* in his edition of Godfrey of Viterbo's *Cronica*. Shakespeare's *Pericles*, in which "Gower" is the commentator, is based only in part on Gower's version of the story. For critical discussion of the story see Dimmick, "'Redinge of Romance,'" pp. 136–37; Donavin, *Incest Narratives*, pp. 64–86; Gallacher, *Love, the Word, and Mercury*, pp. 129–38; Goodall, "John Gower's *Apollonius of Tyre*"; Olsen, "*Betwene Ernest and Game*," pp. 71–86; Olsson, *Structures of Conversion*, pp. 215–25; Peck, *Kingship and Common Profit*, pp. 166–72; Robins, "Romance," pp. 169–72; Scanlon, "Riddle of Incest," pp. 112–27; Watt, *Amoral Gower*, pp. 127–48; and Yeager, *John Gower's Poetic*, pp. 216–29. Because Macaulay's notes on this tale are extensive and excellent I have cited them liberally, supplying translations of the Latin. See notes to lines 404 ff., 542 ff., 679, 767 ff., 866 ff., 1089 ff., 1184 ff., 1248, and 1349 ff.

272 ff.　　☞ **Latin marginalia**: *Hic loquitur adhuc contra incestuosos amantum coitus. Et narrat mirabile exemplum de magno Rege Antiocho, qui vxore mortua propriam filiam violauit: et quia filie Matrimonium penes alios impedire voluit, tale ab eo exiit edictum, quod si quis eam in vxorem peteret, nisi ipse prius quoddam problema questionis, quam ipse Rex proposuerat, veraciter solueret, capitali sentencia puniretur. Super quo veniens tandem discretus iuuenis princeps Tyri Appolinus questionem soluit; nec tamen filiam habere potuit, set Rex indignatus ipsum propter hoc in mortis odium recollegit. Vnde Appolinus a facie Regis fugiens, quamplura, prout inferius intitulantur, propter a-morem pericla passus est.* [Here he speaks moreover against the incestuous coitus of lovers. And he narrates a miraculous instructive example about the great king Antiochus, who after his wife had died violated his own daughter. And because he wanted to prevent the marriage of his daughter with any others, such an edict went forth from him, that if anyone should seek her as a wife, unless he first accurately solved a certain problem of a puzzle which the king himself had proposed, he would receive capital punishment. Whereupon a shrewd youth, Apollonius the ruler of Tyre, arriving, solved the puzzle. Yet he was not able to have the daughter; instead the king, indignant, conceived against him because of this a mortal hatred. Wherefore Apollonius, fleeing from the king's presence, suffered very many dangers, as are described below.]

279–92　　On shared beds and incest after the death of the mother, see Shaw, "Role of the Shared Bed." Shaw cites various accounts in which mothers and sons and fathers and daughters share beds with disastrous results, albeit thinking, as Antiochus does, "that it was no sinne" (line 346).

280　　*deth, which no king mai withstonde.* Proverbial. See Whiting D78, D101.

293–94　　See note to line 54, above.

299 *With strengthe.* "By force." On rape as violence — *violentus concubitus* — see Hanawalt, "Whose Story Was This?" See also the note to line 347.

309–10 *devoureth / His oghne fleissh.* On incest as cannibalism see Donavin, *Incest Narratives*.

312 *This unkinde fare.* See note to 1.2565 on indifference toward the rights of kinsmen as *unkinde* behavior.

347 *sche dorste him nothing withseie.* See Donavin, *Incest Narratives*, pp. 64–94, on the political effects of the incestuous rape of Antiochus' daughter.

374 ff. ☞ **Latin marginalia**: *De aduentu Appolini in Antiochiam, vbi ipse filiam Regis Antiochi in vxorem postulauit.* [Concerning Apollonius' arrival at Antioch, where he requests to have as wife the daughter of King Antiochus.]

376–80 *gret desir . . . hihe mod . . . hote blod . . . lusti knyht . . . musende on a nyht.* Genius presents Apollonius' willful behavior as a phenomenon of youth and nature rather than intemperate or sinful behavior.

402 ☞ **Latin marginalia**: *Questio Regis Antiochi.* [The puzzle of King Antiochus.]

404 ☞ **Latin marginalia**: *Scelere vehor, materna carne vescor, quero patrem meum, matris mee virum, vxoris mee filium.* ["I am conveyed by crime, I feed on maternal flesh, I seek my father, the husband of my mother, the son of my wife."] On the gloss Macaulay observes: "The riddle as given in the Laud MS. is, 'Scelere uehor. Materna carne uescor. Quero patrem meum matris mee uirum uxoris mee filiam, nec inuenio.' Most copies have 'fratrem meum' for 'patrem meum,' but Gower agrees with the Laud MS. I do not attempt a solution of it beyond that of Apollonius, which is, 'Quod dixisti scelere uehor, non es mentitus, ad te ipsum respice. Et quod dixisti materna carne uescor, filiam tuam intuere'" (2:538). The riddle closely resembles riddles from ancient through late medieval times about the cyclical generation of water and ice, which invariably use an incestuous metaphor: e.g., "My mother bore me, and soon my mother is born from me; the daughter whom the mother bore has generated the mother." See Galloway, "Rhetoric of Riddling" (n.b., riddle Ha 11 and analogues, p. 99 and note 108). The riddle in the story of Apollonius, of course, has a literal incestuous meaning, and thus is almost not a riddle at all. But the story presumes that an audience (including previous suitors) would first consider the riddle metaphorically like other ancient and medieval riddles.

405–14 Goolden, "Antiochus's Riddle," offers a detailed comparison of Gower's riddle with the Latin version. See entries in Nicholson (*Annotated Index*, pp. 503–04) for thumbnail summaries of critical discussions of the riddle, and, more recently, Watt (*Amoral Gower*, pp. 129–34).

418 ff. ☞ **Latin marginalia**: *Responsio Appolini.* [Apollonius' response.]

421 *rehersed on and on.* Gower regularly celebrates the individual who can reason well and think problems through step-by-step. Compare, especially, the rational behavior of Peronelle in the Tale of the Three Questions, Florent in his tale, Paulina and her husband in the Tale of Mundus and Paulina, the king in

Trump of Death, and, ultimately, "John Gower," as he once again exercises his reason.

428 ff. ☞ **Latin marginalia**: *Indignacio Antiochi super responsione Appolini*. [Antiochus' indignation over Apollonius' response.]

431 *With slihe wordes and with felle*. Contrast Antiochus' thought process with that of Apollonius as Antiochus uses his reason to subvert truth.

440 ff. ☞ **Latin marginalia**: *De recessu Appollini ab Antiochia*. [Concerning Apollonius' retreat from Antioch.]

466 ff. ☞ **Latin marginalia**: *De fuga Appolini per mare a Regno suo*. [Concerning Apollonius' flight across the sea from his kingdom.]

496 ff. ☞ **Latin marginalia**: *Nota qualiter Thaliartus Miles, vt Appolinum veneno intoxicaret, ab Antiocho in Tyrum missus, ipso ibidem non inuento Antiochiam rediit*. [Note how Taliart the knight, sent by Antiochus to Tyre so that Apollonius might be sickened with poison, returned to Antioch when he was not found there.]

536 *He stinte his wraththe and let him be*. Macaulay notes Gower's variation from the source here, objecting that the change takes away Apollonius' motive for fleeing to Tarsus (3:538).

537 ff. ☞ **Latin marginalia**: *Qualiter Appolinus in portu Tharsis applicuit, vbi in hospicio cuiusdam magni viri nomine Strangulionis hospitatus est*. [How Apollonius arrived at the port of Tharsis, where in the household of a certain great man, Strangulio by name, he was given hospitality.]

542 ff. Macaulay (3:539) notes "In the original Apollonius meets 'Hellanicus' at once on landing, and is informed by him of the proscription. He makes an offer to Strangulio to sell his wheat at cost price to the citizens, if they will conceal his presence among them. The money which he receives as the price of the wheat is expended by him in public benefits to the state, and the citizens set up a statue of him standing in a two-horse chariot (biga), his right hand holding forth corn and his left foot resting upon a bushel measure."

571 ff. ☞ **Latin marginalia**: *Qualiter Hellicanus ciuis Tyri Tharsim veniens Appolinum de insidiis Antiochi premuniuit*. [How Hellican, a citizen of Tyre, coming to Tharsis, forewarned Apollonius about the treacheries of Antiochus.]

575–77 *Hellican . . . preide his lord to have insihte / Upon himself*. In his wandering Apollonius seems at the mercy of Fortune (see 8.585–92). But in Gower Fortune is double-valenced, the good mixed with the bad, with the resolve determined less by chance than by *insihte upon himself*.

585 ff. ☞ **Latin marginalia**: *Qualiter Appolinus portum Tharsis relinquens, cum ipse per mare navigio securiorem quesiuit, superueniente tempestate nauis cum omnibus preter ipsum solum in eadem contentis iuxta Pentapolim periclitabatur*. [How Apollonius, departing the port of Tharsis, sought a more secure one by passage across the sea, but his ship was endangered along with all those aboard it except for himself, when a tempest overtook them near Pentapolis.]

630 *broghte him sauf upon a table*. Earlier, Apollonius was a food supplier as he brought grain to Mittelene. Now he himself is served up as Fortune brings him ashore on a *table* (plank). The felicitous pun comments well on Dame Fortune's movable feasts.

634 ff. ☞ **Latin marginalia**: *Qualiter Appolinus nudus super litus iactabatur, vbi quidam piscator ipsum suo collobio vestiens ad vrbem Pentapolim direxit.* [How Apollonius was thrown naked onto the shore, where a certain fisherman, clothing him with his tunic, directed him to the city of Pentapolis.]

646 *cam a fisshere in the weie*. Just as the sea is a traditional sign of Fortune's instability, so the fisherman figures as an agent who makes a living out of what Fortune provides. N.b. Shakespeare's clever twist on this point in Gower's story to have the fishermen dredge up a suit of "rusty armour" in which Pericles can joust (II.i.119).

666 ff. ☞ **Latin marginalia**: *Qualiter Appolino Pentapolim adueniente ludus Gignasii per vrbem publice proclamatus est.* [How when Apollonius arrived at Pentapolis a gymnastics game was publicly proclaimed through the city.]

678 *comun game*. Gower omits references to the baths in the source (see Archibald, *Apollonius of Tyre*, pp. 74–75 and note to line 679 below) and substitutes a ball game of some sort that is played naked as was the Greek "custume and us (use)" (line 685). "Comun" implies popular, though in this admirable society the king Artestrathes observes the play and rewards the victor.

679 Macaulay observes: "The account in the original story is here considerably different. Gower did not understand the Greek customs. 'Et dum cogitaret unde uite peteret auxilium, uidit puerum nudum per plateam currentem, oleo unctum, precinctum sabana, ferentem ludos iuueniles ad gymnasium pertinentes, maxima uoce dicentem: Audite ciues, audite peregrini, liberi et ingenui, gymnasium patet. Apollonius hoc audito exuens se tribunario ingreditur lauacrum, utitur liquore palladio; et dum exercentes singulos intueretur, parem sibi querit et non inuenit. Subito Arcestrates rex totius illius regionis cum turba famulorum ingressus est: dumque cum suis ad pile lusum exerceretur, uolente deo miscuit se Apollonius regi, et dum currenti sustulit pilam, subtili uelocitate percussam ludenti regi remisit' &c. (f. 207 v°). [And while he was pondering where he would find a means to survive, he saw running through the square a naked boy smeared with oil, wrapped with a towel, bearing equipment for a boys' gymnasium game, uttering in the loudest possible voice, "Hear ye, citizens, hear ye, visitors, freedmen and freeborn: the gymnasium is open!" Hearing this, Apollonius, removing his cloak entered the bath, and used the liquid of Pallas [oil]; and while he observed each man exerting himself, he searched for someone equal to himself and found none. Suddenly Archistrates, the king of the entire region, entered along with his crowd of servants: and while he engaged in a game of ball with his men, by God's will Apollonius participated along with the king: he caught the ball while the king was running and sent the caught ball back with accurate swiftness to the king playing . . . .] The story proceeds to say that the king, pleased

with the skill of Apollonius in the game of ball, accepted his services at the bath, and was rubbed down by him in a very pleasing manner. The result was an invitation to supper. Gower agrees here with the *Pantheon* in making the king a spectator only" (3:539).

696 ff.　　　☞ **Latin marginalia**: *Qualiter Appolinus ludum gignasii vincens in aulam Regis ad cenam honorifice receptus est.* [How Apollonius, winning the gymnastics game, was honorably received for a feast in the king's hall.]

720　　　　*beginne a middel bord. Beginne* suggests that Apollonius is placed at the head of a second table.

729 ff.　　　☞ **Latin marginalia**: *Qualiter Appolinus in cena recumbens nichil comedit, set doloroso vultu, submisso capite, ingemiscebat; qui tandem a filia Regis confortatus cytharam plectens cunctis audientibus citharisando vltra modum complacuit.* [How Apollonius, sitting down to the feast, ate nothing, but instead with a mournful face and lowered head began groaning; finally, being comforted by the king's daughter, he played a harp and pleased all the listeners by his harping.]

767 ff.　　　Macaulay observes (3:539): "In the original all applaud the performance of the king's daughter except Apollonius, who being asked by the king why he alone kept silence, replied, 'Bone rex, si permittis, dicam quod sentio: filia enim tua in artem musicam incidit, nam non didicit. Denique iube mihi tradi liram, et scies quod nescit' (f. 208 vº). [Good king, if you permit I will say what I feel: for your daughter has jumped into the art of music but has not learned it. Command therefore that the lyre be handed to me, and you will learn what she does not.] Gower has toned this down to courtesy."

768　　　　*mesure.* Measure is a technical term in music borrowed from grammar to define the metrics of a line. See Boethius, *De musica* (Augustine's *De musica* makes a similar point), where measure is discussed in terms of mode, duration, accent, and metrical feet. *MED* gives "?melody" and "?harmony" as possible glosses, but such a reading is indeed questionable and misleading. If one thinks of melody as the sequence (the measuring) of a song in a particular mode then the term might apply (see line 783). But if the term were understood to mean a pleasing tune then the gloss would be quite inappropriate. Similarly, if "harmony" means ratio and proportions of intervals, then it might be a suitable gloss, but if "harmony" is taken to mean chord structures then the gloss would be wrong. See note to Prol.1056.

777　　　　*He takth the harpe.* Playing the harp teaches "mesure" (8.773), that is, proportion, moderation, and harmony, all crucial virtues for good kingship. (See note to 8.768.) As a good king Apollonius not only embodies "measure," he teaches it to his people. Of all kingly practices, this brings him closest to the angelic state (see 8.781–83) best suited to good rule.

801 ff.　　　☞ **Latin marginalia**: *Qualiter Appolinus cum Rege pro filia sua erudienda retentus est.* [How Apollonius was kept with the king in order to educate his daughter.]

808–11　　　*preide unto hir fader . . . That sche myhte . . . His lore have.* This is one of the earliest instances of the story of a nobleman in disguise who becomes the teacher of a young noblewoman whom he ultimately marries. In the Renaissance, where the education of noblewomen becomes an important factor in their commodification for desirable marriages, the trope becomes a prominent comic device. In Gower's adaptation of *The Pantheon* the agency of the young woman is heightened as she falls in love with the stranger, chooses him as her tutor, and then insists upon him and no other as her mate. Shakespeare picks up on the idea in *Pericles*, but also, more in the vein of a Plautine comedy, in *Taming of the Shrew*, where it is the men who are suitors and the teacherly role is divided between Lucentio (for Latin studies) and Hortensio (for music) as they disguise themselves to court Bianca. See also the device in *Comedy of Errors*, Berowne in *Love's Labours Lost*, and Gascoigne's *Supposes*, as well as Ariosto's *I Suppositi*. In Gower the girl's eagerness is fulfilled, but at a terrible price, as Fortune "slays" her, then abandons her to years of service to Diana before returning her husband and daughter to her. Other later analogues of the prince in disguise as a philosopher/teacher may be seen in Pierre Marivaux's play *The Triumph of Love* (1732) and in Gioacchino Rossini's *Barber of Seville* (1816), which is based on a play by Beaumarchais (1775).

820 ff.   ☞ **Latin marginalia**: *Qualiter filia Regis Appolinum ornato apparatu vestiri fecit, et ipse ad puelle doctrinam in quampluribus familiariter intendebat: vnde placata puella in amorem Appolini exardescens infirmabatur.* [How the king's daughter caused herself to be outfitted with ornate trappings, and he sought in many friendly ways the teaching of the girl; whereupon the girl, pleased, burned and sickened with love of Apollonius.]

829   *Of harpe, of citole, and of rote.* The citole was a stringed instrument with a rounded belly and neck with frets that is plucked as one might play a banjo or mandolin. The rote was a stringed instrument of the violin class played with a mechanical wheel, like a hurdy gurdy. It also had frets which were measured with one hand while the other cranked the wheel. The instrument was held in the lap. See Sadie, *New Grove Dictionary of Musical Instruments*.

850   *Of hire ymaginacion.* Gower softens "the harshness which pervades much of the traditional account," allowing "Apollonius and his bride to be considerably more tender and emotional than they are in [the Latin source]" (Archibald, *Apollonius of Tyre*, p. 192). Gower's focus on the bride's imagination as she tenders her thoughts characterizes his kind treatment of women throughout the poem.

866 ff.   ☞ **Latin marginalia**: *Qualiter tres filii Principum filiam Regis singillatim in vxorem suis supplicacionibus postularunt.* [How three sons of rulers in turn begged the king's daughter to be their wife.] In the original this incident occurs when the king and Apollonius are together. The king has been approached by the three suitors, but tells them they cannot visit his daughter because she is sick from too much study. He asks each to write his name and the amount of money he is prepared to offer as dowry, and he asks Apollonius to carry these petitions to her. She reads them and asks: "'Master Apollonius, are you not sorry that I am going to be married?' Apollonius said: 'No, I am delighted that now that I have taught you well and revealed a wealth of learning, by God's favour you will also

marry your heart's desire.' The girl said: 'Master, if you loved me, you would certainly be sorry for your teaching'" (Archibald, *Apollonius of Tyre*, p. 133).

875–80   *ech of hem do make a bille . . . And whan sche wiste hou that it stod . . . Thei scholden have ansuere.* Artestrathes' involvement of his daughter in the marriage decision stands in marked contrast to Antiochus' proceedings. He makes sure that she has a detailed resumé of each suitor — his name, his parentage, his wealth, but also *his oghne wille* (line 876; i.e., his personal reasons for wanting her as his bride) — so that she might make an informed decision. Then when she does make her choice her father takes her concerns seriously. See note to lines 889 ff.

889 ff.   ☞ **Latin marginalia**: *Qualiter filia Regis omnibus aliis relictis Appolinum in maritum preelegit.* [How the king's daughter chose Apollonius as husband, leaving all others behind.] In the original her letter has nothing of the suggestion in Gower's version of an agony of love that might lead to death. Instead, the letter is a forthright demand to control her own marriage even to her own economic disadvantage, a demand that does not even use conditional verbs: "volo coniugem naufragio patrimonio deceptum" [I want to marry the man who was cheated out of his patrimony by shipwreck]. Gower's version of her letter is full of conditional verbs: "Bot if I have Appolinus . . . I wol non other man abide . . . . if I of him faile . . . Ye schull for me be dowhterles" (8.898–903). In the original some modesty is recuperated by a slight riddle in her statement, which leads to a scene of discovery: the king does not know which man that is, and must then ask the other suitors if they have been shipwrecked, before asking Apollonius if he has discovered the shipwrecked man, upon which he answers, "Bone rex, si permittis, inueni" [Good king, if you allow, I have]. But in spite of this brief riddle and discovery not in Gower, generally her demand in the original shows a woman in late antiquity asserting personal will (*volo*) in defiance of economic concerns that usually governed marriage in such culture. In Gower's version there is no coy riddle about the identity of her beloved (Apollonius is mentioned outright in the note to the king), and there is no mention of the economic pressures on marriage. There is just her love, whose force is emphasized by the conditional verbs, and the careful efforts of her father to facilitate its realization.

914 ff.   ☞ **Latin marginalia**: *Qualiter Rex et Regina in maritagium filie sue cum Appolino consencierunt.* [How the king and queen consented to the marriage of their daughter with Apollonius.]

930 ff.   Macaulay notes: There is no mention of the queen in the original. The king calls his friends together and announces the marriage" (3:540).

951 ff.   ☞ **Latin marginalia**: *Qualiter Appolinus filie Regis nupsit, et prima nocte cum ea concubiens ipsam impregnauit.* [How Apollonius married the king's daughter, and, sleeping with her on the first night, impregnated her.]

952–74   Macaulay notes that the description of the wedding originates with Gower (3:540).

975 ff.   ☞ **Latin marginalia**: *Qualiter Ambaciatores a Tyro in quadam naui Pentapolim ven-*
ientes mortem Regis Antiochi Appolino nunciarunt. [How ambassadors arriving
from Tyre to Pentapolis in a certain ship announced to Apollonius the death
of King Antiochus.]

1003   In the source Apollonius is named successor to Antiochus. Macaulay observes:
"This was regarded by our author as an unnecessary complication" (3:540).

1020   *nede he mot, that nede schal*. Proverbial. Variant of Whiting N61. Compare Prol.
698 and 1.1714.

1020 ff.   ☞ **Latin marginalia**: *Qualiter Appolino cum vxore sua impregnata a Pentapoli*
versus Tyrum nauigantibus, contigit vxorem, mortis articulo angustiatam, in naui fili-
am, que postea Thaisis vocabatur, parere. [How, when Apollonius with his preg-
nant wife was voyaging from Pentapolis toward Tyre, it happened that the
wife, seized in the grip of death, gave birth in the ship to a daughter, who was
later called Thaisis.]

1054 ff.   Macaulay notes: "So far as the original can be understood, it seems to say that
the birth of the child was brought about by the storm and that the appearance
of death in the mother took place afterwards, owing to a coagulation of the
blood caused by the return of fair weather" (3:540).

1059 ff.   ☞ **Latin marginalia**: *Qualiter Appolinus vxoris sue mortem planxit*. [How Apol-
lonius mourned his wife's death.]

1059–83   Most of this section is original with Gower.

1089 ff.   Macaulay speculates: "Apparently the meaning is that the sea will necessarily
cast a dead body up on the shore, and therefore they must throw it out of the
ship, otherwise the ship itself will be cast ashore with it. The Latin says only,
'nauis mortuum non suffert: iube ergo corpus in pelago mitti' (f. 211 v°)" [a
ship will not bear a corpse: therefore order the body to be tossed into the sea]
(3:540).

1098 ff.   ☞ **Latin marginalia**: *Qualiter suadentibus nautis corpus vxoris sue mortue in qua-*
dam Cista plumbo et ferro obtusa que circumligata Appolinus cum magno thesauro vna
cum quadam littera sub eius capite scripta recludi et in mare proici fecit. [How, with
the sailors persuading him, Apollonius caused his dead wife's body to be
enclosed in a certain coffin hammered shut and wound round with lead and
iron, and, with a great treasure along with a certain letter under her head, to
be thrown into the sea.]

1122 ff.   ☞ **Latin marginalia**: *Copia littere Appolini capiti vxoris sue supposite*. [Copy of
Apollonius' letter deposited at his wife's head.]

1141 ff.   ☞ **Latin marginalia**: *Qualtier Appolinus, vxoris sue corpore in mare proiecto, Tyrum*
relinquens cursum suum versus Tharsim navigio dolens arripuit. [How Apollonius,
when his wife's body was thrown into the sea, abandoning Tyre took his course
toward Tharsis by sea voyage, mourning.]

1151–1217 Along with lines 1833–66 cited by Bullough (*Narrative and Dramatic Sources of Shakespeare*, 1.10–11; 50–54) as a probable source for the discovery of the mother section of Shakespeare's *Comedy of Errors*.

1151 ff. ☞ **Latin marginalia**: *Qualiter corpus predicte defuncte super litus apud Ephesim quidam medicus nomine Cerymon cum aliquibus suis discipulis inuenit; quod in hospicium suum portans et extra cistam ponens, spiraculo vite in ea adhuc inuento, ipsam plene sanitati restituit.* [How a certain doctor, Cerymon by name, along with some of his students, found the body of the aforesaid deceased on the shore at Ephesis; carrying it into his household and taking it out of the coffin, and finding a breath of life still in her, he restored her fully to health.]

1160 *That God wol save mai noght spille.* Proverbial. Variation of Whiting G276.

1172 *Al that schal falle, falle schal.* Proverbial. Variation of Whiting H105: "Hap what hap may."

1184 ff. Macaulay notes (3:540–41): "In the original it is not Cerimon himself, but a young disciple of his, who discovers the signs of life and takes measures for restoring her. She has already been laid upon the pyre, and he by carefully lighting the four corners of it succeeds in liquefying the coagulated blood. Then he takes her in and warms her with wool steeped in hot oil."

1222 ff. ☞ **Latin marginalia**: *Qualiter vxor Appolini sanata domum religionis peciit, vbi sacro velamine munita castam omni tempore se vouit.* [How Apollonius' wife, healed, sought a religious establishment, where she vowed to be chaste for all time, fortified by holy scripture.]

1248 The daughter introduces a kind of Cinderella motif, where, as in the fairy tale, the "stepmother" would destroy the heir for the sake of her own daughter. Macaulay observes that the daughter is apparently Gower's invention, perhaps the result of his misreading of the original "adhibitis amicis filiam sibi adoptauit," that is, in the company of friends he adopted her as his daughter (3:541).

1272 ff. ☞ **Latin marginalia**: *Qualiter Appolinus Tharsim nauigans, filiam suam Thaisim Strangulioni et Dionisie vxori sue educandam commendauit; et deinde Tyrum adiit, vbi cum inestimabili gaudio a suis receptus est.* [How Apollonius, voyaging to Tharsis, placed his daughter Thaisis with Strangulio and his wife Dionisia to be educated; and thereupon he returned to Tyre, where he was received with inestimable joy by his people.]

1295 *Thaise. Tharsia* in the source, bearing the name of the city. Macaulay notes that "the Laud MS regularly calls her Thasia," which may be the link toward Thaise (3:541).

1324 ff. ☞ **Latin marginalia**: *Qualiter Thaysis vna cum Philotenna Strangulionis et Dionisie filia omnis sciencie et honestatis doctrina imbuta est: set Thaisis Philotennam precellens in odium mortale per inuidiam a Dionisia recollecta est.* [How Thaisis along with Philotenna, daughter of Strangulio and Dionisia, was imbued with every doctrine of honorableness and science; but against Thaisis, excelling over Philotenna, was conceived a mortal hatred from Dionisia's envy.]

1349 ff.   Macaulay observes: "Much is made in the original story of the death of this nurse and of the revelation which she made to Tharsia of her real parentage. Up to this time she had supposed herself to be the daughter of Strangulio. The nurse suspected some evil, and advised Tharsia, if her supposed parents dealt ill with her, to go and take hold of the statue of her father in the market-place and appeal to the citizens for help. After her death Tharsia visited her tomb by the sea-shore every day, 'et ibi manes parentum suorum inuocabat' [and there she would invoke the ancestral gods of her parents]. Here Theophilus lay in wait for her by order of Dionysiades" (3:541).

1373 ff.   ☞ **Latin marginalia**: *Qualiter Dionisia Thaysim, vt occideretur, Theophilo seruo suo tradidit, qui cum noctanter longius ab vrbe ipsam prope litus maris interficere proposuerat, pirate ibidem prope latitantes Thaisim de manu Carnificis eripuerunt, ipsamque vsque Ciuitatem Mitelenam ducentes, cuidam Leonino scortorum ibidem magistro vendiderunt.* [How Dionisia sent Thaisis to her servant Theophilus so that she might be killed. When he had sought to kill her at night along the shore very far from town, pirates hiding near there snatched Thaisis from the executioner's hand, and leading her up to the city Mitelene, they sold her to a certain Leonine, a master of prostitutes there.]

1406   *In havene sauf and whan thei be.* "And when they were in safe haven."

1423 ff.   ☞ **Latin marginalia**: *Qualiter Leoninus Thaisim ad lupanar destinauit, vbi dei gracia preuenta ipsius virginitatem nullus violare potuit.* [How Leonine sent Thaisis to a bordello, where by the intervening grace of God no one was able to violate her virginity.]

1451–52   *this weie . . . mi weie.* "The rhyme is saved from being an identical one by the adverbial use of 'weie' in the second line, 'mi weie' being equivalent to 'aweie'" (Mac 3:542).

1477 ff.   ☞ **Latin marginalia**: *Qualiter Thaisis a lupanari virgo liberata, inter sacras mulieres hospicium habens, sciencias quibus edocta fuit nobiles regni puellas ibidem edocebat.* [How Thaisis, freed from the bordello still a virgin, taking hospitality among holy women, there taught the noble girls of the kingdom the sciences she had been taught.]

1480   *Now comen tho that come wolde.* Proverbial variant. See Tilley C529.

1498 ff.   ☞ **Latin marginalia**: *Qualiter Theophilus ad Dionisiam mane rediens affirmauit se Thaisim occidisse; super quo Dionisia vna cum Strangulione marito suo dolorem in publico confingentes, exequias et sepulturam honorifice quantum ad extra subdola coniectacione fieri constituerunt.* [How Theophilus, returning the following morning to Dionisia, affirmed that he had killed Thaisis, whereupon Dionisia, along with her husband Strangulio, dissimulating a grief in public, by treacherous contrivance caused funeral rites and a sepulcher to be made honorifically, as far as the outside world was concerned.]

1541 ff.   ☞ **Latin marginalia**: *Qualiter Appolinus in regno suo apud Tyrum existens parliamentum fieri constituit.* [How Apollonius, remaining in his kingdom at Tyre, convened a parliament.]

1560   *unkinde*. "Disloyal, ungrateful." See note to 1.2565 on lack of loyalty to kin as unnatural (*unkynde*) behavior.

1567 ff.   ☞ **Latin marginalia**: *Qualiter Appolinus post parliamentum Tharsim pro Thaise filia sua querenda adiit, qua ibidem non inventa abinde navigio recessit.* [How Apollonius after the parliament departed for Tharsis to seek his daughter Thaisis; not finding her there, he retreated thence by sea voyage.]

1590 ff.   ☞ **Latin marginalia**: *Qualiter Nauis Appolini ventis agitata portum vrbis Mitelene in die quo festa Neptuni celebrare consueuerunt applicuit; set ipse pre dolore Thaysis filie sue, quam mortuam reputabat, in fundo nauis obscuro iacens lumen videre noluit.* [How Apollonius' ship, tossed by waves, reached the port of the city Mitelene on the day when they were accustomed to celebrate Neptune's feast; but he, for sorrow for Thaisis his daughter whom he judged to be dead, threw himself in the dark hold of the ship and did not want to see the light.]

1614   *hihe festes of Neptune*. Gower provides a felicitous touch by setting the moment of Apollonius' arrival at Mitelene at the sacred feast of Neptune. This is the *peripeteia*, the moment of reversal, the mysterious turning point of the plot. The sea, like Fortune, has seemed to be Apollonius' enemy, having taken from him his ship, then his wife, and then leaving him drowning in the waves of his grief now that his daughter Thais is dead. But, like Fortune, Neptune has also been his friend, enabling him to escape the murderous Taliard, bringing him to safety at Pentapolim where he found his wife, then saving Thais from Theophilus' knife and conveying her mysteriously straight to Mitelene. It also preserved Apollonius' wife, conveying her to Ephesus. Now, through the mysterious sanctity of Neptune, the sea becomes the vehicle of his restoration — first of his lost daughter, then of his lost wife, then his kingdoms. Neptune repeatedly tests him but ultimately rewards him with all his domains.

1618 ff.   ☞ **Latin marginalia**: *Qualiter Athenagoras vrbis Mitelene Princeps, nauim Appolini inuestigans, ipsum sic contristatum nichilque respondentem consolari satagebat.* [How Athenagoras, the ruler of the city of Mitelene, searching Apollonius' ship, tried to console him, while he was sorrowing and answering nothing.]

1622   *Athenagoras*. Archibald observes: "Gower is alone in introducing Athenagoras for the first time only when Apollonius' ship arrives, thus omitting the auction and his shameful visit to the brothel" (*Apollonius of Tyre*, p. 70).

1652 ff.   ☞ **Latin marginalia**: *Qualiter precepto Principis, vt Appolinum consolaretur, Thaisis cum cithara sua ad ipsum in obscuro nauis, vbi jacebat, producta est.* [How by order of the ruler, in order that Apollonius might be consoled, Thaisis, with her harp, was led to him where he was lying in the darkness of the ship.]

1670 ff.   *many a lay*. Macaulay supplies an original example (3:543): "Her song is given in the original; it is rather pretty, but very much corrupted in the manuscripts. It begins thus,

> 'Per sordes gradior, sed sordis conscia non sum,
> Ut rosa in spinis nescit mucrone perire,' &c."

[I walk amidst corruption, but I am not conscious of corruption, / As a rose among thorns does not perish from their sharp points.]

1672–73   *he no more than the wal . . . herde.* Proverbial. See Whiting W26.

1681 ff.   See Macaulay (3:543): "Several of her riddles are given in the original story and he succeeds in answering them all at once. One is this,

> 'Longa feror uelox formose filia silue,
> Innumeris pariter comitum stipata cateruis:
> Curro uias multas, uestigia nulla relinquens.'
> [I am borne swiftly, long shapely daughter of the woods, / With an innumerable crowding horde of companions: / I run over many roads leaving no tracks.]

The answer is 'Nauis' [Ship].

She finally falls on his neck and embraces him, upon which he [strikes] her severely. She begins to lament, and incidentally lets him know her story. The suggestion contained in ll. 1702 ff., of the mysterious influence of kinship, is Gower's own, and we find the same idea in the tale of Constance, ii. 1381 ff.,

> 'This child he loveth kindely,
> And yit he wot no cause why.'"

1700 ff.   ☞ **Latin marginalia**: *Qualiter, sicut deus destinauit, pater filiam inuentam recognouit.* [How just as God had ordained, the father recognized the newfound daughter.]

1705–08   *the fader ate laste / His herte upon this maide caste, / That he hire loveth kindely, / And yit he wiste nevere why.* See Watt (*Amoral Gower*, pp. 138–40) on Gower's adaptation of his sources to heighten the resemblances between Apollonius and Antiochus.

1748 ff.   ☞ **Latin marginalia**: *Qualiter Athenagoras Appolinum de naui in hospicium honorifice recollegit, et Thaisim, patre consenciente, in vxorem duxit.* [How Athenagoras took Apollonius from the ship honorably into his household and, with her father consenting, took Thaisis as wife.]

1777 ff.   ☞ **Latin marginalia**: *Qualiter Appolinus vna cum filia et eius marito nauim ingredientes a Mitelena vsque Tharsim cursum proposuerunt. Set Appolinus in sompnis ammonitus versus Ephesim, vt ibidem in templo Diane sacrificaret, vela per mare diuertit.* [How Apollonius, traveling along with his daughter and her husband, had set his course from Mitelene for Tharsis. But Apollonius, warned in dreams, diverted his sails across the sea toward Ephesis, so that he might offer sacrifice in the temple of Diana.]

1778   *his sone tolde.* Apollonius' referring to Athenagoras here and hereafter (line 1823) simply as his *sone* bespeaks the sanctity of marriage in his piety. His sacrifice itself is given specific Christian overtones as he goes to shrift in his "holi contemplacioun" (line 1838) that leads to the "miracle" (line 1867) of his wife's resurrection. The "hole felaschipe" (line 1886) then returns to Tyre, then Mitelene and the coronation of Thais and Athenagoras, before bringing the law to Tharse.

1793   *To Ephesim*. It is noteworthy that Apollonius, having decided to take vengeance upon Dionise and Strangulio (8.1777–82), would first visit Ephesus to do his sacrifice (line 1795). This giving precedence to piety over vengeance results in the recovery of his wife.

1833 ff.   ☞ **Latin marginalia**: *Qualiter Appolinus Ephesim in templo Diane sacrificans, vxorem suam ibidem velatam inuenit; qua secum assumpta in Nauim, versus Tyrum regressus est*. [How Apollonius at Ephesus, sacrificing in the temple of Diana, found his wife there under the veil; taking her with him on the ship, he returned toward Tyre.]

1887 ff.   ☞ **Latin marginalia**: *Qualiter Appolinus vna cum vxore et filia sua Thyrum applicuit*. [How Apollonius with his wife and daughter reached Tyre.]

1912 ff.   ☞ **Latin marginalia**: *Qualiter Appolinus Athenagoram cum Thaise vxore sua super Tyrum coronari fecit*. [How Apollonius caused Athenagoras along with Thaisis his wife to be crowned over Tyre.]

1928–29   Lewis singles out these lines for their "businesslike" poetry. They could come from a traveler, a ballad, or Homer (*Allegory of Love*, pp. 206–07).

1930 ff.   ☞ **Latin marginalia**: *Qualiter Appolinus a Tyro per mare versus Tharsim iter arripiens vindictam contra Strangulionem et Dionisiam vxorem suam pro iniuria, quam ipsi Thaisi filie sue intulerunt, iudicialiter assecutus est*. [How Apollonius, taking his path from Tyre across the sea toward Tharsis, prosecuted Strangulio and Dionisia his wife for the injury that they had inflicted on his daughter Thaisis.]

1963 ff.   ☞ **Latin marginalia**: *Qualiter Artestrate Pentapolim Rege mortuo, ipsi de regno Epistolas super hoc Appolino direxerunt: vnde Appolinus vna cum vxore sua ibidem aduenientes ad decus imperii cum magno gaudio coronati sunt*. [How, with Artestrates, king at Pentapolis, having died, they sent from the kingdom letters about this to Apollonius; wherefore Apollonius and his wife arriving there are crowned with great joy, to the glory of the empire.]

1993–2002   "Gower's ideas about marriage seem to come together here. A good marriage, based on the existence of honesty, compassion, fidelity, and joy in being together (evidenced by appropriate expressions of physical affection), is the proper end for virtuous lovers" (Rytting, "In Search of the Perfect Spouse," p. 125).

1995–96   *Honesteliche*. See J. A. W. Bennett's discussion of the fitting conclusion to the poem, "Gower's 'Honeste love.'" See also the concept as it is presented in *CA* 4.1455 ff. with its celebration of the "gentil herte" (4.1457).

2009 ff.   *Confessor ad Amantem*. [The Confessor to the Lover.] See Simpson on Gower's ideal philosopher-king as the reader of the poem who "a kingdom hath to justifie" (8.2112) (*Sciences and the Self*, p. 229).

2030 ff.   ☞ **Latin marginalia**: *Confessio Amantis vnde pro finali conclusione consilium Confessoris impetrat*. [The Lover seeks the Confessor's counsel as a final conclusion.]

2039   *Danger*. A defense mechanism of the woman in *RR* who perpetually thwarts the
            ardent lover with aloofness. Guillaume de Lorris presents *Dangier* as somewhat
            gruff and crude but effective in warding off, up to a point at least, male
            aggression.

2040   *moste fere*. "Greatest fear," with an ironic pun on "closest companion." Al-
            though Gower usually spells "fiere" for "companion" (though not always), a
            homophonic pun seems likely.

2055   *leng*. The comparative form, i.e., "longer."

2063–64   Proverbial. See Whiting N49.

2068 ff.   ☞ **Latin marginalia**: *Hic super Amoris causa finita confessione, Confessor Genius
            Amanti ea que sibi salubrius expediunt, sano consilio finaliter iniungit.* [Here, with
            the confession concerning the cause of love finished, Genius the Confessor
            finally adds to his salutary counsel those things which profit him still more
            salubriously.]

2086   *Tak love where it mai noght faile*. The line resonates with the sentiments at the
            end of Chaucer's *TC*, where the narrator, just prior to the dedication to Gower,
            advises "yonge, fresshe folkes" (5.1835) to turn their love to God who made
            humankind "after his ymage" (5.1839) and asserts, "What nedeth feynede loves
            for to seke?" (5.1848).

2102–03   *fot which . . . sporneth . . . his heved hath overthrowe*. Proverbial. See Whiting F466.

2130   *love . . . that blind was evere*. Proverbial. See Tilley L506. See also *CA* 8.2794.

2146–47   *For I can do to thee no more / Bot teche thee the rihte weie*. Genius informs Amans
            that he may attempt to teach, but only Amans can learn, and that must be the
            consequence of Amans' own choice, Robins cites the passage as evidence that
            Genius, with all his exempla, can only suggest, and that otherwise "instruction
            by analogy is unpersuasive" ("Romance," p. 172).

2151 ff.   ☞ **Latin marginalia**: *Hic loquitur de controuersia, que inter Confessorem et Amantem
            in fine confessionis versabatur.* [Here he speaks about the debate between the
            Confessor and the Lover at the end of the confession.]

2189–2209   Amans' debate with Genius is perplexing in that it focuses the tension between
            reason and desire. Though Genius has consistently advocated moderation of
            desire he has, nonetheless, given Amans the opportunity to talk about — even
            indulge in — his fantasies. But now Genius puts an end to that game. Amans
            objects to Genius' looking upon his passions as a game (line 2152) but his
            reason acknowledges that Genius is right. What is most perplexing is the dis-
            covery that both sides of the debate are occurring within him. He is the site of
            the debate.

2189   *Tho was betwen mi prest and me*. Here Gower shifts his narrative point of view
            from that of a dramatic dialogue to that of an onlooking narrator, albeit still
            in the first person. The shift in tone anticipates the Lover's new perspective
            which will enable him to disengage himself from his venial infatuation so that

his love-wound might be healed. This beginning of a new objectivity is a crucial step toward the naming of "John Gower" in line 2321, which is further prelude toward his taking control of his life in full honesty.

2212–13   *teres . . . In stede of enke.* Gower's graphics of the myopic behavior suit well the melodramatic pathos of his letter.

2217 ff.   In his epistle Amans shifts into a rhyme royal stanza (the Chaucerian stanza of *TC, PF,* and the religious tales of *CT*) as if to ennoble his sentiment. See Dean, "Gower, Chaucer, and Rhyme Royal," who sees these stanzas as Gower's most Chaucerian moment. Gower also uses the stanza in his French poems and *In Praise of Peace.*

2218 ff.   ☞ **Latin marginalia**: *Hic tractat formam cuiusdam Supplicacionis, quam ex parte Amantis per manus Genii Sacerdotis sui Venus sibi porrectam acceptabat.* [Here he describes the form of a certain supplication, which, offered on the part of the Lover by the hand of Genius her priest, Venus accepted.]

2224 ff.   In his narcissism Amans imagines that all succeed in love except himself, a position often echoed by lovers in Chaucer (e.g., Aurelius' complaint to Apollo in The Franklin's Tale). As in *PF,* the problem seems to the lover to be one of Nature's doing, not his own. In constructing such debates both Chaucer and Gower draw upon sentiments expressed in Alanus de Insulis' *De Planctu Naturae* and Jean de Meun's *RR,* where Nature tires of hearing the lover's complaints and threatens to discipline his unruliness. See also line 2327, where Venus identifies his complaint not simply against her and Cupid, but against Nature also.

2230   *bot I.* A common trope. To the heartsore man, all creatures seem to have their mates but him. Compare the popular fourteenth-century song, "Fowles in the Frith," where the birds and the fishes have their happy places but "I mon waxe wod" (Luria and Hoffman, *Middle English Lyrics,* #6, p. 7).

2234–35   *and thus betwen the tweie / I stonde, and not if I schal live or deie.* Gower echoes *PF,* where the dreamer knows not whether he floats or sinks (line 7) but like an iron between two magnets of equal power (lines 148–53) is trapped in a kind of error (line 156) he seems incapable of dealing with.

2238 ff.   In this stanza Amans sees himself caught in a *tale,* a fictional circumstance like that of Pan in love. His fictitious comparison of himself with a wrestler, caught in a throw, again echoes *PF,* where Affrican compares the dreamer seeking to understand love to an observer at a wrestling match, who has opinions on the contest even though he "may nat stonde a pul" (line 164).

2264   *Danger.* See note to line 2039.

2275   *Satorne.* In some traditions the reign of Saturn is affiliated with peace and the golden age. But seldom is he benevolent to lovers, even though Venus was generated from his desire-inflamed testicles, after he was emasculated by Jupiter. The lovers in Chaucer's Knight's Tale find him to be cold, dry, devious, and malicious; he takes delight in the ruination of hopes and fantasies — "My lookyng is the fader of pestilence" (see *CT* I[A]2454–69).

2301   *I*. N.b. the shift in first person from Amans the suppliant to the narrator as he returns to a more objective outside view of himself, Cupid, Venus, and "this prest which hihte Genius" (line 2306). Though technically he is still "Amans" (see the Latin speech marker to line 2301), he will forthwith identify himself as "John Gower" (line 2321). See note to line 2320.

2303 ff.   ☞ **Latin marginalia**: *Hic loquitur qualiter Venus, accepta Amantis Supplicacione, indilate ad singula respondit.* [Here he says how Venus, accepting the Lover's supplication, unhesitantly answers point by point.]

2320   *what is mi name*. Venus' question, though "as it were halvinge a game" (line 2319), raises the fundamental identity concern of the protagonist: who exactly is he, caught up amidst his fantasies. His reply, "John Gower" (line 2321), functions as an epiphany that propels the poem's conclusion, with its detailed steps toward anagnorisis.

2330   Venus observes that Nature's domain is sublunary, but within that realm (i.e., all places under the first sphere) she is powerful. Compare Chaucer's description of her in *PF* where she rules as "the vicaire of the almyghty Lord" and stimulates creaturely desire as she would "prike yow with plesaunce" (*PF*, lines 379–89).

2339   *Agein Nature*. See White on the naturalness of the elderly Amans, rather than the unnaturalness, as most have argued. "Gower does not seem to see the universe as a place considerately arranged so that the man of goodwill shall move reasonably smoothly towards salvation; rather he sees it as a battleground on which man in his weakness must face adversaries immensely superior to him and by no means wholeheartedly committed to his spiritual good" ("Naturalness of Amans' Love," p. 321).

2378 ff.   ☞ **Latin marginalia**: *Hic in exemplum contra quoscumque viros inveteratos amoris concupiscenciam affectantes loquitur Venus, huiusque Amantis Confessi supplicacionem quasi deridens, ipsum pro eo quod senex et debilis est, multis exhortacionibus insufficientem redarguit.* [Here Venus tells an instructive example against whichever aged ones affect the lust of love, and, as if ridiculing the supplication of the Lover to Genius, she chastises him as inadequate with many exhortations, because he is old and weak.] Other MSS offer a different Latin gloss, which translates: Here he narrates how Venus, indignantly examining the infirmity of the languishing lover, exhorted him as inadequate with very many examples, as for a medicine, lest he should presume to try anything else in her court.

2379   *Rageman*. A dice game, the play of which apparently involved women and verses. See Macaulay's note (3:544–45).

2398 ff.   *I am Venus*. On Venus' conflation of the vocabulary of rural labor, business, and sexuality to deal with her assessment of Amans' impotence as a lover of the world, see Sadlek, "John Gower's *Confessio Amantis*," especially pp. 157–58.

2412   *'Min herte wolde and I ne may.'* Proverbial. Not in Whiting or Tilley.

2428–32   "When the unmasking of his senile impotence provides an unexpected moment of closure, Amans' sense of himself as a lover is belied. The logic of evaluating his life according to external goods breaks down under its own weight: such an external way of thinking is a 'thing where thou miht non ende winne' (8.2430), making Amans out to be, in Aristotle's phrase, a chameleon and weakly supported" (Robins, "Romance," p. 173). The allusion is to *Nicomachean Ethics* 1.100b6–7.

2435   *The thing is torned into was.* Fowler, *History of English Literature*, sees in this line the culmination of "a moving, terrible vision, of life threatened by irresistable and irrational impulses," where "individual tales, . . . triumphs of *refacimento*, the art of stylish re-presentation," are brought to an end" (p. 12). See also Peck, *Kingship and Common Profit*, p. 178, and Zeeman, "Framing Narrative," p. 230.

2439   *Remembre wel hou thou art old.* Zeeman ("Framing Narrative," pp. 229–33) relates the presentation of "old age as the antidote to erotic love" to the pseudo-Ovidian *De Vetula*, which circulated widely in England in the late thirteenth and fourteenth centuries. See also Burrow, "Portrayal of Amans," especially pp. 17–24; and Echard, "With Carmen's Help," p. 34: "It is not only 'Gower' who is unfit for love, nor is it only Genius who has failed to deal with Amans' dilemma — all of Genius' *auctores* have been part of the effort. None of these old men is, in the end, up to the task of dealing with human nature." The emphasis on the transformation of the lover in old age is strong in all recensions of the poem. Compare 8.*3070 and 8.2827–41. See Illustration 1, which picks up on the idea.

2442 ff.   ☞ **Latin marginalia**: *Qualiter super derisoria Veneris exhortacione contristatus Amans, quasi mortuus in terram corruit, vbi, vt sibi videbatur, Cupidinem cum innumera multitudine nuper Amantum variis turmis assistencium conspiciebat.* [How, saddened over the derisory exhortation of Venus, the Lover fell down to the earth as if dead, where, as it seemed to him, he perceived Cupid with an innumerable multitude of recent lovers with assorted crowds of attendants.]

2450   *And as I lay.* Macaulay (3:545–46) compares the situation to the Prol. to *LGW*, but suggests that it was not Gower's practice to borrow directly from "contemporary poets of his own country" (3:546).

2470   Richard II's new queen was, of course, Anne of Bohemia; thus Bohemian fashions were the current rage.

2500 ff.   *believed.* Macaulay translates *which was believed / With bele Ysolde* as "who was accepted as a lover by Belle Isolde" (2:546), suggesting the root of *believed* here to be *lief* (love) rather than *leve* (belief). In this section on the company of lovers, the lovers and their companions, as Gower presents them, are all defined by their commitments to love; thus, in the instance of traitors in love like Jason, Hercules, or even the "untrewe" Theseus who "ches" Phedra, all are defined by their last commitment, which becomes their final determination.

The effect is not so much to suggest the triumph of love as its limitation. Venus confines with labels, a rather different process of enablement from Amans' recovery of his name "John Gower" and his subsequent release from Venus' constraints.

2501 ff.   ☞ **Latin marginalia**: *De nominibus illorum nuper Amantum, qui tunc Amanti spasmato, aliqui iuuenes, aliqui senes, apparuerunt. Senes autem precipue tam erga deum quam deam amoris pro sanitate Amantis recuperanda multiplicatis precibus misericorditer instabant.* [Concerning the names of those lovers from not long ago, who then appeared, some young, some old, to the convulsed Lover. But the old ones, specifically, pityingly urged with many prayers both the God and the Goddess of love to restore the Lover's health.]

2526–27   *Ector . . . Pantaselee.* Hector is usually presented in Latin tradition as a model husband. But here he is committed to Venus' domain with Pantaselle presented as his beloved. Compare *Cinkante Balades* 43.2:9: "Unques Ector, q'ama Pantasilée."

2531–35   *And Troilus . . . his parconner.* On Gower's representation of Troilus and Criseyde, derived from Chaucer, see Mieszkowski, *Reputation of Criseyde*, pp. 100–03.

2573 ff.   *Cleopatras.* Compare Chaucer's presentation in *LGW*.

2582   *Wo worthe alle slowe.* The line is ambiguous: "Woe to the slain"; or "Woe to those who arrive late" (i.e., all slow). Thisbe has just impaled herself, but she also recognizes that she was late for the appointment.

2617–18   *alle goode / With mariage.* See Olsson, "Love, Intimacy, and Gower," pp. 82–86, on the "Foure Wyves" and their domestic roles and virtues. Olsson stresses their freedom of choosing and its liberating effects within natural and social constraints.

2705   Merry tales of Aristotle and Socrates overwhelmed by love were popular in scholastic satire of the later Middle Ages. See the *Lay of Socrates*, where a girl rides him around the college yard as a four-legged horse. That Aristotle is trapped in a "silogime" (line 2708) simply means that once the two premises (he and she) are in place, the conclusion is inevitable.

2712   *concluded.* "Determined," with an ironic pun on formal logic.

2718   *Sortes.* Macaulay notes: "It is impossible that this can be for 'Socrates,' with whose name Gower was quite well acquainted. Perhaps it stands for the well-known 'Sortes Sanctorum' (Virgilianae, &c.), personified here as a magician, and even figuring, in company with Virgil and the rest, as an elderly lover" (2:547). But Macaulay may be wrong. In *Piers Plowman* B.12.268 Socrates seems to be the one called by that name. The name appears for Socrates in *Amoryus and Cleopes.* See also Bacon, *Communium naturalium*, ed. Steele, p. 87, where Bacon, discussing Aristotle's *Metaphysics* VII on substantial gradation, refers to Socrates as "Sortis."

2749 ff.   ☞ **Latin marginalia**: *Hic tractat qualiter Cupido Amantis senectute confracti viscera perscrutans, ignita sue concupiscencie tela ab eo penitus extraxit, quem Venus postea* *absque calore percipiens, vacuum reliquit: et sic tandem prouisa Senectus, racionem inuocans, hominem interiorem per prius amore infatuatum mentis sanitati plenius restaurauit.* [Here he describes how Cupid, searching through the internal organs of the Lover, shattered by old age, entirely extracted from him the burning darts of his lust; Venus, later perceiving him to be without heat, left him empty. And thus Old Age, finally glimpsed, invoked reason in him, and very fully restored to sanity of mind the interior man who had been previously infatuated by love.]

2810   *byme.* A common single syllable morpheme for *by me*.

2819   *reins.* The kidneys are the physiological seat of the passions. See Bartholomaeus, *De renibus* 5.43, which note that from the *renes* "springiþ þe humour semynal. So seiþ Varro. For veynez and marouȝ sweten out a þynne humour into þe kideneiren [kidneys], and þat liquour is ofte resoloued by hete of Venus, and renneth and comeþ and schediþ itself anon to the place of gendringe" (*De proprietatibus rerum*, 1.254).

2821–31   *A wonder mirour . . . Wherinne anon myn hertes yhe / I caste . . . .* See Schutz's excellent discussion of Gower's application of mirroring technique to the conclusion of his poem, where the Lover (now "John Gower") discovers within himself "a mirror of self-awareness." Acteon found no such mirror and Narcissus only a distortion ("Absent and Present Images," p. 121).

2837 ff.   ☞ **Latin marginalia**: *Quod status hominis Mensibus anni equiperatur.* [That the estate of man is equivalent to the months of the year.]

2857   *erst was hete is thanne chele.* Proverbial. See Whiting H552.

2880   *So goth the fortune of my whiel.* Venus herself becomes fortune-like, yet at the same time a spokesperson of "kinde," as she clarifies her relationship with Amans.

2897   *Forget it thou, and so wol I.* The tone here is reminiscent of the all-things-shall-pass mentality of Ecclesiastes. But, more than this, remembering and forgetting are key components of Boethian psychology, where we must remember what should not have been forgotten, but also to forget what should not have preoccupied us. That Genius links his acts of remembering and letting go with that of Amans heightens the interrelationship of the two at this last point in their bifurcation prior to Genius' disappearance, along with Amans, as they are, in their reintegration in the single psyche of John Gower, to be forgotten.

2904   *A peire of bedes blak as sable.* A set of beads (not just two); a rosary (*MED paire* 2b). With the departure of Genius, and then Venus herself as she disappears "al sodeinly, / Enclosid in a sterred sky" (lines 2941–42), "John Gower" is left in repose with his prayer beads and his thoughts.

2907   *Por reposer.* See Olsson's discussion of "home, intimacy, and repose" ("Love, Intimacy, and Gower," pp. 86 ff.), and of Gower's unusual "retraction" (p. 90) as he explores the uncertainty of ever finding "perfect repose in the 'house of this world'" (p. 91).

2908   *John Gower.* Chandler ("Memory and Unity") sees this line as the culmination
        to the remembering/unity motif. See also Peck, *Kingship and Common Profit*, pp.
        179–82; and Strohm, "Note on Gower's Personas." Strohm uses Donaldson's
        notion of the three persons of Chaucer's pilgrim to explain Gower's staging
        of his threefold persona: "The substitution of John Gower for 'Sone' and
        Amans . . . marks a station on the way to lucidity and reunion of Amans with
        the broader perspective of the Poet" (p. 297). But Simpson puts the matter
        most shrewdly: "In a wonderful irony, which is itself Ovidian, the person who
        will finally be won over in the *Confessio* is not the lady, but Amans himself"
        (*Sciences and the Self*, p. 217).

2909   *ate laste cast. MED cast* n.1b: "at (one's) last throw, with (one's) back to the wall,"
        citing this line.

2926–27 *thi bokes . . . / Whiche.* Macaulay (3:547) sees a reference here to Gower's earlier
        moral treatises (*MO* and *VC*), in which case the effect is akin to Chaucer's
        Retraction as "Gower" is told to put aside his frivolous love complaint to adhere
        to his more serious literary efforts. (Chaucer had retracted his dream visions,
        Troilus, love poems, and those Canterbury Tales "that sownen into synne"
        (X[I]1085), but thanked God for his translation of *Boece*, saints' lives, homilies,
        and devotional works.) But *thi bokes* might also allude to Gower's library in
        general — these old books that still dwell among us and from which we are
        taught (see Prol.1–3), in which case the sense of 8.2927 would be "[Of] which you
        have written for many years." See Mustanoja, *Middle English Syntax*, p. 197n2,
        where *whiche* hearkens back to "an old inflected genitive" comparable to "the
        non-periphrastic dative *which* (instead of *to which*, 'to whom')." If this is the sense
        (it is the certainly the one I prefer), then we might see a different parallel with
        Chaucer than the Retraction; namely, the conclusion to the F Prologue of *LGW*,
        where Alceste and Cupid send Geoffrey back to his books with instructions to
        study them and write of virtuous wives. Here Venus, with Genius at her side,
        sends "Gower" back to his books where "vertu moral" dwells. Compare this
        attitude toward the pedagogical value of old books in Gower with the propo-
        sition on Chaucer's *PF* where old books are compared to "the olde feldes" from
        which "cometh al this newe corn" (lines 22–25). My point is not to suggest that
        one poet borrows from the other, but rather to demonstrate diverse uses of
        rhetorical formulas, particularly for conclusion, that an educated late fourteenth-
        century cohort of readers delight in and play with in like ways. See also the notes
        to 8.3106–37, 8.3138 ff., 8.3165–67, and the *Explicit*.

2938   From this point on, Fairfax 3 is copied in a new hand. The new scribe uses
        slightly different orthography. Particularly noticeable is *y* for the pronoun *I*,
        and *i* or *y* for *e* in inflections.

2940 ff. *Adieu, for y mot fro thee wende.* In the first recension of *CA*, based here on MS
        Bodley 902, lines *2941–*57 dedicate the poem to Gower's friend Geoffrey
        Chaucer, then continue to the end, with acknowledgment once again of the
        commission by King Richard and prayers on behalf of Richard. Although the
        second ending, with its emphasis on good kingship and the sending forth of
        Gower's English poem for the instruction of human kind accompanied by

prayers for England's sake, is essentially different from the first recension, several lines of the earlier conclusion remain essentially intact. Compare *2962 / 2942, *2969–70 / 2969–70 (now inverted), *2971–85 / 2971–85, *3061–63 / 3109–11, *3065–66 / 3115–16, *3067–68 / 3121–22, *3087–3106 / 3151–64, *3111–14 / 3169–72.

*2955   *his testament of love*. Middleton suggests an allusion honoring Thomas Usk's *Testament of Love* through a "fictively-displaced injunction to 'Chaucer'" ("Thomas Usk's 'Perdurable Letters,'" p. 101; see also p. 88n35). Usk was part of a coterie of writers who had celebrated the joy of literature in his addresses to Chaucer — "a *jeu d'esprit*, sheer self-delighting self-display: 'Thou hast delighted me in making'" (p. 100). Upon his brutal execution by the Lords Appellant, Middleton suggests that Usk's literary achievements could not, for fear of reprisal, be acknowledged directly — thus the compliment through their mutual friend Chaucer. If Middleton is right, the dropping of these lines from the Lancastrian version of *Confessio* in 1392, the version of the Fairfax 3 manuscript, may reflect more a political expedience regarding Usk than some breech of friendship between Gower and Chaucer, as some have argued. Henry of Lancaster was one of the Appellants.

*2965   *Hoom fro the wode*. The return home from the wood is a typical romance/dream vision conclusion as the narrator reenters his former estate, perhaps somewhat enlightened by all that has occurred. His prayers and "hole entente" (lines *2966–*67) are signs of hope.

*Notes to Latin verses iv (before line *2971). **Line 2**: The arms of England are three lions *passants guardants*, which in heraldry are also known as leopards. Normally, the plural of "scepters" would be a poetic form for "sovereignty"; but here too there is a specific heraldic referent. The scepters of countries over which a king claimed entitlement (England, Ireland, and France, for a fourteenth-century English king) were sometimes represented as part of the royal arms; the Wilton Diptych, a portable, folding altar whose subject is Richard II amidst the Virgin, Christ, saints, and angels, and which was probably commissioned for the king, shows on its exterior right wing a single crowned lion ("leopard") astride the royal banner and arms of England and France. Gower's heraldic praise of Richard here is matched by his condemnation of Richard elsewhere later. In Gower's Latin work, the *Tripartite Chronicle*, finished after Richard had been deposed by Henry Bolingbroke, Gower punningly states that Richard was "a hare and not a leopard" (*lepus est et non leopardus* — III.160).

Line 4: *What* has been "made perpetual" (*perpetuata*) may, grammatically, be either the songs (by their being sung), or England (by its being sung about).

2973 ff.   ☞ **Latin marginalia**: *Hic in anno quartodecimo Regis Ricardi orat pro statu regni, quod a diu diuisum nimia aduersitate periclitabatur.* [Here in the fourteenth year of King Richard he prays for the estate of the kingdom, which is in danger because of long-held division from excessive adversity.] The date here would be 1390. Some MSS present the marginal gloss in the Prologue, at line 21.

*2973 ff.   ☞ **Latin marginalia**: A Latin gloss appears here in the margin: *Hic in fine libri honorificos que virtuosos illustrissimi Principis domini sui Regis Anglie Ricardi secundi mores, sicut dignum est, laude commendabili describens, pro eiusdem status salubri conseruacione cunctipotentem deuocius exorat.* [Here at the end of the book describing with commendable praise, as it is worthy to do, the honorific and virtuous qualities of the most illustrious ruler his lord king of England, Richard the Second, on behalf of the safe preservation of his estate he very devoutly entreats the Almighty in prayer.]

3080–3105   *For if a kyng wol justifie . . . and be memorial.* This passage, so different from the matter of the first recension's conclusion, sets Gower's political position centrally within the ethos of moral responsibility of people in powerful positions. Compare 8.2109–20. On Gower's later thoughts on the interconnectedness of personal piety and political action, see Peck, "Politics and Psychology of Governance in Gower," pp. 218–38. On Gower's interest in kingship rather than a specific king as part of an "educative dialogue with a courtly audience," see Staley, *Languages of Power*, pp. 25–40.

*3087   *Whan game is beste, is best to leve.* A "quit-while-ahead" proverb akin to "when the game is best yt ys time to rest." See Whiting G26.

3106–37   *And now to speke as in final.* Gower announces his conclusion several times, somewhat like a classical music composition with suspended cadences and other concluding trickery. In this leave-taking he makes use of humility tropes of the sort that Chaucer mocks in the Prologue to the Franklin's Tale. Here, while writing "in Englesch . . . betwene ernest and game" (lines 3108–09), Gower hopes that "lered men" will not scorn him "for lak of curiosité" or "eloquence" (3114–15) or skills in "rethoriqe" (3117) that "Tullius" (3119) would require him "to peinte" (3118). His words are "rude" and "pleyn" (3122), partly because he is old, "feble and impotent" (3127), but in the "symplesse of my poverte" he "Desireth for to do plesance / To hem under whos governance / I hope siker to abide" (3134–37). Compare Chaucer, *CT* V(F)715–27. It is not possible to know which of the two writers wrote first; probably the two passages were written at about the same time. Whether Chaucer is mocking Gower as well as the Franklin, or whether Gower looks on the Franklin as an admirable gentleman, or whether the two writers are simply drawing upon the same conventions but in different ways is anyone's guess.

3108 ff.   ☞ **Latin marginalia**: *Hic in fine recapitulat super hoc quod in principio libri primi promisit se in amoris causa specialius tractaturum. Concludit enim quod omnis amoris delectacio extra caritatem nichil est. Qui autem manet in caritate, in deo manet.* [Here at the end he recapitulates concerning what in the beginning of the first book he promised he would particularly treat in the cause of love. For he concludes that all pleasure of love beyond charity is nothing. "Who remains in love, he remains in God."] The reference is to 1 John 4:16.

3114   *curiosité.* See Echard, "With Carmen's Help," pp. 27–29, on the interconnectedness of curiosity in the English and Latin verses.

3138 ff.   *now uppon my laste tide*. Gower announces his conclusion once again (see notes
to 8.2926–27, 3106–37, and 8.3165–67), but this one is, in truth, the last (ex-
cept for the *Explicit*). The effect is like that of a musical composition with var-
iations on a conclusion as one cadence follows another for a cumulative
ornamental effect. Each utilizes rhetorical conventions for conclusion. In this
instance see note to 8.3165–67.

3140–61   See White on Gower's use of juxtaposition to create uncertainty in the poem.
The shift here from earthly love to Christian charity underscores the sense of
failure in the poem as Amans is obliterated in a "rueful pessimism about the
possibilities of living a life that fulfills our desire to enjoy the world as well as
our obligation to live with our eyes focused on heaven" ("Division and Fail-
ure," p. 615).

3165–67   *Such love . . . Such love . . . Such love . . .* Here compare the use of anaphora for
a conclusive effect with the Epilogue to Chaucer's *TC* 5.1828–32: "Swich fin hath
. . . Swich fin hath . . . Swich fin hath . . . Swich fin hath . . . Swich fin hath."

Explicit. Line 6: *Vade liber purus*. Gower's farewell to his book ties in with a long-established
classical tradition. See Tatlock, "Epilog of Chaucer's *Troilus*," which cites ex-
amples from Ovid, *Tristia* 1.1.1; Martial, *Epigrams* 1.3.70, 3.4.5; Statius, *Silvae*
4.4; and the *Greek Anthology* 12.208; as well as vernacular examples in
Provençal and Old French lyrics, Dante, Petrarch, and, especially, Boccaccio,
whose *Teseida* 12.84, *Filostrato* 9.1, *Fiammetta* 9, and the endings of *Corbaccio*,
Filocolo, and *De Casibus Virorum Illustrum* all served as sources for Chaucer and
other English writers. Tatlock makes no mention of Gower's *Explicit*. Neither
does Schoeck in his "'Go Little Book,'" or Andrews in his "Go Little Book,"
who, after discussion of *TC* 5.1786, proceeds to note examples from Hoccleve,
Caxton, James I (in *Kingis Quair*), Hawes, and other later writers. But it is
important to note Gower's commissioning of his book is not to kiss the steps
of "Virgile, Ovide, Omer, Lucan, and Stace," as in *TC* 5.1792 but rather to
make its way to Henry of Lancaster, count of Derby, whose political influence,
Gower opines, might help to establish a reign of peace and repose — a happy
future that Gower would, with little confidence, presume to imagine.

❦ TEXTUAL NOTES

ABBREVIATIONS: **A**: Bodleian Library MS Bodley 902 (*SC* 27573), fols. 2r–183r; **B**: Bodleian Library MS Bodley 294 (*SC* 2449), fols. 1r–197r; **C**: Corpus Christi College, Oxford MS 67, fols. 1r–209r; **F**: Bodleian Library MS Fairfax 3 (*SC* 3883; copy text for this edition), fols. 2r–186r; **J**: St. John's College, Cambridge MS B.12 (34), fols. 1r–214r; **Mac**: G. C. Macaulay; **S**: Stafford, now Ellesmere 26, fols. 1r–169v; **T**: Trinity College, Cambridge MS R.3.2 (581), fols. 1r–147v.

TEXTUAL NOTES TO PROLOGUE

1	*Of.* F: *Off.* The scribe usually writes *ff* to indicate a capital letter, as in the first letter of the first words of lines 4, 66, 89, etc., which I have simply transcribed as *F.* But he occasionally writes *-ff* for *-f* in medial and terminal positions. Here, as in line 93, where the words begin sections of the poem, the point is, perhaps, to capitalize the whole word as a section marker — i.e., *OF* and *IF.*
29–30	Omitted in S.
*34–*35	☞ **Latin marginalia**: line 2: *Regis Anglie Ricardi secundi.* So Mac. B omits.
*65	*onwrong every.* So Mac. B: *outkrong eny.* J: *outkrong euery.*
*75	*Which.* B: *What.* Most other good MSS, including J and F, read *Which*, so I have followed Mac's emendation here.
*77	*may.* So B. J: *myht.* Mac emends to *myhte*, as in F, though several other manuscripts read *may.* So I have left the subjunctive in the idiom of the Bodley 294 scribe.
80	*office.* So S, Mac. F: *officie.*
83	*amendement.* So S, F. Mac: *amendment.*
113	*word.* So F, J, Mac. S, B: *world.*
147–320	Omitted in S (missing leaf).
149	*whiche.* So F. B, Mac: *which.* J: *wheche.*
173	*resoun.* So B, Mac, F, J: *reson.*
201	*erthly.* So J, Mac. F: *ertly.* B: *eorþely.*
249	*which.* So B, Mac. F: *wich.* J: *wheche.*
280	*pacience.* So B, J, Mac. F: *paciencie.*
370	*argumenten.* So S, B, J, Mac. F: *argumeten.*
419	*com.* So F, S, J. B, Mac: *come.*
495–98	Omitted in S, B, J.
579–84	Omitted in S, B, J.
581	*ben.* So F. Mac: *be.*

588   *sent*. So S, B, J, Mac. F: *send*.
592   *Til*. So F, S, B. J: *Tyl*. Mac: *Till*.
723   *chivalrie*. So F. J: *cheualrie*. Mac emends to *chivalerie* from S, B for purposes
            of meter. The stress would fall on the second syllable.
772   *Lombardy*. F, S: *Lombardȝ*. B: *Lumbards*. J: *Lombardi*. Mac: *Lombardz*.
865   Omitted in B.
957   *mistorneth*. So S, Mac. F: *mistornieth* (or, perhaps, *mistormeth*). B, J: *mystorneþ*.
1046   *ful*. So F, S, B. J: *foll*. Mac: *full*.
1055–end   Omitted in S (lost leaf).
1078   *waxeth*. So J, Mac. F: *waxed*. B: *wexeþ*.

TEXTUAL NOTES TO BOOK 1

1–106   Omitted in S (lost leaf).
17   *no man*. Here and elsewhere in the MS the scribe writes *noman*. I have reg-
            ularly expanded the compound into two words, according to modern
            usage.
19   *to moche . . . to lite*. F: *tomoche . . . tolite*. Here and hereafter I expand such
            compounds into two words. See note to line 17.
125   *Thow*. So F. S, B, J, Mac: *Thou*.
130   *wis man*. F: *wismam*. S, B, Mac: *wisman*. J: *wysmon*.
154   *sone*. F usually capitalizes *Sone* and Mac always does when it refers to Amans.
            I have followed modern practice and ignored the capital.
183   *thanne wold*. So F, S. J: *þenne wold*. B: *þan wold*. Mac emends to *than wolde*.
234   *Mi sone*. So S. F: *Mi sone sone*. B, J, Mac: *My Sone*.
293   *the*. So S, B, J, Mac. F: *ther*.
295   *shryve*. So F. S: *schryue*. B, Mac: *shrive*. J: *schriue*.
298   *mispended*. So F. S: *mysdespended*. B, J: *mysdispended*. Mac emends to *misdis-
            pended*; but *hadde* is disyllabic and the emendation is unnecessary.
310   *manye such a man*. So F. S, A, Mac: *manye suche a man*. B: *many such a man*. J:
            mony such a mon.
334 ff.   ☞ **Latin marginalia**: line 4: *superveniens*. So Mac. F reads *superueveniens* (the
            repetition of *ve* occurs at a line break).
335   *whilom*. So S, B, J, Mac. F: *whilon*.
355   *throstle*. So S, B, Mac. F: *Trostle*. J: *þrestele*.
377   *houndes*. So S, J, B, Mac. F: *hondes*.
393–94   *constellacioun . . . nacioun*. So S, B. F: *constellacioun . . . nacion*. J, Mac: *con-
            stellacion . . . nacion*.
397   *bore*. So S, B, J, Mac. F: *bothe*. I have followed Mac's emendation on the basis
            of other MSS, but also because of the mention of *nativité* in line 392.
483 ff.   ☞ **Latin marginalia**: line 5: *pertransiit*. So F. Mac: *pertransiuit*. Mac's form,
            while certainly the more common, is not necessary given the legitimacy
            of F.
531   *myht*. So S, J, Mac. F: *myhte*. B: *might*.
Latin verses v (before line 575). **Line 1**: *Aquila que*. F: *Aquilaque*.
580   *ferste*. So S, Mac. F, J: *ferst*. B: *first*. I have followed S to maintain the parallel
            in line 585.

584	*I.* So S, B, J, Mac. Omitted by F.
631–814	Omitted in J.
673	Ornamental capital on *Ther*; thus my division at the syntactic break.
823	*wynne.* So B, J, Mac. F: *wynme.* S: *winne.*
1023	*seid.* So S, A, Mac. F: *seide.* B, J: *seyd.*
1068	*tobroken.* So F. S, B, J, Mac: *tobreken.*
1172	*Synon.* So S, B, J, Mac. F: *Symon.*
1216	*which.* So S, B, Mac. F: *wich.* J: *whech.*
1225	*Bot.* So S, Mac. F: *Byt.* B: *But.* J: *Bote.*
1257	*schalt.* So S, B, Mac. F: *schat.* J: *shalt.*
1301	*Mi.* So F, S. B, J, Mac: *My.*
1344 ff.	☞ **Latin marginalia**: line 2: *deseruiunt.* So Mac. F: *deseruiant* (induced by preceding *ut*).
1345	*Compleignte.* So S, Mac. F, J: *Compleingte.* B: *compleynte.*
1378	*Compleignte.* So S, Mac. F, J: *Compleingte.* B: *compleignt.*
1403–06	Lines only in third recension. Others (S, B, J) have: *And in ensample of þis matiere / A tale I fynde as þou schalt hiere* (text from B).
1464	Omitted in B.
1500	*othre.* So F, S. B, J, Mac: *other.* But see 1.1496.
1625	*th'unsemylieste.* So F, S. B: *þunsemelieste.* J: *þe vnsemelieste.* Mac: *thunsemlieste.*
1648	*Gif his ansuere.* So F. S: *ȝive his ansuere.* B, Mac: *Yive his answere.* J: *ȝeue his answere.*
1719	*womanhiede.* So F. S, Mac: *wommanhiede.* B: *wommanhede.* J: *wommonhede.*
1747	*Sche.* So F, S, B. J: *Heo.* Mac: *She.*
1785	*fole.* So F, S, B, J, Mac: *foule.*
1881–82	Omitted in S.
2017–20	S has only two lines: *Wherof þou miht þiselue lere / I þenke telle as þou schalt hiere.*
2043	*Thei.* So Mac. F: *That.* S: *þe.* B: *þey.* J: *They.*
2105	*And.* So S, B, J, Mac. F: *An.*
2159	*Here.* So S, Mac. F: *Hire.* B: *Her.* J: *Heor.*
2171	*sherte.* So F. S: *schert.* B, J, Mac: *scherte.*
2267–74	This transition was altered in the third recension. Others (S, B, J) have: *Forþi eschew it I þe rede / For in Ouide a tale I rede / how þat a man was ouertake / Wherof þou might ensample take* (text from B).
2311–12	*branche . . . stanche.* So F. S, B, J, Mac: *braunche . . . staunche.*
2343–58	Omitted in S, B, J.
2360	*alle.* So F, S, J, B. Mac: *all.*
2369–72	Omitted in S, B, J.
2398	*have his wille.* Mac emends to *have al his wille*, from S, B, J. Metrically the emendation is unnecessary if *scholde* is disyllabic.
2457	*myhte.* So F, S. B: *might.* J, Mac: *myht.*
2460	*ferst.* So F, J. S, Mac: *ferste.*
2462 ff.	☞ **Latin marginalia**: line 14: *Ravenni.* So F. Mac: *Rauennensis.*
2676	*Til.* So F, S, B. J: *Tyl.* Mac: *Till.* See also 8.370.
Latin verses x (before line 2681). **Line 5:** *scit.* So B, Mac. F, S, J: *sit.*
2713–14	Lines only in third recension. Others (S, B, J) have: *So ouerglad þat purgatoire / Ne might abregge his veinegloire* (text from B).

2827	*ek.* So F, S. B: *eek.* J, Mac: *eke.*
2829	*tree.* So F, S, B, J. Mac: *tre.*
2847	*thurghknowe.* So A, Mac. F: *thurgknowe.* S, B: *thurgh knowe.* J: *þorouh knowe.*
2932	*exposicioun.* So S, B, Mac. F, J: *exposicion.*
3068 ff.	☞ **Latin marginalia**: line 5: *obtinuit.* So Mac. F: *obtitinuit.*
3351	*mai.* So S, J, Mac. F: *mar.* B: *may.*
3357	*sesed.* So S, B, J, Mac. F: *seled.*
3398	*sene.* So Mac. F, S: *scene.* B: *seene.* J: *schene* (omits *was*).

TEXTUAL NOTES TO BOOK 8

1–336	Omitted in S (lost leaves).
3 ff.	☞ **Latin marginalia**: line 1: *Postquam ad.* So Mac. F: *Postquam ad ad* (second *ad* repeated after line break).
201 ff.	☞ **Latin marginalia**: line 7: *pudicicia.* So Mac. F: *pudicia* (loss of letters by eye-skip).
237	*grete.* So F, B, J. A, C, Mac: *gret.*
416	*avised of.* F: *auised of of.*
466 ff.	☞ **Latin marginalia**: *mare.* So Mac. F omits at line break.
535	*He.* So S, B, J, Mac. F: *His.*
975	*spousailes.* So S, B, Mac. F: *spousales.* J: *sposailes.*
1024	*lenger.* So S, B, J, Mac. F: *lengerr.*
1029	*schipe.* So F, S, J. B, Mac: *schip.*
1039	*thei.* So F, S. B, Mac: *they.*
1047	*here.* So S, A, C, Mac. F, J: *hire.* B: *her.*
1055	*delivered.* So S, J, B, Mac. F: *deliiled.*
1069	*I.* So S, B, J, Mac. F: *it.*
1088	*take.* So F, S, B, J. Mac: *tak.*
1110	*sich.* So B, J, Mac. F, S: *such. sich* is found nowhere else in F, but I have followed B, J, and Mac for the sake of rhyme.
1177	*thei.* So S, B, J, Mac. F: *þe.*
1212	*Wher.* So F, S, B, J. Mac: *Where.*
1252	Omitted in B.
1498 ff.	☞ **Latin marginalia**: line 3: *confingentes.* So Mac. F: *configentes* (macron omitted or no longer visible).
1575	*Thei.* So F, S, J. B, Mac: *They.*
1650	*were.* So F, S, B, J. Mac: *weren.*
1687	*madd man.* So S, Mac. F: *madd mad man.* B: *mad man.* J: *mad mon.*
1890	*thei.* So F, S, J. B, Mac: *they.*
1999	*as it is write.* So F. S, B, J, Mac: *his lif was write.*
2106	*so befalle.* So B, J, Mac. F: *so be befalle.* Eyeskip from previous line.
2367–68	Omitted in S.
2369–70	Lines altered in S: *Noght al as þou desire woldest / Bot so as þou be resoun scholdest.*
2371–76	Omitted in S.
2462	*sih.* So S, Mac. F, J: *syh.* The line is omitted in B.
2481	*soon.* So F. Mac silently emends to *soun* from S, B, J, which improves the sense but not the rhyme.

2938–3146	A new hand picks up the copying of the poem in F.
2938–66	Written over an erasure in F.
2946	*here.* B, Mac: *hire.*
*2960	*word.* So J, Mac. A: *world,* as in other first recension MSS.
2970	*live.* So S, B, Mac. F: *lieve.*
2989	*live.* So S, B, Mac. F: *lieve.* I have followed Mac's emendation, though *lieve* is certainly possible, especially if the religious rather than the social implication is being emphasized. See also note to line 2970.
2994	*worldes.* So B, Mac. F: *wordles.* S: *worldis.*
3037	*marchandie.* So B, Mac. F: *machandie.* S: *merchandie.*
3094	*wite it.* So S, B, Mac. F: *wite ?t.*
3108 ff.	☞ **Latin marginalia**: line 1: *libri primi.* So Mac. F omits *primi.*
3147–end	Another new hand picks up the copying of the poem in F.

✣ BIBLIOGRAPHY

Aarne, Antti. *The Types of the Folk-Tale: A Classification and Bibliography*. Trans. and enlarged by Stith Thompson. New York: B. Franklin, 1971.

Aers, David. "Reflections on Gower as '*Sapiens* in Ethics and Politics.'" In Yeager, 1998. Pp. 185–201.

Anatomy of Guy de Chauliae. In *An Interpolated Middle English Version of the Anatomy of Guy de Chauliae*. Ed. Björn Wallner. Lund: Lund University Press, 1995.

Andrews, John S. "Go Little Book." *Notes and Queries* 197 (1952), 413.

Archibald, Elizabeth, ed. and trans. *Apollonius of Tyre: Medieval and Renaissance Themes and Variations, Including a Text and Translation of 'The Historia Apollonii Regis Tyrii.'* Cambridge: D. S. Brewer, 1991.

Augustine. *On Christian Doctrine*. Trans. D. W. Robertson, Jr. Indianapolis: Bobbs-Merrill, 1958.

———. *The Trinity*. Trans. Stephen McKenna. Fathers of the Church 45. Washington, DC: Catholic University Press of America, 1963.

———. *Confessions*. Trans. with introduction and notes by Henry Chadwick. Oxford: Oxford University Press, 1991.

Averroës. *Averrois Cordubensis Commentarium Magnum in Aristotelis De Anima Libros*. Ed. F. Stuart Crawford. Cambridge, MA: The Medieval Academy of America, 1953.

Avianus. "The Fables of Avianus." In *Minor Latin Poets*. Ed. and trans. J. Wight Duff. Loeb Classical Library. Latin Authors 284. Cambridge, MA: Harvard University Press, 1968.

———. *The Fables of Avianus*. Trans. David R. Slavitt. Baltimore: The Johns Hopkins University Press, 1993.

Bacon, Roger. *Communium naturalium*. Ed. Robert Steele. Oxford: Clarendon Press, 1909.

Bakalian, Ellen Shaw. *Aspects of Love in John Gower's Confessio Amantis*. London: Routledge, 2004.

Baker, Denise N. "The Priesthood of Genius: A Study of the Medieval Tradition." *Speculum* 51 (1976), 277–91.

Baldwin, John. "The Medieval Merchant at the Bar of Canon Law." *Papers of the Michigan Academy of Science, Arts, and Letters* 44 (1959), 287–99.

Bartholomaeus Anglicus. *De proprietatibus rerum*. See Trevisa, below.

Batchelor, Patricia. "Feigned Truth and Exemplary Method in the *Confessio Amantis*." In Yeager, 1998. Pp. 1–16.

Beidler, Peter G., ed. *John Gower's Literary Transformations in the Confessio Amantis: Original Articles and Translations*. Washington, DC: University Press of America, 1982.

Beidler, Peter G. "Transformations in Gower's *Tale of Florent* and Chaucer's *Wife of Bath's Tale*." In Yeager, 1991. Pp. 100–14.

Bennett, J. A. W. "Gower's 'Honeste love.'" In *Patterns Of Love and Courtesy: Essays in Memory of C. S. Lewis*. Ed. John Lawlor. London: Edward Arnold, 1966. Pp. 107–21.

Bennett, Michael J. "The Court of Richard II and the Promotion of Literature." In *Chaucer's England: Literature in Historical Context*. Ed. Barbara Hanawalt. Minneapolis: University of Minneapolis Press, 1992. Pp. 3–20.

Benoît de Sainte-Maure. *Le roman de Troie*. Ed. Léopold Constans. 6 vols. Société des anciens textes français. Paris: Librairie de Firmin-Didot et cie, 1904–12.

Berchorius, Petrus (Pierre Bersuire). *Ovidius moralizatus*. Werkmateriaal 1. Utrecht: Rijkuniversiteit, Instituut voor Laat Latijn, 1962.

Bloomfield, Morton W. *The Seven Deadly Sins: An Introduction to the History of a Religious Concept, with Special Reference to Medieval English Literature.* East Lansing: Michigan State College Press, 1952.

Boccaccio, Giovanni. *Genealogie deorum gentilium libri.* Ed. Vincenzo Romano. 2 vols. Scrittor d'Italia 200–01. Bari: G. Laterza, 1951.

———. *Boccaccio on Poetry: Being the Preface and the Fourteenth and Fifteenth Books of Boccaccio's Genealogia deorum gentilium in an English Version with Introductory Essay and Commentary.* Ed. and trans. Charles Osgood. New York: Liberal Arts Library, 1956.

Boethius, Anicius Manlius Severinus. *Boethius: The Theological Tractates with English Translation by H. F. Stewart and E. K. Rand; The Consolation of Philosophy with English Translation of "I. T." (1609) Revised by H. F. Stewart.* Loeb Classical Library. London: William Heinemann, 1918.

———. *Philosophiae Consolatio.* Ed. Ludovicus Bieler. Corpus Christianorum, Series Latina 94. Turnholt: Brepols, 1957. [For the Middle English translation that Gower doubtless knew, see Chaucer, "Boece," *Works*, pp. 395–469.]

Bowers, John. *The Crisis of Will in Piers Plowman.* Washington, DC: Catholic University Press of America, 1986.

The Brut, or The Chronicles of England. Ed. Friedrich W. D. Brie. 2 vols. EETS o.s. 131, 136. Bungay, UK: Richard Clay and Co., 1906–08. Rpt. London: Oxford University Press, 1960–71.

Bryan, W. F., and Germaine Dempster, eds. *Sources and Analogues of Chaucer's Canterbury Tales.* London: Routledge and Kegan Paul, 1941.

Bühler, Curt F. "'Wirk alle thyng by conseil.'" *Speculum* 24 (1949), 410–12.

Bullough, Geoffrey. *Narrative and Dramatic Sources of Shakespeare.* 8 vols. New York: Columbia University Press, 1957–75.

Burke, Linda Barney. "Women in John Gower's 'Confessio Amantis.'" *Mediævalia* 3 (1977), 239–59.

———. "The Sources and Significance of the 'Tale of King, Wine, Women, and Truth' in John Gower's *Confessio Amantis.*" *Greyfriar* 21 (1980), 3–15.

———. "Genial Gower: Laughter in the *Confessio Amantis.*" In Yeager, 1989. Pp. 39–64.

Burrow, John A. *Ricardian Poetry: Chaucer, Gower, Langland and the Gawain Poet.* London: Routledge and Kegan Paul, 1971.

———. "The Portrayal of Amans in *Confessio Amantis.*" In Minnis, 1983. Pp. 5–24.

Carruthers, Mary J. *The Book of Memory: A Study of Memory in Medieval Culture.* Cambridge: Cambridge University Press, 1990.

Chance, Jane. See Nitzsche, Jane Chance.

Chandler, Katherine R. "Memory and Unity in Gower's *Confessio Amantis.*" *Philological Quarterly* 71 (1992), 15–30.

Chaucer, Geoffrey. *The Riverside Chaucer.* Third edition. Gen. ed. Larry D. Benson. Boston: Houghton Mifflin, 1987.

Clarke, Edwin, and Kenneth Dewhurst. *An Illustrated History of Brain Function.* Oxford: Sanford Publications, 1972.

Clarke, Maude V. *Fourteenth Century Studies.* Oxford: Clarendon Press, 1937.

Coffman, George R. "John Gower in His Most Significant Role." In *Elizabethan Studies and Other Essays in Honor of George F. Reynolds.* University of Colorado Studies. Series B, Studies in the Humanities vol. 2, no. 4. Boulder: University of Colorado Press, 1945. Pp. 52–61.

———. "John Gower, Mentor for Royalty: Richard II." *PMLA* 69 (1954), 953–64.

Coleman, Janet. *Medieval Readers and Writers 1350–1400.* New York: Columbia University Press, 1981. [See especially "John Gower's Complaint," pp. 126–56.]

Copeland, Rita. *Rhetoric, Hermeneutics, and Translation in the Middle Ages: Academic Traditions and Vernacular Texts.* Cambridge Studies in Medieval Literature 11. Cambridge: Cambridge University Press, 1991.

Correale, Robert M. "Gower's Source Manuscript of Nicholas Trevet's *Les Cronicles.*" In Yeager, 1989. Pp. 133–57.

Craun, Edwin D. *Lies, Slander, and Obscenity in Medieval English Literature: Pastoral Rhetoric and the Deviant Speaker*. Cambridge: Cambridge University Press, 1997. [See, especially, ch. 4: "Confessing the Deviant Speaker: Verbal Deception in the *Confessio Amantis*," pp. 113–56.]

Cursor Mundi: A Northumbrian Poem of the XIVth Century. Ed. Richard Morris. 7 vols. EETS o.s. 57, 59, 62, 66, 68, 99, 101. Oxford: Oxford University Press, 1874–93; rpt. 1961–66.

Damian-Grint, Peter. "*Estoire* as a Word and Genre." *Medium Ævum* 66 (1997), 189–206.

Dean, James. "Gather Ye Rosebuds: Gower's Comic Reply to Jean de Meun." In Yeager, 1989. Pp. 21–37.

———. "Gower, Chaucer, and Rhyme Royal." *Studies in Philology* 88 (1991), 251–75.

———, ed. *Medieval English Political Writings*. Kalamazoo, MI: Medieval Institute Publications, 1996.

Dictys, Cretensis. *Dictys Cretensis et Dares Phrygius De Bello Trojano*. Delphin Classics. London: A. J. Valpy, 1825.

Dihle, Albrecht. *The Theory of Will in Classical Antiquity*. Berkeley: University of California Press, 1982.

Dimmick, Jeremy. "'Redinge of Romance' in Gower's *Confessio Amantis*." In *Tradition and Transformation in Medieval Romance*. Ed. Rosalind Field. Cambridge: D. S. Brewer, 1999. Pp. 125–37.

Donaldson, E. Talbot. *Speaking of Chaucer*. New York: W. W. Norton, 1972.

Donavin, Georgiana. *Incest Narratives and the Structure of Gower's Confessio Amantis*. English Literary Studies Monograph Series 56. Victoria, BC: University of Victoria, 1993.

Early English Versions of the Gesta Romanorum. Ed. Sidney J. H. Herrtage. EETS e.s. 33. London: Oxford University Press, 1962.

Echard, Siân. "Pre-Texts: Tables of Contents and the Reading of John Gower's *Confessio Amantis*." *Medium Ævum* 66 (1997), 270–87.

———. "Glossing Gower: In Latin, in English, and *in absentia*: The Case of Bodleian Ashmole 35." In Yeager, 1998. Pp. 237–56.

———. "With Carmen's Help: Latin Authorities in the *Confessio Amantis*." *Studies in Philology* 95 (1998), 1–40.

———, ed. *A Companion to Gower*. Cambridge: D. S. Brewer, 2004.

Echard, Siân, and Claire Fanger. *The Latin Verses in the Confessio Amantis*. See Gower, John.

Economou, George. "The Character *Genius* in Alain de Lille, Jean de Meun, and John Gower." *Chaucer Review* 4 (1970), 203–10.

Edwards, A. S. G. "Selection and Subversion in Gower's *Confessio Amantis*." In Yeager, 1998. Pp. 257–67.

Emmerson, Richard K. "Reading Gower in a Manuscript Culture: Latin and English in Illustrated Manuscripts of the *Confessio Amantis*." *Studies in the Age of Chaucer* 21 (1999), 143–86.

Esch, Arno. "John Gower's Narrative Art." Trans. Linda Barney Burke. In Nicholson, 1991. Pp. 81–108. First published as "John Gowers Erzählkunst." In *Chaucer und seine Zeit: Symposion für Walter F. Schirmer*. Ed. Arno Esch. Tübingen: Niemeyer, 1968. Pp. 207–39. [Considers narrative practice in "The Tale of Rosiphilee," "Albinus and Rosemund," and "The Tale of Constance."]

Farnham, Anthony E. "The Art of High Prosaic Seriousness: John Gower as Didactic Raconteur." In *The Learned and the Lewed: Studies in Chaucer and Medieval Literature*. Ed. Larry D. Benson. Harvard English Studies 5. Cambridge, MA: Harvard University Press, 1974. Pp. 161–73.

Ferster, Judith. *Fictions of Advice: The Literature and Politics of Counsel in Late Medieval England*. Philadelphia: University of Pennsylvania Press, 1996. [See, especially, ch. 7: "O Political Gower," pp. 108–36.]

Fisher, John H. *John Gower, Moral Philosopher and Friend of Chaucer*. New York: New York University Press, 1964.

Fowler, Alastair. *A History of English Literature*. Cambridge, MA: Harvard University Press, 1987.

Fox, George F. *Mediaeval Sciences in the Works of John Gower*. Princeton, NJ: Princeton University Press, 1931. Rpt. New York: Haskell House, 1966.

Fox, Hilary E. "'Min herte is growen into ston': Ethics and Activity in John Gower's *Confessio Amantis*." *Comitatus* 36 (2005), 15–40.

Fredell, Joel. "Reading the Dream Miniature in the *Confessio Amantis*." *Medievalia et Humanistica* 22 (1995), 61–93.

Gallacher, Patrick J. *Love, the Word, and Mercury: A Reading of John Gower's Confessio Amantis*. Albuquerque: University of New Mexico Press, 1975.

Galloway, Andrew. "The Rhetoric of Riddling in Late-Medieval England: The 'Oxford' Riddles, the *Secretum Philosophorum*, and the Riddles of *Piers Plowman*." *Speculum* 70 (1985), 68–105.

———. "Gower in His Most Learned Role and the Peasants' Revolt of 1381." *Mediaevalia* 16 (1993), 329–37.

———. "The Making of a Social Ethic in Late-Medieval England: From *Gratitudo* to 'Kyndeness.'" *Journal of the History of Ideas* 55 (1994), 365–83.

———. "Middle English Poetics in the Circle of H. E. L." *Studies in Medieval and Renaissance Teaching* 13 (2006). Forthcoming.

Geoffrey of Vinsauf. *Poetria Nova of Geoffrey of Vinsauf*. Trans. Margaret Nims. Toronto: Pontifical Institute of Mediaeval Studies, 1967.

Gesta Romanorum. Trans. Charles Swan. London: George Routledge and Sons, Ltd., 1905. [Latin version; for English versions, see *Early English Versions of the Gesta Romanorum*.]

Godfrey of Viterbo. *Pantheon, sive Memoria Sæculorum*. *Patrologia Latina*. Ed. J.-P. Migne. Paris: Migne, 1855. Parts 16–20. Vol. 198, cols. 871–1044.

———. "Cronica de Apollonio," from the *Pantheon*. In Samuel Singer, *Apollonius Von Tyrus*. Halle: Max Niemeyer, 1895. Pp. 150–77.

Goodall, Peter. "John Gower's *Apollonius of Tyre*: *Confessio Amantis*, Book VIII." *Southern Review* [Australia] 15 (1982), 243–53.

Goolden, P. "Antiochus's Riddle in Gower and Shakespeare." *RES* 6 (1955), 245–51.

Gower, John. *The Complete Works of John Gower*. Ed. G. C. Macaulay. 4 vols. Oxford: Clarendon Press, 1899–1902. Vols. 2 and 3 rpt. as *The English Works of John Gower*. EETS e.s. 81–82. London: K. Paul, Trench, Trubner and Co., Ltd., 1900–01; rpt. Oxford University Press 1957, 1969. [Vol. 1 is the French works; vol. 4 is the Latin works.]

———. *The Major Latin Works of John Gower: The Voice of One Crying [Vox Clamantis], and The Tripartite Chronicle*. Trans. Eric. W. Stockton. Seattle: University of Washington Press, 1962.

———. *Confessio Amantis (The Lover's Shrift)*. Ed. and trans. Terence Tiller. Baltimore: Penguin Books, 1963.

———. *Confessio Amantis, by John Gower*. Ed. Russell A. Peck. New York: Holt, Rinehart & Winston, 1968. Rpt. Medieval Academy Reprints for Teaching. Toronto: University of Toronto Press, 1980. [Selections.]

———. *Selections from John Gower*. Ed. J. A. W. Bennett. Oxford: Clarendon Press, 1968.

———. *The Latin Verses in the Confessio Amantis: An Annotated Translation*. Ed. and trans. Siân Echard and Claire Fanger. With a preface by A. G. Rigg. East Lansing, MI: Colleagues Press, 1991.

———. *Mirour de l'Omme (The Mirror of Mankind)*. Trans. William Burton Wilson. Rev. Nancy Wilson Van Baak. East Lansing, MI: Colleagues Press, 1992.

———. *Confessio Amantis*. Ed. Russell A. Peck, with Latin translations by Andrew Galloway. 3 vols. Kalamazoo, MI: Medieval Institute Publications, 2000–04.

———. *In Praise of Peace*. Ed. Michael Livingston. With *The Minor Latin Works*. Ed. and trans. Yeager.

———. *The Minor Latin Works*. Ed. and trans. R. F. Yeager. Kalamazoo, MI: Medieval Institute Publications, 2005.

Grady, Frank. "Gower's Boat, Richard's Barge, and the True Story of the *Confessio Amantis*: Text and Gloss." *Texas Studies in Language and Literature* 44 (2002), 1–15.

Grant, Mary A., ed. and trans. *The Myths of Hyginus*. Lawrence: University of Kansas Press, 1960. [Includes *Fabulae* 1–277 and *Poetica astronomica*, Book 2.1–43.]

Green, Eugene. "Speech Acts and the Art of the Exemplum in the Poetry of Chaucer and Gower." In *Literary Computing and Literary Criticism: Theoretical and Practical Essays on Theme and Rhetoric*. Ed. Rosanne G. Potter. Philadelphia: University of Pennsylvania Press, 1989. Pp. 167–87.

Green, Richard Firth. *A Crisis of Truth: Literature and Law in Ricardian England*. Philadelphia: University of Pennsylvania Press, 1999.

Griffiths, Jeremy. "*Confessio Amantis*: The Poem and Its Pictures." In Minnis, 1983. Pp. 163–78.

Guido de Columnis [Guido delle Colonne]. *Historia Destructionis Troiae*. Ed. Nathaniel Edward Griffin. Cambridge, MA: The Mediaeval Academy of America, 1936.

———. *Historia Destructionis Troiae*. Trans. Mary Elizabeth Meek. Bloomington: Indiana University Press, 1974.

Guillaume de Deguileville. *The Pilgrimage of the Life of Man*. Trans. John Lydgate. Ed. F. J. Furnivall and Katharine B. Locock. EETS e.s. 77, 83, 92. London: Kegan Paul, Trench, Trübner, 1899, 1901, 1904.

Hahn, Thomas. "Old Wives Tales and Masculine Intuition." In *Retelling Tales: Essays in Honor of Russell Peck*. Ed. Thomas Hahn and Alan Lupack. Cambridge: D. S. Brewer, 1997. Pp. 91–108.

———, ed. *Sir Gawain: Eleven Romances and Tales*. Kalamazoo, MI: Medieval Institute Publications, 1995.

Hamilton, George L. "Gower's Use of the Enlarged *Roman de Troie*." *PMLA* 20 (1905), 179–96.

———. "Some Sources of the Seventh Book of Gower's *Confessio Amantis*." *Modern Philology* 9 (1912), 323–46.

———. "Studies in the Sources of Gower." *Journal of English and Germanic Philology* 26 (1927), 491–520.

Hanawalt, Barbara A. "Whose Story Was This? Rape Narratives in Medieval English Courts." In "*Of Good and Ill Repute*": *Gender and Social Control in Medieval England*. New York: Oxford University Press, 1998. Pp. 124–41.

Harbert, Bruce. "Lessons from the Great Clerk: Ovid and John Gower." In *Ovid Renewed: Ovidian Influences on Literature and Art from the Middle Ages to the Twentieth Century*. Ed. Charles Martindale. Cambridge: Cambridge University Press, 1988. Pp. 83–97.

Higden, Ranulf. *Polychronicon Ranulphi Higden. Monachi Cestrensis; together with English Translations of John Trevisa and an Unknown Writer of the Fifteenth Century*. Vols. 1–2, ed. Churchill Babington; vols. 3–9, ed. Joseph Rawson Lumby. 9 vols. Rolls Series 41. London: Longman & Co., 1865–86. [See also "The English *Polychronicon*: A Text of John Trevisa's Translation of Higden's *Polychronicon*, based on Huntington MS. 28561." Ed. Richard Arthur Seeger. 2 vols. Ph.D. dissertation, University of Washington, 1975.]

Hines, John. *Fabliau in English*. London: Longmans, 1993.

Hiscoe, David W. "The Ovidian Comic Strategy of Gower's *Confessio Amantis*." *Philological Quarterly* 64 (1985), 367–85.

Hyginus. *Fabularum liber*. Basel, 1553. Rpt. New York: Garland, 1976. [Includes *De planetis*.]

———. *Fabulae*. [See Grant, above.]

———. *Poetica astronomica*. [See Grant, above.]

Jacquart, Danielle, and Claude Thomasset. *Sexuality and Medicine in the Middle Ages*. Trans. Matthew Adamson. Princeton, NJ: Princeton University Press, 1988.

Jacques de Vitry. *The Exempla or Illustrative Stories from the Sermones Vulgares of Jacques de Vitry*. Ed. Thomas Frederick Crane. London: D. Nutt, 1890. Rpt. New York: B. Franklin, 1971.

Johannes de Hauvilla. *Architrenius*. Ed. and trans. Winthrop Wetherbee. Cambridge: Cambridge University Press, 1994.

Jonson, Ben. *Ben Jonson*. Ed. C. H. Herford, Percy Simpson, and Evelyn Mary Spearing Simpson. 11 vols. Oxford: Clarendon Press, 1925–52.

Kaeuper, Richard W. *Bankers to the Crown: The Riccardi of Lucca and Edward I*. Princeton, NJ: Princeton University Press, 1973.

Katz, Dennis M., trans. *The Romances of Alexander*. New York: Garland, 1991.

Kelly, Henry Ansgar. *Love and Marriage in the Age of Chaucer*. Ithaca, NY: Cornell University Press, 1975.

Kerby-Fulton, Kathryn, and Steven Justice. "Langlandian Reading Circles and the Civil Service in London and Dublin, 1380–1427." *New Medieval Literatures* 1 (1997), 59–83.

Kibler, William. *An Introduction to Old French*. New York: Modern Language Association, 1984.

Kolve, V. A. *Chaucer and the Imagery of Narrative: The First Five Canterbury Tales*. Stanford, CA: Stanford University Press, 1984.

Langland, William. *Piers Plowman. A Parallel-Text Edition of the A, B, C and Z Versions. Volume I. Text*. Ed. A. V. C. Schmidt. London: Longman, 1995.

Laskaya, Anne, and Eve Salisbury, eds. *The Middle English Breton Lays*. Kalamazoo, MI: Medieval Institute Publications, 1995.

Latham, R. E. *Revised Medieval Latin Word-List*. Oxford: Oxford University Press, 1965; rpt. 1980.

Latini, Brunetto. *Li Livres dou tresor*. Ed. Francis Carmody. Berkeley: University of California Press, 1948.

Lawton, David. "Dullness and the Fifteenth Century." *English Literary History* 54 (1987), 761–99.

Lewis, C. S. *The Allegory of Love: A Study in Medieval Tradition*. Oxford: Clarendon Press, 1936. Pp. 198–222.

Lindahl, Carl. "The Oral Undertones of Late Medieval Romance." In *Oral Tradition in the Middle Ages*. Ed. W. F. H. Nicolaisen. Binghamton, NY: Medieval and Renaissance Texts and Studies, 1995. Pp. 59–75.

Little, Lester. "Pride Goes before Avarice: Social Change in Latin Christendom." *American Historical Review* 76 (1971), 16–49.

Lopez, Robert Sabatino. *The Commercial Revolution of the Middle Ages 950–1350*. Cambridge: Cambridge University Press, 1976.

Luria, Maxwell S., and Richard Hoffman. *Middle English Lyrics*. New York: W. W. Norton, 1974.

Lynch, Kathryn L. *The High Medieval Dream Vision: Poetry, Philosophy, and Literary Form*. Stanford. CA: Stanford University Press, 1988.

Macaulay, G. C. "The *Confessio Amantis*." In *The Cambridge History of English Literature*. Vol. 2: *The End of the Middle Ages*. Ed. A. W. Ward and A. R. Waller. Cambridge: Cambridge University Press, 1908. Pp. 166–76.

Machan, William. "Thomas Berthelette and Gower's *Confessio*." *Studies in the Age of Chaucer* 18 (1996), 143–45.

Mainzer, Conrad. "John Gower's Use of the 'Medieval Ovid' in the *Confessio Amantis*." *Medium Ævum* 41 (1972), 215–29.

Mast, Isabelle. "Rape in John Gower's *Confessio Amantis* and Other Related Works." In *Young Medieval Women*. Ed. Katherine J. Lewis, Noël James Menuge, and Kim M. Phillips. New York: St. Martin's Press, 1999. Pp. 103–32.

Mathew, Gervase. *The Court of Richard II*. London: John Murray, 1968.

McKisack, May. *The Fourteenth Century: 1307–1399*. Oxford: Clarendon Press, 1959.

Middleton, Anne. "The Idea of Public Poetry in the Reign of Richard II." *Speculum* 53 (1978), 94–114.

———. "Thomas Usk's 'Perdurable Letters': The *Testament of Love* from Script to Print." *Studies in Bibliography* 51 (1998), 63–116.

Mieszkowski, Gretchen. *The Reputation of Criseyde: 1155–1500*. Hamden, CT: Archon, 1971.

Minnis, A. J. "Late-Medieval Discussions of *Compilatio* and the Role of the *Compilator*." *Beiträge zur Geschichte der deutschen Sprache und Literatur* 101 (1979), 385–91.

———. "John Gower, *Sapiens* in Ethics and Politics." *Medium Ævum* 49 (1980), 207–29.

———, ed. *Gower's 'Confessio Amantis': Responses and Reassessments*. Cambridge: D. S. Brewer, 1983.

———. *Medieval Theory of Authorship: Scholastic Literary Attitudes in the Later Middle Ages*. Second edition. Philadelphia: University of Pennsylvania Press, 1988.

———. "De Vulgari Auctoritate: Chaucer, Gower and Men of Great Authority." In Yeager, 1991. Pp. 36–74.

Mitchell, J. Allan. *Ethics and Exemplary Narrative in Chaucer and Gower*. Woodbridge, UK: D. S. Brewer, 2004.

Mustanoja, Tauno. *A Middle English Syntax*. Part I: Parts of Speech. Helsinki: Société Néophilologique, 1960.

Myles, Robert. *Chaucerian Realism*. Woodbridge, UK: D. S. Brewer, 1994.

Nicholson, Peter. "Gower's Revisions of the *Confessio Amantis*." *Chaucer Review* 19 (1984), 123–43.

————. "The Dedications of Gower's *Confessio Amantis*." *Mediaevalia* 10 (1984), 159–80.

————. *An Annotated Index to the Commentary on Gower's Confessio Amantis*. Binghamton, NY: Medieval and Renaissance Texts & Studies, 1989.

————, ed. *Gower's Confessio Amantis: A Critical Anthology*. Cambridge: D. S. Brewer, 1991.

————. *Love and Ethics in Gower's Confessio Amantis*. Ann Arbor: University of Michigan Press, 2005.

Nims, Margaret. "*Translatio*: 'Difficult Statement' in Medieval Poetic Theory." *University of Toronto Quarterly* 43 (1974), 215–30.

Nitzsche, Jane Chance. *The Genius Figure in Antiquity and the Middle Ages*. New York: Columbia University Press, 1975.

Oesterley, Hermann. *Gesta Romanorum*. Berlin: Weidmann, 1872.

Olsen, Alexandra Hennessey. "*Betwene Ernest and Game*": The Literary Artistry of the Confessio Amantis. New York: Peter Lang, 1990.

Olsson, Kurt. "Natural Law and John Gower's *Confessio Amantis*." In *Gower's Confessio Amantis: A Critical Anthology*. Ed. Peter Nicholson. Suffolk, UK: Boydell and Brewer, 1991. Pp. 181–213. First published in *Medievalia et Humanistica* n.s. 11 (1982), 229–61.

————. *John Gower and the Structures of Conversion: A Reading of the Confessio Amantis*. Cambridge: D. S. Brewer, 1992.

————. "Love, Intimacy, and Gower." *Chaucer Review* 30 (1995), 71–100.

Owen, Charles A., Jr. *Pilgrimage and Storytelling in the Canterbury Tales*. Norman, OK: University of Oklahoma Press, 1977.

Oxford English Dictionary. Second edition. Ed. J. A. Simpson and E. S. C. Weiner. Oxford: Clarendon Press, 1989.

Parkes, M. B., and A. I. Doyle. "The Production of Copies of the *Canterbury Tales* and the *Confessio Amantis* in the Early Fifteenth Century." In *Medieval Scribes, Manuscripts, and Libraries: Essays Presented to N. R. Ker*. Ed. M. B. Parkes and A. G. Watson. London: Scolar Press, 1978. Pp. 163–210.

Parkes, Malcolm. "Patterns of Scribal Activity and Revisions of the Text in Early Copies of Works by John Gower." In *New Science out of Old Books: Manuscripts and Early Printed Books: Essays in Honour of A. I. Doyle*. Ed. Richard Beadle and A. J. Piper. London: Scolar, 1995. Pp. 81–121.

Paulus Diaconus. *Historia Langobardorum*. [N. p.]: P. Maglione, 1934.

Pearsall, Derek. "Gower's Narrative Art." *PMLA* 81 (1966), 475–84.

————. *Gower and Lydgate*. Harlow, UK: Longmans, Green & Company, 1969.

————. "The Gower Tradition." In Minnis, 1983. Pp. 179–97.

————. "Gower's Latin in the *Confessio Amantis*." In *Latin and Vernacular: Studies in Late-Medieval Texts and Manuscripts*. Ed. A. J. Minnis. York Manuscripts Conferences: Proceedings Series, 1989. Vol. 1, pp. 13–25.

Peck, Russell A. *Kingship and Common Profit in Gower's Confessio Amantis*. Carbondale: Southern Illinois University Press, 1978.

————. "Social Conscience and the Poets." In *Social Unrest in the Late Middle Ages*. Ed. Francis X. Newman. Binghamton, NY: Medieval and Renaissance Texts and Studies, 1986. Pp. 113–48.

————. "John Gower and the Book of Daniel." In Yeager, 1989. Pp. 159–87.

————. "The Problematics of Irony in Gower's *Confessio Amantis*." *Mediaevalia* 15 (1993 for 1989), 207–29.

————. "The Phenomenology of Make Believe in Gower's *Confessio Amantis*." *Studies in Philology* 91 (1994), 250–70.

————. "The Politics and Psychology of Governance in Gower: Ideas of Kingship and Real Kings." In Echard (2004). Pp. 215–38.

————. "Folklore and Powerful Women in Gower's Tale of Florent." Forthcoming in *The English "Loathly Lady" Tales: Boundaries, Traditions, Motifs*. Ed. S. Elizabeth Passmore and Susan Carter. Kalamazoo, MI: Medieval Institute Publications.

Peter, John. *Complaint and Satire in Early English Literature*. Oxford: Clarendon Press, 1956.

Petrarch. *Letters from Petrarch*. Trans. Morris Bishop. Bloomington: Indiana University Press, 1966.

Porter, Elizabeth. "Gower's Third Microcosm and Political Macrocosm." In Minnis, 1983. Pp. 135–62.

Reich, Rosalie, ed. *Tales of Alexander the Macedonian* (ספר אלכסנדרוס מוקדון): *A Medieval Hebrew Manuscript Text and Translation with a Literary and Historical Commentary*. New York: KTAV Publishing, 1972.

Robins, William. "Romance, Exemplum, and the Subject of *The Confessio Amantis*." *Studies in the Age of Chaucer* 19 (1997), 157–81.

Roman de Fauvel. Ed. Arthur Langförs. Paris: Société des anciens textes français, 1914.

Runacres, Charles. "Art and Ethics in the *Exempla* of *Confessio Amantis*." In Minnis, 1983. Pp. 106–34.

Rytting, Jenny Rebecca. "In Search of the Perfect Spouse: John Gower's *Confessio Amantis* as a Marriage Manual." *Dalhousie Review* 82 (2002), 113–26.

Sadie, Stanley. *The New Grove Dictionary of Musical Instruments*. New York: Grove's Dictionaries of Music, 1984.

Sadlek, Gregory M. "John Gower's *Confessio Amantis*, Ideology, and the 'Labor' of 'Love's Labor.'" In Yeager, 1998. Pp. 147–58.

Salisbury, Eve. "Remembering Origins: Gower's Monstrous Body Poetic." In Yeager, 1998. Pp. 159–84.

Saul, Nigel. *Richard II*. New Haven: Yale University Press, 1997.

Scanlon, Larry. *Narrative, Authority, and Power: The Medieval Exemplum and the Chaucerian Tradition*. Cambridge: Cambridge University Press, 1994. Pp. 245–97.

———. "The Riddle of Incest: John Gower and the Problem of Medieval Sexuality." In Yeager, 1998. Pp. 93–127.

Schaff, Philip, ed. *A Select Library of the Nicene and Post-Nicene Fathers of the Christian Church*. First Series. 14 vols. New York: Christian Literature, 1886–90; rpt. Edinburgh: T&T Clark, 1991–97.

Schmitz, Götz. "Rhetoric and Fiction: Gower's Comments on Eloquence and Courtly Poetry." In Nicholson, 1991. Pp. 117–42. First published as "Rhetorik und Poetik: Gowers Äusserungen zur Rede- und Dichtkunst." In *The Middel Weie: Stil- und Aufbauformen in John Gowers "Confessio Amantis."* Studien zur Englischen Literatur, Band 11. Bonn: Bouvier, 1974. Pp. 27–54.

———. "Gower, Chaucer, and the Classics: Back to the Textual Evidence." In Yeager, 1989. Pp. 95–111.

Schoeck, R. J. "'Go Little Book' — A Conceit from Chaucer to William Mededith." *Notes and Queries* 197 (1952), 370–72.

Schueler, Donald G. "Gower's Characterization of Genius in the *Confessio Amantis*." *Modern Language Quarterly* 33 (1972), 240–56.

Schutz, Andrea. "Absent and Present Images: Mirrors and Mirroring in John Gower's *Confessio Amantis*." *Chaucer Review* 34 (1999), 107–24.

Scott, Florence R. "Chaucer and the Parliament of 1386." *Speculum* 18 (1943), 80–86.

Severs, J. Burke. "The Antecedents of *Sir Orfeo*." In *Studies in Medieval Literature in Honor of Professor Albert Croll Baugh*. Ed. MacEdward Leach. Philadelphia: University of Pennsylvania Press, 1961. Pp. 187–207.

Shakespeare, William. *Pericles*. Ed. F. D. Hoeniger. The Arden Edition of *The Works of William Shakespeare*. Cambridge, MA: Harvard University Press, 1963.

Shaw, Judith. "Gower's Illustrative Tales." *Neuphilologische Mitteilungen* 84 (1983), 437–47.

———. "The Role of the Shared Bed in John Gower's Tales of Incest." *English Language Notes* 26 (1989), 4–7.

Sidrak and Bokkus. Ed. T. L. Burton. EETS o.s. 311–12. Oxford: Oxford University Press, 1998–99.

Simpson, James. "Ironic Incongruence in the Prologue and Book I of Gower's *Confessio Amantis*." *Neophilologus* 72 (1988), 617–32.

———. *Sciences and the Self in Medieval Poetry: Alan of Lille's Anticlaudianus and John Gower's Confessio Amantis*. Cambridge: Cambridge University Press, 1995.

Solinus. *The excellent and pleasant worke, Collectanea rerum memorabi lium of Caius Julius Solinus*. Trans. Arthur Golding. A facsimile reproduction with intro. by George Kish. Gainesville, FL: Scholars' Facsimiles and Reprints, 1955.

Sorabji, Richard. *Aristotle on Memory*. London: Dentworth, 1972.

Spitzer, Leo. "Note on the Poetic and Empirical 'I' in Medieval Authors." *Traditio* 4 (1946), 417–18.

Staley, Lynn. "Gower, Richard II, Henry of Derby, and the Business of Making Culture." *Speculum* 75 (2000), 68–96.

———. *Languages of Power in the Age of Richard II*. University Park: Pennsylvania State University, 2005.

Statius. *Statius*. Trans. J. H. Mozley. 2 vols. Loeb Classical Library. Cambridge, MA: Harvard University Press, 1982. [Vol. 1: *Thebaid I–IV*; vol. 2: *Thebaid V–XII*.]

———. *P. Papini Stati Thebaidos Libri XII*. Ed. D. E. Hill. Lugduni Batavorum: E. J. Brill, 1983.

Stow, George B. "Richard II in John Gower's *Confessio Amantis*: Some Historical Perspectives." *Mediaevalia* 16 (1993), 3–31.

Strohm, Paul. "Form and Social Statement in *Confessio Amantis* and the *Canterbury Tales*." *Studies in the Age of Chaucer* 1 (1979), 17–40.

———. "A Note on Gower's Personas." In *Acts of Interpretations: The Text in its Contexts 700–1600. Essays on Medieval and Renaissance Literature in Honor of E. Talbot Donaldson*. Ed. Mary J. Carruthers and Elizabeth D. Kirk. Norman, OK: Pilgrim Books, 1982. Pp. 293–98.

———. "Politics and Poetics: Usk and Chaucer in the 1380s." In *Literary Practice and Social Change in Britain, 1380–1530*. Ed. Lee Patterson. Berkeley: University of California Press, 1990. Pp. 83–112.

———. "The Textual Vicissitudes of Usk's 'Appeal.'" In *Hochon's Arrow: The Social Imagination of Fourteenth-Century Texts*. Princeton, NJ: Princeton University Press, 1992. Pp. 145–60.

Suetonius. *Suetonius*. Trans. J. C. Rolfe. 2 vols. Loeb Classical Library. Cambridge, MA: Harvard University Press, 1998. [Vol. 1 contains *Lives of the Caesars*, Books I–IV; Vol. 2 contains *Lives of the Caesars*, Books V–VIII and *Lives of Illustrious Men*.]

Summers, Joanna. "Gower's *Vox Clamantis* and Usk's *Testament of Love*." *Medium Ævum* 68 (1999), 55–62.

Tatlock, John S. P. "The Epilog of Chaucer's *Troilus*." *Modern Philology* 18 (1921), 625–59.

Thompson, Stith. *Motif-Index of Folk-Literature; A Classification of Narrative Elements in Folktales, Ballads, Myths, Fables, Mediaeval Romances, Exempla, Fabliaux, Jest-Books, and Local Legends*. 6 vols. Bloomington: Indiana University Press, 1955–57.

Thorpe, Lewis. "A Source of the 'Confessio Amantis.'" *Modern Language Review* 43 (1948), 175–81.

Tilley, Morris Palmer. *A Dictionary of Proverbs in England in the Sixteenth and Seventeenth Centuries*. Ann Arbor: University of Michigan Press, 1950.

Tinkle, Theresa. *Medieval Venuses and Cupids: Sexuality, Hermeneutics, and English Poetry*. Stanford, CA: Stanford University Press, 1996. [See ch. 7: *Remedia Amoris*, pp. 178–97, on Gower.]

Trevisa, John. *The Governance of Kings and Princes: John Trevisa's Middle English Translation of the De regimine principum of Aegidius Romanus*. Ed. David C. Fowler, Charles F. Briggs, and Paul G. Remley. Garland Medieval Texts 19. Garland Reference Library of the Humanities 1778. New York: Garland, 1997.

———. *On the Properties of Things: John Trevisa's Translation of Bartholomaeus Anglicus De proprietatibus rerum*. Gen. ed. M. C. Seymour. 3 vols. Oxford: Clarendon Press, 1975–88.

———, trans. *Polychronicon*. See Higden, above.

Usk, Thomas. *The Testament of Love*. Ed. R. Allen Shoaf. Kalamazoo, MI: Medieval Institute Publications, 1998.

Vatican Mythographers I–III. *Scriptores Rerum Mythicarum Latini Tres Romae Nuper Reperti*. Ed. Georgius Henricus Bode. Göttingen: Cellis, 1854; rpt. Hildesheim: Georg Olms, 1968. [Vat. Myth. I–III.]

———. *Mythographi Vaticani I et II*. Ed. Peter Kulcsar. Corpus Christianorum, Series Latina 91c. Turnholt: Brepols, 1987.

Walsingham, Thomas. *The St. Albans Chronicle, 1406–1420*. Ed. V. H. Galbraith. Oxford: Clarendon Press, 1937.

Watt, Diane. *Amoral Gower: Language, Sex, and Politics*. Medieval Cultures 38. Minneapolis: University of Minnesota Press, 2003.

The Westminster Chronicle, 1381–1394. Ed. and trans. L. C. Hector and Barbara F. Harvey. Oxford: Clarendon Press, 1982.

Wetherbee, Winthrop. "The Theme of Imagination in Medieval Poetry and the Allegorical Figure of 'Genius.'" *Medievalia et Humanistica*, n.s. 7 (1976), 45–61.

———. "Genius and Interpretation in the 'Confessio Amantis.'" In *Magister Regis: Studies in Honour of Robert Earl Kaske*. Ed. Arthur Groos. New York: Fordham University Press, 1986. Pp. 241–60.

———. "Constance and the World in Chaucer and Gower." In Yeager, 1989. Pp. 65–94.

———. "Latin Structure and Vernacular Space: Gower, Chaucer, and the Boethian Tradition." In Yeager, 1991. Pp. 7–35.

———. "John Gower." In *The Cambridge History of Medieval English Literature*. Ed. David Wallace. Cambridge: Cambridge University Press, 1999. Pp. 589–609.

White, Hugh. "The Naturalness of Amans' Love in *Confessio Amantis*." *Medium Ævum* 56 (1987), 316–22.

———. "Division and Failure in Gower's *Confessio Amantis*." *Neophilologus* 22 (1988), 600–16.

———. *Nature, Sex, and Goodness in a Medieval Literary Tradition*. Oxford: Oxford University Press, 2000.

Whiting, Bartlett Jere, and Helen Wescott Whiting. *Proverbs, Sentences, and Proverbial Phrases: From English Writings Mainly before 1500*. Cambridge, MA: Belknap Press of Harvard University Press, 1968.

Wills, Garry. "Augustine's Magical Decade." *New York Review of Books* 46, no. 8. May 6, 1999. Pp. 30–32.

———. *St. Augustine*. The Penguin Lives Series. New York: Viking Penguin Group, 1999.

Yates, Frances A. *The Art of Memory*. London: Routledge and Kegan Paul, 1966.

Yeager, R. F. "'Oure englisshe' and Everyone's Latin: *The Fasciculus Morum* and Gower's *Confessio Amantis*." *South Atlantic Review* 46 (1981), 41–53.

———. "John Gower and the *Exemplum* Form: Tale Models in the *Confessio Amantis*." *Mediaevalia* 8 (1982), 307–35.

———. "John Gower and the Uses of Allusion." *Res Republica Litterarum* 7 (1984), 201–13.

———, ed. *John Gower: Recent Readings*. Studies in Medieval Culture 26. Kalamazoo, MI: Medieval Institute Publications, 1989.

———. *John Gower's Poetic: The Search for a New Arion*. Cambridge: D. S. Brewer, 1990.

———, ed. *Chaucer and Gower: Difference, Mutuality, Exchange*. Victoria, BC: University of Victoria, 1991.

———. "Learning to Speak in Tongues: Writing Poetry for a Trilingual Culture." In Yeager, 1991. Pp. 100–14.

———. "'Scripture Veteris Capiunt Exempla Futuri': John Gower's Transformation of a Fable of Avianus." In *Retelling Tales: Essays in Honor of Russell Peck*. Ed. Thomas Hahn and Alan Lupack. Woodbridge, UK: D. S. Brewer, 1997. Pp. 341–54.

———, ed. *Re-Visioning Gower*. Asheville, NC: Pegasus Press, 1998.

York Plays: The Plays Performed by the Crafts of Mysteries of York on the Day of Corpus Christi in the 14th, 15th, and 16th Centuries. Ed. Lucy Toulmin Smith. New York: Russell & Russell, 1963.

Yunck, John A. *The Lineage of Lady Meed: The Development of Medieval Venality Satire*. Notre Dame, IN: University of Notre Dame Press, 1963.

Zeeman, Nicolette. "The Framing Narrative of *Confessio Amantis*." *Medium Ævum* 60 (1991), 222–40.

⚜ GLOSSARY

abide, abyde(n) *wait, remain, endure*
achieve *finish, succeed, settle*
acompten *include; tell; confess; compute; evaluate*
acorde *agree*
adresce *arrange, prepare, array*
affeccioun *inclination*
afferme *fix, confirm, establish*
agein *against*
algate *in every respect, unceasingly, especially*
alther gen. of *all*
and conj., occasionally placed medially rather than at the head of a coordinated clause
appel *appeal to a higher authority; accuse*
aquite *free; repay, give, make amends, relieve; deprive*
asterte *escape*
awaite(n) *watch; lie in ambush*
axe *ask, ask for; demand*

barme *bosom*
be *by*
be(n) *be, been; am, are*
beclippe, beclipt *embrace(d); contain(ed)*
beheste *promise; assurance*
behote *promised, assured, pronounced, dedicated*
benyme *take away*
beschrewe *curse*
beste *beast*
betake *give, deliver, command*
beyete(n) *gain, property, possession; acquire, obtain, provide; beget*

bille *letter*
bot *except, unless, only*
bote *reward, remedy, help*

chiere *face, looks, countenance; welcome*
childinge *childbirth*
clepeth *calls*
coign *coin, money*
colour *color, manner, pretext, reason*
compasse *devise, contrive; undertake; surround; consider, achieve*
comune *common people; commonwealth; ordinary, familiar*
comune(n) *participate, conform; have dealings with; communicate*
conne *know, know how; be able to*
couthe *could; understood; knew how*
covine *company; agreement; devise, conspiracy*
cunnynge *skilled*
cure *charge of a parish; care, help, remedy; trouble, grief*

dai, dawe *day*
dampne *condemn*
dar, dorste, durste *dare(d)*
debat *strive, dispute*
debate *contend*
decas *destruction*
dede *did; dead; deed*
defence, defense *prohibition, protection*
defend *protect, forbid*
del, diel *part, portion*
dele(n) *have to do, consult*
delivere *active; readily*
deme *judge, condemn; decide*
dere *harm, injure*

dere, diere *dear; precious*
descrive *describe*
despuile *rob, strip*
do *cause, make, put*
dom *judgment*
drye *endure, suffer; experience*
duc, duck, duk *duke, leader*

echon *each one*
eft *after*
eir *air*
ek(e) *also*
engin(e) *disposition, ingenuity; deceive,*
    entrap
entaile *form, fashion, sculpture*
entente *meaning; intention, purpose,*
    thought
er(e) *ear; before*

faitour *deceiver, imposter, cheat; one*
    who is false or feigns
feint *false, sluggish, deceitful; faint*
fele *many*
fere, fiere *companion;* **in fiere** *together*
ferst *first*
fette(n) *fetch, get*
finde, fint, fond *find (found),*
    invent(ed), provide(d)
fol *fool; foolish*
fonde *try, attempt*
fordo *destroy; condemn; render useless;*
    blot out
forlore, forlorn *utterly lost*
fre *free person*
fro *from*

gate *gate, gateway; passage; road, path,*
    street
gaude(s) *ornamental beads in a rosary;*
    bawble; finery, fripperies
gere *fighting equipment, harness;*
    clothes; behavior
gesse *infer, conclude; discern; suppose*
gete(n) *get; beget*
glas *mirror*
good *good; wealth; kindness*
gove(n) *give; given*

grucche *complain*

ha *interjection*
haveles *destitute, without possessions*
hele *heal; conceal, cover*
hem *them; themselves*
here *their; here; hear*
heste *command*
heved *head*
hewe *hue*
hie *hasten*
hiere *hear*
hihte *was called*
his *his; its*
hol, hool, hole *whole; wholly*
honeste *honorable, noble, appropriate,*
    truthful
honesté *honorableness, worthiness;*
    splendor, elegance, comeliness; virtue,
    decency
hote(n), hatte *be named; be called;*
    command, order, bid; promise

ilke *same*
Irahel *Israel*
irous *angry, wrathful*
iwiss *truly, certainly*

jape *joke, trick, deception; to behave*
    foolishly; fondle; have sexual
    intercourse
jolif *lusty, frolicsome, amorous*
juel *jewel*
juise *judgment, punishment*

kepe *care*
kesse, kiste *kiss(ed)*
kinde *nature, manner, race; natural,*
    kind
kiste *chest*

lacche *seize*
laghtere *laughter*
large *wide, liberal*
latoun *bronze*
laude *praise*
lawhe *laugh*

leche *physician, remedy*
leiance *allegiance*
leie, lein *lay, set, apply*
lemman *lover*
lere *loss*
lere, liere *learn, teach, guide*
les *lie, falsehood*
lese *lose*
lesinge *lie, lying, falsehood*
lief *dear, pleasant*
lieve *believe, trust*
likned *compared*
list *like, desire*
loenge *praise*
longe *belong*
lore n. *learning, teaching;* v. *lost*
loure *frown*
loute *bow, yield*
low, lowh *laugh*
lust *desire, charm, pleasure*

maister *scholar, tutor, official*
make *mate, match; fashion*
makinge *making, composing*
malgré *in spite of*
manyon *many a one*
marche *border*
mased *amazed, confused*
mede *reward, gift, bribe; worldly gain;*
  meadow
medle *mingle*
memoire *memory*
men *people*
mete *food*
mete(n) *meet; dream*
mochel *great*
molde *earth; fashion*
mone *moan, lament; moon; companion*
mote *must*
mowe *may, be able to, might*
muable *changing, easily moved*
myht *might; strength, prowess*

n- sometimes attached to words to
  indicate the negative: e.g., **not** =
  ne+wot (knows not); **nyste** =
  ne+wyste (knew not)

nacioun *country, people, group, race*
nam *am not*
nam, nom *took*
nest *nest; next*
newe *new; renew; newly*
niht, nyht(e) *night; become night*
non *noon*
nyce, nice *foolish, fastidious, delicate*
nyh *near*

of *of, from, by, by reason of*
of *off*
oghne *own*
on *on, in*
on *one;* **in on** *united, without ceasing*
or, er(e) *before*
or *or;* **or . . . or** *either . . . or, whether*
  . . . or

paie *pay, please, satisfy*
part(e) *part; divide, distribute, depart,*
  share
parti *variegated; colorful*
pas *step, pace, gait; road, passageway*
peine *pain, punishment, endeavor;*
  suffer, take pains, be troubled
peise *weigh*
per, par *by, for, through or by means of*
pes *peace*
plat *plainly, flatly, entirely, frankly*
plein *full; plain, smooth, simple; fully,*
  plainly
pourchace *procure, seek; endeavor,*
  succeed
prest *priest*
pris *value, prize, fame, renown, praise*
privé *secret*
propre *proper, own, appropriate*
pure *unalloyed, excellent, honest,*
  absolute; entirely

queinte *clever, wise; curious, crafty,*
  cunning, gentle
querele *dispute, altercation, cause,*
  claim, enterprise
qweme *please, be pleasing*

rape *haste; hasten; rape*

rathere *sooner*

real *royal*

recche, rowhte, roghte *care for, heed*

rede(n) *read, take counsel, contemplate; advise*

rote *custom, condition*

rote *a medieval musical instrument, probably of the violin class*

roune *whisper*

routhe *pity, compassion*

rowe *row, company; dawn;* **be rowe** *in order*

ryht *right; justice*

sawe *saying, speech*

schape(n), schope(n) *shape, contrive, prepare, bring about; create*

sche, scheo *she*

schent *harmed, ruined*

schrifte *confession*

schrive(n) *confess, hear confession, absolve, receive absolution*

se, seth, sih(e); sawh; sen, sein *see, saw, seen*

seie, sein; seid, sayde *say; declare; said; spoken*

sek, siek, sik *sick*

siete *sit, sat*

sih *saw*

sike, syke *sigh*

siker *certain, sure, secure; surely*

sithe *time(s)*

siththe *since*

skile *reason*

sleihte *skill, deceit, trickery*

slyh *cunning, sly*

sodeinliche *suddenly*

solein *alone, lonely, strange*

sonde *message, sending, decree; messenger*

soth(e) *truth*

stede *place; horse*

stevene *voice; promise*

such on *such a person*

suie *follow*

swevene, swefne *dream*

take(n) *take, give; betake*

teene, tene *sorrow, injury, hardship, vexation, anger*

th- *often affixed to words for* the *as in* thapostel (the apostle), thair (the air), *and* thastat (the estate). *In such constructions I have used an apostrophe to differentiate the article from the noun (i.e.,* th'apostel)

that *that, which, so that;* **that . . . ne** *but that, than that, lest, almost*

ther(e) *there, where, whereas, at that point, thereby, therefore*

tho *those; then*

thrinne *therein*

thurgh *through*

tobreke *break to pieces*

tofore *before; formerly*

totore *torn to bits*

tour *tower*

unavised *unwise, unwisely*

unbuxom *disobedient*

unethes *scarcely, hardly*

unkinde *unnatural, ungrateful*

unsely *unhappy*

upon *on, upon, into, with regard to, by reason of*

vois *voice, rumor, vote*

war *aware, careful*

wawe *wave*

wede *dress, cover*

wene *think, expect, believe*

werne *refuse, prevent*

wif *woman, wife*

wight *person; creature*

will(e) *will, pleasure, willfulness*

wise *manner*

wiste *knew*

wit *mind, reason, senses*

wite(n), wot *know*

wod *mad, wild*

worthe(n) *become*

wreche *wretch; vengeance; avenge;*
    satisfy
wyle *cunning*
wyte *blame, censure*

yare *ready*
ye, yhe *eye*
ynowh *enough*
ywiss *certainly, truly; indeed*

REFERENCE INDEX TO VOLUME 1

N.b.: All reference citations are by page number.

MIDDLE ENGLISH TEXTS SERIES

The Floure and the Leafe, The Assembly of Ladies, The Isle of Ladies, edited by Derek Pearsall (1990)

Three Middle English Charlemagne Romances, edited by Alan Lupack (1990)

Six Ecclesiastical Satires, edited by James M. Dean (1991)

Heroic Women from the Old Testament in Middle English Verse, edited by Russell A. Peck (1991)

The Canterbury Tales: Fifteenth-Century Continuations and Additions, edited by John M. Bowers (1992)

Gavin Douglas, *The Palis of Honoure*, edited by David Parkinson (1992)

Wynnere and Wastoure and The Parlement of the Thre Ages, edited by Warren Ginsberg (1992)

The Shewings of Julian of Norwich, edited by Georgia Ronan Crampton (1994)

King Arthur's Death: The Middle English Stanzaic Morte Arthur and Alliterative Morte Arthure, edited by Larry D. Benson, revised by Edward E. Foster (1994)

Lancelot of the Laik and Sir Tristrem, edited by Alan Lupack (1994)

Sir Gawain: Eleven Romances and Tales, edited by Thomas Hahn (1995)

The Middle English Breton Lays, edited by Anne Laskaya and Eve Salisbury (1995)

Sir Perceval of Galles and Ywain and Gawain, edited by Mary Flowers Braswell (1995)

Four Middle English Romances: Sir Isumbras, Octavian, Sir Eglamour of Artois, Sir Tryamour, edited by Harriet Hudson (1996)

The Poems of Laurence Minot 1333–1352, edited by Richard H. Osberg (1996)

Medieval English Political Writings, edited by James M. Dean (1996)

The Book of Margery Kempe, edited by Lynn Staley (1996)

Amis and Amiloun, Robert of Cisyle, and Sir Amadace, edited by Edward E. Foster (1997)

The Cloud of Unknowing, edited by Patrick J. Gallacher (1997)

Robin Hood and Other Outlaw Tales, edited by Stephen Knight and Thomas Ohlgren (1997); second edition (2000)

The Poems of Robert Henryson, edited by Robert L. Kindrick with assistance of Kristie A. Bixby (1997)

Moral Love Songs and Laments, edited by Susanna Greer Fein (1998)

John Lydgate, *Troy Book Selections*, edited by Robert R. Edwards (1998)

Thomas Usk, *The Testament of Love*, edited by R. Allen Shoaf (1998)

Prose Merlin, edited by John Conlee (1998)

Middle English Marian Lyrics, edited by Karen Saupe (1998)

John Metham, *Amoryus and Cleopes*, edited by Stephen F. Page (1999)

Four Romances of England: King Horn, Havelok the Dane, Bevis of Hampton, Athelston, edited by Ronald B. Herzman, Graham Drake, and Eve Salisbury (1999)

The Assembly of Gods: Le Assemble de Dyeus, or Banquet of Gods and Goddesses, with the Discourse of Reason and Sensuality, edited by Jane Chance (1999)

Thomas Hoccleve, *The Regiment of Princes*, edited by Charles R. Blyth (1999)

John Capgrave, *The Life of Saint Katherine*, edited by Karen A. Winstead (1999)

John Gower, *Confessio Amantis*, Vol. 1, edited by Russell A. Peck; with Latin translations by Andrew Galloway (2000; second edition 2006); Vol. 2 (2003); Vol. 3 (2004)

Richard the Redeless and Mum and the Sothsegger, edited by James M. Dean (2000)

Ancrene Wisse, edited by Robert Hasenfratz (2000)

Walter Hilton, *The Scale of Perfection*, edited by Thomas H. Bestul (2000)

John Lydgate, *The Siege of Thebes*, edited by Robert R. Edwards (2001)

Pearl, edited by Sarah Stanbury (2001)

The Trials and Joys of Marriage, edited by Eve Salisbury (2002)

Middle English Legends of Women Saints, edited by Sherry L. Reames, with assistance of
    Martha G. Blalock and Wendy R. Larson (2003)

The Wallace: Selections, edited by Anne McKim (2003)

Richard Maidstone, *Concordia (The Reconciliation of Richard II with London)*, edited by
    David R. Carlson, with a verse translation by A. G. Rigg (2003)

Three Purgatory Poems: The Gast of Gy, Sir Owain, The Vision of Tundale, edited by Edward
    E. Foster (2004)

William Dunbar, *The Complete Works*, edited by John Conlee (2004)

Chaucerian Dream Visions and Complaints, edited by Dana M. Symons (2004)

Stanzaic Guy of Warwick, edited by Alison Wiggins (2004)

Saints' Lives in Middle English Collections, edited by E. Gordon Whatley, with Anne B.
    Thompson and Robert K. Upchurch (2004)

Siege of Jerusalem, edited by Michael Livingston (2004)

The Kingis Quair and Other Prison Poems, edited by Linne R. Mooney and Mary-Jo Arn
    (2005)

Chaucerian Apocrypha: Selections, edited by Kathleen Forni (2005)

John Gower, *The Minor Latin Works*, edited and translated by R. F. Yeager, with *In Praise
of Peace*, edited by Michael Livingston (2005)

*Sentimental and Humorous Romances: Floris and Blancheflour, Sir Degrevant, The Squire of
Low Degree, The Tournament of Tottenham, and The Feast of Tottenham*, edited by Erik
    Kooper (2006)

DOCUMENTS OF PRACTICE SERIES

Love and Marriage in Late Medieval London, selected, translated, and introduced by
    Shannon McSheffrey (1995)

Sources for the History of Medicine in Late Medieval England, selected, introduced, and
    translated by Carole Rawcliffe (1995)

A Slice of Life: Selected Documents of Medieval English Peasant Experience, edited, translated,
    and with an introduction by Edwin Brezette DeWindt (1996)

Regular Life: Monastic, Canonical, and Mendicant Rules, selected and introduced by
    Douglas J. McMillan and Kathryn Smith Fladenmuller (1997); second edition,
    selected and introduced by Daniel Marcel La Corte and Douglas J. McMillan (2004)

Women and Monasticism in Medieval Europe: Sisters and Patrons of the Cistercian Reform,
    selected, translated, and with an introduction by Constance H. Berman (2002)

Medieval Notaries and Their Acts: The 1327–1328 Register of Jean Holanie, introduced,
    edited, and translated by Kathryn L. Reyerson and Debra A. Salata (2004)

COMMENTARY SERIES

Haimo of Auxerre, *Commentary on the Book of Jonah*, translated with an introduction and
    notes by Deborah Everhart (1993)

Medieval Exegesis in Translation: Commentaries on the Book of Ruth, translated with an intro-
    duction and notes by Lesley Smith (1996)

Nicholas of Lyra's Apocalypse Commentary, translated with an introduction and notes by
    Philip D. W. Krey (1997)

Rabbi Ezra Ben Solomon of Gerona, *Commentary on the Song of Songs and Other Kabbalistic Commentaries*, selected, translated, and annotated by Seth Brody (1999)

John Wyclif, *On the Truth of Holy Scripture*, translated with an introduction and notes by Ian Christopher Levy (2001)

Second Thessalonians: Two Early Medieval Apocalyptic Commentaries, introduced and translated by Steven R. Cartwright and Kevin L. Hughes (2001)

The Glossa Ordinaria on the Song of Songs, translated with an introduction and notes by Mary Dove (2004)

MEDIEVAL GERMAN TEXTS IN BILINGUAL EDITIONS SERIES

Sovereignty and Salvation in the Vernacular, 1050–1150, introduction, translations, and notes by James A. Schultz (2000)

Ava's New Testament Narratives: "When the Old Law Passed Away," introduction, translation, and notes by James A. Rushing, Jr. (2003)

History as Literature: German World Chronicles of the Thirteenth Century in Verse, introduction, translation, and notes by R. Graeme Dunphy (2003)

VARIA

The Study of Chivalry: Resources and Approaches, edited by Howell Chickering and Thomas H. Seiler (1988)

Studies in the Harley Manuscript: The Scribes, Contents, and Social Contexts of British Library MS Harley 2253, edited by Susanna Fein (2000)

The Liturgy of the Medieval Church, edited by Thomas J. Heffernan and E. Ann Matter (2001); second edition (2005)

TO ORDER PLEASE CONTACT:

Medieval Institute Publications
Western Michigan University
Kalamazoo, MI 49008-5432
Phone (269) 387-8755
FAX (269) 387-8750

http://www.wmich.edu/medieval/mip/index.html

Medieval Institute Publications is a program
of The Medieval Institute, College of Arts
and Sciences, Western Michigan University

Typeset in 10/13 New Baskerville
with Golden Cockerel Ornaments display
Designed by Linda K. Judy
Manufactured by Edwards Bros., Inc.—Ann Arbor, Michigan

Medieval Institute Publications
College of Arts and Sciences
Western Michigan University
1903 W. Michigan Avenue
Kalamazoo, MI 49008-5432
http://www.wmich.edu/medieval/mip

 WESTERN MICHIGAN UNIVERSITY